LAW, PROCESS AND CUSTODY
Prisoners and Patients

LAW IN CONTEXT

Editors: Robert Stevens (Covington & Burling, London)
William Twining (University College, London) and
Christopher McCrudden (Lincoln College, Oxford)

Law, Process and Custody: Prisoners and Patients

GENEVRA RICHARDSON

Reader in Law at Queen Mary and Westfield College,
University of London

Weidenfeld and Nicolson
London

Weidenfeld and Nicolson
Orion Publishing Group Ltd
Orion House, 5 Upper St Martin's Lane,
London, WC2H 9EA

ISBN 0 297 82146 6 paperback

Photoset by Deltatype Ltd, Ellesmere Port, Cheshire
Printed in Great Britain by
Butler & Tanner Ltd, Frome and London

CONTENTS

PREFACE

This book has emerged from a long-standing interest in the administration of prisons and special hospitals and the treatment of those detained within them. It represents an attempt to analyse the current impact of public law regulation on the processes of decision-making within these custodial institutions, and to consider the direction such regulation might take in the future. While the book draws chiefly on existing research material rather than presenting fresh empirical data, the discussion of special hospitals is informed by my own experience, as a member of the Mental Health Act Commission, of visiting one particular special hospital regularly over a period of six years. I have endeavoured to rely on published material to substantiate points in the text wherever possible, but some references appear to cases and incidents known to me personally. In all such cases I have taken great care to respect the confidence of all those concerned. The conclusions drawn from the material, however, represent my own views, not those of the Mental Health Act Commission.

While writing this book I have enjoyed enormous help and support from colleagues on the Mental Health Act Commission and at Queen Mary and Westfield College, and to them all I owe many thanks. I should also like to thank all those at the Home Office who have patiently answered my queries. Special thanks, however, must go to Denis Galligan, whose help and advice in relation to the analysis in Part I was invaluable, to William Bingley and Lucy Scott-Moncrieff, who provided most useful comments on the draft of Part III, and to Rod Morgan and Christopher McCrudden, who kindly and most helpfully read and commented on the whole manuscript. Finally, I should like to thank Sophia Oliver for her considerable help in producing the final version, and Oliver Thorold and Sandra Talton, who offered a constant mix of professional and domestic support throughout.

Genevra Richardson
December 1992

TABLE OF CASES

TABLE OF STATUTES

ABBREVIATIONS

BNF	British National Formulary
CI	Circular Instruction
CNA	Certified Normal Accommodation
CPS	Crown Prosecution Service
CRC	Control Review Committee
DHSS	Department of Health and Social Security/Services
DoH	Department of Health
ECHR	European Court of Human Rights
HMCIP	Her Majesty's Chief Inspector of Prisons
HSC	Health Service Commissioner
LOR	loss of remission
LRC	local review committee
MHAC	Mental Health Act Commission
MHRT	Mental Health Review Tribunal
MIND	National Association for Mental Health
MQP	minimum qualifying period
NACRO	National Association for the Care and Rehabilitation of Offenders
NHS	National Health Service
PMS	Prison Medical Service
RAG	Research and Advisory Group on the Long-term Prison System
RPS	reconviction prediction score
RSU	regional secure unit
SHSA	Special Hospital Service Authority
SI	Statutory Instrument
SO	Standing Order
SUSC	Special Units Selection Comittee

I

Introduction

A structure of criminal law exists in this country, and some of those who offend against it are identified, charged, prosecuted, tried and convicted. They are then sentenced to one of a variety of forms of official sanction, including both custodial and non-custodial penalties, and are required to fulfil the demands of such sanctions until final release is achieved. As many have pointed out, it is misleading to call this sequence of events a system if 'system' is taken to imply the existence of some over-arching purpose and consistent plan. On the other hand there is now a growing recognition of the necessary inter-dependence of the various stages within the structure and their close relationships one with another, and this recognition is increasingly being used to inform accounts of the separate stages. Even accounts of the substantive criminal law itself are beginning to discuss questions of enforcement, and Ashworth has recently produced an analysis of sentencing which seeks to place it in the broader context of criminal justice.[1]

However, within this move towards a wider understanding of the criminal justice system as a whole, the administration of prisons and, more particularly, secure hospitals has been largely omitted from the legal literature at least. Any relevant discussion tends to be limited to a description of the parole system and the powers of the Mental Health Review Tribunals, and to an account of prisoner's rights. There is little analysis of the nature or purpose of the powers exercised by the various custodial authorities, or of the mechanisms, whether judicial or extra-judicial, designed to regulate that exercise. From the point of view of both those who work and those who are detained within custodial institutions this omission is unfortunate. In both prisons and secure hospitals, extensive areas of discretion are granted to the relevant authorities, who are empowered to intervene most directly in the lives and liberties of individuals.

1 A. Ashworth, *Sentencing and Criminal Justice* (1992, London: Weidenfeld and Nicolson). In relation to the substantive criminal law, see N. Lacey, C. Wells and D. Meure, *Reconstructing Criminal Law* (1990, London: Weidenfeld and Nicolson). The inter-dependence of the various stages was also clearly recognised in the Woolf Report, *Prison Disturbances April 1990* (1991, Cm 1456, London: HMSO).

Borrowing heavily from the tools of public law analysis, this book represents an attempt to remedy these omissions.

Any full analysis of the origin and exercise of powers must involve some consideration of the purposes for which those powers are granted and, when the agency in question is part of a larger system, its purposes cannot be understood in isolation from the purposes of the system itself. Although the criminal justice system as presently constituted may have no single over-arching aim, some such aims have been suggested,[2] and one central element within the system – the proper role and function of criminal punishment – has inspired constant and energetic debate.[3] This book, however, does not seek directly to contribute to these debates, it is concerned more specifically with the role and purpose of imprisonment and compulsory hospital detention. Unfortunately even here there is great uncertainty.

Imprisonment is, in practice, the most severe punishment available to the criminal courts in England and Wales but there is little agreement as to its underlying purpose. At various times, and in reflection of the purposes traditionally attributed to criminal punishment in general, the purposes of imprisonment have been seen in terms of deterrence, rehabilitation, retribu-tion – or, more recently, desert – and social protection, in a variety of combinations. However, the restrictions placed on both the imposition and length of imprisonment by sections 1 and 2 of the Criminal Justice Act 1991 would suggest that its main purpose is now to be understood in terms of retribution, or desert, and social protection. While such a combination of aims may not pose undue difficulties as far as the nature of imprisonment is concerned, provided it is agreed that both desert and social protection can be accommodated simply by the segregation of the prisoner from the rest of society, such a combination can lead to confusion with regard to duration of sentence and release.

With regard to the hospital detention of convicted offenders, a similar duality of goals can occur. Section 37 of the Mental Health Act 1983 allows a court to impose a hospital order where it is satisfied that a convicted offender is suffering from a mental disorder under the 1983 Act to a nature or degree which makes it appropriate for him or her to be detained in hospital for medical treatment. Section 41 permits additional restrictions to be imposed where necessary for the protection of the public from serious harm. Thus, the main purpose of hospital detention would appear to be the facilitation of treatment, with an additional element of social protection where relevant. While the fundamental validity of such official purposes is ripe for further discussion, this book is primarily concerned with the implications flowing from the implementation of those purposes once either form of custody has

---

2 See, particularly, J. Braithewaite and P. Pettit, *Not Just Deserts* (1990, Oxford: Oxford University Press).

3 See, particularly, H. L. A. Hart, *Punishment and Responsibility* (1968, Oxford: Oxford University Press), N. Lacey, *State Punishment* (1988, London: Routledge), and D. Garland, *Punishment and Modern Society* (1990, Oxford: Oxford University Press).

been imposed. Attention will thus be concentrated on the decisions taken after sentence.

The administration of either a sentence of imprisonment or a period of hospital detention involves the exercise of public power, whether the detaining institution itself is publicly or privately owned. The use of the law to regulate the administration of custodial institutions therefore raises issues similar to those which are raised with regard to the use of the law to regulate the exercise of any public function. In recent years the proper role and function of the law in general, and the courts in particular, in the regulation of government has come under increased scrutiny. Within this wider debate a distinction is sometimes made between the regulation of the process of public decision making and the control of the substantive outcome of such decisions.

In the first part of this book an attempt will be made to explain what is meant by process in this context, to consider how the law's involvement in its regulation might be justified, and to examine the form any legal regulation might take. To this end, chapter 2 opens with a brief description of the ways in which the law is currently involved in the regulation of the processes of policy implementation within the custodial sphere. It then examines the constitutional justifications for such involvement, with reference to both orthodox and alternative constitutional theory. In chapter 3 an account is given of the justifications traditionally provided for the law's involvement in procedural regulation at a more individual level, and an attempt is made to identify the predominant judicial view. In an attempt to move beyond the limitations imposed by this established view and to encourage the realisation of the law's regulatory potential, an alternative, broader approach to process is suggested, which sees the pursuit of 'full process' as essential to the legitimate exercise of public authority. Chapter 4 describes the forms of decision making commonly adopted in the implementation of custodial policy and their current distribution. With reference to the alternative approach to process suggested in chapter 3, chapter 4 then considers the factors which should be used to guide the choice of decision making form at each of the three main stages of policy implementation: formulation, application and validation.

In the light of the introductory discussion, the remaining chapters of the book seek to provide an account of the processes of decision making within both prisons and secure hospitals, in an attempt to further our understanding of the custodial elements within the criminal justice system. The decision making processes at each stage of policy implementation are examined with particular reference to the law's involvement in their regulation, and the current position is compared to that which might be required to fulfil the demands of 'full process' as described in the first three chapters.

Chapters 5 to 8 concern the implementation of selected areas of prison policy. Chapter 5 deals with the formulation of the policies to be applied within prison establishments, while chapter 6 considers the processes through which polices are applied, and the mechanisms available to provide review. Chapter 7 deals more specifically with the structure of prison discipline, and chapter 8 describes the evolution and application of release policy with regard to both fixed-term prisoners and those serving life sentences.

Chapters 9 to 12 are concerned with mentally disordered offenders. Chapter 9 describes official policy with regard to such offenders, and pays particular attention to the evolution of the Mental Health Act 1983, and to the mechanisms provided for the identification of mentally disordered offenders and their diversion from penal custody. Concentrating on the regime within special hospitals, chapters 10 and 11 consider the processes for both the application and the validation of policy in relation to such issues as the imposition of medical treatment and the recognition of residual freedoms. The process of release from hospital is then considered in chapter 12, with particular regard to the role played by the Mental Health Review Tribunal and the Secretary of State. Finally, chapter 13 attempts to provide a summary of the main issues and to draw some tentative conclusions.

Part I
Process

2
Process, Custody and the Constitution

Decision making with regard to the administration of custody within the criminal justice system, and the law's involvement in the regulation of the process of such decision making, provide the main focus of this book. The notion of process, however, needs some initial explanation. It is being used here in a very broad sense to cover both the structure and the procedure of all the bodies involved in the evolution and application of policy. It thus includes process in the narrow sense of the procedures adopted by administrative and judicial bodies when applying policies to individuals, but it extends far further, not only to include the structure of these policy implementing bodies, but also to encompass the structure and procedure of the bodies providing accountability, and of those responsible for the formulation of the original policy itself.[1]

In a later chapter an attempt will be made to provide a more comprehensive classification of decision making processes by reference to both the nature of the outcome sought and the form of decision making adopted, but here it is necessary merely to emphasise the breadth of the overall notion of process. Such a definition of process, which extends to cover equally the principle of universal adult suffrage and the rules concerning hearsay evidence, may well be thought too wide to retain any real analytic value. The discussion presented here will seek to argue otherwise, and will suggest that involvement in matters of process, thus broadly defined, constitutes a most significant role for the law within the criminal justice system.

In this part of the book the many justifications provided for the law's involvement in the regulation of process will be examined and the role and potential of the various forms of process will be discussed. By way of introduction this chapter will consider the constitutional context of the legal regulation of process. It will provide a very brief outline of the basic constitutional structure of custodial decision making (a shorthand adopted to refer to decisions relating to the administration of custody) in England and

1 For a discussion of process in this broad sense see L. Tribe, *Constitutional Choices* (1985, Cambridge, Mass.: Harvard University Press), and P. Craig, *Public Law and Democracy in the United Kingdom and the United States of America* (1990, Oxford: Oxford University Press).

Wales, and will describe the ways in which the law can be involved in matters of process. The justifications provided by traditional constitutional theory for that involvement will then be considered, and some discussion offered of alternative constitutional bases for the claim to fair process.

(a) The Constitutional Structure of Custodial Decision Making

(1) Parliament

(a) Empowering

According to orthodox constitutional principle, Parliament provides the ultimate lawmaking authority within the United Kingdom. It creates the primary legislation setting up and empowering the various agencies which exercise public power within the state. Thus, in the present context, the Parole Board was originally created and empowered by the Criminal Justice Act 1967. The degree of specificity with which this empowering task is performed, however, can vary enormously.

Occasionally the primary legislation is very precise, as in the case of the Murder (Abolition of the Death Penalty) Act 1965, section 1 of which imposes a mandatory sentence of life imprisonment for those convicted of murder. But such precision is rare. More often the statute itself is general in form, leaving to delegated legislation, codes of practice and departmental guidelines the provision of more detailed guidance as to the manner in which the agency is to fulfil its function. The Prison Act 1952, for example, contains few detailed provisions governing the daily operation of prison establishments. Such matters are left to delegated legislation in the form of the Prison Rules, and to Standing Orders and Home Office Circulars, with only the Prison Rules having statutory force.[2] Alternatively, the primary legislation may set a standard leaving significant interpretational latitude to the agency. Section 41 of the Mental Health Act 1983, for example, empowers a Crown Court to impose restrictions on a hospital order when it considers it necessary to do so in order to protect the public from serious harm. Finally, the legislation may remain entirely silent on the principles according to which the agency is to perform its task, and may make no provision for their formal identification. As will be described in chapter 8, the Criminal Justice Act 1967 provided no guidance as to the basis on which the Parole Board should recommend the early release of prisoners. Parliament, it would appear, is willing to delegate wide policy making powers to inferior bodies.

(b) Overseeing

Despite the common lack of specificity in the empowering statute, Parliament's ability directly to oversee the performance of the agency, once empowered, is strictly limited. Two mechanisms for achieving accountability,

2 Prison Rules 1964, SI 1964/388 with amendments.

in the sense of scrutiny after the event, should, however, be mentioned. In the first place, statutory agencies are typically required to report to Parliament annually, either directly or through the responsible minister.[3] This offers Parliament some record of the agency's activities, and can provide a trigger for debate. Secondly, in 1978 the House of Commons decided to establish a system of departmentally related select committees charged with examining the performance of particular central government departments. There is thus a Select Committee for Home Affairs, and also of relevance in this area, a Select Committee for Social Services and for Education, Science and Arts. These select committees are composed of back-bench MPs and perform a largely investigative role, calling witnesses and examining documents, and eventually reporting to the whole House. In the course of subsequent chapters the impact of such reports in relevant policy areas will be considered; here it is necessary merely to remark that, while valuable, select committees cannot be expected on their own to provide the oversight necessary to ensure the strict adherence of central government departments to the often obliquely expressed intentions of Parliament.[4]

In addition to these mechanisms for direct control, Parliament relies on the doctrine of ministerial responsibility. Each central government department is headed by a member of the government – a minister – and by constitutional convention that minister is responsible to Parliament for the workings of his or her department. Thus the responsible minister must account to Parliament, must answer questions, and in the final analysis may have to resign if his or her department is seen to be seriously deficient in some respect.

The formal management structure of the Prison Service, excluding for the moment the question of privatisation, can be used to illustrate the application of the traditional concept of ministerial responsibility. The Prison Act 1952 makes the Home Secretary responsible for the maintenance and organisation of prisons and requires him (we have yet to have a female Home Secretary) to report annually to Parliament. It also gives him the power to appoint prison personnel and to issue rules for the management of prison establishments. Thus, in the words of the Woolf Inquiry, 'the Home Secretary, assisted by one of his junior ministers, is directly responsible and accountable to Parliament for all aspects of the Prison Service work'.[5]

In practice the Home Secretary acts through the Director General of the Prison Service, who chairs the Prisons Board. The Board is not a statutory body but was created within the Prison Department of the Home Office to

3 Section 5, Prison Act 1952 requires the Secretary of State to report annually to Parliament, while s.121(10), Mental Health Act 1983 requires the Mental Health Act Commission, every two years, to report to the Secretary of State who shall lay the report before both Houses of Parliament.

4 For discussion of the role of select committees generally, see G. Drewry, 'Select Committees and Back-Bench Power', in J. Jowell and D. Oliver (eds), *The Changing Constitution* 2nd edn (1989, Oxford: Oxford University Press), ch. 6, and G. Drewry (ed.), *The New Select Committees* 2nd edn (1989, Oxford: Oxford University Press).

5 *Prison Disturbances April 1990* (The Woolf Inquiry) (1991, Cm 1456, London: HMSO), para. 12.35.

monitor the performance of the Prison Service and to act as a consultative forum. Over the last 20 years the structure of senior management within the Prison Service has been regularly reviewed and reorganised, and the debates underlying the various changes will be considered in more detail later. Here it is necessary merely to note that at present the Board has nine members, three of whom possess operational as well as policy responsibilities. Between these three directors and the individual establishments there are 15 area managers, each of whom is responsible for approximately nine establishments. Each individual establishment has a governor appointed by the Home Secretary who, by section 7 of the 1952 Act, is made responsible for good order and discipline within the prison. Other duties, including the hearing of disciplinary charges and the hearing of complaints brought by prisoners, are outlined in the Prison Rules.[6] Section 4 (2) of the Act, however, makes the Home Secretary responsible for insuring 'that the provisions of this Act and of any rules made under this Act are duly complied with'. Thus, although a governor can be held directly responsible to the courts for the way in which he or she exercises certain of his or her powers, governors are generally regarded as the servants or agents of the Home Secretary, and act under his direction.[7] In 1984 a new management framework for the accountability of individual establishments was introduced, requiring an annual 'contract' to be drawn up between each governor and his or her area manager.[8] These contracts are intended to define the function and goals of each prison establishment. Thus, whatever the merits of the present system, it is evident that a formal line of responsibility extends out from the Home Secretary, through the Director General and the Board, via the area managers, to the governors of individual establishments.

While the above account suggests that the Prison Service can be viewed as an arm of the Home Office, many tasks within the criminal justice system are entrusted to agencies which do not formally constitute part of a central government department. Indeed it is now clear that the Prison Service itself is to be devolved from the Home Office to be transformed into a 'Next Steps' executive agency.[9] Such developments aside, however, many fringe organisations already exist, performing statutory functions within the criminal justice system. In recognition of this phenomenon, the doctrine of ministerial responsibility extends beyond the strict limits of the central government department itself to cover agencies which, while not formally part of the department, are none the less within its patronage and sphere of influence. The responsible minister is typically given some direct means of control over

6 These two functions are discussed in greater detail in chapters 6 and 7. By virtue of rule 98 a governor may, with the agreement of the Secretary of State, delegate any of his or her powers and duties under the rules.

7 The House of Lords finally allowed judicial review of the governor's disciplinary award in *Leech* v. *Deputy Governor of Parkhurst Prison* [1988] AC 533.

8 See Prison Department, *Annual Report 1984–5* (1985, Cmnd 9699, London: HMSO), and see C.I. 55/1984 reproduced therein.

9 The issue is discussed in ch. 5.

such fringe bodies, the power to issue regulation, for example, or to make appointments, to call for inquiries or to withhold finance, and in return is responsible to Parliament for the performance of the agency. The Home Secretary, for example, is responsible to Parliament for the activities of the Parole Board, as is the Secretary of State for Health responsible for the Mental Health Act Commission.

Thus, in formal constitutional terms, Parliament creates and empowers the various public agencies operating within the criminal justice system and achieves oversight of their operations primarily through the device of ministerial responsibility. Indeed, despite the scepticism of numerous observers in whose eyes the concept has long since ceased to command respect,[10] ministerial responsibility is still regarded as crucial to the constitutional propriety of the agencies. When the creation of a prison ombudsman was considered by the May Inquiry the Home Office argued strongly that such a figure would interfere with the Home Secretary's direct responsibility to Parliament.[11] More recently, the Woolf Inquiry has been at pains to emphasise that its favoured 'structured stand-off' between the Home Secretary and the Director General of the Prison Service would in no way diminish the Home Secretary's responsibility to Parliament.[12] Whatever its efficacy, however, ministerial responsibility is clearly insufficient on its own to render the various actors within criminal justice accountable to the public through Parliament. Accordingly, Parliament has created a variety of specialised agencies entrusted with the task of overseeing specific aspects of the system.

Within the custodial sphere these watchdog agencies include, for prisons, Her Majesty's Chief Inspector of Prisons, boards of visitors, the Parliamentary Commissioner or Ombudsman, and the new independent complaints adjudicator; and for hospitals, the Mental Health Act Commission and the Health Services Ombudsman. With the exception of the independent prison complaints adjudicator, each is set up by statute with specific powers and responsibilities, and their respective roles will be considered in later chapters. Each, with the exception of boards of visitors and the complaints adjudicator, has a duty to report to Parliament, directly in the case of the Parliamentary Commissioner, and via the relevant minister in the other cases.[13]

10 See, for example, N. Lewis and I. Harden, *The Noble Lie: the British Constitution and the Rule of Law* (1986, London: Hutchinson); C. Turpin, 'Ministerial Responsibility: Myth or Reality?', in Jowell and Oliver, *supra*, n.4; and D. Oliver, *Government in the United Kingdom: the Search for Accountability, Effectiveness and Citizenship* (1991, Buckingham: Open University Press).
11 *Committee of Inquiry into the U.K. Prison Services* (1979, Cmnd 7673, London: HMSO).
12 *Supra*, n.5, ch. 12. Ministerial responsibility and the Prison Service is discussed further below in chapter 5.
13 For the duty of the Parliamentary Commissioner, see s.10(4), Parliamentary Commissioner Act 1967, and for the duties of the HSC and HMCIP see s.119(4)(b), National Health Service Act 1977, and s.5A(5), Prison Act 1952, respectively.

(2) Beyond Parliament

(a) The Independent Sector

While it is true that Parliament is the primary creator and empowerer of actors within the criminal justice system, there are exceptions. There is a growing independent or private sector even within the custodial sphere. There are, for example, private hospitals which specialise in the provision of accommodation for patients detained under the provisions of the Mental Health Act 1983. Such establishments, while exercising statutory powers with regard to those within their care, are not directly created by Parliament, nor are their activities the direct responsibility of any central government department or minister. They are, however, typically subject to public control with regard to certain functions, *ex ante* through the imposition of minimum standards or codes of practice, and *ex post* through inspection by a watchdog body. Private hospitals wishing to take detained patients, for example, have to be registered with the local health authority, are subject to the Code of Practice issued by the Department of Health and fall within the remit of the Mental Health Act Commission.[14] The development of private prisons is discussed in chapters 5 and 6.

(b) Crown Prerogative

A small number of powers still derive from Crown prerogative rather than Act of Parliament. These powers are now exercised by the executive in the name of the Crown. The Home Secretary, for example, can advise the Crown to grant an absolute or conditional pardon to a person convicted of a criminal offence.[15] It has also been affirmed by the Court of Appeal that the Crown still retains a prerogative power to maintain the peace and keep law and order, and that this power is sufficient to entitle the Home Secretary to supply plastic baton rounds and CS gas to a chief constable, despite opposition from the local police authority.[16] In theory, of course, the executive remains answerable to Parliament for the way in which it exercises such powers.

(c) International Law

The United Kingdom is party to international treaties which create obligations in international law. Of these the European Convention on Human Rights and Fundamental Freedoms is the most relevant here. Although not incorporated into domestic law, the European Convention does

14 A mental nursing home must be registered with the local health authority under Part II of the Registered Homes Act 1984, and if it wishes to take detained patients, it must be specifically registered to do so – s.23(5). For discussion of the Code of Practice and the role of the Mental Health Act Commission see chapters 9 and 11.

15 For a general Account of the Crown prerogative see O. Hood Phillips and P. Jackson, *Constitutional and Administrative Law* 7th edn (1987, London: Sweet and Maxwell), ch. 14.

16 *R.* v. *Home Secretary, ex p. Northumbria Police Authority* [1988] 2 WLR 590.

carry a right of individual petition, endorsed by Parliament, which enables an individual to challenge domestic law before the European Commission and Court of Human Rights. This right has been used effectively by both prisoners and patients who have had aspects of the law relating to their custody condemned by the European Court of Human Rights (ECHR) as contrary to the obligations imposed by the Convention.[17] Thus a body of rules exists which in international law must take precedence over Parliamentary legislation, and to which individuals have access.

(3) The Courts

Finally, the judiciary act as significant decision makers within the criminal justice system. Essentially the courts perform three distinct roles within the system. In the first place, they act as front-line decision makers themselves, operating crucial aspects of the system. Magistrates' Courts, for example, play a central role in the operation of the remand system, committal proceedings, trial and sentence. Secondly, senior courts also act as watchdogs in the sense that they hear appeals from the courts below. When performing these two functions the courts, like the bodies described above, are acting under specific statutory powers, they are effectively empowered by Parliament.[18] In their final role, however, the courts exercise a non-statutory power deriving from the common law. The common law empowers the High Court to review the actions of both inferior courts and other public bodies to insure that they act within their powers, whether these powers be statutory, prerogative, or in some other sense public in nature.[19]

(b) The Law's Involvement in Process and its Place in Orthodox Constitutional Theory

Using the broad definition offered above, it is clear that the law is extensively involved in matters of process. The majority of bodies operating within the criminal justice system are created, or at least empowered, by statute. Their structure, membership, and relationship with other agencies, all aspects of process, are thus provided for by law. These bodies range in function from those with a primarily policy making role, such as the Home Secretary, to the largely adjudicatory bodies such as Magistrates' Courts, and agencies like the boards of visitors, designed to provide a means of review. In the case of each

17 For an introduction to the Convention see F. G. Jacobs, *The European Convention on Human Rights* (1980, Oxford: Oxford University Press). See also A. Drzemczewski, *European Human Rights Convention in Domestic Law: A Comparative Study* (1983, Oxford: Oxford University Press). Individual cases are discussed in later chapters.

18 See, generally, Magistrates' Court Act 1980, and Criminal Appeal Act 1968.

19 This common law power of review is discussed further below. For a general account of the law see H. W. R. Wade, *Administrative Law* 6th edn (1988, Oxford University Press), and P. Craig, *Administrative Law* 2nd edn (1989, London: Sweet and Maxwell).

body the law will stipulate the procedures to be followed in the exercise of its powers, and will use a range of different mechanisms to do so, including primary legislation and principles of the common law. These techniques will be examined further in later chapters, but first it is necessary to consider the constitutional background.

(1) Constitutional Fundamentals

As will be suggested below, much of the law's current involvement with process can be explained by reference to orthodox constitutional principles. The United Kingdom has no written constitution. Instead constitutional lawyers have identified certain fundamental principles which are said to govern the relationship between public bodies and between individuals and public bodies. Briefly stated, these principles include: the legislative supremacy of Parliament, the separation of powers, and the rule of law.[20] At the heart of the system lies the supremacy of Parliament. In domestic law there are no limits on the legislative competence of Parliament. Parliament may pass what laws it wishes, and all other bodies, including the courts, are subject to the will of Parliament.[21] Thus the United Kingdom has no body comparable to the Supreme Court in the United States, with authority to declare Parliamentary legislation unlawful. Indeed there are no formally established criteria by which a notion of lawfulness could be judged. Such criteria do exist in relation to custodial policy in international law, in the form of the European Convention on Human Rights and Fundamental Freedoms, and are applied to Parliamentary legislation by the ECHR. But the rulings of that court, although extremely influential, as will be seen in subsequent chapters, do not form part of domestic law.

While the legislative function of the state in the United Kingdom is performed by Parliament, administration and adjudication are the responsibility of the executive and the judiciary respectively. The United Kingdom has never purported to adhere strictly to the separation of powers. Indeed the executive is comprised of members of the legislature. Nevertheless, aspects of the doctrine retain a significant influence. For example, belief in the legislative monopoly of Parliament, that is that all legislative instruments must bear the stamp of Parliamentary approval, has affected the courts' attitude to administrative rule making. Further, at the rhetorical level at least, the need for checks and balances between the three organs of government is recognised, even though it is widely accepted that in recent years the executive has significantly extended its powers.

Despite the absence of a written constitution, and the presence of a flexible

20 British constitutional lawyers tend to start with the works of A. V. Dicey, particularly, *An Introduction to the Study of the Law of the Constitution* (1885, London: Macmillan). For more contemporary accounts, see R. Heuston, *Essays in Constitutional Law* 2nd edn (1964, London: Stevens); G. Marshall, *Constitutional Theory* (1971, Oxford: Oxford University Press); C. Munro, *Studies in Constitutional Law* (1987, London: Butterworths); Jowell and Oliver, *supra*, n. 4; and Oliver, *supra*, n. 10.
21 For a discussion of Dicey's views on the supremacy of Parliament see Craig, *supra*, n.1, ch. 2.

attitude towards the separation of powers, the United Kingdom would still claim to possess a limited government, even if in McAuslan and McEldowney's terms it is a question of 'auto-limitation'.[22] According to Dicey, such limitation derives from the presence of constitutional conventions, and from the adherence of the government to the rule of law. Of the two, the concept of the rule of law is the more significant here. At its narrowest the rule of law expresses the principle of adherence to the law. All citizens are required to act within the law, but so also are all public bodies and organs of government. No single organ of the state is entitled to act outside the law. Dicey's three elements of the rule of law – the supremacy of the ordinary law, the virtual condemnation of broad discretionary powers, and the common law origins of all civil liberties – are well-known, and their influence over public law in this country widely discussed.[23] Whatever the origins and impact of Dicey's views, however, there is an alternative approach to the rule of law which, in an attempt to enhance its neutrality, gives it a more obviously procedural bias. The rule of law is seen as a constraint on the form of law and its implementation. To be deserving of respect and obedience, law must comply with certain rules. It must, for example, be certain, non-retrospective, as specific as possible, and non-selective in application.[24] This and other interpretations of the rule of law will be discussed further below.

(2) Process Broadly Understood

In order to set the law's involvement in process in its orthodox constitutional context it is important to appreciate the implications of these constitutional principles for the role of the courts. Process in its broad sense, encompassing both the structure of policy implementing bodies and the structure and procedure of policy formulating bodies, will be taken first. With regard to Parliament, although the electoral system is regulated by the law and supervised by the courts, the ordinary law has little influence within the Houses of Parliament themselves. According to established legal doctrine no court can inquire into the procedures adopted by the legislature during the conduct of a bill through the two Houses of Parliament.[25] Parliamentary process itself is therefore outside the jurisdiction of the ordinary courts. Secondly, when Parliament sets up a decision making structure, no court can challenge the lawfulness of that structure. Thus, if Parliament wished to exclude the accused from the criminal trial or to insist that the Parole Board be comprised exclusively of prisoners serving life sentences, no domestic court

---

22 P. McAuslan and J. McEldowney (eds), *Law, Legitimacy and the Constitution* (1985, London: Sweet and Maxwell), ch. 1.

23 See, for example, *Public Law* Seminar on Dicey and the Constitution, reported in *Public Law* (1985), 583–723; J. McEldowney, 'Dicey in Historical Perspective: A Review Essay', in McAuslan and McEldowney, *supra* n. 22, ch. 2; and Craig, *supra*, n. 1, ch. 2.

24 See J. Jowell, 'The Rule of Law Today', in Jowell and Oliver, *supra*, n. 4, ch. 1, and J. Raz, 'The Rule of Law and its Virtue' (1977) LQR 195.

25 *Edinburgh and Dalkeith Railway* v. *Wauchope* (1842) 8 Cl. and F 710.

could object. Parliament is legislatively supreme: it expresses the will of the people.

Thus, ostensibly at least, the courts have to accept the process requirements provided by Parliament. The position is different in international law where Parliament has ratified our adherence to an international convention. Thus in *X* v. *United Kingdom*,[26] a mentally disordered offender, compulsorily detained in hospital, was able to challenge the structure provided by the Mental Health Act 1959 to govern decisions concerning his discharge. Subsequent to the ruling of the ECHR that domestic law failed to comply with the obligations imposed by the European Convention on Human Rights, the relevant statutory provisions were changed.[27] The process requirements imposed by the European Convention which are relevant to custodial decision making, typically, as in *X*, involve the prescription of adjudication in circumstances where the domestic law relies upon some form of executive or administrative decision making, and the imposition of more stringent procedural safeguards before existing adjudicatory bodies. However, the requirements of the Convention do also relate to the way in which the law itself is articulated, and they have been used to impose conditions of certainty and publicity on administrative rules.[28]

Once Parliament has created the basic structure of decision making, the High Court, in the exercise of its supervisory jurisdiction, has the power to intervene to ensure that the empowered bodies perform the tasks allotted to them.[29] The common law doctrine of *ultra vires* enables the High Court to strike down a decision that it considers to be outside the powers of the inferior body. It is a very expansive doctrine that can impinge on questions of process, broadly defined, in a number of ways. In the first place, in its substantive guise the doctrine of *ultra vires* requires that a public body act within its powers: it must make only those decisions it is empowered to make and must not act unreasonably nor irrationally. The application of these rules, despite the substantive label, can touch on matters of process. In *Ex p. Hanscomb* the court held that the Home Secretary's policy of delaying, for up to three to four years, consultation with the trial judge over the earliest date for the release of a life-sentence prisoner was unreasonable.[30]

Secondly, a body which is vested with discretionary powers must exercise those powers itself, it cannot delegate them to another body, nor can it fetter itself by adopting a pre-ordained, inflexible policy. If it does so it is acting *ultra vires*: it is failing to use a discretion given to it.[31] The case of *Re Findlay* provides an example of the operation of this principle in a custodial context.[32] There an attempt was made to challenge the Home Secretary's introduction of a new

26 (1981) 4 EHRR 181.
27 For further discussion see chapter 12.
28 *Silver* v. *The United Kingdom* (1980) 3 EHRR 473. The case is discussed further in chapter 5.
29 See reference at, *supra*, n. 19.
30 *R* v. *Secretary of State, ex p. Handscomb* (1987) 86 Crim. Ap. R 59.
31 *British Oxygen Co Ltd* v. *Board of Trade*, [1971] AC 610.
32 *Re Findlay* [1985] AC 318.

parole policy on the ground that the new policy, by applying a restrictive attitude to certain categories of prisoner, constituted an unlawful fetter on the Home Secretary's discretion. In the event, the House of Lords rejected this contention and upheld the policy.

Traditionally the application of the common law doctrine of *ultra vires* by the High Court has been justified by reference to all three fundamental principles described above. In the first place, the legislative supremacy of Parliament suggests that any inferior body that seeks to extend its powers beyond those granted to it by Parliament is defying Parliament's legislative monopoly. It is seeking to empower itself. The rule of law demands that a public body act within the law, within the powers given to it by Parliament, and it is for the courts, not the public body itself, to provide the definitive statement of the law's requirements. Similarly, the separation of powers suggests that it is for Parliament to empower the public body, for the body to exercise those powers, and for the courts to insure that it does so within the law. If the body itself were entitled conclusively to interpret the extent of its powers it would be assuming the functions of the legislature. However, as is suggested in the following section, these justifications are not entirely convincing.

(3) Process Narrowly Defined

The involvement of the law with process more narrowly defined is extensive. The criminal trial is not directly relevant to the present study but can usefully be mentioned as an example of the extensive legal regulation of process. The rules concerning procedure and evidence have perhaps been more highly developed in the context of a criminal trial than for any other forum. Criminal procedure is largely covered by statute, while criminal evidence, that is, the rules which determine what facts may be proved in a trial and what evidence may be called to prove those facts, has been developed by the common law and significantly codified by statute.[33] The Police and Criminal Evidence Act 1984, for example, replaces the common law on improperly obtained evidence (section 78) and confessions (section 76), while at the same time retaining the court's common law power to exclude evidence in their discretion – section 82(3).

The tight control imposed by the law on the criminal trial can be seen as directly required by the rule of law. A finding of guilt by a criminal court commonly results in the imposition by the state of punishment on the individual. According to the classic notion of the rule of law, a citizen can only be punished for an infringement of the pre-existing criminal law. The sophisticated procedural and evidential requirements imposed on the criminal courts can be justified as a means of insuring that this requirement of the rule of law is met.

33 For an explanation of criminal procedure see C. Hampton, *Criminal Procedure* 3rd edn (1982, London: Sweet and Maxwell), and C. Emmins, *A Practical Approach to Criminal Procedure* 3rd edn (1985, London: Blackstone Press). On criminal evidence see C. Tapper, *Cross on Evidence* 7th edn (1990, London: Butterworths).

Outside the criminal trial, the law is also involved in the direct imposition of procedural requirements on the various custodial agencies, even though the requirements imposed may vary greatly in their stringency and specificity. Primary legislation in the form of the Prison Act 1952, section 47, requires merely that a prisoner, facing a disciplinary charge, 'be given a proper opportunity of presenting his case'. This bare requirement is echoed in the Prison Rules. The Criminal Justice Act 1967 was similarly unspecific in the procedural requirements it imposed on the Parole Board, while its successor, the Criminal Justice Act 1991, although reticent on the matter itself, has provided for procedural issues to be dealt with by rules, section 32(5). In the context of mentally disordered offenders, delegated legislation is used to stipulate in some detail the procedures to be followed by Mental Health Review Tribunals when considering the discharge of a patient from hospital.[34]

The direct imposition of procedural requirements in this way by statute or delegated legislation is clearly quite justifiable, in orthodox constitutional terms, by reference to the supremacy of Parliament. It can also be said to promote the rule of law by helping to insure that the relevant agencies fulfil their functions in a rational, non-arbitrary manner. To demand that reasons be given, for example, as is the case for Mental Health Review Tribunals, should encourage a decision maker to insure that proper grounds exist for the decision.

In addition to the direct imposition of procedural requirements by statute, the High Court, in the exercise of its common law supervisory jurisdiction, can insure that public bodies meet the requirements of natural justice and the duty to act fairly.[35] These requirements may be applied both where there are no statutory provisions as to procedure and where the High Court considers the statute to be either inadequate or in need of clarification. The rules of natural justice, and more recently the duty to act fairly, have been evolved gradually by the supervisory courts. In the earlier part of this century natural justice was applied mainly to quasi-judicial bodies, and the rules tended to reflect an adjudicatory model of decision making, occasionally emulating the criminal trial. In recent years the requirements have been extended to apply to more 'administrative' decision making and some attempt has been made to break away from the adjudicatory model. The wide use of the term 'duty to act fairly' rather than 'natural justice' reflects this development. Whatever term is used, however, the common law procedural requirements are notoriously flexible, and will vary significantly according to the nature of the body, the context in which it is operating, the function it is performing, and the interests at stake. They encompass the right to a fair hearing and the rule against bias. In very broad terms, the former involves the right to be given notice of the decision – either the criteria to be met or the charges to be faced – the right to know the nature of the evidence, to respond and to put your own case, and the right to a

34 Mental Health Review Tribunal Rules 1983, SI 1983/942.
35 The origins and the nature of the common law requirements are discussed in greater detail in chapter 3. But see Wade, *supra*, n. 19, pt V, and Craig, *supra*, n. 19, chs 7 and 8, for an account of the law.

decision based on that evidence. At present there is no general common law right to reasons. The rule against bias provides the right to an impartial decision maker who neither has, nor appears to have, a personal interest in the outcome of the decision.

In recent years the High Court has regularly been asked to assess the legality of the procedures adopted by custodial agencies and, in certain contexts, has been prepared to intervene. While the individual cases will be further analysed below, a few can be mentioned here by way of illustration. Commonly, the empowering legislation will contain some procedural stipulations, but even where it is silent the courts have occasionally been prepared to imply a duty to act fairly. In *Ex p. Hickling*,[36] a prison governor was said to have a duty to act fairly when excluding a female prisoner from a mother and baby unit. More commonly the court will be asked to build on some express, albeit loose, statutory requirement. The history of court intervention in relation to prison disciplinary hearings provides a useful illustration. As mentioned above, both the Prison Act 1952 and Prison Rules make reference to the right of the prisoner to a proper opportunity of presenting his case when facing a disciplinary charge, and the court was able to argue in *Ex p. St Germain* that this illustrated a statutory intention that the rules of natural justice should be applied.[37] In other contexts, however, the court has refused to expand the bare words of the statute.[38] The requirements imposed by section 62(3) of the Criminal Justice Act 1967 were not held by the Court of Appeal to entitle a recalled life licensee to written reasons for his recall, nor did the Divisional Court consider that natural justice required disclosure to the prisoner of his medical records.[39] Similarly, where the statute has imposed procedural requirements in one context, the court has refused to extend those requirements beyond the specific context.[40] This reluctance to intervene in the context of release and recall, however, has recently been superseded by a much greater willingness on the part of the judiciary to impose the procedural requirements of the common law, as will be seen in chapter 8.

It is perhaps harder to find a justification in orthodox constitutional theory for the imposition of common law procedural requirements, whether through the doctrine of substantive *ultra vires* or by the imposition of duty to act fairly, than it is for any of the other forms of the law's involvement in process. In the case of the duty to act fairly, the courts are prepared to impose requirements in excess of those demanded by the statute: the statute may be entirely silent on the question of procedure, or may impose procedures which the judges then amplify. In either case the courts could be seen as usurping the functions of Parliament. In answer to such fears, reliance is sometimes placed on the concept of an implied statutory requirement that the rules of natural justice be followed. In some cases such a concept may be persuasive, but when rapidly

---

36 *R* v. *Home Secretary, ex p. Hickling* (1985) *The Times*, November 7.
37 *R* v. *Board of Visitors Hull Prison, ex p. St Germain* [1979] QB 425.
38 *R* v. *Deputy Governor of Parkhurst Prison, ex p. Hague* [1990] 3 All ER 687.
39 *R* v. *Home Secretary, ex p. Gunnell*, (1984) CLR 170 and (1985) CLR 105.
40 *Payne* v. *Lord Harris* [1981] 1 WLR 754.

evolving common law rules are applied to venerable statutory structures it becomes less plausible.

The application of the principles of substantive *ultra vires* can leave the courts similarly vulnerable to orthodox constitutional challenge. The courts have effectively assumed the right to determine when a public body is acting unreasonably or irrationally, arguing that there is an implied statutory requirement that power be exercised reasonably. However, when the Divisional Court in *Ex p. Handscomb* held that the Home Secretary's delay of three to four years was so unreasonable as to render his decision unlawful, it might be argued that it was acting unconstitutionally by imposing limits to the Home Secretary's discretion where Parliament had imposed none.

(c) A Broader Approach to Constitutional Fundamentals

The argument just offered is not intended to suggest that there can be no justification for the court concerning itself with the Home Secretary's delay or the detailed procedures adopted by the board of visitors. The suggestion is merely that the constitutional doctrines of Parliamentary supremacy and the rule of law in its narrowest sense are insufficient on their own to provide such a justification. The next chapter will consider possible bases for the regulation of process on a more individual level. Here it is appropriate to provide some preliminary constitutional thoughts, and later chapters will seek to establish that there is a link between the constitutional basis for process regulation and the true justification for an individual's claim to procedural protection.

The issues raised in the last section are not exclusive to the law's involvement in process. The judicial review of the exercise of power by public authorities on any grounds which are not expressly and unambiguously stipulated in the empowering legislation raises questions of the proper relationship between the legislature and the courts, and of the true legitimacy of judicial review – legitimacy in terms of the validity of any claim by the reviewing courts to obedience and respect. Such issues have long been of central concern to public lawyers, and have generated considerable literature, extending far beyond our present inquiry.[41] However, within that broader literature a significant theme has emerged, relating the legitimacy and constitutional propriety of judicial review directly to the courts' concern with matters of process. Process has acquired a vital role.[42]

In the United States, where the constitution permits judicial review of primary legislation as well as judicial review of administrative action, the proper basis for such review is a particularly controversial issue. When a

41 See, for example: T. Prosser, 'Towards a Critical Public Law' (1982) 9 Jo. of Law and Soc. 1; Harden and Lewis, *supra*, n. 10; McAuslan and McEldowney, *supra*, n. 22; and Craig, *supra*, n. 19, ch. 1, and *supra*, n. 1.

42 See: Prosser, *supra*, n. 41; D. Galligan, 'Judicial Review and the Textbook Writers' (1982) 2 Ox. Jo. of Leg. Studies 257; and M. Partington, 'The Reform of Public Law in Britain: Theoretical Problems and Practical Considerations', in McAuslan and McEldowney, *supra*, n. 22.

Supreme Court composed of appointed judges can declare a piece of Congressional legislation unlawful the apparent conflict between legality and democracy is inescapable. Considerable thought has therefore been given, both to the proper basis for the Supreme Court's power to overturn the legislative will, and to the principles which should govern the application to administrative action of the due process guarantees contained within the constitution.[43]

While in public law in general, and in constitutional law in particular, there are real dangers in trying to draw too close a parallel between the experience of the United States and that of the United Kingdom, the literature does share common concerns and develop common themes. On the central issue of the constitutional basis for the courts' intervention in matters of process in the absence of express statutory authority, there would appear to be two main lines of approach. The first is the more descriptive and, certainly in its British guise, remains more faithful to the orthodox principles as traditionally understood by lawyers. The second is the more prescriptive and critical of existing constitutional structures.

(1) Principles

The foundations of the first approach are to be found in the writings of Ronald Dworkin.[44] According to Dworkin, courts should be, and indeed are, concerned with the application of principle rather than policy. They are concerned with the identification of rights rather than the identification of the best means of promoting the general welfare. The latter task is properly pursued by the legislature and implemented by the administration. The identification of what rights exist in any given case involves the courts in the interpretation of existing rules. Do existing legal practices confer the rights in question? This interpretive task, according to Dworkin, requires the court to consider whether the existence of the right in issue is supported by the most favourable meaning attributable to existing legal rules in the light of the general principles of justice, fairness, integrity and procedural due process. The approach thus recognises the creative nature of judicial interpretation, and at the same time claims a significant role for legal adjudication in the consistent application of the 'political ideals' of justice, fairness and procedural due process.[45] The law plays a crucial part in the maintenance of the integrity of political ideals which might bring it into conflict with the majoritarian will. But such conflict is both inevitable and proper.

43 The literature is extensive, but on the question of review of the legislature see, particularly, J. H. Ely, *Democracy and Distrust: A Theory of Judicial Review* (1980, Cambridge, Mass.: Harvard University Press), and L. H. Tribe, *supra*, n. 1. And on the review of administrative action see R. B. Stewart, 'The Reformation of American Administrative Law' (1975) 88 Harv. LR 1667. Craig, *supra*, n.1, provides an excellent discussion of the main trends within the US literature.

44 See, generally, *Taking Rights Seriously* (1977, London: Duckworth), and *Law's Empire* (1986, London: Fontana Press), and, particularly, see 'The Forum of Principle' (1981) 56 New York Univ. LR 469.

45 *Supra*, 1986, p. 164.

According to the principle approach, therefore, the recognition of certain process rights in individuals affected by the decisions of custodial agents may be seen as no more than the performance of the courts of their proper role, the application of principle. Where the relevant statute is silent as to a particular procedural right, the courts may look to existing legal practices to determine whether, when interepreted in the light of justice, fairness, procedural due process and integrity, those practices support the existence of the right in question.

There is a striking similarity here between Dworkin's 'political ideals' and some current interpretations of the rule of law. In the last section it was remarked that some commentators see the rule of law as an essentially procedural concept, concerned with the form of law and its application.[46] Others see it as reflecting shared and fundamental notions of justice and fairness.[47] Jowell, while recognising that the rule of law is primarily procedural in effect, argues that it also possesses a substantive content:

'[i]t is a principle that promotes the virtues of regularity, rationality and integrity on the part of officials, and thus protects the legitimate expectations (to both future procedures and substance) of affected individuals. Because it does not itself provide specific content, it requires elaboration in the light of the practical reasons of each generation'.[48]

Understood in any of these senses, the rule of law falls well within the territory covered by Dworkin's political ideals. Accordingly, it is possible to view the imposition of procedural requirements by the reviewing courts both as the judicial enforcement of the rule of law and as the application of the principle approach to creative judicial review. In the British context, however, principles can never be applied in opposition to the express wording of a statute: the supremacy of Parliament must ultimately prevail.[49]

(2) Democracy

In the United Kingdom the doctrine of Parliamentary supremacy, whatever its historical origins and whatever its precise legal implications, is based on some notion of democratic government. Parliament is properly the supreme lawmaker because Parliament is comprised of representatives elected by universal adult suffrage. Democracy is fundamental to our constitution. It is, however, representative democracy in the sense that it is government by representatives elected by the general population.[50] Indeed, in a complex

46 *Supra*, n. 24.
47 T. R. S. Allan, 'Legislative Supremacy and the Rule of Law' (1985) 44 CLJ 111.
48 *Supra*, n. 24, p. 21.
49 For an interesting discussion of this issue see, I. Harden, 'Review Article: The Constitution and its Discontents' (1991) 21 Brit. Jo. of Pol. Sci. 489.
50 J. S. Mill, *Considerations on Representative Government* (1911, London: Longmans). See also W. N. Nelson, *On Justifying Democracy* (1980, London: Routledge and Kegan Paul), and for contemporary accounts of British democracy see A. Birch, 'The Theory and Practice of Modern British Democracy', ch. 4 in Jowell and Oliver, *supra*, n. 4, and C. Harlow, 'Power from the People? Representation and Constitutional Theory', in McAuslan and McEldowney, *supra*, n. 22, ch. 3.

modern state any other form of democracy may be thought infeasible. There is a strong argument that representative government is best able to achieve the proper balance of interests within a pluralist society by encouraging deliberative decision making by representatives insulated from the influence of factions.[51] Political reality in the United Kingdom is, of course, very far from this ideal. The emergence of strong party discipline and political patronage have done nothing to reduce the influence of powerful factions, nor to encourage true deliberative decision making.

Whatever the political reality, however, in a representative democracy the law might properly be concerned with ensuring that no faction achieves disproportionate influence, nor suffers undue exclusion from the process of government. Court intervention to enforce such law would be supportive of democracy, not opposed to it.[52] Indeed, this is the position taken by many who espouse some pluralist conception of democracy. Pluralism comes in many guises, both here and in the United States, but essentially it rejects the unitary notion of the state as portrayed by Dicey.[53] Society is understood as being comprised of a multitude of groups, each with their own interests and values, and legislation is seen as a product of bargaining and negotiation between them. In such a scheme the law might properly be used to redress any inequality in bargaining power. More specifically, it could be argued that the judiciary, being better insulated than elected representatives from the influence of factions, are particularly well suited to policing the processes of bargaining and negotiating, and thus to promoting democracy, despite their unelected and apparently undemocratic status.[54] A persistent problem is caused, however, by the lack of any independent criteria for deciding between competing interests.

Alternatively, there is a more participatory and communal model of democracy. Such a view recognises a public good which is independent of the product of bargaining between interest groups, and it emphasises individual participation and de-centralised decision making structures. It springs in part from the republican, anti-federalist opposition to the US constitution, and has enjoyed a recent revival in the United States.[55] The idea of deliberative decision making seems to be at the centre of the concept. Individuals participate in decision making, not in order to champion their own self-interest, but to evolve through a process of 'scrutiny and review' a notion of the public good.[56] Thus process, or more specifically deliberation, has both a procedural and a substantive dimension: the process will have been procedurally fair, and the

---

51 C. Sunstein 'Interest Groups in American Public Law' (1985) 38 Stan. LR 29.

52 See Ely, *supra*, n. 43, and Tribe, 'The Puzzling Persistence of Process-Based Constitutional Theories' (1980) 89 Yale LJ 1063.

53 See Craig, *supra*, n. 1, for an interesting account of various forms of pluralism in both Britain and the United States.

54 Sunstein, *supra*, n. 51.

55 *Ibid*. See also F. Michelman, 'Foreword: Traces of Self-Government' (1986) 100 Harv. LR 4; and Craig, *supra*, n. 1, ch. 10.

56 C. Sunstein, 'Beyond the Republican Revival' (1988) 97 Yale LJ 1539, p. 1548.

outcome emerging from it will be substantively correct in that it will have been achieved through agreement between political equals.[57]

While this revival of interest in republicanism is not generally used to advocate major constitutional change, there are those who take a much more radical approach to participatory democracy. Barber, for example, espouses 'strong' democracy.[58] It rests on the idea of self-governing communities and direct self-rule: individual citizens participate directly in the creation of the rules that govern them. Although the implementation of strong democratic processes will lead to a sense of the common good, there are no independent, pre-existing values, the very process of democracy itself is the governing ideal. Decisions are reached through a process of direct participation between autonomous individuals and, although conflicts will arise, they are transformed through the deliberative process. Exploitation by the majority is avoided by self-regulation. Through education and participation in accessible centres of decision making the individual acquires the skills necessary for self-government.[59]

Barber, and others who support similar views, stress the importance of small-scale, localised decision making in the realisation of strong or directly participatory democracy.[60] However, in certain spheres it is accepted that such direct participation will not be feasible, and that decisions will have to be taken by some form of bureaucratic structure through processes designed to ensure adherence to the principles of strong democracy. Thus some mechanism of external control will be required to monitor the efficacy of those processes. Further, in all areas the free flow of information will be crucial to the realisation of strong democracy, and might need to be guaranteed through some form of external supervision. If individual citizens are to participate directly in policy making they must have access to all relevant information and the technology necessary to utilise it.

Thus it is possible to argue that even in a system of strong democracy, where direct participation prevails, some external controls, even if they are non-judicial, will be required to ensure adherence to democratic principles.[61] In our existing system of government, of course, democratic aspirations are set much lower, but similar arguments can be made to justify the intervention of courts in the regulation of process within our present constitution. If the creation and policing of fully open and accountable decision making processes is seen as fundamentally supportive of democracy, it might properly take precedence over the faithful application of the Parliamentary will. Indeed, it has been

---

57 The possibility of disagreement is, however, recognised.

58 B. Barber, *Strong Democracy: Paricipatory Politics for a New Age* (1984, Berkeley: University of California Press). See also C. Pateman, *Participation and Democratic Theory* (1970, London: Cambridge University Press).

59 T. Prosser, 'Democratisation, Accountability and Institutional Design: Reflections on Public Law', in McAuslan and McEldowney, *supra*, n. 22, ch. 8, makes a similar point.

60 Pateman, *supra*, n. 58.

61 Craig, *supra*, n. 1, pp. 399–400, provides an interesting discussion of the likely attitudes of strong democracy to the constitutional role of the judiciary in the United States.

suggested in the domestic context that, despite the doctrine of Parliamentary supremacy, the courts should act as the ultimate 'quality controllers' to ensure that the legislatively ordained structures fully comply with the demands of true democracy and the rule of law.[62] According to such a view, court intervention directed towards the improvement of process would be supportive of the democratic foundations of the constitution, not hostile to them.

62 Harden and Lewis, *supra*, n. 10, p. 274.

3
Approaches to Process

The purpose of this chapter is to examine how commentators have sought to justify the law's involvement in process at a more individual level. It is possible to classify decision making in a variety of ways, but for present purposes it is necessary merely to distinguish between policy formulation, policy application and policy validation. The first two are self-explanatory, if not mutually exclusive: a decision to apply a policy in a particular way to a specific set of circumstances may act as a precedent to guide future application decisions, thus constituting policy formulation in addition to application. Policy validation occurs when an application, or possibly formulation, decision is challenged. For reasons that will be considered below, the common law regulation of process at present is primarily concerned with application and validation, and it is with those decisions that most of the literature is concerned. It is also primarily concerned with matters of process narrowly defined: process in the sense of procedure.

(a) Approaches to Process Narrowly Defined

Broadly speaking, there are two basic approaches within the literature. The first, which comes in a wide variety of guises, views the insistence on 'fair' process as justified primarily by reference to the beneficial effect of process on the direct outcome of the decision. Thus strict procedural requirements can be justified if they encourage accurate decisions. The second sees 'fair' processes as justified in so far as they protect values which exist independently of the direct outcome of the decision. My right to be heard before a decision which affects me is taken is essential in order to protect my personal dignity and autonomy, and is thus justified irrespective of the impact of my participation on the ultimate decision.

(1) Instrumentalism

The first approach emphasises the link between process and direct outcome. Thus, assuming it is possible to identify the 'correct' outcome, a procedural requirement is justified to the extent that it encourages such an outcome. So, if the sole purpose of the criminal trial is to reach an accurate finding of guilt or innocence, then any procedural requirement that encourages accuracy is justified and any which fails to do so is not.[1] Procedures are not, however, free, and if an efficiency objective is introduced the ideal level of procedural regulation will be that which minimises both the cost of the procedure itself (direct costs) and the costs of reaching a wrong – for example, inaccurate – decision (error costs). Any attempt to calulate this ideal level, however, is likely to encounter major difficulties.

In the first place, as implied above, it is not always relevant to talk in terms of correct outcomes. Even in the context of application and validation, the policies to be applied may often involve standards requiring interpretation, judgment and opinion. There may be no uniquely correct outcome. Further, while the facts may be agreed, the precise implications of the policy in relation to them may be hotly contested. The biographical details of a detained patient's background, for example, may be fully and accurately documented, but the implication to be drawn from them and the application of the discharge criteria to them by the Mental Health Review Tribunal may be highly controversial, and hard to assess as correct or incorrect. Secondly, while the identification of direct costs may be fairly straightforward – the salaries to paid to an adjudicator and the necessary clerical staff, for example – the calculation of error costs can give rise to considerable difficulties. This familiar criticism of the economic approach can be usefully illustrated by further reference to the discharge decisions of Mental Health Review Tribunals, where the range of 'incorrect' decisions available is very wide. A patient who is discharged when insufficiently recovered may fail to cope with conditions within the community, and may suffer a significant reduction in quality of life until recalled to hospital, while another prematurely discharged patient may commit a serious offence of violence shortly after leaving hospital. Alternatively, a patient whose discharge is inappropriately refused will suffer prolonged and significant loss of liberty. While each of these decisions can be regarded as wrong, any sensible assessment of their relative error costs will be hard to achieve.

The stark economic approach, as described, also fails to recognise any benefit in process beyond the facilitation of correct outcomes. Thus, in considering the role of procedures, Dworkin introduces another element to the notion of error costs. Using the criminal trial as an example, he distinguishes between two types of harm: bare harm and moral harm.[2] The innocent suspect who is mistakenly convicted and punished suffers bare harm in being sent to prison: a direct cost of the error. In addition, he or she also suffers moral harm by being wrongly deprived of the right not to be punished when innocent. It is

---

1 See, for example, J. Bentham, *A Treatise on Judicial Evidence* (1825), extracted by M. Dumont (1981, Littleton, Colorado: Rothman). For further discussion of Bentham's views see W. Twining, *Theories of Evidence: Bentham and Wigmore* (1985, Stanford, California: Stanford University Press).

2 R. Dworkin, *A Matter of Principle* (1986, Oxford: Oxford University Press), ch. 4.

these additional moral costs deriving from the infringement of a right which, according to Dworkin, justify greater expenditure on procedures designed to avoid wrongful convictions than on procedures designed to avoid wrongful acquittals. It seems that to deprive someone of a right is to treat that person unfairly: to have a right is to have some undertaking from society that certain interests will be protected; to breach that undertaking is to act unfairly towards the right-holder. Thus, with the notion of moral costs Dworkin moves beyond the bare economic analysis of process, and in so doing introduces the concept of rights. For Dworkin the possession of a substantive right triggers a secondary right to procedural protection.

This is a powerful argument for procedural rights in relation to substantive rights. The corollary is, however, that there are no procedural rights in relation to bare interests.[3] The harm which may result from interference with bare interests is bare harm; there is no moral harm since nothing has been lost to which there is a right, and it is only moral harm that attracts procedural protection. It seems that for Dworkin, once outside the sphere of substantive rights, procedures are essentially matters of policy, with any claim to specific procedures being so weak as to be negligible.

(2) Process Values

Both the economic and the moral costs approach to process are instrumental, in the sense of regarding the primary purpose of procedural requirements as facilitating correct decisions: processes are related directly to decision outcomes. The economic approach can be described as 'single-value instrumentalism' and the moral cost approach as 'multi-value instrumentalism'.[4] An alternative approach is to see processes as designed to protect values which are independent of the direct outcome of the decision, such as participation, fairness and the protection of individual dignity. While such values may contribute to correct outcomes, that may not be their primary justification. Respect for individual dignity may be regarded as a value worthy of protection in decision making structures irrespective of its impact on the direct decision outcome. As Bayles describes it, in the case of the instrumental approach the causal chain from procedure to economic or moral error cost goes through the decision outcome, whereas in the process-values approach the causal link from procedure to process value does not go through the decision outcome.[5]

This emphasis on the role of process as the protector of independent values is common to the dignitary approach to process which has been influential in the United States. The precise details of the approach vary. For some commentators the requirement that an individual be treated fairly is grounded

---

3 But see D. J. Galligan, in D. J. Galligan and C. J. Sampford, *Law, Rights and the Welfare State* (1986, London: Croom Helm).

4 M. Bayles, *Procedural Justice: Allocating to Individuals* (1990, Dordrecht: Kluwer Academic Publishers), ch. 6.

5 *Ibid.*, p. 128.

in a notion of justice derived from social contact theory,[6] for others it springs from natural rights,[7] from fundamental liberal values,[8] or from Kant's injunction condemning the treatment of individuals merely as means.[9] Whatever the precise foundation of the approach, however, the claim is made that the need to provide procedural fairness, particularly in the form of participation, springs from the obligation to respect a person's dignity and autonomy as a human being. To deny an individual the opportunity to participate in decisions affecting her is to deprive her of the conditions necessary for continued moral agency.[10] The primary justification for a claim to fair process, accordingly, lies not in the ability of such processes to achieve correct outcomes, but in the respect that they afford to the dignity and autonomy of individuals. The instrumental value of fair procedures is not denied by dignitary theorists, it is merely viewed as secondary.

Bayles has attempted to develop a means of evaluating processes that combines features of both the instrumental and the dignitary approaches.[11] Together with the dignitary theorists, he assumes that process benefits exist which are independent of the direct decision outcome, but he does not derive them exclusively from the dignity and autonomy of individuals. Such benefits, according to Bayles, are those that a 'fully rational person would accept',[12] and he lists participation, fairness in the sense of equality, intelligibility, timeliness and confidence in the decision making process. Some of these benefits would further the instrumental accuracy objective, but their value is accepted even if they have no such effect. Thus, Bayles argues that procedures should be evaluated in terms of the extent to which they reduce error, moral and direct costs, and promote process benefits. Bayles uses this 'norm' to evaluate the characteristics of procedural justice which he sees as impartiality, the provision of a hearing, the provision of grounds for decisions and the principles of formal justice. Impartiality may increase accuracy, but even if it fails to do so, it will provide a process benefit in the form of an increase in confidence in the decision making process. Thus Bayles' formula enables factors beyond the directly instrumental and those immediately related to the protection of

6 R. Saphire, 'Specifying Due Process Values: Towards a More Responsive Approach to Procedural Protection' (1978) 127 Univ. of Penn. LR 111, and W. Van Alstyne, 'Cracks in "The New Property": Adjudicative Due Process in the Administrative State' (1977) 62 Cornell LR 445.

7 J. Mashaw, 'Dignitary Process: A Political Psychology of Liberal Democratic Citizenship' (1987) 39 Univ. of Flo. LR 433.

8 J. Mashaw, *Bureaucratic Justice: Managing Social Security Disability Claims* (1983, New Haven: Yale University Press).

9 E. Pincoffs, 'Due Process, Fraternity, and a Kantian Injunction', in J. R. Pennock and J. W. Chapman (eds), *Due Process. Nomos 18* (1977, New York: New York University Press), ch. 5, and J. Mashaw, 'Administrative Due Process: The Quest for a Dignitary Theory' (1981) 61 Bos. Univ. LR 885.

10 Mashaw, *supra*, n. 7.

11 *Supra*, n. 4.

12 *Ibid.*, p. 130.

individual dignity to be taken into account when assessing or selecting procedures and, as such, it helps to widen the debate.

Three main justifications for the regulation of process are to be found in the existing literature, therefore: the instrumental approach which regards process regulation as designed primarily to reduce direct, error and moral costs; the dignitary approach which sees fair process as essential to the maintenance of the dignity and autonomy of individuals; and Bayles' broader process-values approach. It is now necessary to look at judical practice in the light of these approaches.

(b) Judicial Practice

The previous chapter gave a brief description of the procedural requirements imposed by the High Court in the course of its review jurisdiction. While the general principles of *ultra vires* contain procedural aspects in the guise of unreasonableness, for example, or the rule against self-fettering, the common law requirements are primarily contained in what are traditionally referred to as the rules of natural justice: namely, the rule against bias and the right to a fair hearing. It was suggested, particularly with reference to natural justice, that in certain circumstances the interference of the common law might be hard to justify by reference to orthodox constitutional principle. In an attempt to understand how the judges themselves view – and presumably justify – their role, judicial practice will be considered with reference to the conceptual approaches described above. The majority of the discussion will relate to the rules of natural justice, but some reference will be made to other common law procedural principles.

The criteria of the imposition of the rules of natural justice, or more recently the duty to act fairly, can be said to involve two elements: interference with the right or interest of an individual, and the decision of a body exercising a public function. Each requires further consideration. First, it is evident from the case law that the requirements of the common law, especially those incorporated in the right to a fair hearing, are triggered by the existence of a right or interest in an individual.

(1) The Rights or Interests of Individuals

Since *Ridge* v. *Baldwin* and subsequent case law it is quite clear that the protection afforded by common law procedures extends beyond the legally recognised rights of individuals: the old distinction between rights and privileges has finally disappeared.[13] In the *Council for Civil Service Unions*, Lord Diplock explained that, to be subject to procedural requirements, a decision must affect some person, either by affecting his or her private law rights or obligations, or by depriving that person of a benefit or advantage which he or she legitimately expected to enjoy.[14] Such a legitimate expectation can arise

13 [1964] AC 40.
14 *Council for Civil Service Unions* v. *Minister for the Civil Service* [1985] AC 374 at p. 408.

through past practice or a specific undertaking. The expectation may be to a substantive benefit which then attracts procedural protection, or it may refer directly to the procedure itself, as when an individual or a group is promised consultation.

Thus, while the extent to which the recognition of a legitimate expectation can guarantee the receipt of a substantive benefit may be open to some doubt,[15] the relevance of the concept to the application of common law procedural protection is considerable. According to Wade, the concept is flexible enough to be used to trigger procedural protection 'in any of many situations where fairness and good administration justify the right to be heard'.[16] On the other hand, its flexibility could just as readily allow it to be used restrictively. The court may deny the existence of a legitimate expectation in certain circumstances, as it did in *U.S. Tobacco*,[17] or may define the extent of the expectation very restrictively, as was arguably the case in *Re Findlay*,[18] where the House of Lords adopted a very restricted view of the legitimate expectations possessed by life-sentence prisoners.

Finally, the interest of the individual must be *affected* by the decision. Strictly speaking, this requirement exempts preliminary recommendations from procedural regulation, and may partially explain the courts' slightly ambivalent attitude to the procedural regulation of statutory inquiries.[19]

Thus, the application of common law procedures is triggered by the existence in an individual of a substantive interest which stands to be affected, and which is deemed worthy of procedural protection. One exception to this substantive interest requirement, however, is created by the legitimate expectation doctrine when it is applied, not to provide a substantive interest with some procedural protection, but directly to enforce an undertaking to follow a certain procedure.[20] Here the expectation deemed worthy of protection relates to a procedural rather than a substantive benefit. In such cases the common law is prepared directly to enforce the non-statutory procedures promised by public bodies. The strong connection which, apart from this one exception, exists between the substantive interest of an individual and the procedural obligations of the decision maker is reinforced by the rule that only the person denied the fair hearing can sue for breach of common law procedures. So a third party with a general interest in the maintenance of fair procedures cannot challenge the validity of a decision made in breach of the duty to afford a fair hearing. Only the person denied the hearing, who inevitably is the person whose substantive interests have been affected, can issue the challenge. The requirement is similar to that contained in the idea of standing, namely that an individual seeking judicial review of an agency's

15 C. Forsyth, 'The Provenance and Protection of Legitimate Expectations' (1988) 47 CLJ 238.
16 H. W. R. Wade, *Administrative Law* 6th edn (1988, Oxford: Oxford University Press), p. 522.
17 *R. v. Secretary of State, ex p. U.S. Tobacco* [1992] 1 All ER 212.
18 [1985] AC 318.
19 See, for example, *Bushell v. Secretary of State for the Environment* [1981] AC 75, and *R v. Secretary of State for Transport, ex p. Gwent* [1987] 2 WLR 961.
20 See, for example, *A-G of Hong Kong v. Ng Yuen Shiu* [1983] 2 AC 629.

action must first possess sufficient interest in the matter to which the application relates, but Wade suggests the requirement is also 'inherent in the principle of natural justice itself'.[21]

In practice, most of the case law seems to reflect an instrumental approach to the role of process regulation, particularly with regard to the right to a fair hearing. The common law seeks to encourage informed and accurate decision making by insisting that before a decision is made a fair hearing is afforded to those whose interests stand to be affected. Commom law intervention is thus designed to protect the interests of individuals from interference consequent upon incorrect decisions. Orthodox judicial rhetoric, by contrast, displays an additional concern for process, possibly dignitary, values. According to this orthodoxy, reviewing courts will intervene to insure adherence to the requirements of the common law, even if such adherence would have made no difference to the decision outcome:

If the principles of natural justice are violated in respect of any decision it is, indeed, immaterial whether the same decision would have been arrived at in the absence of the departure from the essential principles of justice. The decision must be declared to be no decision.[22]

Such an approach would suggest a desire to insure fair procedures which is independent of any impact on the direct outcome of the individual decision. In practice this orthodoxy is often avoided, either by a refusal by the court to grant a remedy for the alleged breach,[23] or by a denial that any breach occurred.[24] Nevertheless, whatever its practical significance, the emphasis placed on process values in judicial rhetoric is still firmly linked to the possession by an individual of a substantive interest worthy of protection: the obligation to provide fair procedures and to treat a person with dignity may be independent of the direct outcome of the decision, but it only arises when that person's substantive interests are at stake.

To some extent the judges' approach towards the rule against bias differs from their approach towards the right to a fair hearing. The rule against bias has traditionally been regarded as being more concerned with appearances than is the right to a fair hearing. It extends beyond actual to presumptive bias. No actual bias need be present, merely a 'reasonable suspicion' or a 'real likelihood' of bias. Thus the rule appears to be designed not only to protect the interests of individuals from interference flowing from biased decision making, but also to safeguard process benefits through supporting the principle that justice be seen to be done. On this basis it is closer to Bayles' process-values approach than to narrow instrumentalism. In line with this broader concern with the appearance, if not the reality, of the decision making structure, a greater willingness to allow third parties to complain might be anticipated in

21 *Supra*, n. 16, p. 537.
22 *General Medical Council* v. *Spackman* [1943] AC 627, per Lord Wright at p. 644.
23 *Fullbrook* v. *Berkshire Magistrates' Court Committee* (1970) 69 LGR 75, and *Glynn* v. *Keele University* [1971] 1 WLR 487.
24 *Cinnamond* v. *British Airports Authority* [1980] 1 WLR 582.

relation to the rule against bias than exists with regard to the right to a fair hearing.

To some extent the case law does indeed reflect a more flexible approach: the decision of a biased planning authority to grant planning permission, for example, has been quashed at the instance of an interested party other than the applicant.[25] But that flexibility is very limited. Even in the example given, the successful challenger had a substantive interest: he owned property neighbouring the development land. Further, the doctrine of waiver enables an individual to waive the presence of a biased decision maker and, having done so, to be barred from any subsequent challenge on ground of bias.[26] Such a doctrine tends to reflect the narrower interest-protection approach by regarding the directly affected individual as the only person properly concerned: if he or she accepts the presence of bias, so be it. It does little to support any broader concern with the fairness of the decision making structure itself, whether apparent or real.

Thus the interpretation of the first criterion, the existence of a decision affecting the rights or interests of an individual, tends to indicate an essentially instrumental approach: fair process is required in order to encourage accurate decisions, and thereby to protect the substantive interests of individuals. Further, even where a concern with process values is expressed, that concern is inspired by the presence of a vulnerable substantive interest. This is not to contend that the desire to protect substantive interests cannot be outweighed by a concern to maintain the integrity of the process itself. In *Ex p. Beniam and Khaida* the interests of the individual applicants were outweighed by the perceived need to protect the future efficacy of the decision making process.[27] It is merely to suggest that an instrumental approach, in the form of a desire to protect the substantive interests of individuals from interference as a result of inaccurate decision making, appears to dominate the case law in practice.

(2) The Decision of a Body Exercising a Public Function

The second criterion for the application of the common law procedural requirements – that there be a decision by a body exercising a public function – is, for present purposes, less significant. While it is now clear that susceptibility to common law procedures is not restricted to the exercise of statutory powers, the powers must be public in the sense that they must not derive exclusively from contract, and the decision maker must be operating with some government recognition.[28] In the days prior to *Ridge* v. *Baldwin*, even with regard to obviously public bodies, the courts had developed a distinction between administrative and judicial bodies. The latter were susceptible to procedural regulations, the former were not: a decision had not only to be public but judicial or quasi-judicial as well. *Ridge* v. *Baldwin* was thought to

25 *R* v. *Hendon Rural District Council, ex p. Chorley* [1933] 2 KB 696, and see Wade, *supra*, n. 16, p. 476.
26 *R* v. *Secretary of State for Health, ex p. Prison Officers Assoc.* [1991] *The Times*, 28 October.
27 *R* v. *Gaming Board of Great Britain, ex p. Benaim and Khaida* [1970] 2 QB 417.
28 *R* v. *Panel on Takeovers and Mergers, ex p. Datafin* [1987] QB 815.

have destroyed the distinction, at least in so far as it affected the *application* of natural justice. In *King*, however, the Court of Appeal revived the distinction in order to deny judicial review and the application of natural justice to the disciplinary decisions of prison governors.[29] Governors, unlike boards of visitors, were said to be administrative bodies. Four years later, in a similar context, the House of Lords categorically denied the existence of such a distinction, and it can only be hoped it is now dead and beyond all resurrection.[30] The nature of the body and its functions will, however, continue to affect the nature of the procedural requirements imposed on it by the common law.

Until the early 1970s the procedural requirements of the common law were described generally as the rules of natural justice. In the late 1960s, however, the courts began to develop the notion of a duty to act fairly,[31] and it is now common for the courts to talk in terms of the duty to act fairly in preference to the rules of natural justice. To an extent this development mirrored the whittling down of the old administrative/judicial distinction. While natural justice in its traditional form might properly apply to judicial and quasi-judicial decisions, a less formal set of requirements incorporated in the duty to act fairly might be more appropriate in a primarily administrative context. Considerable debate has surrounded the precise nature of the duty to act fairly and the implications that can be drawn from its introduction,[32] but it is at least clear that it, like its traditional counterpart, is primarily concerned with the protection of the interests of individuals. A public body may be under a duty to act fairly but such a duty will attach to its activities primarily in so far as they directly affect the interests of individuals.

(3) The Influence of Adjudication

It is often remarked that the procedural requirements of the common law are closely modelled on the adjudicatory format, particularly the adversarial adjudicatory form familiar to the British courts. Accordingly, the common law insists, with varying degrees of formality, on adequate notice of the impending decision, an opportunity to see the evidence, an opportunity to be heard, and a decision from an impartial decision maker which is based on the revealed evidence. Through this form of participation the vulnerable individual is given the opportunity to improve the accuracy of the decision and to facilitate informed decision making. In the eyes of the judiciary, who are familiar with the adjudicatory model, such a procedural form may represent the most suitable process available for the protection of individual interests from the inaccurate application of public policy.[33]

Although it is true that the duty to act fairly has introduced greater

29 *R* v. *Deputy Governor of Camphill Prison, ex p. King* [1985] QB 735.
30 *Leech* v. *Parkhurst Prison Deputy Governor* [1988] AC 533.
31 *Re HK* [1967] 2 QB 617.
32 M. Loughlin, 'Procedural Fairness: A Study of the Crisis in Administrative Law Theory' (1978) 28 Univ. of Toronto LJ 215, and R. A. Macdonald, 'Judicial Review and Procedural Fairness in Administrative Law: I' (1979–1980) 25 McGill LJ 520.
33 M. D. Bayles, *Principles of Law: A Normative Analysis* (1987, Dordrecht: Kluwer Academic Publishers), and Bayles, *supra*, n. 4.

flexibility into the common law, the content of the requirements still tends to derive from the adjudicatory model, and their impact only rarely extends beyond application decisions. Admittedly, in recent years the courts have shown a greater willingness to entertain claims to consultation, a potentially encouraging development. However, such claims tend to relate to application or very specific policy formulation decisions, and tend to be most successful where the alleged consultee is also the person directly affected by the decision outcome.[34] They therefore add little to the traditional adjudicatory format and emphasis on application decisions.

(4) Implications and Limitations

In the light of the above discussion it is possible to argue that the common law's involvement in the regulation of process is based on a mutually supportive structure containing three elements: instrumental justification for involvement, an emphasis on the application and validation stages of policy evolution, and the adoption of an adjudicatory model of procedure. Without extensive research it is not possible to attribute cause and effect between these three elements, but the links between them are clear. In the first place, the attitude of the courts to the basis for their imposition of procedural requirements seems, in the main, to reflect the instrumental approach. Procedures are required in order to protect individuals', largely substantive, interests: the possession of such an interest triggers the procedural require-ment. The need to protect the individual's interest may, in the result, be outweighed by the need to promote the integrity of the system, but the whole question of procedural propriety is triggered by the existence of a vulnerable interest in an individual initially deemed worthy of protection. Similarly, on the rare occasions when the dignitary approach prevails, the emphasis on individual rights is still strong, since it would seem that it is only when a person's interests are involved in a decision that dignity and respect require the participation of that person.[35] Secondly, the common law rules are applied predominately at the application and validation stages, where these individual interests are most likely to be directly affected. Thirdly, and finally, the adjudicatory model which prevails is widely regarded as particularly well-designed for the protection of individual interests from interference resulting from uninformed and inaccurate decisions.

Arguably, the present character of the common law procedural require-ments imposes two significant limitations on their potential. In the first place, the emphasis placed on the protection of individual interests by the common law, and especially by the right to a fair hearing, has provided no incentive to extend procedural regulation beyond the application and validation stages of policy evolution and implementation. The substantive interests of individuals are most vulnerable to direct interference as a result of decisions to apply policy and by subsequent attempts to challenge such applications. With

---

34 *R* v. *Secretary of State for the Environment, ex p. Brent LBC* [1982] QB 593, *R* v. *Secretary of State for Transport, ex p. GLC* [1986] QB 56, and *supra*, n. 14.

35 Mashaw, *supra*, n. 7.

regard to policy formulation in the form of rule making, the common law has traditionally been reluctant to become involved. According to established principle, natural justice does not apply to decisions of a legislative nature. There is, for example, no common law right to be heard before the making of legislation, whether primary or delegated.[36] A duty to consult may, of course, be created by statute in relation to delegated legislation but, while such duties are regarded as mandatory and may be interpreted quite strictly by the courts,[37] non-compliance will not necessarily lead to invalidation of the relevant regulations.[38]

With regard to administrative rule making, the position seems now to be governed by the doctrine of legitimate expectation. Thus, if an interest group has always been consulted in the past or has been promised consultation in the future, they might argue that they have a legitimate expectation to consultation which they should not be denied in the absence of a hearing and of strong public interest in favour of denial. In the absence of such a legitimate expectation, however, neither interested groups nor individuals have a right to consultation prior to the formulation of administrative rules. The common law seems unwilling, whether through duty to act fairly or through the general principles of *ultra vires* which require the decision maker to act reasonably, to demand consultation where none is required by statute, or by promise, or by established practice. The House of Lords, for example, had no hesitation in denying the claim that the Home Secretary had a duty to consult the Parole Board prior to the introduction of a new policy on parole.[39]

The second major limitation derives directly from the emphasis on individual interest protection. Before the procedural requirements can be triggered, the court must recognise a substantive right or legitimate expectation in need of protection. The judicial approach thus closely resembles that of Dworkin: procedural rights are secondary to the protection of substantive interests. Admittedly, with the development of legitimate expectations the courts have signalled a willingness to go beyond Dworkin and to protect interests which do not constitute rights, but they do still demand some *legitimate* expectation. This requirement immediately raises the familiar problem of selection: who selects the expectations worthy of protection and on what basis? Is it really appropriate that the judges should do so?[40]

(c) A Broader Approach

In the light of the limitations flowing from the traditional approaches to

36 See, Wade, *supra*, n. 16, and *Leech*, supra, n. 30, at p. 578.
37 See *U.S. Tobacco*, *supra*, n. 17.
38 *R* v. *Secretary of State, ex p. A.M.A.* [1986] 1 WLR 1, and *R* v. *Secretary of State for Health, ex p. Natural Medicines Group* [1991] COD 60.
39 *Re Findlay*, *supra*, n. 18, and *R* v. *Secretary of State, ex p. Cox* (1991) *The Independent*, 8 October.
40 See J.A.G. Griffith, *The Politics of the Judiciary*, 4th edn (1991, London: Fontana).

process as reflected in current judicial attitudes, it becomes relevant to consider whether an alternative can be found which moves beyond the secondary role typically attributed to 'rights' to fair process. At the beginning of this chapter it was remarked that most of the literature discussing the bases for the involvement of the common law in the regulation of process within the United Kingdom tends to concentrate on decisions at the application and validation stages. There is, of course, a separate and extensive literature concerned with the processes involved in the constitution of governments, some of which was touched on in the previous chapter. In this country, however, the two debates tend to run in parallel: there is little exchange between the two.[41] As Craig has pointed out in the context of participation, there is no satisfactory theory recognising the possibility of participation, other than as a voter or as a litigant, in the broadest sense.[42] While no attempt will be made here to provide a single such comprehensive theory, an attempt will be made to argue that a sufficiently close relationship exists between the ideas referred to in the previous chapter and the regulation of process in the more individual context to suggest an alternative basis for the latter which moves beyond the mere protection of substantive interests.

At the centre of the argument lies the notion of legitimate authority. The decisions of officials exercising public power should comply with certain principles of justification. It can be argued that such a justification require-ment applies to all those whose decisions affect others – parents, teachers, employers etc. In the public sphere, however, where the power exercised emanates ultimately from the state, special principles of justification apply. While the precise identification of the 'public' sphere or the 'state' is a complex and highly contingent exercise, it will be assumed here that the ultimate authority to impose and administer judicial punishment must fall within the public sphere, however defined, and that this will remain unaffected by privatisation.

Thus criminal justice is one aspect of state power exercised through the law, and only by establishing the authority of the law is it possible to establish the authority of the individual decision maker operating within that law. The issue is a large one, but for present purposes it is sufficient to concentrate on one specific question: under what condition is law authoritative, in the sense of being deserving of support and respect? An institution may be authoritative in a purely formal sense when it acts properly within the powers granted to it. So the Parole Board may be authoritative in that sense when it makes the kinds of decisions which it has been empowered to make by legislation and does so according to relevant legal principles. This is an important sense of authority

---

41 See, however, T. Prosser, 'Democratisation, Accountability and Institutional Design: Reflec-tions on Public Law', in P. McAuslan and J. McEldowney (eds), *Law, Legitimacy and the Constitution* (1985, London: Sweet and Maxwell), ch. 8.

42 P. Craig, *Public Law and Democracy in the United Kingdom and the United States of America* (1990, Oxford: Oxford University Press), p. 175. But see contributions to J. Pennock and J. Chapman (eds), *Participation in Politics: Nomos 16* (1975, New York: Atherton).

since, in a legal dispute, it is only these formal issues that typically arise. However, a broader question is being raised here concerning the conditions necessary to persuade the citizen that the law deserves her respect in more than a purely formal sense.

The question can be taken in two stages: first, why is state authority necessary? And secondly, under what condition ought it to be accepted? In answer to the first part it can be argued that, even if a society and its members wish merely to survive, they would be wise to introduce some regulation of the exploitation and distribution of resources, and of the actions of one person in relation to another.[43] Coordination is required for survival and, indeed, coordination is often used to express the general, overriding function of a legal system.[44] As societies become more complex and diverse, the need for coordination becomes more intense but more difficult to achieve.[45] If, in addition, mere survival is rejected in favour of higher levels of order and welfare, then the task of coordination is ever more demanding and, arguably, the case for state authority ever more compelling.[46]

An acceptance of the practical case for state authority, however, still leaves open the question of the conditions of its exercise. A government charged with coordinating social activities will be authoritative only if it acts reasonably in accordance with certain acceptable principles. While the precise identification of these principles will vary widely, depending on the overall approach taken to fundamental issues of moral and political theory, it is sufficient here to consider briefly just two alternative approaches.

(1) Liberal Pluralism

According to the first approach, which is essentially grounded in the Western liberal tradition, it is convenient to separate the 'acceptable principles' into three different categories by reference to their origins and levels of specificity. In the first place, even liberals, who deny that any particular conception of the good should take automatic priority, accept that there are some principles that are so fundamental that compliance is a necessary condition of authority within any society. Among such principles are ideas of respect for persons and their liberty: ideas about autonomy, privacy and personal responsibility: about the protection of individuals from harm, and the provision of basic welfare. To some extent these principles reflect the primary goods considered as the bare essentials by Rawls' thin theory of the good.[47] Such abstract

43 H. Hart, *Concept of Law* (1961, Oxford: Oxford University Press).

44 J. Finnis, *Natural Law and Natural Rights* (1980, Oxford: Oxford University Press), and J. Raz, *The Morality of Freedom* (1986, Oxford: Oxford University Press).

45 Connolly, 'Modern Authority and Ambiguity', in J. Pennock and J. Chapman (eds), *Authority Revisited: Nomos 29* (1987, New York: New York University Press).

46 G. Teubner, 'Substantive and Reflexive Elements in Modern Law' (1983) 17 L and Soc. R 239.

47 J. Rawls, 'The Basic Liberties and their Priority', in S. M. McMurrin (ed.), *Liberty, Equality and Law* (1987, Salt Lake City: University of Utah Press). And see the discussion in Craig, *supra*, n. 42, p. 249.

precepts have to be interpreted and made concrete, but they are nevertheless regarded as the foundation stones of a justifiable social order.

At a second level, each community is likely to be committed to more specific values which are implicit in day-to-day life, and which become embedded in its political structure, its form of government, and its legislation, administration and adjudication. These working values might include a commitment to democratic principles, representative government, duties of care towards others, entitlements to property, and rights to welfare. Working values are discovered by examining the laws and practices of the society, thus a study of the criminal law, for example, would provide a guide to a host of values.[48] Indeed, a level of consensus about such intermediate or working values is important in securing social cohesion. The working values of a community, of course, might be repugnant and merit no support. But, provided that they meet the first layer of principles and can be seen to be the historical products of a humane society which is open to change, then there is virtue in preserving those values and in encouraging consistency between them. That virtue is expressed by Dworkin in the idea of integrity, and for Dworkin integrity is of cardinal importance in the legitimation of a legal system.[49] Part of its importance lies in the stability and certainty which flows from integrity; but part is also to be found in the way that it preserves and perpetuates a sense of community.

The third category of principle which contributes to the authority of a legal system, according to this approach, is of particular relevance to the role of process, and thus is of special interest here. The argument is pluralist in so far as it accepts that modern societies are complex and diverse.[50] They are complex in the sense that the task of coordinating their many activities cannot be forced into a single master plan: effective coordination will depend on more localised action, on responding to issues and disputes, on accommodating interests and groups, and on finding compromises amongst them. Societies are diverse in the sense that groups and individuals vary across a wide spectrum in their activities and interests, their values and preferences. Within such a society one of the principle liberal values must be 'the freedom of the citizen and of associations freely chosen by citizens'.[51] Such a value recognises personal freedom and the diversity that follows from it: it allows for differing concepts of the good. In addition, principles of equality, often expressed in terms of democracy, suggest that each person counts in the decisions of government.

In order to satisfy these two principles of freedom and equal political significance, any exercise of government power must demonstrate that full regard has been paid to the diversity of values and interests represented within society. Coordination requires some subordination of individual interests to the public good: individual or group freedom cannot be absolute. But,

48 Bayles, *supra*, n. 4.
49 *Law's Empire* (1986, London: Fontana Press).
50 The sense is thus more general than that adopted in chapter 2.
51 P. Hirst and P. Jones, 'The Critical Resources of Established Jurisprudence' (1987) 14 Jo. of Law and Soc. 21, p. 24.

arguably, subordination should only occur after full consideration of the plurality of interests and values at stake. A decision which evolves through such a process of consideration should reflect a broad public interest, and in doing so should match the third category of principles contained in the notion of authoritative governmental power.

According to this third category of principle, legal and administrative institutions at every level of government, from legislation to individualised decisions, must be designed to ensure that all interests are represented, and that none is accorded automatic priority. Through the full participation of individuals and groups and the responsiveness of public decision makers, decisions can be reached which reflect the public interest in its broadest sense, a public interest which is refined from the wealth of group and individual interests. So the requirements of freedom and equal political significance carry with them implications for the process through which governmental decisions evolve, and any governmental decision which evolves through a process designed to facilitate, if not to guarantee, the full reflection of the public interest will have a further claim to authority.

In sum, according to the traditions of liberal pluralism, the principles necessary for the authoritative exercise of state power fall into three categories. The first of these principles demands compliance with fundamental moral values: the second reflects a concern for the stability and continuity of values within the system, and the third, recognising the complex and plural nature of modern society, places particular importance on the process of public decision making. While this third principle is not regarded as sufficient on its own to provide full authority for the exercise of governmental power, it is seen as a necessary condition. Thus, according to this approach the claim to full process, at whatever stage in policy implementation it is being made, whether it be in relation to individual application decisions or with regard to policy formulation, is grounded ultimately on the citizen's entitlement to the legitimate exercise of public power, and exists independently of any vulnerable 'substantive' interest possessed by that citizen. Further, any external mechanism – such as legal regulation through the courts – which is designed to ensure compliance with the demands of full process would be justified as serving to promote the legitimacy of governmental power, irrespective of silence on the part of the legislature. The enforcement of common law principles reflective of full process in this sense would be supportive of democracy rather than hostile to it: they would be constitutional in the most fundamental sense.

(2) Strong Democracy

There is an alternative, more radical, approach which accords process an even more central role. According to Barber's theory of strong democracy, the co-ordination required within a society is achieved by way of direct participation and self-regulation. The authority of 'state' action is achieved through the 'active consent of participatory citizens'.[52] While, in the more liberal approach

---

52 B. Barber, *Strong Democracy: Participatory Politics for a New Age* (1984, Berkeley: University of California Press), p. 137.

described above, the individual and the state are distinct and the relationship between the two requires a balance of control and accountability which is often understood in contractual terms, within strong democracy there is no clear divide between individual and government: the individual, as a direct participant, is part of government. Further, within strong democracy there are no prior values. Conflicts will be resolved and decisions reached through a process of public deliberation, and any values that evolve will emerge from discussion between the citizens themselves.

In the absence of prior rights, tyranny by the majority is to be avoided, not by external controls, but through the process of self-regulation. Process is therefore at the heart of strong democracy: it is process that protects the substance of decisions. According to this approach, the process through which a decision evolves is the fundamental source of its authority. The role of the law as a mechanism for ensuring the maintenance of strong democratic processes, however, is more uncertain. Ideally, direct self-regulation requires no external control. As mentioned in the previous chapter, however, Barber recognises that direct participation and self-regulation will not always be possible, and that certain agencies with decision making powers will be required even within strong democracy. In relation to these agencies some external mechanisms may be necessary to guarantee their adherence to the principles of participatory democracy. Further, even though the presence of prior values is denied by strong democrats, the commitment to strong democratic principles could itself, as Craig argues, be seen as such an independent value, and some system of external review might be advisable to safeguard adherence to it.[53]

(3) Conclusions

These two alternative, broader approaches to process, although coming from different traditions, share common characteristics. They both see full process as fundamental to the authority of state action, and they both recognise that participation is required at every stage of government in order to legitimate the decisions reached. According to liberal pluralism, the individual is distinct from the state and is entitled to expect the legitimate exercise of state authority, *one* component of which demands that all decisions be taken in the full reflection of the public interest. According to strong democracy, on the other hand, where there is no clear line between individual and state the authority of action is derived exclusively from the process of direct participation and self-regulation through which decisions evolve, and from the substantive implications of that process.

Thus, despite the differences in emphasis, under either approach the individual who claims a fair hearing before a policy application decision is made affecting her, is relying essentially on the same principle as that which entitles her to participate in the legislative process of policy formulation. The nature of the participation required at either point will depend on the precise

---

53 Craig, *supra*, n. 42, p. 382.

stage in the process of policy implementation at which the decision occurs, but the basis of the claim remains essentially the same. It is not to protect her independent substantive interests that the citizen participates, but to promote the true authority of the decision. Admittedly, the two approaches reflect very different attitudes towards the role of government, but both emphasise the fundamental role of process in the legitimation of governmental decisions, and thus provide an alternative view of the law's involvement in the regulation of process which could encourage the law to develop beyond the narrow parameters of interest protection set by the more traditional approaches. Most significantly, a broader approach of this nature would break the essential link between substantive interests and procedural protection: claims to fair procedures would no longer be secondary, and would carry the demands for fair process into the realm of policy formulation.

Some of the practical difficulties likely to be encountered by any attempt to implement such an approach will be considered in the following chapters, where the broad approach will be referred to generally as 'full process' or the 'full reflection of the public interest'. Only where particularly relevant will the differences between the two 'broad' approaches be emphasised.

4
Forms of Process

(a) The Stages of Policy Evolution

In the previous chapter two approaches to the notion of full process were described and, while the two differ significantly in many respects, both would support a broad notion of process requiring sufficient participation at all levels of public decision making to enable decisions to be reached which fully reflect the public interest. The practical impact of this argument, in terms of the nature of the processes demanded and the extent of the law's involvement in the regulation of those processes, will vary widely, emphasising at one extreme 'full' participation in the creation of policy and, at the other, the rational application of closely defined rules to individual circumstances. The purpose of this chapter is to consider the factors which might influence the selection of the precise process requirements to be applied to any particular decision within criminal justice, or more particularly, within custodial policy.

As a preliminary it is necessary to consider again the stages at which decisions occur in the creation and implementation of criminal justice policy. Broadly speaking, decisions may be required at three distinct but interrelated stages: (a) policy making, frequently involving the development of rules, principles or standards; (b) the initial application of a policy to individual circumstances, and (c) the checking or validation of decisions at stages (a) or (b).

Stage (a) decisions concerning policy creation must always occur, since application decisions cannot be reached in a vacuum. In structure, and particularly in degree of formality and openness, however, such decisions will vary enormously. The creation of the rules of substantive criminal law, a necessary precursor to determinations of guilt or innocence, is, for example, commonly accompanied by the whole formality of the Parliamentary legislative process, whereas the identification of the criteria to be applied in assessing a mentally disordered offender's suitability for unescorted walks around the grounds of a secure hospital is an extremely informal and unstructured procedure. Further, in the evolution of any particular policy, stage (a) decisions may themselves occur at a number of different points as policies are devised, refined and redefined. Any individual decision to prosecute, for example, is preceded by a long chain of policy formulation decisions involving Parliament, the Director of Public Prosecutions, the Crown Prosecution Service and the local police force. In general, however, stage (a) decisions can be differentiated from decisions at stages (b) and (c) by reference to the generality and prospectivity of the former.

Decisions at stage (b) involving the individual application of policy will similarly vary widely in terms of formality, openness and participation, from the criminal trial, for example, to the decision of medical staff forcibly to inject a special hospital patient, but all should be based on a recognisable policy, thus presupposing the existence of a prior stage (a) decision. However, as the literature has long recognised, the formulation of policy may result in the creation of rules, principles or standards of varying degrees of specificity, with the result that the task involved in application, particularly in terms of the degree and nature of the discretion residing in the decision maker, will vary significantly depending on the form in which the policy has been drafted.[1] Further, except in the case of very specific and clearly defined rules, application decisions are likely to involve some elements of policy formulation. The difficulty lies in identifying the appropriate degree of formulation to be entrusted to stage (b). Typically, in a strictly legal sense the formulation involved in applications is relevant only to the individual case, but occasionally, as in the case of the criminal courts, formulation occurring in the course of one application can bind future applications. At a more informal level, notions of fairness and consistency can also vest application decisions with a precedent-setting role. In all such cases stage (b) decisions play a clear part in policy formulation; they, like stage (a) decisions, become prospective rather than exclusively retrospective.[2] It is also important to note at this early stage that the task imposed on stage (b) decision makers can vary widely, from truthfinding and issue resolution to resource allocation, or, as Bayles calls them, burden/benefit decisions.[3]

Stage (c) decisions can be introduced to check the validity of decisions at both stage (a) and stage (b). Traditionally, a distinction has been drawn between validation decisions which check the substance of earlier decisions and those which check an earlier decision's compliance with process requirements.[4] Whatever the original validity of such a distinction it can be argued that, while it may always be necessary, in recognition of human frailty,

1 See, particularly, J. Jowell, 'The Legal Control of Administrative Discretion' (1973) *Public Law* 178, and C. Harlow and R. Rawlings, *Law and Administration* (1984, London: Weidenfeld and Nicolson). For a general discussion of the relevant literature see D. Galligan, *Discretionary Powers: A Legal Study of Official Discretion* (1986, Oxford: Oxford University Press).

2 See Galligan, *supra*, pp. 117–28 for an interesting discussion of the theories of administrative process.

3 M. Bayles, *Procedural Justice: Allocating to Individuals* (1990, Dordrecht: Kluwer Academic Publishers), ch. 1.

4 See, for example, P. Craig, *Admininstrative Law* 2nd edn (1989, London: Sweet and Maxwell), ch. 10.

to have some method of *ex post* enforcement of process requirements, the more comprehensive those requirements become at stages (a) and (b), the less pressing will be the need for checks as to substance.

(b) Decision Making Structures

In the discussion that follows, a distinction is made between decision making structures and procedures. Structure is used to refer to the mechanism adopted to reach a particular decision – adjudication, for example, or mediation – whereas procedure refers to the practices adopted by a given decision maker in reaching a decision, whether an oral hearing is held, for example, or cross examination allowed. While certain procedures are commonly associated with particular decision-making structures – adjudication with oral hearings, for example – no such automatic relationships will be assumed.

At present a variety of decision-making structures are employed within criminal justice. They include: parliamentary legislation; ministerial or administrative decision; adjudication; contract; mediation or conciliation, and commissions of inquiry.[5] Certain of these structures are exclusive to a single stage of decision making, while others may be found at all three stages. Within criminal justice, the first three structures are the most significant.

Parliamentary legislation, including both primary and delegated legislation, is, within criminal justice, exclusive to policy formulation. Legislation evolving from the Parliamentary process creates rules and standards, some of which may be sufficiently precise to require no further specification before being applied to individual circumstances, but most of which require considerable amplification by way of subsidiary rules and guidelines.

Ministerial or administrative decision making is perhaps the most common structure within criminal justice. To an extent it is a residual category, and encompasses all decisions made by executive or administrative agents which are not merely preliminary or advisory and where the agent is not acting as an impartial adjudicator. It is thus wide enough to include both the decision of the Home Secretary to release a life-sentence prisoner on licence, and the decision of a charge nurse to seclude a special hospital patient. While ministerial and administrative decisions occur most commonly, as in the above two examples, at the application stage, they are often found in policy formulation in the form of ministerial circulars, managerial directives etc., and can also be used to provide validation at stage (c). In this latter role they may be implemented automatically as part of the decision making structure: if the seclusion of a patient extends beyond a certain period, for example, the responsible medical officer will be automatically required to endorse the nurse's original decision. Alternatively, administrative decisions may act as a means of appeal at the instigation of those affected by the initial decision: a

5 For an interesting discussion of Fuller's account of the processes of socio-legal ordering see R. Summers, *Lon L. Fuller* (1984, London: Edward Arnold), chs. 6–8.

prisoner's petition to the area manager against a governor's decision, for example.

Adjudication constitutes the third structure of decision making, and the structure which is at present most commonly connected with the legal regulation of process. While it is hard to identify the precise essence of adjudication, its main distinguishing features would appear to be the existence of a particular dispute between identifiable parties, and the involvement of a third party who 'hears' evidence concerning the dispute and imposes a decision on the parties by applying pre-existing rules or principles to the evidence received.[6] Arguably, arbitration shares similar features, and is distinguishable from adjudication solely on the basis of the status of the decision maker and the pre-ordained rules. As a general rules these tend to be public in origin in the case of adjudication, and to spring from private agreement in the case of arbitration. Further, it is important to emphasise that adjudication, thus identified, can be either adversarial or inquisitorial in character. Within the criminal justice system the adjudicatory structure, which clearly includes the criminal trial, is present at both the application and the validation stage and, to the extent that application decisions can involve the formulation of policy for future application, adjudication can also perform a stage (a), or policy formulation, role.

Contract has not traditionally been a common form of decision making within criminal justice. It involves the specification of obligations through bargaining, and can occasionally be involved in the application of policies to individuals by the definition of obligations or rules specific to that individual. A therapist and client, or a social worker and child, may articulate the rules of their relationship in a form of contract. However, 'contracts' of a sort may start to play a more important role in the specification and monitoring of prison conditions. In the first place, if the privatisation of custodial services continues, the government may increasingly include minimum performance standards within the contract. Secondly, minimum standards may be expressed in 'contracts' between individual prisoners and their holding establishment.

Mediation and conciliation, the processes whereby a third party seeks to achieve agreement between two opposing parties, are rare at present but are occasionally employed at the application stage. They have been introduced, for example, in relation to complaints against the police and, to a lesser extent, with regard to complaints in special hospitals. They have been considered in connection with the treatment of victims, and exist more informally in relation to police decisions to arrest and charge.

The final category, commissions of inquiry, is not strictly speaking a distinct structure of decision making, being typically a hybrid possessing characteristics of both administrative decision making and adjudication. The category is perhaps descriptive of the function of the decision maker rather

6 See L. Fuller 'The Forms and Limits of Adjudication' (1978) 92 Harv. LR 353; M. Bayles, *Principles of Law: A Normative Analysis* (1987, Dordrecht: Kluwer Academic Publishers), ch. 2; and Bayles, *supra*, n. 3.

than the structure. It includes all inquiring and advisory bodies. In preparation for the making of binding decisions at any of the three stages, advisory bodies are used to perform a factfinding role, and are often required to provide information and to make recommendations. In general, such bodies are required to be independent of the main interests at stake. The Woolf Inquiry into Prison Disturbances April 1990 provides a clear example.[7]

For any particular decision, therefore, a range of possible structures is available, but each category of structure is itself flexible enough to encompass a broad spectrum of formality, openness, etc., and the precise nature of the procedure required will vary according to the particular context of the decision. The identification of the preferred process for any decision within criminal justice will therefore require the choice of a fully complementary structure and procedure, appropriately suited to the stage at which the decision occurs in the evolution of policy and to the nature of the task expected of the decision maker: issue resolution, for example, or truthfinding.

The purpose of this chapter is to examine the factors which should govern the identification of the preferred decision-making process in any given custodial context. The discussion will start with a brief account of the three structures of greatest current significance and the extent of their respective roles within custodial decision making. A consideration of the factors relevant to the choice of both structure and procedure at the policy formulation stage will follow. Section **e** will then concentrate on the application and validation stages, and will consider the potential for adjudication, whether adversarial or inquisitorial, and its relationship to administrative decision making.[8]

(c) Adjudication, Legislation and Administrative Decision Making: Their Existing Distribution

In considering the range of processes, lawyers have tended to concentrate on adjudication, which they have traditionally regarded as the epitome of fair procedure. Indeed, the direct links between adjudication and common law notions of fair process are now well-recognised. In the United States the content of the constitutional guarantee of fair process has been strongly influenced by the adjudicatory model,[9] while in the United Kingdom the principles of natural justice, comprising the right to a fair hearing and the rule against bias, were expressly based on the court model with regard to both their content and the circumstances in which they were applied.[10] Indeed, even in the first part of this century there had to be a '*lis inter partes*', or a specific

7 *Prison Disturbances April 1990* (The Woolf Report) (1991, Cm 1456, London: HMSO).
8 For an interesting comparative discussion of the factors influencing the evolution of processes see M. Damaska, *The Importance of Structures and Ideologies for the Administration of Justice* (1986, New Haven: Yale University Press).
9 An interesting discussion is provided by M. Redish and L. Marshall, 'Adjudicatory Independence and the Values of Procedural Due Process' (1986) 95 Yale LJ 455.
10 Craig, *supra*, n. 4, ch. 7.

dispute between identifiable parties, before the right to a fair hearing could be asserted.[11] As was seen in the previous chapter, the emergence of the duty to act fairly has introduced greater flexibility to the common law rules, but the influence of the adjudicatory model is still strong.

Many attempts have been made to identify the essential elements of adjudication and to specify the proper limits of its role. At the centre of this debate lie the works of Lon Fuller.[12] Fuller dedicated considerable energy to analysing the processes of legal ordering. He was anxious to break down the rigid separation between means and ends, and the study of legal processes was central to his approach to jurisprudence. Fuller identified various forms of socio-legal process, and believed that each possessed its own moral force or source of legitimacy. Furthermore, he felt that each form of process had its own appropriate sphere, and that it was important to identify that sphere and to ensure that processes were not employed for tasks for which they were not specifically suited.

Adjudication can be seen primarily as a structure for the resolution of disputes. According to Fuller, adjudication enables those directly affected by the outcome to present arguments to an impartial third party, and to receive in return a decision based on those arguments. In this classic sense, adjudication requires full adversarial participation, since all parties must be allowed to present arguments in support of their case and to answer the arguments of all other parties. It also requires the adjudicator to be strongly responsive and to base her decision on the arguments presented by the parties; it does not invest the adjudicator with an inquisitorial function. Adjudication in this sense is regarded as being better suited to cases where a finite number of people stand to be affected by the application of pre-ordained principles or rules rather than to the evolution of general policy or the resolution of polycentric issues. A polycentric issue has been defined as one which involves

a complex network of relationships, with interacting points of influence. Each decision made communicates itself to other centres of decision, changing the conditions so that a new basis must be found for the next decision.[13]

Undoubtedly Fuller, with his interests in the civil courts, did provide a very narrow and predominately adversarial definition of adjudication, and one that can presently be applied to only a small range of criminal justice decisions. In the case of such decisions, adjudication is principally designed to produce correct (in the sense of accurate) outcomes through the participation of those most directly affected. Thus, in terms of the analysis described in the previous chapter, Fuller's classic adjudicatory model is designed to reduce the error costs of decisions. The extent to which it is able to do so in practice is considered further below. However, arguably, the purpose of adjudication

11   *Franklin* v. *Minister of Town and Country Planning* [1948] AC 87.
12   See, especially, *supra*, n. 6; *The Morality of Law* (1969, New Haven: Yale University Press), and Summers, *supra*, n. 5.
13   Jowell, *supra*, n. 1, p. 213. See Fuller, 'Adjudication and the Rule of Law' (1960) 54 Proceedings of the Am. Society of International L 1, pp. 3–5.

should not be seen exclusively in terms of truthfinding and the pursuit of accuracy. It may be that the important, and additional, task of issue resolution would be better served by some more flexible approach to adjudication, which might promote those process benefits that are independent of the truthfinding goal.[14] The interesting question for present purposes is whether the scope of adjudication within custodial policy implementation can and should be enlarged to cover areas of less formal, or more complex, decision making. The answer will depend on the extent to which adjudication can, in the appropriate circumstances, fulfil the role of full process and facilitate the reflection of the full public interest.

At present only a narrow range of criminal justice decisions, and an even narrower range of custodial decisions, adopt adjudication even in a liberalised form. They include, at the application stage, the criminal trial itself, pre-trial hearings before magistrates, prison disciplinary hearings, and Mental Health Review Tribunal hearings; and at the validation stage, appeals against verdict and sentence, and applications for judicial review. Outside these specific areas a multitude of decisions are made affecting both individual and collective interests. A small proportion are legislative in structure, in the narrow sense of Parliamentary legislation being adopted here; but the vast majority are administrative.

Parliamentary legislation, in a formal sense, includes all primary and delegated legislation. Primary legislation emanating straight from Parliament should be seen as the direct outcome of the democratic process. It constitutes rule making or policy formulation by Parliamentary legislation in the fullest sense. However, as was suggested earlier, such primary legislation is seldom sufficient on its own to guide custodial decision makers without further amplification. Delegated legislation, which is often used as one means of providing this necessary service, is more difficult to classify as true Parliamentary legislation. It is typically drafted through a process of administrative decision making within the relevant government department, and is often subjected to only the most cursory Parliamentary scrutiny. It is thus the product of Parliament in little more than a formal sense.

While there is no space here to consider how the Parliamentary element might be strengthened, it is worth noting Wallington's quite pessimistic view. He sees the dilemma of delegated legislation as consisting of two crucial elements: 'the nature of delegated legislation itself, and the operation of Parliament as an institution', and, as he is sceptical of Parliament's general ability to provide 'a systematic check on a government's legislative ambitions', he feels any reform of the process for the scrutiny of delegated legislation is likely to be constrained in its effects by the more fundamental inadequacies of the system as a whole.[15] Whatever the problems with the Parliamentary system in general and its role with regard to delegated legislation in particular, however, any assessment of Parliament as a policy formulator is far outside the

14 See generally Bayles, *supra*, n. 3.
15 J. Hayhurst and P. Wallington, 'The Parliamentary Scrutiny of Delegated Legislation' (1988) *Public Law* 547.

scope of this book. Our present concern is with the existing role of Parliamentary legislation in the implementation of custodial policy and, once a strict definition is adopted, it becomes clear that that role is, in practice, strictly limited.

In fact, the vast majority of custodial decisions fall into the residual category of administrative or ministerial decision making. As explained earlier, these administrative decisions can occur at any stage in the evolution of custodial policy, and are subjected to widely varying procedural requirements depending on the nature of the task to be performed. Ultimately, they are identifiable through their negative characteristics: they are not adjudicative, neither are they legislative in the Parliamentary sense. While at a formal level it is easy to distinguish administrative decision making from Parliamentary legislation, even at the policy formulation stage, the distinction between administrative decision making and adjudication at the application and validation stages is sometimes harder to identify. Here, in theory at least, it is possible for the administrative decision maker to emulate the procedures required of an adjudicator and, where the resolution of an individual dispute is involved, the two structures can be very similar. However, as will be suggested later in the chapter, the administrative decision maker will inevitably lack the impartiality required of an adjudicator, and it may be this distinction which should ultimately determine their respective roles at application and validation.

Whatever the fine distinctions between adjudication and administrative decision making at the margin, it is evident that vast areas of the implementation of custodial policy are currently left to administrative decision. According to the present argument, all public decision making, through whatever structure and at whatever stage, should be bound by processes designed to ensure that decisions are reached in reflection of a broadly defined notion of public interest. Even before examining aspects of the present system in detail, however, it seems reasonable to assume that, whatever the possibilities in theory, in practice much administrative decision making within the custodial sphere falls far short of satisfying these requirements of full process. Much of it is hidden from public view, and decisions are taken in the absence of any real attempt to identify the public interest. If the current processes of custodial policy implementation, dominated as they are by administrative decision making, are to be improved, therefore, and the ideal of full process pursued, thought must be given, both to possible alternatives to administrative decision making as the basic structure, and to the procedures best suited to the particular decision, whatever structure is ultimately chosen.

(d) Policy Formulation: Rule Making

According to orthodox constitutional theory, the proper structure for policy formulation should start with the full articulation of policy in primary legislation. Any necessary technical detail could be delegated to the minister for introduction by way of delegated legislation, while any further specification that might from time to time become necessary could properly be undertaken by either the minister or her delegate, subject to the chain of ministerial responsibility. In practice the picture is very different. Even with regard to the relationship between primary and delegated legislation, delegated legislation is no longer merely entrusted with the technical details, but is becoming increasingly involved with the policy behind the legislative scheme.[16]

Beyond the realm of Parliamentary legislation, in criminal justice as in other areas of public administration, the practice of rule making by administrative bodies is widespread. Administrative decision making is being adopted as a structure not merely for the application of rules but for their creation.[17] In criminal justice, as elsewhere, the form, function and legal effect of these rules varies widely, from Leon Brittan's statement to the House of Commons with regard to parole for long-term prisoners, to the codes of practice issued under the Police and Criminal Evidence Act. Sometimes the chain of ministerial responsibility remains firmly intact, as in the case of Prison Service Circular Instructions and Standing Orders, while in other contexts the link is far more tenuous: local police policy guidelines, for example, or the policies governing seclusion and search in individual special, or even private, hospitals.

To some extent, whatever the form or legal effect of such rules, their existence is to be welcomed. Rules or standards can be regarded as a means of structuring administrative decision making, of ensuring that the individual application of policies is consistent, rational, and predictable, and of facilitating the control of administrative agents by the provision of bench-marks according to which individual decisions can be judged.[18] Rule making, therefore, can provide a means of improving the process of administrative decision making at the application stage. The benefits claimed are not, of course, above question, and the debate fuelled by Davis in the late 1960s concerning the proper relationship between discretion and rules shows no signs of burning itself out.[19] However, for the present we may bypass that debate and simply assume that the creation of some rules and standards by administrative agents is essential in the furtherance of policy implementation. Indeed, the inevitability, if not the desirability, of administrative rule making

16 *Ibid.*, p. 551.
17 The literature on administrative rule making is extensive. In this country, see particularly: G. Ganz, *Quasi-Legislation: Recent Developments in Secondary Legislation* (1987, London: Sweet and Maxwell); D. Miers and A. Page, *Legislation* 2nd edn (1990, London: Sweet and Maxwell); R. Baldwin and J. Houghton, 'Circular Arguments: The Status and Legitimacy of Administrative Rules' (1986) *Public Law* 239; and R. Baldwin, 'Governing with Rules: The Developing Agenda', in H. Genn and G. Richardson (eds), forthcoming.
18 See, primarily, K. C. Davis, *Discretionary Justice* (1969, Urbana: University of Illinois Press). For a general discussion see Galligan, *supra*, n. 1, chs 3 and 4; M. Adler and S. Asquith (eds), *Discretion and Welfare* (1981, London: Heinemann); K. Hawkins (ed.), *The Uses of Discretion* (1992, Oxford: Oxford University Press), and J. Jowell, *Law and Bureaucracy* (1975, New York: Dunellen Publishing Co).
19 Davis, *supra*. For reviews see A. Reiss, 'Book Review of *Discretionary Justice*', 68 Michigan LR 994; R. Baldwin and K. Hawkins, 'Discretionary Justice: Davis Reconsidered' (1984) *Public Law* 570; Galligan, *supra*, n. 1; and Hawkins, *supra*, n. 18.

is now recognised by the common law.[20] The issues of significance here, however, centre on the identification of the rule maker, the selection of the decision making structure, and the choice of precise procedure to be adopted.

(1) Identification of Rule Maker

(a) Expertise

With regard to Parliamentary legislation, constitutional orthodoxy allows for the creation of delegated legislation provided the basic policy is contained in the primary legislation and the rule making power is specifically authorised.[21] Such delegation of the legislative function is regarded as particularly appropriate when detailed and technical regulations are required. In such circumstances it is seen as justified since it both saves Parliamentary time and makes use of the special expertise on which government departments can draw. This attitude to delegated rule making emphasises two distinct aspects of authority.[22] In the first place, the rule making body must be formally empowered: it must have institutional or legal authority. Secondly, it should have relevant expertise or competence and, arguably, it is this issue of competence which should govern the selection of one particular rule maker over any other.

In the realm of administrative rule making the formal grant of authority to the rule maker is typically implied rather than express. The agency responsible for the implementation of a particular policy will create rules or guidelines to assist it in its task, and the common law, within limits, now recognises its authority to do so. But ideally, as in the case of delegated legislation, the choice of the particular rule maker should be governed by questions of competence. Sometimes it is technical expertise that is required where, for example, codes of practice are necessary to cover the conduct of professional or specialised bodies. Alternatively, at a more minute level, expertise, in the sense of local experience or knowledge, is essential where rules or standards are required for the running of individual institutions.

(b) Accountability

Accountability is another factor relevant to the choice of rule maker. Traditionally, the issue of accountability has been seen in terms of accountability to Parliament through the doctrine of ministerial responsibility. Thus constitutional theory assumes a chain of accountability from rule maker via the minister to Parliament, and thus to the public. In this sense the practice of empowering government departments to draft delegated legislation fulfils the

---

20 *British Oxygen* v. *Board of Trade* [1971] AC 610.
21 For an account of the constitutional position see H. W. R. Wade, *Administrative Law* 6th edn (1988, Oxford: Oxford University Press).
22 For a general Discussion of the question of authority see J. Pennock and J. Chapman (eds), *Authority Revisited: Nomos 29* (1987, New York: New York University Press).

accountability criterion. However, in many cases of administrative rule making the expertise criterion will indicate a rule maker who is independent of the minister and her department. In some circumstances direct local knowledge will be required, while in others independence from central government will itself be a condition of competence, as, for example, where an independent view on policy is required, or where it is thought advisable to allow the market rather than government to determine priorities.[23] In these cases traditional ministerial responsibility may be either impractical or inappropriate. Tensions can thus arise between the potentially conflicting demands of expertise and accountability.

To an extent the answer to this dilemma may lie in the nature of the primary legislation itself. Clearly, the more precise the primary legislation becomes with regard to the policies to be pursued and the issues to be covered by the administrative rules, the greater will be the scope for Parliamentary control, both in the creation of the rules and in the subsequent scrutiny of administrative action. Further, in addition to strengthening Parliamentary control, detailed primary legislation can increase the opportunity for judicial scrutiny of the subsequent rules through the ordinary principles of judicial review, and can thus facilitate an alternative, *ex post*, form of accountability at the validation stage. However, there is both a limit to the detail which it is either feasible or desirable that the primary legislation should contain, and a limit to the extent to which accountability should be seen solely in terms of accountability to Parliament.

In chapter 2 the limitations of the doctrine of ministerial responsibility were briefly referred to, and it was suggested that such a doctrine cannot provide an adequate mechanism for accountability in a modern state, whose functions are performed by a multitude of independent and quasi-independent agencies. In theory, ministerial responsibility provides a channel for accountability to the public through their representatives in Parliament. In practice, answerability to the public might be better achieved by encouraging public participation at the rule making or policy formulation stage itself. Thus, in the selection of rule makers, less attention should be paid to creating the appearance of answerability to Parliament, and more emphasis should be placed on facilitating wide participation in the process of rule making itself. The end result might not meet strong democracy's ideal of self-regulation, but it would help more accurately to reflect the public interest.[24]

Finally, a particular problem of accountability is revealed in politically sensitive areas of the criminal justice system. It might be argued that because of the sensitivity of an issue – the treatment of violent criminals for example – rules should be made by a politically accountable figure rather than an anonymous panel of experts. Several problems are raised by this argument, not least the suspicion that the reaction of politically accountable figures to

23 For an interesting discussion of the implications arising from the growth in fringe organisations see P. Craig, *Public Law and Democracy* (1990, Oxford: Oxford University Press) chs 5 and 6.
24 B. Barber, *Strong Democracy: Participatory Politics for a New Age* (1984, Berkeley: University of California), and see chapter 3 for further discussion.

politically sensitive areas is unlikely to be entirely objective; but behind the argument lie the very real difficulties presented in criminal justice by the need accurately to interpret and reflect the public interest. The issue is considered further in later chapters.

(2) Choice of Structure and Procedure

In the context of policy formulation or rule making it is convenient to consider the question of structure and procedure together. The only decision making structure within criminal justice that is designed exclusively for rule making is Parliamentary legislation but, as has been suggested, its role in everyday policy formulation is relatively insignificant, particularly when restricted to primary legislation. In practice, much policy formulation is undertaken either by government departments, with or without resort to delegated legislation, or by other agencies, which may be more or less independent of central government. In terms of structure these bodies, both governmental and non-governmental, operate by means of administrative decision making. In order to examine whether this structure is appropriate it is necessary first to consider the nature of the procedures that should be adopted. According to the model of full process being developed here, the procedures adopted by rule makers should be those that are best able to encourage the full reflection of the public interest. At the very least this suggests that rule making procedures should be open, and should permit wide participation.

(a) Interest Representation

At present in this country little attention has been paid to administrative rule making procedures. Outside the realm of delegated legislation, statutes rarely impose procedural requirements and, as has already been described, the common law has traditionally been reluctant to become involved. This is in marked contrast to the position in the United States. There the Administrative Procedure Act 1946 imposes notice and comment requirements on certain forms of agency rule making, and strict adjudicatory-style hearings on others.[25] The opportunity for participation is thus formally provided.

Experience in the United States has led many commentators to question the wisdom of increasing participation in administrative rule making. Participation is seen as the means whereby interests may be represented before the decision maker, and thus requires the identification of relevant interests. Further, the success with which any interest is represented is likely to be related to the resources available to the interested party. Thus, as Stewart has forcefully argued, general rights of participation tend to favour the powerful and well-organised interests over the small, more informal, groupings.[26] Doubts have also been raised as to the quality of the rules emerging from

25 5 USC 553, 556, 557. See S. Breyer and R. Stewart, *Administrative Law and Regulatory Policy* 2nd edn (1985, Boston: Little Brown).
26 R. Stewart, 'The Reformation of American Administrative Law' (1975) 88 Harv. LR 1667.

participatory proceedings. Such rules, it is feared, may be rendered less effective as a result of the compromises required by the negotiating process.[27] Increased participation, it is also argued, can lead to over-formalised proceedings, additional cost, and unwarranted delay.[28] Finally, as in all contexts where greater openness is urged, some have predicted that strategies will develop to bypass the formal procedures, and that the real rules will continue to evolve in private.

Without denying the force of these cautionary arguments, it is possible to respond to the majority of them. In the first place, with regard to the fear that powerful interests will dominate, Craig has drawn attention to the influence of lobby groups within the central legislative process.[29] He points out that any criticism of interest representation before administrative rule makers on the basis of the disproportionate influence of certain interests can as well be applied to central Parliamentary legislation. The answer is not to discourage participation, but to devise means of neutralising the inequalities of influence. Secondly, it is by no means self-evident that rules evolving from a participatory decision making process will be less effective. On the contrary, there is a strong argument that they will be more sensitive to the relevant pressures, and will be more acceptable to those affected. A perceived need to encourage feelings of 'ownership' towards the proposed code of prison standards encouraged the authorities to consult widely within the Prison Service before drafting the new code.[30] Thirdly, as will be suggested below, wide interest representation does not necessarily involve the introduction of formal adjudicatory structures if such are not appropriate. Finally, any additional delay or cost caused by increased interest representation at the policy formulation stage might well be outweighed by smoother decision making at subsequent stages in the implementation of the policy.

(b) Full Participation

While it is possible to answer many of the fears aroused by the present experience of interest group participation in agency rule making, it is still necessary to examine further the basis on which any participation is being urged, because only then is it possible to consider the form that participation ideally should take. In the previous chapter two possible bases for the claim to full participatory processes were suggested, one grounded in notions of liberal pluralism, the other in strong democracy. Under the former approach, full process is one of the conditions necessary for the legitimate exercise of governmental power. Governmental decisions must reflect the public interest in its broadest sense, and must therefore evolve from processes designed to enable them to do so. However, since the public interest is to be distilled from the multitude of relevant individual and group interests, it becomes necessary

27 Baldwin and Houghton, *supra*, n. 17.
28 See Craig, *supra*, n. 23, chs 4 and 6, where he provides an interesting discussion of the problems involved in ensuring proper representation before administrative rule makers.
29 *Ibid.*, pp. 128–32.
30 See chapter 5.

in practice to identify the relevant interests and to determine the nature of their participation in order to enable such distillation to occur.

As mentioned above, problems of interest identification and weighting are already manifest within existing procedures where, according to one view, they can be seen as a reflection of the allegedly inevitable conflict within liberalism between the subjective and the objective.[31] The subjective element would emphasise the right of individual groups to represent their own factional interests, while the objective element would stress the needs of the administration to conduct its business justly and efficiently. That such tensions might persist, even within a full participatory system, should be recognised, but their impact will be reduced if it is remembered that the purpose of participation under the proposed model is to facilitate the reflection of the full public interest, not merely to assist fair bargaining between interested parties. Similarly, Craig's claim that the identification of relevant interests, and the weight attaching to their representations, must be dependent on the political doctrines prevailing within the centre of government at any given time would lose much of its relevance under the proposed approach.[32] According to the notion of full process being suggested here, which applies to all stages of governmental decision making, the political doctrines of central government will themselves have evolved in the full reflection of the public interest, and can properly be used to define the scope of the decisions made at later stages within the process of policy implementation.

Under this ideal approach, questions of the identification and weighting of interests will be resolved by reference to the stage in the implementation process at which the rule making occurs. If the object of the participation is to ensure the full reflection of the public interest, the nature of the interests requiring representation will vary according to the context – that is, the subject matter and the stage – of the decision. Thus, for the creation of national policy or guidelines it might be appropriate to provide for the reflection of individual preferences through democratic representation, and to combine that with the open consideration of technical information and the views of experts and groups with an interest at the national level. On the other hand, once it could be assumed that national policy guidelines were appropriately created, the participation in the creation of more specific and directly applicable rules should be designed to ensure that the general policy was accurately distilled in the light of 'local' circumstances, whether those be defined according to geography, institution or subject matter. In many cases a series of these subsidiary rule making stages will be required in order to render national policy operational at a local level, but at each stage participation could be limited to those with immediately relevant interests. The notion of selective representation is relevant here. As Galligan points out:

> representation can occur in different ways and degrees at different levels of political

31 G. Frug, 'The Ideology of Bureaucracy in American Law' (1984) 97 Harv. LR 1276.
32 *Supra*, n. 23, pp. 179–82.

activity; while all interests may join in the political process at the macro level, greater selectivity is necessary at the micro level.[33]

Whatever the subject matter, however, and whatever the stage in the implementation process, the rule making body must justify its decision to the various participants in the light of their individual contributions. It need not be controlled by the participants, but it must be responsive to them. Participation is being required here not merely to satisfy some notion of individual dignity but to ensure the full reflection of the public interest. Participation of this sort not only affects the substance of decisions but provides a form of *ex ante* accountability. It might also be relevant at this stage to draw a distinction between participation and consultation. Participation in the present sense occurs when the interested individual or group volunteers the contribution, whereas consultation occurs at the instigation of the decision maker. In terms of the decision maker's duty to respond, however, the two are similar. Thus, even with wide participation, it may still be appropriate occasionally to impose a duty to consult, and to oblige rule makers to seek contributions from otherwise silent interests.

The above discussion provides no comprehensive answers to the dilemmas confronted by the need to ensure full participation. It does not purport to do so. The aim at this stage is merely to identify the appropriate questions to be asked, by providing a broad account of the purposes of participation that goes beyond mere interest representation. The issue will be dealt with in greater detail with regard to specific instances of rule making in the chapters that follow.

The second approach to full participation is that grounded in strong democracy. Here participation is central. Citizen action and self-legislation are at the heart of the theory: there are no independent grounds on which to validate government action, no prior goods. However, since the theory accepts the need for agencies in which direct participation is infeasible, there will have to be some means of identifying those interests entitled to participate, and some system of external control to ensure the congruity of agency decisions with the general legislative will.

Within strong democracy Craig identifies three competing dispositions:[34] the individualist, the mediatory, and the communitarian, and he suggests that the nature of the participation provided for within any particular agency will depend on the relative weighting given to each of the three dispositions. Thus one option, giving considerable weight to the individualist disposition, would be to preserve the highest levels of citizen participation and self-legislation within the agency. Rules would be required to maximise citizen access and the process of dialogue before the agency would be prolonged. Alternatively, greater weight could be accorded to the communitarian disposition. Here the agency's authority is provided by its democratic origins, its creation by

33 *Supra*, n. 1, p. 346. See later chapters for the application of the principle of selective representation to specific contexts.
34 *Supra*, n. 23, pp. 400–407.

legislation, and by the presence on it of democratic representatives. The agency itself can then become the 'primary guardian of the common good', reducing the need for citizen participation and dialogue.[35] Thus, even within strong democracy, alternative approaches to the dilemma of participation before agency decision makers exist. The tensions operating within strong democracy may be different from those at play within liberalism, but they are none the less influential in determining the details of participation.

(3) Preliminary Conclusions: Policy Formulation

The above argument has assumed that an increase in the use of rule making will help to structure and constrain decisions at the application and validation stages. In this endeavour Parliamentary legislation should play a dual role. In the first place, it should be more specific in its statements of policy and, of particular relevance to the application and validation stages, more specific as to the legal impact of the rules it contains. Section 117 of the Mental Health Act 1983, for example, stipulates that it shall be the duty of the relevant health authority, together with the local social services department, to provide after-care for a detained patient on discharge from hospital. No further statutory guidance is given, and no indication of the legal consequences of a failure to comply. In the context of scarce resources such vague statutory exhortations have little practical relevance.

Secondly, where Parliamentary legislation is not the preferred rule making structure, such legislation should determine, with as much precision as possible, the powers, structure and procedure of the chosen rule making body. Such a body should be selected with reference to its expertise, and special attention should be paid to the question of accountability to the public, whether that be achieved via strengthened Parliamentary scrutiny and ministerial responsiblity or by increased public participation, either within or before the rule making agency itself. The procedures adopted by the agency should be such as to best facilitate the making of rules which fully reflect the public interest. Here full participation and its inevitable corollary, openness, will be central, although the precise details of the participation required for any particular instance of rule making will depend on the subject matter and the stage in the evolution of the policy, as well as on the precise approach to full process adopted. Arguably, such participatory rule making could often, with the necessary procedural strictures, be accommodated within the basic structure of administrative decision making. This might be the case where the rules were of limited application, either in terms of geography or subject matter.

In other circumstances, where rules of more general application were proposed, a structure similar to that associated with commissions of inquiry might be preferred. Such a commission could draft rules for submission to Parliament. Its composition would be chosen on the basis of relevant

35 *Ibid.*, p. 404.

expertise, and accountability could be achieved, both through openness and wide participation at the policy formulation stage itself, and through submission of the results to Parliamentary scrutiny and approval. As suggested earlier, a commission of inquiry can be seen as a hybrid structure, sharing characteristics of both adjudication and administrative decision making, but, in the context of policy formulation, possessing advantages over both. In particular, a commission of inquiry might be preferable to administrative decision making in so far as the independence of the decision maker from government influence, at least, could be more readily guaranteed. Further, a commission would not be bound by the procedural expectations associated with a traditional adjudicatory structure designed primarily for the resolution of disputes. It would thus be better able to adopt the flexible and far-reaching approach to participation necessary for the proper formulation of policy.

(e) Application and Validation Decisions

In this section the requirements of full process at the later stages of policy evolution will be considered. It is in this context that adjudication has typically been regarded as most relevant, and the ensuing pages will consider the various forms of adjudication and their proper relationship with administrative decision making. In section c a narrow model of adjudication, taken essentially from Fuller, was described. This model is adversarial in form in so far as it places emphasis on the participation of the opposing parties, and their control over the submission of evidence to an impartial third party. An alternative inquisitorial model would reduce the control exercised by the parties themselves, and would include an obligation on the adjudicator to seek out information and call for evidence. Within such a model the strict responsiveness requirement stipulated by Fuller would be waived.[36]

(1) Adversarial v. Inquisitorial, and the Traditional Principles of Fair Procedure

Before attempting to evaluate the relative merits of these two models of adjudication and to consider their relationship to administrative decision making, however, it will be useful to consider the characteristics that are traditionally regarded by lawyers as constituting fair procedure. Bayles lists these characteristics in terms of four principles: that a decision maker should be impartial; that a person affected by a decision should have the opportunity to be heard; that decision makers should provide grounds for their decisions; and the principles of formal justice, namely adherence to rules, and consistency over time and between subjects.[37] According to Bayles, these principles can be drawn from human rights statements, constitutions,

36 See M. Eisenberg, 'Participation, Responsiveness and the Consultative Process' (1978) 92 Harv. LR 410, for an interesting discussion.
37 *Supra*, n. 3.

common law requirements and model statutory codes, and can thus be presumed to be justifiable, although subject to rebuttal by sound argument.[38]

The principle of impartiality is designed both to guard against partial decision makers and to ensure the independence of decision makers. A partial decision maker is one possessing a predisposition to one outcome rather than another, and such a predisposition can arise from personal interest in an outcome, from preconceived conclusions of fact, or from personal feelings either for or against a particular party. It is seldom thought to arise from an adjudicator's previous involvement in similar legal or policy judgments. However, because of the difficulty of establishing actual partiality, and because of the impact of any suspicion of partiality, both on the parties and on observers, the principle also seeks to avoid the mere *appearance* of partiality. The independence sought by the principle includes the absence of control by interested parties, and the absence of any potentially conflicting function in the decision maker. According to the analysis described in chapter 3, the principle of impartiality, thus interpreted, should serve to reduce costs in cases of actual bias by guarding against inaccurate decision making. Further, in cases of both actual and apparent partiality, it should promote the process benefit of confidence in the decision making structure.[39]

The principle of impartiality is clearly reflected in the common law rule against bias. The second principle, that a hearing should be provided, equates to the other pillar of traditional natural justice. This principle specifies that a person likely to be affected by 'a determination of government action' should be entitled to an opportunity to know and to answer any unfavourable evidence.[40] It requires an open and prompt hearing, preceded by notice providing the affected person with sufficient information and time to prepare. The hearing, however, need not always be oral. This principle is also seen as being designed to reduce error costs ensuring that all relevant information is before the decision maker and is adequately tested. It is also said to promote process benefits by protecting individual dignity through the provision of participation, and by increasing the intelligibility of decision making.[41]

The third principle, that the grounds for a decision be provided, is not yet directly reflected in the procedural requirements of the common law.[42] It requires that grounds be given for decisions, and that those grounds be reasonable. It thus presupposes some system of validation. The detail and the specificity of the reason will, however, depend on the degree of discretion given to the decision maker. Again, adherence to this principle can be expected to reduce error costs by ensuring that decision makers have rational reasons for their decisions. It can further be seen to promote intelligibility and the

38 *Ibid.*, pp. 9–13.
39 *Ibid.*, ch. 2 and p. 136. For a discussion of the importance of impartiality see Redish and Marshall, *supra*, n. 9.
40 K. Davis, *Administrative Law Text* 3rd edn (1972, St Paul, Minn.: West Publishing Co), p. 160.
41 See Bayles, *supra*, n. 3 and p. 136.
42 See Craig, *supra*, n. 4, pp. 221–2.

'psychological resolutions' of disputes: a party is thought more likely to accept a decision if he or she is given the reasons for that decision.[43]

The final principle, that of formal justice, is, according to Bayles, comprised of the requirements of consistency, adherence to precedent and conformity to rules. These requirements are deemed necessary in order to limit the scope of discretion, and are described as requirements of justice 'because they promote equality of treatment of those subject to decisions'.[44] While such requirements may reduce the direct costs of decision making, they do not necessarily reduce error costs. They may, however, promote the values of fairness and intelligibility.[45]

These four traditional principles have so far been considered only in terms of the error cost plus process benefit approach of Bayles, described in chapter 3. It is necessary now to consider them against the notion of full process being developed here. According to this notion the four principles may still be relevant, but the approach will differ from that just recounted. First, it would appear that impartiality in terms of actual bias is essential, because a biased decision maker, being predisposed to one particular interest, is unlikely to reflect the public interest in its fullest sense. However, under a strict notion of strong democracy, the concept of bias might be regarded as meaningless. In a system of direct participation and self-legislation the public is the decision maker; a decision evolving through a process of true public deliberation cannot be biased.

Secondly, the traditional notion of a hearing tends to be limited to those directly affected: it is the individual 'who has a sufficient interest or right at stake in a determination' who is entitled to the hearing.[46] While it is clear that full process requires openness and the participation of directly interested individuals, it seldom rests there. The requirements of full process, even when short of those demanded by strong democracy, are significantly more expansive, as has been described above. Thirdly, the provision of grounds for a decision is certainly essential to full process.[47] Full process requires a decision maker to justify her decision against all proposed alternatives. The giving of reasons is thus fundamental to this approach. Finally, formal justice might be relevant to full process to the extent that consistency with properly created existing rules and policies is necessary for any application decision – or further refining policy formulation – to be justifiable, just as any apparent inconsistency of treatment between subjects must be specifically justified. However, it does not stand as a separate principle, but rather is subsumed in the notion of justifiability. Its relevance within traditional theory seems to be related to appearances as much as to substance, and to that extent it is no longer relevant within full process.

43 See Bayles, *supra*, n. 3, ch. 4 and p. 137.
44 *Ibid.*, p. 110.
45 *Ibid.*, ch. 5 and pp. 137–8.
46 See Davis, *supra*, n. 40, p. 160.
47 For a discussion of the significance of the provision of reasons see G. Richardson, 'The Duty to Give Reasons: Potential and Practice' (1986) *Public Law* 437.

Returning to traditional theory, the four principles are clearly realisable within the adversarial model of adjudication. Indeed, their content is significantly influenced by it. Arguably, they can also be met within a more inquisitorial approach. A hearing is plainly essential to a fair inquisitorial system, although the form taken by such a hearing might differ from that appropriate to the adversarial model. Not all the evidence and information will be provided at the instigation of the parties, and the adjudicator will be playing a more proactive role. Similarly, the obligation to provide grounds for a decision applies equally to both models. It is sometimes suggested that impartiality is harder to achieve within an inquisitorial system, since adjudicators who are responsible for investigating and presenting evidence may find the maintenance of a neutral position difficult.[48] While such reservations might be well grounded, they would appear to be applicable to all situations where hypotheses are tested, and in the present context might be no more significant than the opportunities for unconscious bias arising within the adversarial system from an adjudicator's preference for the style of one party's presentation. Formal justice, with its emphasis on the following of rules and precedents, on the other hand, is traditionally associated with adversarial systems, although there would seem to be no fundamental reason why it should not apply to inquisitorial structures as well. Consistency between similar subjects is a separate issue, and could apply equally to inquisitorial systems.

(2) Adversarial v. Inquisitorial, and the Purposes of Adjudication

While adversarial and inquisitorial adjudicatory systems may have a similar capacity to comply with the traditional principles of procedural justice in all significant respects, their ability to perform the various tasks currently asked of adjudication is not necessarily the same. Truthfinding, and the consequent reduction of error costs, is seen as one of the primary tasks of adjudication. The argument in favour of the adversarial approach in relation to truthfinding is typically based on the belief that the parties directly involved have every incentive to discover evidence in their favour and to challenge evidence in favour of the opposing party. In this way, it is thought, the truth is likely to be uncovered. One psychological study found that, when the preponderance of the evidence was unfavourable to their clients, advocates who were client-orientated sought evidence more thoroughly than their colleagues who saw their role as that of investigator for the court.[49] However, as Bayles points out, such assiduity on the part of client-orientated advocates might not be productive of the truth:

48 See Fuller, *supra*, n. 6, pp. 382–3. See also J. Thibaut and L. Walker, *Procedural Justice: A Psychological Analysis* (1975, Hillside NJ: Laurence Erlblaum Associates, Publishers), p. 49, and Bayles, *supra* n. 3, p. 33.

49 See Thibaut and Walker, *supra*, p. 38. For a thorough discussion of research on the impact of procedural fairness see E. A. Lind and T. R. Tyler, *The Social Psychology of Procedural Justice* (1988, New York: Plenum Press).

side A, which the evidence supports, will present, say, five items, while side B will also present five items. Since of the total evidence perhaps only twenty-five percent supports side B, the decision maker is then presented with a skewed sample.[50]

Further, partisan advocacy may lead a party to seek to discredit an opposition witness, despite knowing that witness's evidence to be true. Finally, there is the perennial problem of the unequal distribution of resources between parties. In an adversarial system, where the outcome depends so much on the arguments put by the opposing sides, that inequality can be particularly significant.

On the basis of these arguments it is appropriate to be suspicious of the adversarial system's capacity for truthfinding. Indeed, as Bayles concludes, 'so far as determining factual matters, it is probably pretty poor'.[51] However, truthfinding in the present context does not consist solely of factfinding. Facts, once established or agreed, often require interpretation. The factual evidence before a Mental Health Review Tribunal may be agreed by all, but the interpretation placed on it might be hotly contested: is the patient likely to be a danger to himself or to the public, or is he not? Here it might be helpful for the decision maker to be presented with competing and contradictory interpretations.[52] If so, then there is an argument that, for these types of decision, an adversarial model might be preferred.

The alternative systems of adjudication should not be evaluated solely by reference to truthfinding, however. As described in chapter 3, a decision making process may produce benefits that are independent of truthfinding, and may therefore be irrelevant to the reduction of error costs. The psychological resolution of disputes, which is itself linked to the perceived fairness of the procedure, may be seen as such a benefit. Parties may feel better about a decision, even if it is adverse, if they have been able to 'have their say'. A study by Thibaut and Walker suggests that adversarial adjudication produces more satisfaction with the decision than inquisitorial adjudication, and concludes that party control – a defining characteristic of adversarial adjudication – is closely related to the participant's favourable assessment of the fairness of a procedure.[53] On the other hand, the adversarial system, which emphasises the differences between parties, may serve to exacerbate rather than to resolve disputes, particularly in a domestic situation or in the context of any continuing relationship.

From the above it is clear that neither the adversarial nor the inquisitorial model should *always* be preferred. Each context will need to be considered individually. While the Mental Health Review Tribunal's decision whether or not to discharge a patient might seem suitable for an adversarial approach on the basis of the nature of the judgments involved, the existence of a continuing

50 *Supra*, n. 6, p. 35.
51 *Ibid.*, p. 36.
52 See M. Frankel, *Partisan Justice* (1980, New York: Hill and Wang), where he considers the possible benefits of the adversarial model in situations requiring implications to be drawn from facts.
53 *Supra*, n. 48.

relationship between patient and doctor might indicate that a more inquisitorial approach would be preferable. The choice of decision making structure at the application and validation stages is not, however, limited to the choice between adversarial and inquisitorial adjudication. As has been consistently emphasised, the majority of routine criminal justice decisions evolve through a process of administrative decision making.

(3) Adjudication v. Administrative Decision Making

The original definition of adjudication adopted at section **b** was neutral with regard to the adversarial and inquisitorial models, and, before deciding which of the alternative adjudicatory models should be adopted, it is necessary to ask the question whether, in any given context, adjudication is to be preferred over administrative decision making. As described earlier, the presence of a dispute between identifiable parties, and the intervention of an impartial third party which imposes a decision according to preordained rules and principles, are the essential characteristics of adjudication, both inquisitorial and adversarial. Such a structure for the resolution of disputes is designed to find facts, to find truth, and to resolve issues. In considering the relative merits of adjudication and administrative decision making it is important to keep these characteristics and purposes in mind: not all application decisions involve the resolution of a dispute between defined parties. Where a patient or prisoner is applying for a resource, for example, the initial decision will involve the application of criteria to a set of circumstances; although factfinding and truthfinding may be involved, there will not be a dispute unless that initial decision is challenged.[54]

Nevertheless, a number of application and validation decisions currently dealt with by administrative decision makers might be potentially susceptible to adjudication, and it is therefore useful to consider how far, in such cases, administrative decision making can meet the four traditional principles of procedural justice commonly associated with adjudication. In the first place, an administrative decision maker can give grounds for her decision, and can also follow the principles of formal justice in so far as they are relevant, whether she is resolving a dispute or making an initial resource allocation. Similarly, in so far as simple disputes and allocative decisions are concerned – the determination of a special hospital patient's application for ground parole, for example – the administrative actor is as capable as the adjudicator of providing an opportunity of being heard where the interests directly at stake are few in number.

The demands of impartiality, however, are less likely to be met by the administrative decision maker. Although impartiality – in the sense of the absence of personal interest and bias – might be achievable by an administrative actor, within a static administrative structure some prejudgement of facts will be hard to avoid where the subject and the decision maker are well-known

54 Such decisions might fall within Bayles' burden/benefit classification.

to each other: a prisoner and deputy governor, for example. Impartiality, in the sense of independence, might present even greater difficulties. In the first place, within an administrative hierarchy junior officials, such as prison officers and special hospital nurses, are frequently required to make decisions which affect not only the individual subjects of the decision, but also the agency for which they themselves work. To that extent they are controlled by one of the interested parties. Secondly, co-mingling of functions is a common phenomenon within prisons and hospitals. A prison governor may be involved in submitting reports concerning a prisoner's parole or transfer and in conducting disciplinary hearings. Similarly, a detained patient's responsible medical officer will be involved in, if not solely responsible for, discharge, transfer and treatment decisions.

Arguably, however, the difficulties encountered in achieving full impartiality in the case of administrative decision making are matched, at least with regard to the resolution of simple disputes and the initial allocation of resources, by the benefits to be gained by the selection of an informed decision maker who can act swiftly. It might therefore follow that administrative decision making should be the preferred structure for simple allocation decisions where no dispute exists, and clear advantages in terms of speed and expertise are to be gained by the selection of an internal decision maker. Adjudication is designed for the resolution of disputes, and in the case of simple allocation decisions, where no dispute exists, there would seem little to be gained by introducing adjudication, provided adequate procedures are adopted by the internal structure. For the resolution of simple disputes, administrative decision making modelled on adjudication might also be considered where the advantages of speed are thought to outweigh the benefits of impartiality and independence which would follow from the introduction of an outside adjudicator. Where administrative actors adopt strict adjudicatory procedures for the resolution of disputes, the essential distinction between administrative decision making and adjudication is provided by the impartiality and independence of the latter. Thus, for any given circumstance, the choice between the two may properly depend upon the relative values of impartiality and independence on the one hand, and speed and local expertise on the other.

Whatever the preferred structures for application decisions with regard to simple allocation and dispute resolution, however, there are strong arguments for introducing independent adjudication as a mechanism for validation. The requirements of full process are designed to facilitate the truly authoritative exercise of public power: the exercise of public power that fully reflects the public interest. The process of validation should therefore provide a means of checking that each formulation or application decision is authoritative in this sense.[55] In the case of many application decisions, the validator will be required to check that the decision represents either an accurate application of the policy, or an appropriate application in the light of the surrounding

55 See the argument in J. Braithwaite and P. Pettit, *Not Just Deserts* (1990, Oxford: Oxford University Press), p. 87.

circumstances. In either case the task might best be performed by an independent adjudicator who can reach an impartial determination on the arguments presented, in the case of adversarial adjudication, or invited, in the case of an inquisitorial approach. Independent adjudication might thus be used where the initial allocation decision is challenged, or where the speedy internal resolution of a simple dispute has not satisfied the parties.

In contrast with the position regarding simple application and validation decisions, however, neither independent adjudication, nor administrative decision making modelled upon it, will necessarily be appropriate where polycentric disputes and more complex allocative decisions are concerned. Both structures would be constrained by the limits of adjudication, and would not have sufficient flexibility, either to examine interests beyond those immediately involved, or to reach conclusions without the benefit of clear, preordained standards or rules. A number of special hospital patients may, for example, object to the prohibition imposed on the receipt of home-made food from visitors. Here a wide range of interests is involved, from management's need to deter the import of illegal drugs into the hospital to the therapeutic advantages to be derived from maintaining positive family links, and the desire of patients from minority groups to receive appropriate food, not to mention the commercial interests of the hospital shop. In such a case the demands of full participation are unlikely to be met merely by the provision to each patient of an opportunity to be heard under the traditional adjudicatory approach. A more flexible structure would be required which was specifically designed to consider the wider implications of all available outcomes, and to encourage active investigation on the part of the decision maker. Such a structure might be internal in the case of initial allocative decisions of a complex nature, and independent in the case of polycentric disputes and validation decisions. Indeed, the requirements of such complex application or validation decisions are similar to those considered above in the context of administrative policy formulation, and, in practice, formulation can become virtually indistinguishable from application or validation. An independent commission of inquiry might, for example, be required to examine allegations of mistreatment of patients within a special hospital following the dismissal of complaints by the internal mechanism (validation), and to make recommendations as the future structure of internal grievance procedures (formulation).

(4) Conclusions

The above discussion suggests that administrative decision making should be the preferred structure at the application stage, where no dispute exists, or where clear advantages in terms of speed and expertise are to be gained from the selection of an internal decision maker, as may be the case for simple first-instance allocative decisions and disputes. Independent adjudication, whether adversarial or inquisitorial, would be required for application decisions involving a dispute and the application of preordained standards where the presence of impartiality and independence is of particular value. The role of adjudication at the validation stage, where it can provide a means of checking the authority of earlier decisions, however, would be greatly extended. Such a development would not detract from the speed and the expertise of the original decision, but would provide an independent means of resolving any subsequent disputes that might arise between subject and front-line decision maker. With regard to more wide-ranging application or validation decisions, where neither adjudication nor administrative decision making modelled upon it might be appropriate, a more flexible procedure should be developed that would facilitate the full reflection of the wide interests involved. Such a structure should be internal in the case of complex allocative application decisions, and independent in the case of polycentric disputes and validation decisions.

With regard to policy formulation, administrative decision making would also seem to be indicated in the first instance where the issues are not too complex or far-reaching, provided the demanding requirements of openness and participation are met. Where rules of more general application are concerned, the independent commission model would be more appropriate. At the validation stage, while it might be possible to provide a system of adjudication to which appeal could be made by those dissatisfied by the outcome of the original rule making, the dispute between the rule maker and the interested party is likely to be polycentric in nature, and a more flexible non-adjudicative but independent structure might be preferred.

Thus it would seem that adjudication, whether adversarial or inquisitorial, should continue to play – in numerical terms at least – a relatively minor role as a structure for application decision making within criminal justice. It is designed for the resolution of disputes, and no clear advantage is to be gained by extending its use, either by contriving to present more issues as disputes, or by using it for other types of decision making. As a structure for validation decisions, however, its use should be extended.[56]

If these tentative conclusions are correct, administrative decision making will continue to play an important part in custodial policy implementation, bounded at one end by more specific legislative policy formulation and, at the other, by adjudicative validation. In order to fulfil the requirements of full process, however, the procedures of administrative decision making will require radical improvement, particularly in relation to openness and participation, whether the decision maker is formulating, applying or validating policy.

---

56 The precise nature of the validation required on specific situations is considered in later chapters. But see Craig, *supra*, n. 23, pp. 121–2 and 182–7, for a discussion of some of the problems presented by court validation in general and the 'hard look' doctrine in particular.

Part II
Prisoners

5
Internal Prison Decisions: Policy Formulation

This chapter and the next are concerned with the processes of internal decision making within prisons: the processes whereby decisions affecting the daily life of individual prisoners are reached. The discussion does not purport to be comprehensive, it would not be feasible to cover all aspects of prison life. Instead, specific topics have been selected for attention on the basis of their significance to those they affect. Further, since only limited data are available concerning internal prison decision making, whether it be policy formulation, application or validation, it is not possible to present a full picture of decision making even regarding the selected topics. However, within the constraints imposed by the nature of the published data, an attempt will be made to examine internal prison decision making in the light of the approaches to process examined in the previous chapters.

This chapter will concentrate on the process of policy formulation with regard to two broad areas: the security categorisation of prisoners, and their transfer between establishments and between regimes within a single establishment; and decisions relating to a prisoner's access to resources, privileges, education, correspondence, etc. By way of introduction, however, it is necessary briefly to return to the structure of prison management and its evolution.

(a) The Aims and Management of the Prison Service

In previous chapters both the general aims of imprisonment and the broad constitutional position of the Prison Service have been briefly discussed. It is now appropriate to consider in more detail the way in which the specific aims of the Prison Service have evolved, and the place of Parliamentary legislation, both in that process of policy formulation and in the creation of the rules governing the routine management of prison establishments.

The current management structure and the formal aims of the Prison Service, as described in chapter 2, have evolved rapidly over recent years. The current Statement of Purpose for the Prison Service was issued in 1988, and the existing structure at headquarters was introduced in September 1990, together with the creation of administrative areas in the place of regions. The decision to contract out the management of a remand prison to the private sector was announced in 1990, invitations to tender were sent out in May 1991, and the first private prison, the Wolds, opened in 1992. The structure of management between the regions (as they were then) and individual governors was introduced in 1984, and the structure within individual establishments was reorganised according to the 'Fresh Start' initiative in 1987/88. The basic statutory framework, however, has remained largely unchanged since its introduction in 1952. In 1963 the Prison Act was amended to take account of the abolition of the Prison Commission, and in 1991 was further amended by the Criminal Justice Act in order to authorise private sector involvement in prison management.[1] These adjustments apart, the evolution of the present structure of prison management has been characterised by the absence of primary legislative intervention.

(1) The Formal Purposes of the Prison Service

The Prison Act 1952 says nothing about the nature and purpose of imprisonment. Apart from the emphasis on desert and social protection contained in sections 1 and 2 of the Criminal Justice Act (see chapter 1), such legislative guidance as does exist is thought to reside in Prison Rules 1 and 2.[2]

Rule 1:

The purpose of the training and treatment of convicted prisoners shall be to encourage and assist them to lead a good and useful life.

Rule 2:

(1) Order and discipline shall be maintained with firmness, but with no more restriction than is required for safe custody and well ordered community life.

(2) In the control of prisoners, officers shall seek to influence them through their own example and leadership, and to enlist their willing cooperation.

(3) At all times the treatment of prisoners shall be such as to encourage their self-respect and a sense of personal responsibility, but a prisoner shall not be employed in any disciplinary capacity.

The May Committee of Inquiry into the United Kingdom Prison Service was set up in 1978 following a number of industrial disputes in prison establishments, and it published its report in 1979.[3] At that time there had been a loss of confidence in treatment as a justification for imprisonment, and

---

1 The Prison Commission was abolished by the Prison Commission Dissolution Order 1963, SI 1963/597, while the amendments necessary to facilitate private sector involvement were introduced through sections 84/88, Criminal Justice Act 1991.

2 Prison Rules 1964, SI 1964/388 as amended.

3 *Report of the Committee of Inquiry into the UK Prison Service*, (The May Report) (1979, Cmnd 7673, London: HMSO).

the May Report reflects that mood in its recommendations. It proposed that the aim of the Prison Service should be to provide 'positive custody' for convicted prisoners, and it recommended the rewriting of rule 1. This recommendation was never followed. Instead the Circular Instruction published in 1984, CI 55/1984, set out the aims of the Prison Service in the following terms:

to keep in custody untried or unsentenced prisoners;
to keep in custody, with such degree of security as is appropriate . . . sentenced prisoners . . .
to provide for prisoners as full a life as is consistent with the facts of custody, in particular making available the physical necessities of life . . .
to enable prisoners to retain links with the community and where possible assist them to prepare their return to it.

This formulation was first published in the Annual Report of the Prison Service for 1983.[4] It had been developed by the Prisons Board in 1983 and was intended to be 'a tool of analysis at Board level', and to provide a 'baseline from which the terms of reference of regions and establishments can be developed'.[5] Reproduced in the 1984 Circular, this definition of the task of the Prison Service was quoted in each successive Annual Report until 1990, but was omitted from the report for 1990–91.

In 1988, after a similar process of administrative decision making, a much more succinct Statement of Purpose was issued:

Her Majesty's Prison Service serves the public by keeping in custody those committed by the courts.
Our duty is to look after them with humanity and to help them to lead law-abiding and useful lives in custody and after release.

This statement was first announced at the Prison Governors' Conference in 1988, was published at the front of the Annual Report 1988–89,[6] and has appeared in all subsequent Annual Reports. It is also displayed in all prison establishments. While the Woolf Report was largely supportive of the Statement of Purpose as far as it related to convicted prisoners, it noted that the Statement failed to recognise the obligation to treat prisoners with justice, and recommended that the Prison Rules be amended to make that obligation clear.[7] The 1991 White Paper makes no reference to that suggestion, and merely states that the Statement of Purpose recognises the Prison Service's 'duty as part of the criminal justice system to ensure that prisoners are treated with justice, humanity, dignity and respect'.[8]

Thus the formal aims of the Prison Service are left untouched by primary legislation, and the contribution of delegated legislation, in the form of the

4 1984, Cmnd 9304 (London: HMSO).
5 *Ibid.*, para. 8.
6 1989, Cm 835 (London: HMSO).
7 *Prison Disturbances April 1990* (The Woolf Report) (1991, Cm 1456, London: HMSO), pp. 240–2.
8 *Custody, Care and Justice: The way ahead for the Prison Service in England and Wales* (1991, Cm 1647, London: HMSO), p. 9.

Prison Rules, has been effectively marginalised. The May Report's suggested amendment to rule I was apparently ignored, and the redrafting recommended by the Woolf Report has yet to happen. Instead, the purposes have been formulated by administrative decision, with little public debate and even less Parliamentary involvement.

These internal processes of policy formulation and the absence of Parliamentary involvement have attracted some criticism, particularly with regard to CI 55/1984. In its 1986/87 report on Prison Education, the House of Commons Select Committee on Education, Science and Arts argued that, in the light of the disagreement surrounding the purpose of imprisonment, the Home Office had a duty to set out its aims, but that this should not be done by internal Circular Instruction.[9] The Select Committee was highly critical of what it saw as the use of a departmental Circular Instruction to define the tasks of the Prison Service. In its reply the government argued that CI 55/1984 did not conflict with Parliamentary intention, and so no amendment was necessary.[10]

While the government's response was no doubt technically correct, it serves merely to underline the absence of Parliamentary involvement. CI 55/1984 could hardly conflict with Parliamentary intention where no relevant intentions had been expressed. In terms of full process, the mechanisms through which the present aims of the Prison Service have evolved are grossly inadequate. While, according to the philosophies of management prevailing at the time, it might have been considered important to create a 'mission statement' towards which all Prison Service personnel could feel ownership, it is of far greater importance that society as a whole should be involved in any debate concerning the purpose and role of imprisonment and the Prison Service. According to the present constitutional structure, Parliament must provide the appropriate forum for such a debate.

(2) The Relationship Between Headquarters and Ministers

While there is the strongest argument that the specification of the fundamental task of a public agency such as the Prison Service should involve broad public participation, it might be thought appropriate that the detailed structure of such an agency should evolve through a process of internal decision making. That process should be able to claim internal authority and legitimacy, but would not generally require extensive external participation and consultation, even when the agency is performing a public task. Accordingly, this book is not concerned with the various processes of internal reorganisation within the Prison Service, save in so far as they carry wider constitutional implications or, as discussed in a later chapter, purport to provide mechanisms for public accountability.

9 *Second Report of the Education, Science and Arts Committee, Session 1986–7 Prison Education* (1987, HC 138–1 London: HMSO).
10 *Prison Education* (1988, Cm 298, London: HMSO).

(a) Agency Status

As was described in chapter 2, the concept of ministerial responsibility is central to the formal constitutional position of the Prison Service. In recent years the precise relationship between the Prison Service and the Home Secretary has come under increasing scrutiny, not only as a result of its apparent limitations, as illustrated by the 1991 Brixton Prison escapes, but also as part of a general move towards increased managerial independence in the public sector.

In Feburary 1989 the Home Secretary announced a review of the organisational structure of the Prison Service above establishment level, and a report was published in August that year.[11] After a brief period of consultation, the Home Secretary announced that the Prisons Board was to be restructured and the four regions replaced by 15 areas. Despite opposition from the Prison Governors' Association these changes were effected in September 1990. The Prisons Board now has nine members, including the Director General and Directors of Inmate Administration, Custody and Inmate Programmes, who have policy as well as operational responsibilities. Its 'role is to decide the Service's priorities – within the framework of policy and resources agreed by ministers – and to set goals and performance targets to ensure this work is carried out'.[12] Each year, to focus the work of the Prison Service, the Board sets and publishes priorities. Formally, these changes have had no impact on the position of the Secretary of State, who still remains responsible to Parliament for the work of the Prison Service. However, the 1990 restructuring, particularly with regard to the role of the Director General, should be seen against the background of the debate, within the public sector generally, concerning the creation of 'Next Steps' agencies.

The 'Next Steps' initiative was launched in 1988, based on the report of the Cabinet Efficiency Unit, *Improving Management in Government: The Next Steps*.[13] The policy was aimed at vesting the service-delivery aspects of government in departmental agencies which would be semi-autonomous, would be run by chief executives, and would be free to operate on the basis of a framework negotiated with the relevant department. From the beginning the proposals have raised fears concerning the implications for ministerial responsibility to Parliament.[14] While the parent minister remains formally responsible, considerable autonomy is granted to the agencies themselves, with inevitable consequences for the minister's obligations to answer directly to Parliament. According to Drewry,

[T]he implicit rationale (or possibly an unintended consequence) of Next Steps is to

11 The Woolf Report, *supra*, n. 7, describes the history of these reforms, pp. 286–88.
12 *Report of the Work of the Prison Service, April 1990–March 1991* (1991, Cm 1724, London: HMSO), p. 53.
13 K. Jenkins, K. Caines and A. Jackson, *Improving Management in Government: The Next Steps* (1988, London: HMSO).
14 R. Baldwin, ' "The Next Steps": Ministerial Responsibility and Government by Agency' (1988) 51 Mod. LR 622.

weaken an already weak mechanism of ministerial responsibility to Parliament by creating a series of arm's length relationships between ministers and the deliverers of public services.[15]

For the Prison Service, while emphasising the importance of ministerial responsibility, the Woolf Report recommended a relationship of 'structured stand-off' between the Prison Service and the minister.[16] Such a relationship would enable the Prison Service to be seen as

an operational organisation which can be expected to work under the clear leadership of the Director General to the policies, priorities and with the resources established by Ministers. Once those policies, priorities and resources have been established, the Prison Service should expect and be expected, to get on with the job. The Director General should expect to answer for his stewardship to Ministers and to explain the work of the Service to the public through the media. Ministers would remain answerable to Parliament.[17]

In furtherance of this objective, Woolf recommended the publication of an annual statement setting out both the tasks and objectives of the Prison Service, and the available resources for the coming year. The Director General would then be expected to account for the extent to which he either was or was not able to meet those objectives. On the question of agency status, the Woolf Inquiry remained neutral, believing that the changes it wanted to see could be achieved as well with agency status as without it.

In its 1991 White Paper the government reserved the question of agency status, but emphasised that the ministers should continue to remain directly responsible to Parliament 'for the policies and objectives of the Service and for the resources made available to it',[18] although the Director General was to adopt a more public role. The question of agency status was finally addressed with the publication of the Lygo Report, *Management of the Prison Service*,[19] later that year. Lygo recommended the introduction of agency status, and the government accepted that recommendation.[20] While, at the time of writing, the details of the new structure are uncertain, the introduction of agency status should bring greater publicity and specificity to the objectives and principles governing the Prison Service. Through an annual 'contract' the targets to be met by the Director General or Chief Executive will be spelt out, together with the resources available. As with all the new agencies, however, the additional autonomy granted to the Chief Executive will be seen to erode the traditional notion of ministerial responsibility, particularly with regard to operational matters. On the other hand, the reaction of the Secretary of State to the Brixton escapes in 1991 provides ample evidence of the weakness of that

15 G. Drewry, 'Next Steps: the Pace Falters' (1990) *Public Law* 322, p. 327.
16 *Supra*, n. 7, p. 291.
17 *Ibid.*.
18 *Supra*, n. 8, p. 28.
19 Sir Raymond Lygo (1991, London: Prison Service).
20 On 11 March 1992, in response to a Parliamentary question from John Wheeler, the then Home Secretary announced that the Prison Service was to become a 'Next Steps' agency from April 1993, Parl. Debs. 1991–92, vol. 205, Written Answers, 11 March 1992, col. 563.

traditional structure. Even without the benefit of agency status, the minister was able to rely on the distinction between operational and policy matters. By maintaining throughout that the escape was an operational issue, Kenneth Baker managed to survive the storm of protest calling for his resignation.[21]

While an increase in the publicity attaching to the responsibilities of the Chief Executive will not solve the problem of differentiation between policy and operational issues, it might make obfuscation more difficult to achieve. Parliamentary Questions can now be channelled to the Chief Executives of executive agencies and the written answers will be published in *Hansard*.[22] Further, it might be possible for the Chief Executive of the Prison Service to be examined periodically by the Home Affairs Select Committee.[23] The traditional system of direct ministerial responsibility to Parliament does not provide the necessary accountability, and rather than mourning its dilution through the introduction of agency status, it is necessary to consider possible alternative or supplementary mechanisms. The changing role of the Director General or Chief Executive may provide the basis on which to build an alternative structure. However, if this is to be done, it should be achieved through Parliamentary debate, not solely through administrative initiatives.

(b) Privatisation

Of arguably even more obvious constitutional importance are the moves to introduce the private sector into various aspects of prison management. This development has generated considerable controversy, but 'privatisation' is clearly to be reflected in government policy for the foreseeable future. Following the Fourth Report of the House of Commons Home Affairs Committee in 1987, which recommended private sector participation in remand centres, the government published a GreenPaper.[24] In 1989, after a period of consultation and the publication of a report by management consultants, the government announced their intention to introduce the necessary legislation.[25]

Initially, provisions enabling the government merely to involve the private sector in escort services and the management of remand centres were introduced in the Criminal Justice Bill 1990; but in the course of the Bill's passage these provisions were extended potentially to include the management of all types of prison. Section 84 of the Criminal Justice Act 1991 enables the Secretary of State to amend that Act by way of statutory instrument in order to permit the privatisation of other types of prison. The contract to run

---

21 See, for example, reports in *The Independent*, 22 November 1991, and 5, 11 and 12 December 1991.

22 Parl. Debs. 1991–92, vol. 211, Written Answers, 16 July 1992, col. 941.

23 This suggestion was made by R. Morgan, 'Prison Accountability Revisited', paper presented at a *Public Law* workshop, London, June 1992.

24 *Private Sector Involvement in the Remand System* (1988, London: HMSO).

25 Deloitte, Haskins and Sells (Accountants), *A Report to the Home Office on The Practicality of Private Sector Involvement in the Remand System* (1989, London: Deloitte, Haskins and Sells).

the first privately managed remand prison, the Wolds, was awarded in November 1991, and the prison was opened in April 1992. In July 1992 a statutory instrument was passed extending the contracting out power to any type of newly established prison, and Blakenhurst, the second establishment to be privatised, will open in 1993 as an ordinary local prison, holding sentenced prisoners.[26] The Home Secretary has further indicated his intention to offer all new prisons to competitive tender, and to begin market-testing existing establishments.[27]

While these developments raise the politically contentious issue of the privatisation of punishment, their initial introduction was at least debated in Parliament, and in that formal sense is beyond constitutional criticism. The early extension of privatisation beyond the remand sector is, however, more vulnerable to criticism. In the debate preceding the amendment of what is now section 84, Angela Rumbold, Minister of State at the Home Office, described the new section as providing the Secretary of State with the power to come back to the House for an extension of his powers 'if, and only if, the remand centre contracting out proved to be a success'.[28] In the event the statutory instrument extending the privatisation programme to any type of newly established prison came into effect on 9 July 1992, just two and a half months after the opening on the Wolds. Ministerial undertakings to the House, it seems, must be treated with caution.

(3) Establishments and Headquarters

The system of managerial accountability that now exists was introduced by CI 55/1984. Each year the regional director, now area manager, agrees a 'contract' or 'compact' with each governor which sets out targets and resources for the coming year, and each year the governor reports on his fulfilment of that compact. The issue will be considered further in the context of validation decisions. As mentioned above, the management structure within each establishment was reorganised through 'Fresh Start' in 1986/87. Although, for the reasons mentioned at the beginning of section **2** above, it is not proposed to analyse either the substance of 'Fresh Start' or the method of its introduction, it could be argued that the latter lacked internal legitimacy.[29]

(4) The Governing Rules

The primary legislation governing the administration of prisons is now 40

26 The Criminal Just Act 1991 (Contracted Out Prisons) Order 1992, SI 1992/1656. See chapter 6 for a discussion of the management of private sector establishments.
27 *The Independent*, 22 December 1992. The choice of Derek Lewis, a businessman with no experience of the Prison Service, as the new Chief Executive, is thought to indicate a desire to promote further privatisation.
28 Parl. Debs. 1990–91, vol. 186, 25 February 1991, col. 720.
29 For discussion of the implementation of 'Fresh Start', see the Woolf Report, *supra*, n. 7, pp. 343–8.

years old and, as explained earlier, it is general and enabling in form. The relevant delegated legislation, the Prison Rules, date from 1964 in the main and, although considerably more detailed than the Prison Act 1952, still leave significant areas of discretion in the hands of the administration. In order to provide some guidance to the ultimate decision makers, therefore, the Prison Service has clarified and supplemented the Rules with Circular Instructions, Standing Orders and Prison Service Headquarters Memoranda to Governors. As will be seen below, these subsidiary rules are typically formulated through a process of administrative decision making with little or no Parliamentary involvement. Indeed, the examples described in this chapter provide ample evidence of the extent of the policy making power granted to administrators by generous enabling legislation.

Whatever their limited scope, however, the Prison Rules and their amendments, as statutory instruments, have formally obtained Parliamentary approval and are public documents. By contrast, the non-statutory administrative rules are issued internally by the Prison Service, and until the mid-1980s were regarded as classified. The secrecy surrounding these documents gave rise to considerable criticism, because it was said to be impossible for prisoners or other interested parties to gain access to the rules and guidance governing routine decisions.[30] Thus, not only was the process of policy formulation hidden and effectively unaccountable to the general public, but the official criteria according to which application decisions might be judged were unavailable. Following criticism by the European Commission of Human Rights in the *Silver* case,[31] however, the veil of secrecy has been partially lifted.

Silver involved interference with prisoners' correspondence, and in order to show that such interference was justifiable under the European Convention, the government had to establish, among other things, that the interference was 'in accordance with law'.[32] To meet this requirement the rules governing the interference had to be reasonably accessible to, and foreseeable by, ordinary citizens. As far as accessibility was concerned, the Prison Rules, as statutory instruments, easily met the requirement, but the unpublished Standing Orders and Circular Instructions, which provided detailed guidance for those running the system, clearly did not. As a result of the Commission's view, the government amended and published the relevant Standing Order, and embarked on a general programme of amendment and publication. By 1990–91 this task was completed and all Standing Orders are now published and should be available in prison libraries.[33] Circular Instructions and Headquarters Memoranda, however, remain inaccessible to the general public. They are 'management documents issued on a restricted basis of official circulation' and, though they are not classified, copies are only sent on request

30 See, for example, the criticism in S. Cohen and L. Taylor, *Prison Secrets* (1979, London: National Council for Civil Liberties and Radical Alternatives to Prison).
31 *Silver* v. *United Kingdom* (1980) 3 EHRR 475.
32 Article 8(2), European Convention on Human Rights.
33 Prison Service, 1991, *supra*, n. 12, p. 30.

to interested parties.[34] Thus the intervention of the European Commission forced a change in policy leading to greater openness regarding the governing rules. The change did not relate directly to the process whereby those rules evolved but, particularly with regard to the Standing Orders, the openness has increased public understanding of application decisions and has greatly facilitated accountability at that stage.

Whatever the impact of *Silver*, it does little to alter the fact that prisons are still run largely according to rules which have evolved internally and, in so far as the majority are concerned, have not been directly approved by Parliament. According to any model of full process, this is hard to justify. Full process, as understood here, requires that the process of policy formulation be such as to facilitate the creation of rules and policies which fully reflect the public interest. In chapter 4 it was accepted that such an ideal did not demand full public participation in the creation of every detailed rule. Indeed, the notion of selective representation, allowing for the representation of different interests at different levels in the formulation process, was suggested as a means of ensuring the participation of the various interests at the most appropriate point.[35] In the prison context this might mean the formulation of general policy by Parliament, and the express delegation of more detailed rule making to appropriately expert bodies bound by strict requirements of openness and consultation.

The reality, as described above, is very different. Parliament has had no noticeable input to the formulation of the overall aims of either imprisonment or the Prison Service, and the primary formal delegation of rule making powers is that contained in section 47 of the 1952 Act. While section 47 authorises the Secretary of State to make rules for the regulation and management of penal establishments, and for 'the classification, treatment, employment, discipline and control of prisoners', by way of statutory instrument, it provides little guidance as to the substance of those rules, and imposes no procedural requirements on the rule maker beyond those implied by the requirement that the rule be subject to annulment in pursuance of a resolution of either House.[36] Indeed, originally under section 52, the rules had merely to be laid before Parliament; the annulment procedure was added by section 66(4) of the Criminal Justice Act 1967.

In sum, the existing statutory framework is inadequate and a new, more considered structure is urgently required. Parliament must be given the opportunity to generate an informed public debate on the purposes of imprisonment, and ultimately to reflect the outcome of that debate in an appropriate legislative structure. For no doubt understandable tactical

---

34 Prison Governors' Association, *Evidence to the Woolf Inquiry*, (1990), part 2, policy document 2, p. 11.

35 *Supra*, chapter 4.

36 For an explanation of the annulment procedures, see Erskine May, *Parliamentary Practice* 21st edn (1989, London: Butterworths), p. 547. As for the content of the rule, section 47 does stipulate that anyone charged with any offence under the rules be given 'a proper opportunity of presenting his case'.

reasons, the Woolf Report decided against advocating major legislative reform,[37] although it did recommend a wholesale revision of the Prison Rules. However, the 1991 White Paper, *Custody Care and Justice*, does refer to the need for new primary legislation,[38] and it must be hoped that, having recognised the need, the government will now take the necessary steps to meet it.

(b) Transfer of Prisoners

Section 12 of the 1952 Act vests the final authority for both the initial allocation of prisoners to specific establishments and their transfer between establishments with the Secretary of State. On remand the prisoner is normally sent to the remand centre or local prison serving the remanding court and, if finally sentenced to imprisonment, will return there for security assessment and allocation. At this stage the sentence planning process should begin, and an assessment should be made of the prisoner's various needs. The Woolf Inquiry, in its final report, emphasised the importance of sentence planning, and the notion is now firmly encorporated in Prison Service policy.[39] Indeed the existence of sentence planning is assumed by the release structure introduced by the Criminal Justice Act 1991.[40] This chapter will not rehearse the arguments surrounding the introduction of sentence planning, but will concentrate on security categorisation, transfers under rule 43 in its various forms, and transfers to a special unit.

(1) Security Categorisation

Security categorisation was introduced in 1967 following the recommendations of the Mountbatten Report, and since then all adult male prisoners serving sentences of over three months have been placed in one of four security categories, A to D, reflecting the degree of risk their escape is thought to pose.[41] The existence of security categorisation has an enormous impact on the lives of individual prisoners, particularly those serving medium and long terms. It powerfully influences the type of establishment to which they are allocated, since establishments are also classified according to the level of security they provide, from dispersal training prisons, which can accept category A prisoners, through to open establishments, to which category D prisoners might immediately be allocated. Indeed, in its evidence to the Woolf Inquiry, the Prison Service explained that, in cases of conflict between security categorisation and other factors influencing a prisoner's allocation, the

37 *Supra*, n. 7, p. 383.
38 *Supra*, n. 8, p. 107.
39 See *supra*, n. 7, pp. 378–82, for the views of the Woolf Inquiry. For initial government reaction see *supra*, n. 8, p. 76, and see Prison Service, *supra*, n. 12, p. 26.
40 See, further, chapter 8.
41 *Report of the Inquiry into Prison Escapes and Security* (The Mountbatten Report) (1966, Cmnd 3175, London: HMSO).

demands of security would prevail.[42] Security allocation will also affect an individual's access to privileges and to work, and will affect his ability to communicate with the outside world.

Despite its significance, however, security categorisation is not specifically ordained by statute. The 1952 Act, as described above, allows for the making of rules for the classification of prisoners (section 47), and the Prison Rules require prisoners to be classified 'having regard to their age, temperament and record and with a view to maintaining good order and facilitating training', rule 3(1). While such statutory language clearly allows for security categorisation, it was, officially at least, equally concerned with classification for the purposes of treatment and training.[43] The actual procedure governing categorisation is currently contained in CI 7/1988, which evolved following criticism of the earlier system from a number of official bodies in the early 1980s.[44] Thus both the primacy given to security and the highly developed system of categorisation which now applies have evolved essentially through administrative practice and decision. Indeed, most of the main participants in the debates preceding the introduction of categorisation and the revision of the necessary procedure were internal to the Home Office, if not to the Prison Department itself.[45]

Since 1988 most of the debate relating to categorisation has centred on the position of remand prisoners. At present, unless a remand prisoner is given a provisional category A categorisation, he is regarded as if he were category B. Circular Instruction 7/1988 declares that there is no reason in principle why a remand prisoner should not be held in category C conditions, provided the necessary information and facilities are available. In practice this means that category B will be assumed unless there is evidence to the contrary, and many remand prisoners will be placed in conditions of unnecessary security.

Here as elsewhere, the creation of the Woolf Inquiry provided an excellent opportunity to air the issues involved before a wider audience. Despite receiving evidence from the Prison Service reflecting a preference for the status quo, the Woolf Report itself effectively proposed a reversal of the burden of proof.[46] It recommended that all remand prisoners be treated as category C unless there were specific reason to prefer category A or B, and argued strongly that such a position would be not only just but practical. Following the publication of the Woolf Report, however, the focus of the debate was altered by the escape of two category A remand prisoners from Brixton.[47] The need to

42 Prison Service, *Evidence to the Woolf Inquiry, Phase 2* (1990, London: Home Office), part 4.
43 M. Fitzgerald and J. Sim, *British Prisons* 2nd edn (1982, Oxford: Basil Blackwell), ch. 2.
44 See, for example, H.M. Chief Inspector of Prisons, *Prison Categorisation Procedures* (1984, London: Home Office), and *Managing the Long-Term Prison System: The Report of the Control Review Committee* (1984, London: Home Office). CI 7/1988 established an algorithm, or decision tree, according to which a sentenced male prisoner's security category is determined.
45 The Chief Inspector, although formally independent of the Prison Service, is employed within the Home Office. The membership of the Mountbatten Committee, on the other hand, was largely external, containing only one ex-member of the Prison Service, but the evidence received came predominantly from within the Prison Service.
46 Prison Service (1990) *supra*, n. 40, and the Woolf Report, *supra* n. 7, p. 327.
47 See: *Inquiry by H.M. Chief Inspector of Prisons into the Escape of Two Category A Prisoners from H.M.P. Brixton on 7 July 1991* (1991, published in part, London: Home Office), G. Lakes and R. Hadfield,

ensure security took priority on the political agenda. Thus in the White Paper, published in September 1991, the only timescale provided by the government concerning the categorisation of remand prisoners related to the review of the classification and treatment of category A remands which was announced following the Brixton escape. Otherwise, although the categorisation of remand prisoners was supported by the White Paper, and its introduction promised, no timetable was provided.[48] Further, despite the strong argument presented in the Woolf Report, the government appears to favour the existing assumption in favour of category B: 'there is no evidence or reason to believe that prisoners remanded in custody by the courts can, as a group, be held securely in category C conditions'.[49] The government's priority, whether or not affected by the Brixton escapes, is clearly the maintenance of security. Categorisation of the remand population will eventually be introduced, but it seems the onus will be on the prisoner to establish that he does not merit category B.

(2) Segregation under Rule 43, Good Order and Discipline

In addition to the career transfer of prisoners in the course of their sentence, transfer is used as a means of control. Disruptive or potentially disruptive prisoners can be transferred to other establishments, either to provide them with more secure accommodation or merely to diffuse a difficult situation within their original establishment, or they may be transferred out of association with other prisoners within their own establishment. Removal from association, as this latter form of internal transfer is called, has a specific statutory base, being governed by rule 43 of the Prison Rules. Rule 43 allows a governor to remove a prisoner from association 'where it appears desirable, for the maintenance of good order or discipline or in his own best interests, that a prisoner should not associate with other prisoners'. In addition to good order cases, therefore, the rule enables a governor to remove a prisoner from association in that prisoner's own interests, and its use in that way will be considered below.

Removal from association, even in good order cases, is distinct from the disciplinary structure. It can be used preventatively to segregate prisoners who are seen as potentially disruptive, and no disciplinary charge needs to be brought. Segregation under rule 43, however, carries significant implications for the prisoner, since the conditions he will experience in segregation are likely to be considerably more harsh than those prevailing throughout the rest of the prison. During the 1970s and 1980s concern grew over the conditions experienced by prisoners on rule 43, and over the adequacy of the procedural safeguards provided. The rule then in force stated merely that segregation

'Interim Report of a Security Audit of Arrangements for Holding and Managing Category A prisoners in Custody' (1991, London: Home Office), and *Report of an Audit of the Custody of Category A Prisoners and of an Inquiry into DOC 1 Division* (1991, London: Home Office).

48 *Supra*, n. 8, p. 53.
49 *Ibid.*

could not extend beyond 24 hours without the authority of the board of visitors or the Secretary of State. The authority given by either of those bodies could not extend beyond one month, but could be renewed from month to month. Indeed, some prisoners were held on rule 43 for prolonged periods. There was no right to a hearing at either the initial segregation, nor at its subsequent authorisation, and no right in the prisoner to reasons. This bare procedure was amplified by Circular Instruction.

In 1986 Her Majesty's Chief Inspector of Prisons examined segregation under rule 43 and recommended that the Circular Instruction be revised and the conditions for rule 43 prisoners be improved.[50] With regard to safeguards, he recommended that the governor be able to segregate initially for up to three days, giving reasons in writing to the prisoner. Thereafter the case should be referred to an adjudicatory body. Following the Chief Inspector's report and growing unease concerning the use of rule 43 in 'own protection' cases, an internal Prison Department Working Group was set up, primarily to consider the treatment of vulnerable prisoners, but its examination and recommendations extended to cover the use of rule 43 in both its guises.[51] The working group agreed with the Chief Inspector that the governor's initial power to segregate be extended to three days, but it resolved to recommend retention of the board of visitors as the primary authorising body. It did not agree with the Chief Inspector that reasons should always be given to the prisoner in writing, nor did it feel that the authorising member of the board of visitors should always see the prisoner.

The government accepted the working group's proposals in all significant respects, and in December 1989 rule 43 was amended to enable the governor to segregate for three days in the first instance. In 1990 a new Circular Instruction was issued, CI 26/1990, covering the procedure in more detail. This Circular encourages the giving of reasons, but it fails to recognise any entitlement in the prisoner to reasons. Further, although boards of visitors have been reminded that authorisation need not be for the full month and should be for the minimum time possible, there is no obligation on them to interview the prisoner before making the authorisation, and thus no guarantee of a 'hearing', either at initial segregation or at subsequent authorisation. The Circular also makes it clear that segregation for good ordeer and discipline can still be used preventatively.

Although the Woolf Inquiry accepted that segregation for good order and discipline would continue to be necessary, it felt that the board of visitors was not the appropriate authorising body, and preferred the area manager.[52] It also felt that the Circular should give firmer guidance on reasons, and that the governor should be expected to give reasons in writing at the time. In the 1991 White Paper, although the government indicated that it would retain the board of visitors, it did accept that 'the prisoner should wherever possible be given the reasons for these decisions in writing'.[53]

---

50 *A Review of the Segregation of Prisoners under Rule 43* (1986, London: Home Office).
51 *The Management of Vulnerable Prisoners: Report of a Prison Department Working Group* (1989, London: Home Office).
52 *Supra*, n. 7, pp. 321–2.
53 *Supra*, n. 8, p. 55.

Thus the current policy on segregation for good order and discipline has been formulated through administrative decision making, endorsed where necessary by Parliamentary approval. To an increasing extent the debate has been conducted openly, and on certain issues, the giving of reasons for example, the government has indicated that it is willing to respond to views expressed from outside. On the question of the role of the board of visitors, however, the government has remained faithful to the views of its own internal working group. As will be suggested in subsequent chapters, the retention of the boards of visitors as the body responsible for authorising continued segregation can only compromise their position as independent watchdogs and monitors.

(3) Transfer Under CI 37/1990

Until 1990 the governor of a dispersal prison was empowered by CI 10/1974 to transfer a prisoner to a local prison under rule 43 segregation for up to 28 days. According to the 1974 Circular this type of transfer could be used in the case of a prisoner who 'needs to be removed from normal location because of an imminent explosive situation caused by his actual or impending disruptive behaviour', and where removal to segregation within the dispersal prison would not be sufficient to defuse the situation. It was thus an extension of the statutory rule 43 procedure created by administrative decision without Parliamentary approval.

Within the prison system this procedure was known as 'ghosting' and was deeply resented by prisoners because of the disorienting impact of unplanned transfer and the absence of review. Boards of visitors at some of the receiving prisons also resented the system, which effectively deprived them of any authority in relation to the segregation of the transferred prisoners. The use of CI 10/1974 was considered by the working group mentioned above, which in May 1989 recommended that the decision whether or not to segregate the transferred prisoner should be left to the governor of the receiving prison, and should be subject to local authorisation.[54]

The following year the pressure for change was given added impetus by the decision of the Court of Appeal in *Ex p. Hague*.[55] Hague, a sentenced prisoner held at Parkhurst Prison, was transferred to Wormwood Scrubs in July 1988 under the provisions of CI 10/1974. He sought judicial review of the deputy governor's decision to transfer him on a number of grounds. Most relevantly for present purposes, he argued that CI 10/1974 was *ultra vires* the Prison Rules. This argument was confirmed by the Court of Appeal, which held that the Circular was *ultra vires* in two respects: in the first place rule 43, unlike the Circular, contemplated the decision to segregate being taken by the governor of the prison in which the prisoner was actually held, and secondly, the Circular implied that the regional Director, on behalf of the Secretary of State, would endorse the full 28-day period of segregation as a matter of routine,

54 *Supra*, n. 51.
55 *R* v. *Deputy Governor of Parkhurst Prison, ex p. Hague* [1990] 3 All ER 687.

whereas rule 43 assumed that a reasoned decision would be taken. The judgment of the Court of Appeal was delivered in May 1990, and in September that year a new Circular Instruction was issued, CI 37/1990.

The 1990 Circular envisages two types of transfer, one short-term, where segregation at the receiving prison is anticipated, and one for up to six months on normal location at the receiving prison. In both cases the decision whether or not to segregate is left with the receiving governor, and in both cases it is expected that the prisoner will return to his original prison. In this respect, therefore, the policy has been amended to meet the concerns of outside bodies and, more particularly, the direct finding of illegality by the Court of Appeal: the new Circular now complies with the express provisions of rule 43.

With regard to the strengthening of the procedural safeguards, however, the court's role has been more chequered. As far as the right to a hearing is concerned, the Court of Appeal refused to recognise a right to be heard, either before the initial segregation under rule 43 or before the renewal. The context was distinguished from that of a formal disciplinary charge, where the Prison Rules specifically require a hearing, and it is evident that the Court of Appeal felt there were sound policy reasons against extending such procedural rigour to the decision to segregate. The court further refused to recognise a legal right in the prisoner to be given the reasons for his segregation, although Taylor LJ states that '[no] doubt in many cases the governor will be able, as here, to give reasons at the time of the decision or shortly after'.[56] The new Circular, while denying any absolute right to reasons, declares that the prisoner should be told the reasons for his transfer, before it is effected if possible, and if segregated at the receiving prison, should again be given reasons. In either case the reasons should be in writing if the prisoner so requests. CI 37/1990, which the Woolf Report regards as adopting 'an exemplary standard in respect of the requirement to give reasons',[57] certainly seems to endorse an admirably generous approach in the light of the rather grudging interpretation presented by the Court of Appeal of the requirements of the common law. Clearly there is still no right to be heard – these transfers are not regarded as disciplinary decisions – but if the reasons requirements specified in the Circular are respected, the prisoner will now have a better understanding of what is happening to him. Quite how far the courts can be credited with influencing these procedural reforms, however, is hard to assess.[58]

Whatever the precise influence of the courts in relation to the procedures contained in CI 37/1990, the introduction of that new Circular following the Court of Appeal decision in *Hague* raises broader questions concerning the role of the courts in policy formulation. In chapter 12 the propriety of achieving policy formulation through judicial adjudication in relation to matters of

---

56 *Ibid.*, p. 698.
57 *Supra*, n. 7, p. 319.
58 The relationship between the decisions in *Hague*, at both first instance and appeal, and the introduction of the procedural reforms to both rule 43 itself and the old CI 10/1974, is not clear. The timing alone is inconclusive. The nature of the resulting procedures themselves is discussed further in the next chapter.

substance is questioned on the ground that such adjudication is not the appropriate forum for the full reflection of the public interest. In the present context the Court of Appeal, acting in its role as supervisor of the legality of administrative decision making, issued a declaration that CI 10/1974 was unlawful. It thus returned the task of policy formulation to the original policy maker, here the Prison Service, drawing attention to the relevant statutory constraints. Further, by adopting a strict interpretation of the statutory framework, the court was effectively requiring the prison authorities to seek further Parliamentary intervention if they wished to continue operating the impugned policy. The implications of such an approach, which apparently reduces the court's role in the formulation of the substance of policy to the policing of the legislative boundaries, are discussed further in subsequent chapters.

In relation to the introduction of procedural requirements by the courts, on the other hand, it is arguable that, despite the reservations expressed above in relation to substance, the judicial role should not be restricted to the strict policing of the expressed legislative will, and that positive judicial policy making should be encouraged. In chapter 2 it was suggested that a broad approach to process would support intervention by the courts in the furtherance of full process, even in the face of legislative silence: such intervention should be seen as supportive of democracy, not hostile to it.

In *Hague* the Court of Appeal clearly declined to make such an intervention. In the first place, Taylor LJ, finding 'powerful support' from the presence of an obligation in the Prison Rules to provide a hearing in relation to disciplinary charges and its corresponding absence from rule 43, refused to impose full procedural stringency on those acting under rule 43.[59] Arguably, such an attitude, although impeccable in orthodox constitutional terms, would, if generally adopted, greatly limit the scope of common law procedural regulation in prison. Secondly, the Court of Appeal held that the prisoner had no right to be given the reasons for his segregation or transfer, even after the event. The denial of any right in the prisoner to reason has a long history in prison litigation, and Taylor LJ was clearly unwilling in *Hague* to break the mould, although he has now done so in the context of release.[60] The Court of Appeal thus declined the opportunity to further the pursuit of full process. While such an approach must be regretted where it leaves untouched an unacceptable statutory decision making process, the positive imposition of procedural regulation by the judiciary brings with it its own problems as will be seen in the context of prison discipline.

(4) Segregation Under Rule 43, Own Protection

The protection of vulnerable inmates from persecution by other prisoners presents considerable difficulties to the Prison Service. The victimisation of sex offenders by other prisoners was a central feature of the Strangeways

59 *Supra*, n. 55, pp. 697–9.
60 *R* v. *Parole Board, ex p. Wilson* [1992] All ER 576.

Prison riot in 1990. At present most vulnerable prisoners are placed under rule 43 for their own protection and, as a result, they experience harsher conditions than prisoners on normal location, and suffer the stigmatising effects of being on rule 43. There are a number of special vulnerable prisoner units throughout England and Wales but they have insufficient capacity to accommodate all vulnerable prisoners. During the 1980s the population of vulnerable prisoners grew fast. The Prison Department working group report referred to in relation to good order and discipline cases shows that, while the total male sentenced population increased by 17.4 per cent between 1983 and 1988, the number of rule 43 prisoners increased by 156 per cent over the same period.[61] At the time of the Strangeways riot it was estimated that 8 per cent of the prison population were either on rule 43 or in a vulnerable prisoner unit: 2,280 were on rule 43, and 880 in a vulnerable prisoner unit.[62]

The Woolf Inquiry recognised that vulnerable prisoners would continue to need protection, but felt that it should not be provided through rule 43. Governors should be required to consider other options. The Woolf Report recommended a new Prison Rule which would place an obligation on the governor to take reasonable steps to protect vulnerable prisoners, and to allow removal from association 'only to the extent which is reasonable'.[63] The government has accepted these proposals and has undertaken to allocate sex offenders to one of 20 prisons and to devise special programmes for their treatment. However, it recognises that there will still be a need to segregate some vulnerable prisoners, albeit for a short period, and has undertaken to amend the Prison Rules in line with the Woolf recommendations.[64] The Prison Service is of the view that there is a difference between those prisoners on rule 43 for reasons of good order and discipline and those segregated for their own protection: 'Prisoners segregated for their own protection should be able to take part in normal activities, as far as practicable'.[65]

Although the policy on the use of rule 43 in own-protection cases has not been the subject of direct court intervention, as was the case with the old 'ghosting' procedures and *Hague*, that policy nevertheless appears to have been strongly influenced by court action. The Prison Department working group, in discussing what they saw as the over-use of rule 43 in own-protection cases, referred to the statement in CI 32/1979 that all members of staff concerned

owe a duty to the inmate to take reasonable care in the circumstances to protect him from injury, and they are liable in law for damages if they fail to take reasonable precautions to prevent an attack on him by another inmate or inmates.

In the view of the working group, this 'stark and uncompromising'

---

61 *Supra*, n. 51.
62 *Supra*, n. 7, p. 313, At the end of March 1991, 1,767 adult males were segregated for their own protection, Prison Service (1991), *supra*, n. 12, p. 8.
63 *Supra*, n. 7, p. 313.
64 *Supra*, n. 8, p. 54.
65 Prison Service, *supra*, n. 12, p. 8.

statement inclined staff to have immediate recourse to rule 43 in order to protect their own legal position, and was thus partially responsible for the increased use of rule 43.[66] It can only be assumed that the caution expressed by CI 32/1979 was in part a reflection of the decision in *Egerton* v. *The Home Office*, where the court recognised that the Home Office could be liable if its officers failed to take reasonable care to protect one prisoner from the assaults of another.[67] The prisoner in the case was assaulted after coming off rule 43. Thus, if the working group is correct in its attribution of responsibility for the increase in rule 43 to the officers' perception of their legal position, court action would seem indirectly to have contributed to the present reforms: in the face of the increasing numbers of own-protection cases, pressure for change was mounting long before the events of April 1990. It is ironic, however, that judging from the *Egerton* case itself, the statement in CI 32/1979 was unnecessarily alarmist. As has been pointed out elsewhere, although the court recognised the existence of a duty of care, it showed itself most reluctant to find that duty breached.[68]

(5) Transfer to Special Units

Since 1968 it has been government policy to disperse category A prisoners among a wider population of prisoners at specially selected establishments known as dispersal prisons. The history of the dispersal system has, however, been troubled, not least by a number of serious disturbances between October 1969 and May 1983.[69] In September 1983 the Home Secretary set up the Control Review Committee (CRC), comprised of senior Prison Service personnel from headquarters, the regions and individual establishments, 'to review the maintenance of control in the prison system, including the implications for physical security, with particular reference to the dispersal system and to make recommendations'. The CRC reported in 1984 and, in its attempt to find solutions to the problems of control within the long-term prison system, recommended the setting up of a number of small special units to hold prisoners who persistently presented serious control problems.[70] The CRC felt that the units should be carefully designed, and should cater for different sorts of prisoner. Since 1984 three such units have been opened: C Wing at Parkhurst, catering for long-term prisoners with a history of troublesome behaviour and psychiatric disturbances; a unit at Lincoln taking difficult inmates who are not psychiatrically disturbed, and a unit at Hull. A further unit is due to open in 1993 at Milton Keynes.[71] The CRC had recommended

66 *Supra*, n. 51, p. 20.
67 (1978) Crim. LR 494.
68 G. Richardson, 'Judicial Intervention in Prison Life', in M. Maguire, J. Vagg and R. Morgan (eds), *Accountability and Prisons: Opening up a Closed World* (1985, London: Tavistock), ch. 3. See discussion in the next chapter.
69 A full list of disturbances at dispersal prisons is given in J. Ditchfield, *Control in Prisons: A Review of the Literature*, Home Office Research Study 118 (1990, London: HMSO), p. 3.
70 Control Review Committee Report, *supra*, n. 44.
71 Prison Service (1991), *supra*, n. 12, p. 8.

that allocation to these units should be undertaken by sentence planning units set up at selected local prisons, but such units have not been created. Instead the Prison Department set up the Special Units Selection Committee (SUSC) to arrange allocation both in and out of the special units, and a special procedure has been established which will be considered in the next chapter.

Despite the rejection of some of its recommendations, the CRC's report, which was greeted by the Home Secretary in 1984 as 'a positive agenda for establishing a better framework of control in our longterm prison system', has been highly influential. It would seem to have been the spur for the increase in privileges at low-security establishments (see below), and for the creation of the special units. It has also led to some opening up of the policy making process in certain areas. The CRC placed considerable emphasis on the value of research into some of the problems confronting the prison system. It recommended a programme of Prison Department-initiated research and the involvement of outside academics. Both recommendations were followed, and a Research and Advisory Group on the Long-Term Prison System (RAG), comprising senior outside academics, was been set up to

provide the prison department, on request, with a source of advice on the research needs arising from the report of the C.R.C., and how they might be met, and, in particular, to advise on the planning, co-ordination and evaluation of the proposed long-term prisoner units.

Before its final meeting in January 1990, RAG itself had published one report discussing C Wing at Parkhurst and future options, and four other pieces of research were either completed or under way.[72] The RAG report stated: 'it is essential that the Prison Service should be completely open about the establishment of the units and their operation',[73] and it recommended that the aims and objectives of the units should be available to all those who wish to see them.

Whatever reservations might be expressed about the role of the special units,[74] the openness accompanying their creation and operation is in marked contrast to the secrecy surrounding the operation of the control units in 1974 through CI 35/1974. In this respect they also compare favourably with the planning and operation of the earlier security units which had originally evolved during the 1960s.[75]

---

72 *Special Units for Long-Term Prisoners: Regimes, Management and Research*, Report of the Research Advisory Group, (1987, London: HMSO). The other relevant research is reported in Ditchfield, *supra*, n. 69; R. Walmsley, *Special Security Units*, Home Office Research Study 109 (1989, London: HMSO); R. Walmsley, *Managing Difficult Prisoners: The Parkhurst Special Unit*, Home Office Research Study 122 (1991, London: HMSO), and W. Hay, R. Sparks and A. Bottoms, *Control Problems and the Long Term Prisoner* (not yet published).

73 *Ibid.*, p. 17. By the time RAG was disbanded in 1990 the practice of commissioning independent research was well-established.

74 Some reservations concerning the special units are expressed in The Woolf Report, *supra*, n. 7, pp. 322–5.

75 See the conclusions in Walmsley (1989), *supra*, n. 72.

(6) Preliminary Conclusions: Transfer

The policies discussed here under the heading of 'transfer' have evolved through a variety of processes in response to a host of different pressures. Pressure has come from within the Prison Service itself, as in the case of the special units; to a limited extent it has come from the courts, directly as in the case of CI 10/1974, and indirectly as in the case of vulnerable prisoners; and to a significant extent from public opinion, the expression of which found a focus in the Woolf Inquiry. In response to these pressures, the policies have been evolved through administrative decision making. Parliamentary legislation has not been used as a process for policy formulation. The breadth of the discretion vested in the administration by the 1952 Act has enabled the authorities to create and amend policy without recourse to primary legislative intervention or full Parliamentary debate. Parliamentary involvement has been limited to those cases where the proposed changes have involved amendment to the Prison Rules, as in the case of segregation under rule 43. Here it was necessary to seek Parliamentary approval for proposed amendments, but only after the details of the amendments had been resolved by administrative decision.

Similarly, as described above in relation to CI 37/1990, even where court action has been influential in promoting change, the new policy itself has evolved through administrative decision making. In some cases the administrative decision making has been both open and responsive – as in the case of the special units and, more recently, in the case of vulnerable prisoners – while in other cases – the security categorisation of remand prisoners for example – the debate may have been open, but the government's response has been muted.

(c) Access to Resources

Whatever the fundamental justification for imprisonment, the government now appears to accept that people are sent to prison *as* punishment, not *for* punishment: segregation from the rest of the community is punishment enough.[76] On this basis the rights and freedoms possessed by an individual who is subject to imprisonment can be restricted only to the extent demanded by the need to segregate.[77] The need to segregate, in turn, is said to consist of two elements: the maintenance of security and the maintenance of control. Security refers to the containment of prisoners within prison, while control, according to the Woolf Report, deals with 'the obligation of the Prison Service to prevent prisoners being disruptive', and might be better described as 'order'.[78] Consequently, prisoners

---

76 See the 1991 White Paper, *supra*, n. 8.
77 For further development of this argument see G. Richardson, 'The Case for Prisoners' Rights', Maguire *et al.*, *supra*, n. 68, ch. 1.
78 Woolf Report, *supra*, n. 7, p. 226. Understood in Woolf's sense, the ultimate objective of 'control' must be to ensure a safe and lawful prison environment, and 'order' is arguably a better term.

should retain all of the rights possessed by other, non-imprisoned citizens, apart from those which are necessarily restricted by the demands of security and control, or perhaps more accurately, order.

Apart from this significant residue of rights, it can also be argued that prisoners possess additional special entitlements *by virtue* of their imprisonment. When someone is subjected to imprisonment, her dependence on the relevant authorities is greatly increased. As a direct consequence of imprisonment the prisoner is no longer in a position to provide her own shelter, food or clothing, neither can she select her own employment, health care or educational facilities. This increase in dependence on the part of the prisoner should impose certain obligations on the prison authorities to provide facilities: obligations which must go further than those currently imposed on the state in relation to non-prisoners. Such an approach to the consequences of imprisonment would require the clear recognition of both the retention by prisoners of their ordinary legal rights despite the fact of their imprisonment, and the acquisition by prisoners of an entitlement to the provision of certain additional facilities.

As already described, the formal legal framework for imprisonment in England and Wales contains little detail. It neither expressly removes rights from prisoners nor does it expressly recognise their retention, and on the subject of additional entitlements it is most unspecific. The Prison Act 1952 is peculiarly silent on the subject, and the Prison Rules, even at their most specific, have not been interpreted as vesting prisoners with directly enforceable rights in private law.[79] Thus, in formal legal terms, an individual prisoner has the right to very few resources. In practice a prisoner's access to resources such as work, education, personal possessions, health, and even association with other prisoners, is governed by administrative rules and guidance derived from the Circular Instructions and Standing Orders drafted internally to amplify the Prison Rules. The extent to which these administrative rules reflect the approach to the implications of imprisonment outlined above will be considered in the discussion which follows.

(1) Privileges

Rule 4 of the Prison Rules requires that there be established at every prison a system of privileges approved by the Secretary of State, which shall include arrangements under which money earned by prisoners may be spent. Standing Order 4, as published in 1985, described 'the range of privileges available and the conditions under which they may be granted', and went on to explain that

a privilege may be defined as a facility or activity approved by the Secretary of State and permitted at the discretion of the governor, whose decision will be based on the availability of resources and the management requirements of his establishment. A

79 See, most recently, *Hague* v. *Deputy Governor of Parkhurst Prison* [1991] All ER 733.

privilege may be forfeited as a punishment for an offence against discipline or may be withdrawn as specified below, but not otherwise.

The privileges were listed in two categories. The first, which included possession of such items as books, newspapers, radios and notebooks, were privileges 'for which inmates are eligible wherever located', while the second category 'for which inmates are normally eligible where conditions permit', included both personal possessions ranging from wedding rings to caged birds, and association with other prisoners. Thus, by administrative order, association was defined as a privilege, the grant of which was 'subject to the availability of accommodation and other resources'.

Whatever the attitude towards association at individual establishments, and however much emphasis was placed on the importance of association by the Standing Order, it is revealing to note that the provision of a resource as fundamental as association was left to administrative discretion. The question whether prisoners should serve the majority of their sentences locked in a single cell or should spend them in some form of voluntary association with other prisoners is central to the whole nature of imprisonment. The debate between the advocates of the 'separate' system of cellular isolation and those favouring treatment and association lay at the heart of much late nineteenth- and early twentieth-century penal policy making.[80] Yet, although government policy, as expressed in the 1991 White Paper, has moved a long way from the strict separate system of the nineteenth century, Parliament has effectively left the choice between a regime of open association and one of cellular isolation in the hands of the administration. The formal statutory structure contents itself merely with a reference in the Prison Rules to daily exercise (rule 27), to religious services (rule 13), to the provision of work for inmates 'where possible outside the cells and in association with one another' (rule 28), and to evening classes (rule 29). In the absence of any firm statutory requirements, therefore, the decision whether prisoners will serve their sentences 'banged up' in their cells for 23 out of every 24 hours, or will serve them in association with one another, will in practice be taken by local management, dictated, not by any considered penal objective, but by the adequacy of the available resources.

The report of the Chief Inspector for 1990–91 describes the factors leading to the significant variations in the amount of association available across different establishments.[81] According to the approach to imprisonment described above, a prisoner's entitlement to voluntary association with his fellows should be restricted to the extent specifically required by the maintenance of security and control or order. Outside prison, people are free to associate with one another, and that same freedom should be restricted in prisoners only to the extent necessary to achieve safe segregation from the rest of society. Association should be regarded as a 'right', the restriction of which

80 For relevant discussion see The May Report, *supra*, n. 3, and L. Radzinowicz and R. Hood, *The Emergence of Penal Policy* (1990, Oxford: Oxford University Press).

81 *Report of H.M. Chief Inspector of Prisons January 1990–March 1991* (1991, London: HMSO).

must be specifically justified, not as an additional privilege to be made available where possible.

The *de facto* delegation of policy formulation to the administration in relation to association illustrates yet again the minimal role played by the formal democratic element in the formulation of custodial policy. Hard-pressed prison governors operating within tight budgets are not in the best position to reflect the true public interest when choosing between association and effective cellular confinement. More specific guidance must be given by the legislature, and clearer priorities set in advance after open and informed debate. The Woolf Report urged that the term 'privilege' be dropped:

> In the past it has been argued on behalf of the Prison Service that privileges imply something which prisoners are given out of grace and favour. It should not be a matter of grace and favour that prisoners are allowed to associate, or that they are able to buy books, newspapers, or have radios.[82]

The report argued that the Prison Service can, and should, be under a duty to provide 'privileges' where practicable, and although that duty would not imply a legally enforceable right in the prisoner to the privilege in question, a failure to provide the 'privilege' could be challengeable through judicial review. The term 'privilege' is inconsistent with this duty and should not be used. The Woolf Report recommended that both rule 4 and Standing Order 4 should be amended to make clear the facilities which should normally be provided for prisoners, and should recognise those facilities, not as privileges, but as a prisoner's normal expectations.[83] To date, the government's response has been half-hearted. Following an undertaking in the 1991 White Paper, Standing Order 4 has now been revised: 'Privileges' have become 'Facilities', and the list of those available to all prisoners has been expanded.[84] The position of association, however, has not been altered, and no attempt has been made to involve Parliament in the debate.

(2) Education and Work

Rule 29 of the Prison Rules states:

'(1) Every prisoner able to profit from the educational facilities provided at a prison shall be encouraged to do so.

(2) Programmes of evening educational classes shall be arranged at every prison and, subject to any directions of the Secretary of State, reasonable facilities shall be afforded to prisoners who wish to do so to improve their education by correspondence courses or private study, or to practise handicrafts in their spare time.'

The value of education is thus recognised, and its promotion encouraged

---

82 *Supra*, n. 7, p. 375.

83 The possible legal implications arising from the creation of an expectation are discussed further in chapter 6.

84 For the government's undertaking, see, *supra*, n. 8, p. 82. The revision of SO 4 has been achieved by way of CI 41/1992 and Standing Order Amendment 499/1992. The Prison Service has, however, started consultation on the introduction of prisoners' compacts, see *Prisoners' Compacts* (1992, London: Prison Service). See also the discussion on standards below, pp.104–7.

but, although the Secretary of State could be in breach of his duty if he failed to arrange any evening educational classes at a prison, there is plainly no right to education. There is also no mention of payment for attendance at educational classes, although prisoners in full-time education are currently paid at a standard rate, usually below that which they could earn in the workshops.

On a number of occasions since 1983 the House of Commons Select Committee on Education, Science and Arts has considered the question of education within prisons. In 1983 it first recommended the introduction of a Prison Regimes Act, which would require the provision of sufficient work or education to keep prisoners actively employed for a normal working day, and would introduce a right of access to education throughout a prisoner's sentence.[85] In reply the government argued that it would be inappropriate to single out education and 'specifically reject[ed] the proposal to confer on prisoners a right which is not available to law-abiding members of the community'.[86] Prisoners, in other words, were to have no additional entitlements by virtue of their exceptional dependence. In 1987 the Select Committee returned to the issue, restating the case for education, but declaring itself prepared to call it a privilege rather than a right.[87] The proposals were again rejected by the government.[88] However, it was in the course of this second exchange of views that the interesting argument concerning the aims of the Prison Service described above emerged.

While the Woolf Inquiry endorsed many of the recommendations of the House of Commons Select Committee and placed considerable emphasis on education, arguing that it should be given an equal standing to work within the activities of the prison, it did not recommend a Prison Regimes Act. As the Woolf Report explained, it had attempted to structure its proposals in a way that avoided having to rely on legislation.[89] The Select Committee, however, remains faithful to its proposed Act.[90] The government's response, contained in the 1991 White Paper, expressed support for education and mentioned the intention to establish guidelines for governors for the provision of balanced regimes within their individual prisons. No legislative change is anticipated immediately, and the government has rejected Woolf's proposal that prisoners in education should receive pay commensurate to that earned elsewhere in the prison.[91] It is, however, proceeding with a programme of contracting out prison education.

The provision of work within prison is covered by rule 28, which states:

(1) A convicted prisoner shall be required to do useful work for not more than ten hours

85 *First Report of the Education, Science and Arts Committee Session 1982–3 Prison Education* (1983, HC 45–1, London: HMSO).

86 *Prison Education* (1983, Cmnd 9126, London: HMSO).

87 *Supra*, n. 9.

88 *Supra*, n. 10.

89 *Supra*, n. 7, pp. 384–5.

90 *The Third Report of the Education, Science and Arts Committee, Session 1989–90, Prison Education* (1990, HC 482. London: HMSO).

91 *Supra*, n. 8, ch. 7.

a day, and arrangements shall be made to allow prisoners to work, where possible, outside the cells and in association with one another . . .

(5) An unconvicted prisoner shall be permitted, if he wishes, to work as if he were a convicted prisoner.

(6) Prisoners may be paid for their work at rates approved by the Secretary of State, either generally or in relation to particular cases.

A sentenced prisoner may, therefore, be required to work, although he has no right to do so, and both the sentenced and the unsentenced may be paid. The debate regarding work centres on the allegedly low-grade nature of the work typically provided, the absence for many prisoners of the opportunity to work at all, or to work a full day, and the unrealistically low wages paid.[92] The government has promised improvements on all three points, but again no timetable is provided, and no extra resources guaranteed.[93]

Here, as in relation to privileges in general, the relevant legislation is enabling rather than mandatory in any effective sense. The authorities possess a wide area of discretion within which they can create their own policies. While the Parliamentary system in the shape of the select committees, has become involved and this involvement has raised awareness of the issues, it has not proved directly influential, particularly with regard to the education committee's call for legislative change.

(3) Correspondence, Access to Lawyers, and Family Ties

For an individual confined to prison the ability to maintain contact with the outside world is of crucial importance. Further, the ability to obtain independent legal advice is essential to the full protection of the prisoner's legal rights and interests. In terms of the approach outlined above, the ability to communicate with the outside world should be seen as a residual right. Prisoners should have the same freedom to communicate with others as is posssessed by non-prisoners, save in so far as the proper demands of security and control require additional restrictions. Perhaps in reflection of the importance of the issues involved, the Prison Rules are relatively detailed on the subject of letters and visits, but nevertheless require supplementing by Standing Order 5, running to 29 pages.

(a) Access to Lawyers

Present policy on access to lawyers has been significantly influenced by court action, both domestic and European. Arising from an incident in 1969, Sydney Golder, a sentenced prisoner, wished to consult a solicitor about possible proceedings in libel against a prison officer. Under the regulations then in force, a prisoner wishing to seek legal advice, unless he was already a party to legal proceedings, had first to petition the Secretary of State. Further, if the

---

92 See *First Report of the Employment Select Committee Session 1991–2 Employment in Prisons and for Ex-offenders* (1991, HC 30, London: HMSO).

93 *Supra*, n.8, ch.7.

potential action concerned treatment by the prison authorities, the prisoner was obliged first to make a formal complaint through internal channels, the prior ventilation rule. When Mr Golder's request to contact his solictor was refused he petitioned the European Commission on Human Rights, and his complaint was ultimately upheld by the European Court of Human Rights.[94] The ECHR held that the action of the Home Secretary was in breach of both article 6 of the European Convention, guaranteeing a right of access to court, and article 8, guaranteeing a right of respect for correspondence. In grudging recognition of the ruling the government amended the relevant Prison Rules to enable prisoners to contact lawyers concerning actions to which they might become a party, but such access was made 'subject to any direction of the Secretary of State'. Significantly the relevant directions, in the form of a Circular Instruction, maintained the prior ventilation rule. The government's commitment to compliance with the European Convention, it seems, was minimal.

In 1980 the whole question of prisoners' correspondence came before the European Court again in *Silver* v. *UK*.[95] In addition to access to legal advice, this case involved the whole question of the stopping and the censorship of prisoners' correspondence. In *Silver* the European Commission doubted the propriety of the prior ventilation rule and, following its report, the UK government amended the relevant Standing Order, replacing 'prior' with 'simultaneous' ventilation. At this point the domestic courts intervened. The Divisional Court, emboldened by the case of *Raymond* v. *Honey*, in which the House of Lords had upheld a prisoner's right of access to court and declared the Prison Rules to be subject to normal constitutional principles,[96] declared the simultaneous ventilation rule to be an impediment to the prisoner's right of access to the courts, and thus *ultra vires* the Prison Rules.[97] The Standing Orders were amended once more, and the simultaneous ventilation rule finally abandoned. Rule 37A and Standing Order 5 combine now to provide that letters to and from lawyers concerning current legal proceedings will not be read or stopped, unless the governor has reason to doubt that the letter is indeed what it purports to be,[98] while letters concerning potential legal action may be read to ensure that they comply with the general restrictions on correspondence.[99]

Adjudication in the form of court action, therefore, has proved an important factor in the evolution of current policy on a prisoner's right to correspond with a lawyer. The courts were asked to judge the legality of existing policy using pre-ordained standards contained in either the European Convention or the

94 *Golder* v. *United Kingdom* (1975) 1 EHRR 524.
95 *Silver* v. *United Kingdom* (1980) 3 EHRR 475 [Comm.]; (1983) 5 EHRR 347 [Crt].
96 [1983] 1 AC 1.
97 *R.* v. *Home Secretary, ex p. Anderson* [1984] QB 778.
98 Standing Order 5 B 32(3).
99 Standing Order 5 B 35. The legality of this practice was unsuccessfully challenged in *R* v. *Secretary of State, ex p. Leech* [1992] COD 168, but successful challenge before the ECHR remains a possibility.

common law. In the three cases described, the contested policy was declared unlawful and the government had little choice but to revise it in order to achieve compliance with those pre-ordained standards. That it appears to have done so reluctantly in the first instance suggests that the court intervention was significant: without it the government would have been unlikely to have acted. Here, as in the case of CI 10/1974, the courts, both European and domestic, were declaring existing policy to be unlawful, and were returning the issue to the original policy maker.

(b) Letters and Phone Calls Generally

The impact of the *Silver* case was not exclusive to the prisoner's right of access to lawyers. It led to the publication of Standing Orders generally, as described above, and forced a revision of Order 5 leading to a significant reduction in the restrictions on all prisoners' correspondence. The recent liberalisation of practice regarding a prisoner's access to the outside world has not, however, been a response to judicial pressure alone. In 1984 the Control Review Committee expressed concern that the system sent the wrong signals to long-term prisoners.[100] Most of the valued and identifiable privileges were concentrated in the high-security training prisons, where overcrowding was less intense and regimes more liberal, thus prisoners had no incentive to seek transfer to a less secure establishment.

In the years following the CRC report the Prison Service has responded to this concern by withdrawing the routine reading of correspondence, first in open prisons and then, in March 1988, in category C prisons. A similar reduction in censorship was initiated in a sample of more secure establishments in February 1990. While encouraged by these moves, the Woolf Inquiry advocated the end of routine censorship, and in 1991 the government announced the intention to abolish the routine reading of letters in all establishments, except dispersal prisons. Incoming mail will still be searched for contraband, and the letters of specific prisoners may still be read for security reasons.[101] Also following the CRC report, cardphones were installed in open prisons, and then extended to category C establishments. Pressure for further extensions came from the Parliamentary All-Party Penal Affairs Group, the Prison Governors' Association and, finally, from the Woolf Report. In response the government has now undertaken to extend cardphones to all establishments which do not yet have them. Guidelines regulating their use are set out in Circular Instructions.

Interestingly, it seeems that once the government's reluctance to abandon strict control over prisoners' correspondence was broken down by the court cases of the 1970s and early 1980s, the climate was right for further liberalisation. The CRC report pointed to the management advantages of relaxing censorship and facilitating the maintenance of family ties and, spurred on by outside bodies, the Prison Service has now agree to extend that

100 *Supra*, n. 44.
101 White Paper, *supra*, n. 8, p. 83.

liberalisation widely throughout the system, and has thus strengthened the prisoner's residual rights.

(c) Visits

Until April 1992 a convicted prisoner was entitled 'to receive a visit once in four weeks', rule 34(2) (a), while an unconvicted prisoner could 'receive as many visits as he wishes within such limits and subject to such conditions as the Secretary of State may direct', rule 34(1). These rules were supplemented by Standing Orders. Following the publication of the Woolf Report recommending longer and more frequent visits, the government announced that all convicted adult prisoners could now receive two visits every four weeks, while unconvicted prisoners should, wherever practicable, receive three one-hour visits a week. A new Circular Instruction, CI 11/1991, reflecting these changes was issued in May 1991, and the Prison Rules were amended in spring 1992 so that rule 34(2) (b) now entitles a convicted prisoner to receive 'a visit twice in every period of four weeks, but only once in every such period if the Secretary of State so directs.'[102]

In 1990 the Scottish Prison Service published *Opportunity and Responsibility*, concerning the management of the long-term prison population in Scotland.[103] The document noted the increasing practice in other western European countries of allowing private family visits, and recommended that the possibility of introducing such visits in Scotland be considered. In response to questions from the Woolf Inquiry, the Prison Service in England and Wales expressed the view that the priority should be the extension of home leave. In its final report, the Woolf Inquiry nevertheless recommended that thought be given to the provision of private family visits, at least for those long-term prisoners who were not eligible for home leave. In its response the government promised to extend the system of day visits of children to their mothers to all female prisons, and undertook to consider the feasibility of extending such arrangements to some male establishments, and the eventual introduction of private family visits.[104]

In contrast to the position in relation to correspondence, there has been no significant judicial pressure for change of the visiting rules. In 1984, in a case relating to the transfer of a remand prisoner, the High Court confirmed that the Secretary of State must consider his obligations under the Prison Rules with regard to visits when transferring a prisoner, but there was no suggestion that the rules themselves required change.[105] Pressure, instead, has come from management concerns as expressed by the CRC, informed by comparisons from other jurisdictions, and more recently from the conclusions of the Woolf Inquiry. As was the case in relation to correspondence, however, the policy formulation in response to this pressure has been achieved by way of

102 Prison (Amendment) Rules 1992, SI 1992/514.
103 (1990, Edinburgh: Scottish Prison Service).
104 White Paper, *supra*, n. 8, p. 83.
105 *R* v. *Home Secretary, ex p. McAvoy* [1984] 1 WLR 1408.

administrative decision making, supplemented by Parliamentary approval only where amendment to the Prison Rules was required.

(d) Home Leave

A prisoner's 'entitlement' to home leave is covered by Circular Instruction. Section 47(5) of the 1952 Act allows for the creation of rules to provide for the temporary release of sentenced prisoners, while the Prison Rules merely state that a prisoner 'may be temporarily released for any period or periods and subject to any conditions', rule 6(1). At present a prisoner may receive short (two-day) or long (five-day) home leave, and eligibility is dependent on security categorisation and length of sentence. In response to the CRC's recommendation that contacts with the family needed to be developed as part of an incentive scheme, the government extended the availability of home leave in open prisons, and the Woolf Inquiry has recommended further extensions throughout the system. To date, the government has merely extended again the opportunities for home leave in open prisons, from three times to six times a year, but has promised to consider other extensions.[106]

Even more clearly than has been the case in relation to the policy on visits to prisoners, where changes to delegated legislation have had to be made, there has been no direct Parliamentary involvement in relation to home visits since the orginal enactment of section 47(5) and the creation of rule 6. The legislative structure is so general that no amendment has been required.

(4) Medical Services

The Prison Act requires every prison to have a duly qualified medical officer (section 7) who, according to rule 17(1) 'shall have the care of the health, mental and physical, of the prisoners in that prison'. The medical officer is employed by the Prison Service and is part of the disciplinary structure. Therefore, although in practice many medical officers are local general practitioners seconded on a part-time basis, the Prison Medical Service (PMS) is formally distinct from the National Health Service (NHS). This location of health care within the prison hierarchy has given rise to considerable concern relating to the standard of medical provision in prisons, to the alleged misuse of sedative drugs and, more recently, to the increase in suicide and self-harm among prisoners. This concern has, if anything been exacerbated by the ruling of the High Court in *Knight*,[107] that standards similar to those found in the NHS cannot be expected of medical care in prisons.

In response, a series of official bodies have looked into the position of the

106 White Paper, *supra*, n. 8, p. 83. The government has published a new Circular Instruction, CI 43/1992, explaining the calculation of eligibility for home leave for those sentenced from October 1992. The arrangements are said to be transitional pending the outcome of a review of home leave.
107 *Knight* v. *Home Office* [1990] 3 All ER 237.

PMS. They include the House of Commons Select Committee on the Social Services, the Chief Inspector and a departmental efficiency scrutiny.[108] One frequently canvassed option has been the intergration of the PMS into the NHS, but this option was excluded from the terms of reference of the efficiency scrutiny, which in the event concluded that there should be closer links between the PMS and the NHS, and that the PMS should purchase the necessary medical care from the NHS and other providers. Plans are now under way for greater contracting out of prison medical care, and for the articulation of health standards.

In relation to suicides, the government has responded to two reports by the Chief Inspector by, among other things, recognising the link between suicides and poor conditions within prison, by improving the design of cells to remove suicide risks, by issuing new guidance on suicides, and by encouraging the involvement of the Samaritans.[109] The notorious F Wing at Brixton, where a number of suicides had occurred in recent years, was also closed. While the seriousness with which the government now appears to be taking the question of prison suicides is most welcome, the problem has been evident for some time. The risk posed by the presence of bars on the inside of cell windows, for example, was one of the factors in contention in the *Knight* case, involving a suicide at Brixton in 1982.

For the government to act, it seems public concern must reach a critical point. It is also no doubt helpful if domestic pressure is reinforced by the threat of international disapproval. The decision to close F Wing was believed to have been connected with the report of the committee established under the European Convention for the Prevention of Torture and Inhuman and Degrading Treatment or Punishment. The committee visited Brixton and four other English jails in 1990, and its highly critical report was published by the government in December 1991, shortly after the Director General had announced the plans to close the wing.[110] Certainly the publication of the Chief Inspector's report on Brixton did not elicit such an immediate response.

(5) Remand Prisoners

In the years 1987/88 and 1988/89 nearly a quarter of the total prison population were remand prisoners. The figure dropped to 21 per cent in the

108 *Third Report of the Select Committee for Social Services, Session 1985-6 Prison Medical Services* (1986, HC 72-2, London: HMSO); *Report of a Review by H.M. Chief Inspector of Prisons of Suicide and Self-harm in Prison Service Establishments in England and Wales* (1990, Cm 1383, London: HMSO), and *Report on An Efficiency Scrutiny of the Prison Medical Service* (1990, London: Home Office).

109 In addition to the Suicide Report (*ibid.*) HMCIP commented adversely on the provision of medical services in the report of his inspection of Brixton Prison in 1990, *H.M.P. Brixton*, (London: Home Office). An account of the government's response can be found in the 1991 White Paper, *supra*, n. 8, pp. 86-7 and in Prison Service (1991), *supra*, n. 12, pp. 28-9.

110 *The Report to the United Kingdom Government on the Visit to the United Kingdom by the European Committee for the Prevention of Torture and Inhuman or Degrading Treatment or Punishment* (1991), and *The Response of the United Kingdom Government* (1991); both are available from the Home Office. The role of the committee is discussed further in the next chapter.

years 1989/90 and 1990/91, but remains a significant proportion.[111] The majority of remand prisoners are not convicted, and must therefore be presumed innocent. Further, not all prisoners held on custodial remand ultimately receive custodial sentences. The Prison Statistics appear to show that, of those received on remand in 1989, 4 per cent were acquitted and 28 per cent received non-custodial sentences;[112] but commentators agree that the precise proportion are extremely hard to calculate.[113] Both the Prison Rules and the European Standard Minimum Rules for the Treatment of Prisoners recognise the special position of remand prisoners. Rule 3(2) of the Prison Rules requires that unconvicted prisoners be kept out of contact with the convicted population as far as is practicable, and a number of the rules make special provision for unconvicted prisoners: for example, rule 17(4), access to outside doctors; rule 20(1), clothing; rule 28(5), work; rule 34(1), personal letters and visits, and rule 41(1), prisoners' property. However, in practice, remand prisoners tend to be concentrated in the local prisons, where the conditions and the overcrowding are at their worst, and it has been the tendancy of the Prison Service to focus most of its limited energy and resources on the sentenced population.

In recent years the public has been made increasingly aware of the position and size of the remand population as a result of the attention focused by the media on the use of police cells,[114] the incidence of suicide and self-harm in the remand population, the plight of the mentally disordered, and the role of remand prisoners in the 1990 riots. In its report the Woolf Inquiry emphasised the need to recognise the special position of remand prisoners, and recommended that the Prison Service adopt an additional statement of purpose dealing specifically with its duties with regard to the remand population.[115] The government appears to have accepted this recommendation, and has undertaken to produce a separate statement of purpose for remand prisoners to ensure that the statements of tasks relating to all establishments holding remand prisoners refer to the need to reflect their special status, and to revise the Prison Rules so that separate rules will apply to remand prisoners.[116]

With regard to the treatment of the remand population, the government has been faced not only with mounting domestic pressure and uncomfortable international comparisons, but also with the unanswerable argument that remand prisoners possess a different status both legally and morally. That it has finally agreed to act must be welcomed, but the nature of that proposed

---

111   Prison Service (1991), *Supra*, n. 12.

112   *Prison Statistics England and Wales 1990* (1990, Cm 1800, London: HMSO), Table 2.10. According to the Howard League, on the other hand, 59 per cent of those sent to prison on remand in 1989 did not receive a custodial sentence: *Remands in Custody* (1992, London: Howard League).

113   See R. Morgan and S. Jones, 'Bail or Jail?', in E. Stockdale and S. Casale (eds), *Criminal Justice Under Stress* (1992, London: Blackstone Press), ch. 2.

114   On 30 April 1992 the Law Society wrote to the Home Secretary drawing attention to the use of police cells. On that date 1,708 people were in police cells rather than in prison.

115   *Supra*, n. 7, pp. 245–8. And see S. Casale and J. Plotnikoff, *Regimes for Remand Prisoners* (1990, London: Prison Reform Trust).

116   *Supra*, n. 8, p. 70.

action – an amendment to the Statement of Purpose, an entirely administrative document, and a revision of the Prison Rules – emphasises yet again the absence of direct Parliamentary involvement in the formulation of matters of central importance to the nature of imprisonment and the administration of the prison system. The government's decision in 1988 to abolish the right of remand prisoners to receive food illustrates the breadth of discretion granted to the authorities by the 1952 Act. The abolition, effected by the Prison (Amendment) Rules 1988, was challenged in *R* v. *Secretary of State, ex p. Simmons*, where the court upheld the government's decision.[117] According to the court section 47(4) of the 1952 Act, which authorises the provision of special treatment for remand prisoners, leaves the nature of the special treatment up to the Secretary of State, whose decision can only be impugned if it is perverse.

(6) Minimum Standards and Overcrowding

In its Statement of Purpose the Prison Service announces its duty to look after prisoners 'with humanity', and yet the appalling conditions and gross overcrowding that prevail in many prison establishments deny the possibility of humane treatment to many prisoners in England and Wales. The sharing of cells designed for single occupancy, the lack of integral sanitation, the 'banging up' of prisoners in their cells for 23 out of 24 hours, and the absence of all but the most basic 'privileges', are all well-publicised aspects of the conditions prevailing in Britain's prisons and, to date, the law has declared itself unable to intervene.

The law as set out in Parliamentary legislation makes few demands on the prison system when it comes to the conditions in which prisoners and staff are required to live and work. The special entitlements which, arguably, should should flow from the prisoner's additional dependence are effectively ignored by the existing legislative scheme. A combination of section 14 of the 1952 Act and rule 23 requires an officer of the Secretary of State to certify that the 'size, lighting, heating, ventilation and fittings' of any cell used for the confinement of a prisoner 'are adequate for health', section 14(2), and to specify the maximum number of prisoners 'who may sleep or be confined at any one time' within it, rule 23(3). Rule 23(2), however, also allows that number, the Certified Normal Accommodation (CNA), to be exceeded with leave of the Secretary of State. The Secretary of State may thus condone overcrowing, and consistently does so. In July 1987, according to the Annual Report of the Prison Service 1987–88, the number of prisoners sharing cells designed for one reached its peak: 5,091 inmates shared three to a cell and 13,892 shared two to a cell.[118]

Admittedly, the Prison Rules make certain stipulations concerning the provision of beds, hygiene, exercise etc., but these give rise to no rights directly enforceable by way of an action for breach of statutory duty, as will be

117 [1989] COD 332. For the amendment to the rules see SI 1988–89.
118 *Annual Report of the Prison Service 1987–88* (1988, cm 516, London: HMSO).

discussed below. Futher, Crown immunity still applies to exempt the Prison Service from prosecution should their kitchens and workshops fail to comply with the relevant regulatory schemes under the Health and Safety at Work Act 1974, for example. However, by virtue of the Food Safety Act 1990, prison kitchens are now open to inspection by the relevant enforcement agencies, and in cases of non-compliance a declaration can be sought.[119] Against this unpromising legislative background the courts have generally declined to become involved, holding that the conditions, or a deterioration in the conditions, in which a prisoner is held cannot amount to the tort of false imprisonment.[120]

(a) Minimum Standards

In the face of the prevailing regulatory vacuum a wide variety of interest groups have argued for the imposition of some form of minimum standards, and for the lifting of Crown immunity. Reporting on the state and use of prisons in 1987, the House of Commons Home Affairs Committee claimed that all its witnesses, other than the Home Office, 'supported the imposition of legally enforceable standards as a step towards improving prison conditions'.[121] The list of witnesses included not only NACRO and the Prison Reform Trust, but also the Prison Governors' Branch of the Society of Civil and Public Servants (now the Prison Governors' Association) and the Prison Officers' Association. The committee itself concluded 'that legislation should be introduced to phase out Crown immunity for prisons and that this should be accompanied by the introduction of a code of minimum standards'.[122]

The precise arguments used in favour of minimum standards have varied depending on the nature of their proposed legal status. Many refer to the opportunity for public debate that the formulation and imposition of standards would provide. If standards were to be included in primary legislation, or even in delegated legislation, Parliament would become directly involved, and if Crown immunity were lifted, external inspectors would gain access.[123] The task of formulating standards and achieving compliance, it is thought, would enable the Prison Department and individual establishments to set priorities and accurately calculate required expenditure.[124] The enunciation of clear standards, it is argued, would also provide a bench-mark against which boards of visitors could assess the conditions within their own establishments, and according to which the Chief Inspector could compare establishments.[125] Those in favour of directly legally enforceable standards also

119 Section 54(2), Food Safety Act 1990. For further discussion see chapter 6.
120 *Hague* v. *Deputy Governor of Parkhurst Prison* [1991], 3 All ER 733. See discussion in chapter 6.
121 *Third Report of the Home Affairs Select Committee, Session 1986–7, The State and Use of Prisons* (1987, HC 35–1, London: HMSO).
122 *Ibid.*, para. 23.
123 L. Gostin and M. Staunton, 'The Case for Prison Standards', in Maguire *et al.*, *supra*, n. 68, ch. 5.
124 Prison Reform Trust, *Evidence to the Home Affairs Committee* (1987), published in *supra*, n. 121, HC 35–2, p. 71.
125 *Report of H.M. Chief Inspector of Prisons 1984* (1985, HC 589, London: HMSO).

see the courts as a useful spur to compliance, and as a means of winning the necessary resources.[126] Finally, in evidence to the Home Affairs Committee, some pointed to the UK's lack of compliance with the European Standard Minimum Rules for the Treatment of Prisoners, and to the use of minimum standards in certain states in the USA, to illustrate the UK's lack of conformity with international developments.[127]

The government's response to this mounting pressure has been slow. In 1982 modest enthusiasm was expressed by the then Home Secretary, and the Prison Department was asked to prepare a draft code for consultation. In the event, however, although it published a summary of building standards and agreed to abide by the European Rules (a letter was sent to all governors in 1988 enclosing the revised European Rules and stating the government's policy of support and compliance), the government felt that the creation of a code of minimum standards would interfere with the programme it had devised for the improvement of prison conditions.[128] The government's priorities lay in an extensive prison building programme and, after pressure from the Chief Inspector, in the introduction of integral sanitation. Indeed, in its evidence to the Woolf Inquiry the Prison Service stated

the Government's present view is that the provision of a code (or codes) of minimum standards would be an enormously complex and time-consuming task, with no guarantee that the end result would lead to an improvement in conditions. The Government has preferred to concentrate on practical steps to improve prison conditions through such measures as its major building and refurbishment programme and improved managerial performance and accountability through initiatives such a Fresh Start and the CI 55/84 procedures.[129]

More specifically, the Prison Service objected that a significant body of standards already existed in the form of the Prison Rules and the Standing Orders (SOs), and it quoted particularly SO 14, which it claimed contained minimum standards relating to health and safety matters. Further, it argued that it would be hard to determine what should be included in a code, and whether a single code should apply to all establishments. It claimed that if the code were not legally enforceable it would be merely aspirational and of limited value, and that if it were merely minimum it would fail to encourage excellence.

The Woolf Inquiry was 'not impressed by any of these arguments'.[130] It received a quantity of evidence advocating enforceable minimum standards and was satisfied that

if the Prison Service were to consult the Prison Governors' Association, the Prison

126 Gostin and Staunton, *supra*, n. 123.
127 *Supra*, n. 121, HC 35–1, para. 21.
128 Prison Governors' Association, *supra*, n. 34, policy document 2, p. 10, describes the letter that was sent to all prison governors in 1988 enclosing the revised European Rules and stating the government's policy of support and compliance.
129 Prison Service (1990), *supra*, n. 40, part 5, p. 25.
130 *Supra*, n. 7, p. 299.

Officers' Association, the other bodies to whom we have already made reference [NACRO and the Prison Reform Trust], and other individuals and bodies who took part in our public seminar which dealt with this subject, they would soon be provided with a shopping list of what is to be included.[131]

The Woolf Report accordingly recommended that the Prison Service, in consultation, prepare a code of standards. Once the code was drafted a timetable should be agreed for compliance with each standard. Some establishments would be expected to achieve compliance more quickly than others, and the targets for each establishment would be included in the govenor's annual 'contract'. The Woolf Report also envisaged a system of accreditation which would enable an establishment ultimately to apply for Accreditation Status when it had achieved compliance with every standard. However, the Accredited Standards would not be legally enforceable, in the first instance, although the Inquiry expected that when they were widely achieved they would be the subject of a Prison Rule, and so subject to judicial review.

The government's response has been broadly supportive of the Woolf Inquiry's view. Although the White Paper effectively repeated the claim that standards already exist, it did promise codification, in consultation with the unions, outside bodies and the prisoners.[132] In furtherance of this undertaking, a Code of Standards Steering Group was established, and a discussion document published in 1992, considering the aims, coverage and possible model to be adopted by the code, and proposing a timetable for its introduction.[133] This document was widely distributed, and was discussed at two seminars attended by representatives from both within and without the Prison Service in May 1992.

While these moves by the prison authorities to involve interested parties in the formulation of a code of standards indicate a welcome opening up of the policy formulation process, significant doubts remain with regard to the legal status of the standards. The question of legal status raises not only the issue of enforceability, which is dealt with in the next chapter, but also the role of Parliament in the formulation processs. The Woolf Report, while content to leave the question of enforceability until the standards could be met, assumed that, at that stage, the standards 'would anyway be the subject of a Prison Rule':[134] they would, in other words, have been before Parliament. The 1991 White Paper, however, whether advertently or inadvertently, slants this conclusion and declares that

the Government agrees with the Woolf Report that questions relating to enshrining the standards in the Prison Rules, and to their enforceability, should be considered when the standards can be met consistently in all establishments.[135]

131 *Ibid.*, p. 300. See, particularly, S. Casale and J. Plotnikoff, *Minimum Standards in Prison: A Programme of Change* (1989, London: NACRO).
132 *Supra*, n. 8, p. 62.
133 *A Code of Standards for the Prison Service: A Discussion Document Produced by the Code of Standards Steering Group* (1992, London: Prison Service).
134 *Supra*, n. 7, p. 301.
135 *Supra*, n. 8, p. 62.

Parliamentary involvement is to be delayed until compliance is achieved. According to the Code of Standards Steering Group, the main value in having standards 'is that it enables those responsible to say clearly what level of service they aim to provide',[136] and it is evident from the discussion document, which makes no mention of the Prison Rules in its provisional timetable, that the emphasis is being placed on wide consultation within the Prison Service and between interested groups rather than on Parliamentary debate. The aim is to 'promote "ownership" of the standard' among those directly involved, rather than within society as a whole.[137] Prisons, it seems, are finally to achieve a code of standards, but Parliament will be effectively excluded from the formulation of that code.

(b) Overcrowding

[T]he life and work of the Prison Service have, for the last 20 years, been distorted by the problems of overcrowding. That single factor has dominated prisoners' lives, it has produced often intolerable pressure on staff, and as a consequence it has soured industrial relations. It has skewed managerial effort and it has diverted managerial effort away from positive developments. The removal of overcrowding is, in my view, an indispensable pre-condition of sustained and universal improvement in prison conditions.[138]

Thus, in his contribution to one of the Woolf Inquiry seminars, did the then Director General describe the effect of overcrowding. The extent of the problem and its impact on all who live or work in prisons cannot be denied.

Prisons are required to accept all those committed to them by order of the court. Therefore, while the Prison Service should be expected to make the best use of the accommodation it has, it can do little to prevent the overcrowding caused by any shortfall between existing accommodation and the number of prisoners entering its custody. Two obvious routes to the reduction of overcrowding thus present themselves: the imposition of restrictions on input through the control of judicial discretion, and the increase in existing accommodation. Until recently, the government has focused most of its efforts on the latter option by investing significant resources in a prison building programme, and in 1991 regarded itself as being 'in sight of providing sufficient places to match the average size of the prison population'.[139]

While evidence was presented to the Woolf Inquiry to the effect that the system would soon be in equilibrium, the Inquiry was anxious to recommend measures designed to insure that gross overcrowding would not be allowed to recur. In interpreting his terms of reference, Lord Justice Woolf excluded sentencing policy from his inquiry, and therefore concentrated his efforts on proposing a structure designed to enhance the Home Secretary's account-

---

136 *Supra*, n. 133, p. 2.
137 *Ibid.*, p. 8.
138 *Supra*, n. 7, p. 281.
139 *Supra*, n. 8, p. 61. The restrictions on the use of custody imposed by the Criminal Justice Act 1991 represent the latest in a series of, to date, not very successful legislative attempts to control input.

ability to the public. The Woolf Report proposed that a new Prison Rule be introduced, to take effect from the end of 1992, the date at which the system was expected to be in equilibrium, which would provide that no establishment should hold prisoners in excess of its CNA, save for very short periods. Any significant increase would only be permitted if the Home Secretary issued a certificate, which he would be required to lay before both Houses of Parliament, stating the necessary increase, the period of its duration, up to a maximum of three months, and the reason for it. Shortly after the publication of the Report, the government's alleged intention to reject this proposal was leaked to the press. In the event, the 1991 White Paper acknowledged the need for greater public awareness of the problem of prison overcrowding, but promised no specific structure nor timetable, merely a consideration of the Woolf proposals once the system had come into equilibrium.[140]

In November 1991, only two months after the publication of the White Paper, an 'unprecedented surge' in the prison population meant that there were 3,000 more prisoners than the Home Office had predicted. On 1 November 1991, 45,572 prisoners were in prison, with a further 1,777 in police cells. The total of 47,349 was 1,814 more than at the same data in 1990.[141] While the situation has since improved, there is still serious overcrowding in individual establishments. However, it is clear that the government does not wish even to consider rendering itself accountable to Parliament in any serious way until overcrowding has receded. Again, Parliament is to be invited in once the problem has been solved and further embarrassment avoided.

(d) Conclusions

The most outstanding feature of the policy formulation described in this chapter must surely be the sparsity of legislative involvement. The Prison Act and the Prison Rules combine to place large areas of policy formulation in the hands of the administrative authorities, on whom they impose few procedural constraints. Thus, although there have been significant changes in internal prison policy over the last two decades, these have necessitated little change to the legislative structure. The changes which have occurred have been inspired by pressure from a variety of sources, including international courts, domestic courts, senior management and public opinion. Most significantly, in recent years pressure for change has found expression through the Woolf Inquiry into the prison disturbances of April 1990. While it is still too early to assess the impact of the Woolf Report on Prison Service policy, and whatever doubts might be voiced on that subject,[142] it is clear that the approach to its task

140 *Supra*, n.8, p.61.
141 *The Independent*, 6 November 1991, Parl. Debs. 1991–92, vol. 198, 5 November 1991. According to the Prison Service (1991), *supra*, n. 12, the prison population rose throughout the whole of 1991. Immediately after the coming into force of the Criminal Justice Act 1991 in October 1992, however, the population fell.
142 For an assessment see *Implementing Woolf: The Prison System One Year On* (1992, London: Prison Reform Trust).

adopted by the Inquiry, particularly at Stage II when the wider applications of the disturbances were examined, has done much to open up the process of internal prison policy formulation.

As the above discussion has illustrated, once, for whatever reason, the need for change is recognised within the Prison Service, the process of policy formulation itself is one of administrative decision making. In the past, although this process might have been informed by an 'independent' report, from the Chief Inspector for example, it was essentially internal and, typically, little systematic consultation would take place outside the Prison Service. In other words, little effort was made to facilitate the full reflection of the public interest. In marked contrast, the Woolf Inquiry made every attempt to consult widely and to respond to and initiate debate when formulating its own views and recommendations.

Inquiries such as that conducted by Lord Justice Woolf are commonly confronted by significant inequalities in the resources, influence and information available to the various interested parties.[143] In the case of the Woolf Inquiry the most obvious danger was that the views of the Prison Service would be accorded disproportionate weight in comparison to that given to the views of prisoners and outside interests. It was a danger of which the Inquiry team was apparently well aware, and Morgan describes a number of the strategies adopted by the Inquiry in an attempt to redress the balance and to involve as many interests as possible.[144] In the first place, all prisoners known to have been in the relevant establishments were written to and their replies analysed. Further, although no single organisation sought to represent the interests of prisoners at Stage I, a counsel to the Inquiry was appointed and was in a position, to some degree, to protect the interests of prisoners through the cross-examination of witnesses.[145] Secondly, positive steps were taken to encourage outside individuals and groups to submit evidence to Stage II, and public seminars were held to discuss specific topics. Outside interests were invited to participate at these seminars, the written evidence of all participants was made available, including that of the Prison Service, and briefing papers were distributed in advance indicating the focus of the Inquiry's interest. While the seminars might not have inspired incisive debate, they did provide an opportunity for the informed exchange of views, and, on some topics, enabled a surprising level of consensus to emerge. In combination, these strategies, particularly at Stage II, the stage most relevant to policy formulation, helped to counteract the potentially disproportionate influence of the Prison Service, by encouraging other sources of opinion to contribute and,

---

143 For further discussion of the problems of interest representation see chapter 4. On the specific difficulties facing inquiries see T. O'Riordan, R. Kemp and M. Purdue, *Sizewell B: An Anatomy of the Inquiry* (1988, London: Macmillan).

144 R. Morgan, 'Woolf: In Retrospect and Prospect' (1991) 54 Mod. LR 713.

145 For consideration of the questions of fairness between parties and between parties' views see O'Riordan *et al.*, *supra*, n. 143. For further discussion of the inquiry as a means of validation, see chapters 6 and 11.

most significantly, by providing those sources with the necessary information to enable them to do so effectively.

The Woolf Inquiry was not, of course, empowered to impose its policy conclusions on government. It could merely make recommendations to the Secretary of State. To that extent it could not fulfil the role of the broad policy formulator considered in chapter 4. Nevertheless it is possible that by its example it has encouraged the policy formulators within the Prison Service to adopt a more open and responsive approach. Certainly the publication and circulation of consultative documents on the code of standards and the Independent Complaints Adjudicator for Prisons, and the holding of seminars on the former, are encouraging signs. It remains to be seen how far the apparent openness will be taken, and how responsive the government will in fact prove to be.

Whatever will prove to have been the impact of Woolf on the process of prison policy formulation, however, it must be remembered that these steps towards openness and responsiveness have been introduced administratively; Parliament has played little part. Indeed, the fate of the proposal to introduce Parliamentary monitoring with regard to overcrowding, and the form taken by the proposed code of standards, would suggest that there is considerable reluctance to involve Parliament, either as an overseer or as a policy formulator. Under our present constitutional arrangements such a position cannot be acceptable. Whatever the actual shortcomings of Parliament, and however far it falls below the demands of full process, it represents at present the primary forum for the identification of the public interest. It must therefore be involved both in the formulation of fundamental prison policy and in the creation of subsidiary structures for the evolution of detailed policies and rules. The prison system, its aims and governing principles, belong to society at large, not just to those who work and live within it.

6
Internal Prison Decisions: Application and Validation of Policy

This chapter is divided into two main parts. Part **a** deals with the application and validation of transfer policy, while part **b** covers a prisoner's access to resources, broadly interpreted. In relation to transfer decisions the discussion of validation centres mainly on the role of the courts, while in part **b** extra-judicial mechanisms are also considered.

(a) Transfer

(1) Application Decisions

In the previous chapter the formulation of policy concerning security categorisation was considered, together with that relating to the subsequent transfer of prisoners. In view of the sparsity of the available data, however, in this chapter the discussion of the processes of application and validation will generally be restricted to the use of rule 43 in its various forms, and to the transfer of prisoners to a special unit.

(a) Segregation Under Rule 43, Good Order and Discipline

Segregation under rule 43 for good order and discipline is not formally a punitive measure. It is an option available to governors to be used 'where it appears desirable, for the maintenance of good order and discipline'. It may be used as a preventive measure and, since no formal charge is laid, its use is not regulated by the same procedural stringency as is applied to the imposition of punishment following a disciplinary charge. Nevertheless, the conditions experienced by many prisoners on rule 43 are comparable to those suffered by prisoners segregated following a disciplinary award. When Her Majesty's Chief Inspector of Prisons considered the operation of rule 43 in 1986, under regulations then in force, he reported the claim by headquarters and regional staff that prisoners were usually told the reasons for their segregation and given the chance to reply.[1] However, several of the prisoners segregated on grounds of good order who were interviewed in the course of the Chief Inspector's research denied that they had been given reasons.

Under the provisions of the amended rule 43 and CI 26/1990 the governor may now authorise segregation for up to three days. If segregation is to continue beyond that period, the authorisation of the board of visitors, or exceptionally the Secretary of State, must be sought. Such authority can extend for up to one calender month and may be renewed. However, the segregation must be ended if at any time the medical officer so advises on medical grounds. It is not essential that the board member interview the prisoner before authorising continued segregation, but it is clearly anticipated that he or she will do so as soon as practicable. The Circular also emphasises that the board member should not automatically authorise continuation for the full month, but should consider the minimum period necessary. Finally, although the Circular details the obligation to record the reasons for segregation on the official records, it states 'inmates have no entitlement to be given reasons for their segregation under rule 43' (Annex C). The giving of reasons to inmates is merely encouraged as 'a sensible practice'. It should also be noted here that within contracted out, or private, prisons the powers of the governor under rule 43 are exercised by the controller.[2]

A number of points arise from these procedures. In the first place there is the question of the proper role of the boards of visitors. There is evidence that under the old procedure authorisation by the boards of visitors was often no more than a formality. Maguire and Vagg suggest that boards of visitors were seeing rule 43 prisoners regularly, but that refusal to authorise continued segregation was very rare.[3] Indeed, they report that many board members saw their involvement as purely token, since the governor could always appeal to the region if the board refused authorisation. Admittedly, CI 26/1990 seeks to emphasise the real role to be played by the board of visitors, and it is to be hoped that members' confidence will increase. However, there remains the fundamental ambiguity of the boards' role. If, as will be discussed below, the boards' watchdog role is to be strengthened then, according to the Woolf Report, board members should not be involved in authorising extensions of segregation:

> [W]hatever is the true position, when a board member gives such authority, prisoners do not see him as acting to safeguard their interests, but as the arm of management. This is not consistent with or helpful to the board's watch-dog role. We propose that, in future therefore, it should be the responsibility of the area manager to give the authority.[4]

1 H.M. Chief Inspector of Prisons, *A Review of the Segregation of Prisoners under Rule 43* (1986, London: Home Office).
2 Section 85(3)(b), Criminal Justice Act 1991, and rule 98A, Prison Rules, inserted by Prison (Amendment) Rules 1992, SI 1992/514. For the role of the controller and the director of private prisons see below, pp. 130–31.
3 M. Maguire and J. Vagg, *The 'Watchdog' Role of Boards of Visitors* (1984, London: Home Office).
4 *Prison Disturbances April 1990* (The Woolf Report) (1991, Cm 1456, London: HMSO), p. 322.

In the event, this argument has been rejected by the government.[5] From the point of view of full process, however, Woolf's view has much to recommend it. In chapter 4 it was suggested that, although true independent adjudication might frequently be the most appropriate mechanism for the initial resolution of disputes, administrative decision making modelled on adjudication might provide an appropriate alternative for simple disputes and allocative decisions where speed, for example, or internal expertise were important. In relation to rule 43 segregation, a dispute exists between the prison governor and the prisoner, but since speed is perceived as essential, there may be good reason to seek resolution through administrative decision making in the first instance. The location of the initial decision in an internal decision maker, however, increases the need for true independence at the validation stage. Thus, if the board of visitors is to play any part in that validation process, it cannot be involved in the application decision itself. If it were so involved it would cease to be truly independent. The issue will be discussed further below.

Whatever the role of the board of visitors, however, it is essential to full process that both the initial decision to segregate and any subsequent decision to authorise extension be taken as openly and on the basis of as much information as possible. If such decisions are to be taken by internal administrative actors, they should at least be modelled on adjudication. Indeed, since the preventive measures allowed by rule 43 must often be based on opinion rather than fact – does the prisoner pose a threat to good order and discipline? – there is a case for arguing that the ideal procedure would be adversarial.

In chapter 4 it was suggested that, while adversarial adjudication might not be the best process for establishing fact, it might be more appropriate where matters of opinion are in dispute. In any event there should, as a minimum, be an assumption that *before* the initial decision is taken the prisoner will be given the reasons why segregation is thought necessary, including the evidence on which that opinion is based. The prisoner should then be given the opportunity to respond to any allegations, the exchange should be fully recorded, and a copy given to the prisoner. A similar procedure requiring the authorities to justify the need for continued segregation should be applied at any subsequent decision to extend segregation. If this further authorisation is most appropriately the responsibility of the area manager, then the area manager should be required to visit the prison in furtherance of his or her management role. Only on very specific grounds – the protection of sources for example – should these procedures be waived, and then only to the minimum extent necessary. The reasons for any waiver should be fully recorded. Judged against these preferred procedures the present Circular's bland encouragement to give reasons *after* the event appears wholly inadequate, even when supplemented by the government's belated acceptance 'that the prisoner should wherever possible be given reasons for these decisions in writing'.[6]

5 *Custody, Care and Justice: The Way Ahead for the Prison Service in England and Wales* (1991, Cm 1647, London: HMSO), p. 94.
6 *Ibid.*, p. 55.

(b) Transfer Under CI 37/1990

Circular Instruction 37/1990 replaces the old procedure for transfer to segregation in a local prison under CI 10/1974. As is the case with simple segregation under rule 43, this procedure did not in the past, and still does not, require the bringing of a formal disciplinary charge. It is designed to enable the governor of a dispersal prison to transfer a disruptive prisoner right out of the prison for a 'cooling off' period in a local prison. From the prisoner's point of view it is a highly significant move that can cause considerable dislocation and resentment: '[t]he evidence before the Inquiry . . . suggests that a transfer against the wishes of a prisoner is one of the most resented actions which the Prison Service can take'.[7]

Under the old Circular Instruction there were minimal procedural safeguards for the prisoner. The authorities were not obliged to provide reasons, and in practice it seems prisoners were not kept fully informed. The Chief Inspector recorded that the two prisoners transferred to local prisons under the old Circular who were interviewed in the course of his study of rule 43 were resentful of their treatment and claimed that they did not know the reasons for their transfer.[8] Further, although both the Divisional Court and the Court of Appeal found that Christopher Hague must have known the reasons for his transfer, Hague himself clearly felt that they had not been satisfactorily explained to him.[9]

The main structural changes to the policy introduced in 1990 have already been described. Under CI 37/1990 the decision whether or not to segregate must be made by the governor of the receiving prison, and any subsequent continuation must be authorised by the local board of visitors. The Circular also describes the required procedures, and imposes a relatively stringent obligation to give reasons. The prisoner must, as far as is practicable, be told the reasons both for transfer and for subsequent segregation, if possible before the event, and those reasons should be given in writing if requested. This represents a marked improvement on the old requirements, and on those specified in CI 1990 relating to simple segregation under rule 43. However, these new procedures still fail to match the preferred requirements described above in relation to rule 43: CI 37/1990 still uses phrases such as 'as far as is practicable', whereas the assumption must be in favour of a full prior explanation, save in specific circumstances. Transfer under CI 37/1990 is designed to be used rarely, and only when the prisoner's immediate removal from the prison is judged to be essential. In such circumstances a full hearing at the moment of transfer might be thought infeasible, but the requirement of some dialogue should not impose an unreasonable burden. At the very least a full explanation and a chance to respond prior to the decision to transfer should be provided in all cases, unless there are specific grounds to justify a

7 The Woolf Report, *supra*, n. 4, p. 227.
8 *Supra*, n. 1.
9 *R* v. *Deputy Governor of Parkhurst Prison, ex p. Hague* (1989) *Independent*, 11 August (Divisional Court), and [1990] 3 All ER 687 (Court of Appeal).

waiver. The assumption must be in favour of such a procedure, subject only to specific exception. Unplanned compulsory transfer is a disruptive event, and its impact is made all the more difficult for prisoners to accept if they have been given an inadequate explanation and little chance to respond. Even with these suggested safeguards the initial decision to transfer would still be taken by administrative decision and, as argued above, the prisoner should be entitled to some mechanism for independent adjudicatory validation.

The provision of adequate validation in the circumstances surrounding a transfer under CI 37/1990, however, is likely to pose some serious practical difficulties. In order to be effective such validation would have to be immediately available and would have to take the form of appeal rather than review. The validator would also have to possess executive powers to return the prisoner to his original prison. The issue is developed further below, but it is hard to see how such a mechanism would operate in practice, with the prisoner far from his home prison. It may be, therefore, that the process requirements necessary to ensure the true authority of decisions taken in application and validation of CI 37/1990 are so stringent and yet so essential as to render the underlying policy either unworkable if they are met, or unacceptable if they are ignored.[10]

(c) Segregation Under Rule 43, Own Protection

Under the present provisions of the Prison Rules, vulnerable prisoners, including but not exclusively sex offenders, can be placed in segregation under rule 43 for their own protection, and the process under which such decisions are taken has come under considerable criticism. The victimisation suffered by sex offenders in particular is well-known, both within and without the prison system, and consequently many potentially vulnerable prisoners request rule 43 segregation immediately on reception in prison. They may justifiably fear that they will be unable to keep the nature of their offences secret. In making the request they are often acting on advice from lawyers, probation officers, police officers, or even judges. According to the working group report on vulnerable prisoners, such requests are frequently acceded to almost automatically, with little thought being given to other possible ways of dealing with the prisoner's legitimate fears.[11] The governor may feel that he or she has no alternative means of guaranteeing even partial physical protection and, in light of the increased sensitivity of prison staff to their legal liability in this context, may feel disinclined to take any risks.

Once on rule 43, however, prisoners may suffer significantly inferior conditions to those experienced by the rest of the prison population. Further, whatever the physical conditions, they will suffer stigmatisation merely as a result of being on the rule. The Woolf Report describes the practice in

10 A similar position is, arguably, reached in relation to the seclusion of disturbed patients, see chapter 10.
11 *The Management of Vulnerable Prisoners: Report of a Prison Department Working Group* (1989, London: HMSO).

Wandsworth Prison, where three wings are used to accommodate rule 43, own protection, cases. The prisoners employed to clean those wings put notices 'not on rule 43' on their doors to protect themselves from the treatment directed at those on the rule.[12] Elsewhere in the Report the experience of those rule 43 prisoners caught up in the disturbances at Strangeways in April 1990 is described, and provides horrific justification for the fear of victimisation.[13]

While the victimisation of sex offenders is a grim reality within prisons in England and Wales, segregation under rule 43 does nothing to solve the problem. It merely seeks to meet the symptoms, and even there it cannot guarantee success. Indeed, rather than tackling the problem of victimisation, it may increase it by adding to the stigmitisation of the prisoner and by institutionalising the discrimination. It is the vulnerable prisoner who suffers the deprivations of segregation under the present system, not the aggressor.

Under the procedures indicated by CI 26/1990, a prisoner who fears victimisation will discuss the situation with the governor and, if the prisoner is himself requesting segregation, he will record his reasons for doing so in writing. The governor will also record his reasons for ordering segregation, and these should be full reasons: a mere reference to 'the nature of the offence' is insufficient. The Circular also encourages the giving of reasons to the prisoner 'as good practice'. As with segregation for good order and discipline, the board of visitors must authorise any extension of segregation after the initial three days. Further, the medical officer should see the prisoner, if possible, every day, and the segregation must be terminated if the officer so advises on medical grounds.

Any consideration of the ideal requirements of full process in this context becomes particularly difficult in the light of the very far from ideal realities against which these application decisions must in practice be made. The ultimate policy with regard to vulnerable prisoners must be to facilitate the free, voluntary and safe association of all prisoners whatever their offence, and at the same time to provide the necessary protection and help for vulnerable individuals. Arguably, therefore, any procedure which granted automatic priority to the prisoner's desire for segregation might not facilitate the full reflection of the public interest. It might rather serve to perpetuate the current, unacceptable, position. Instead, a specific obligation should be imposed on the authorities to provide alternatives to segregation, and the procedure for dealing with the location of vulnerable prisoners should be designed, against that background, to achieve considered agreement between the prisoner and the governor. Further, it should be supplemented by an effective mechanism for independent validation should the prisoner feel that his views have been unjustifiably discounted.

12 *Supra*, n. 4, p. 311.
13 *Ibid.*, pp. 71–2.

(d) Transfer to a Special Unit

As described in the previous chapter, the Prison Service is developing special units for prisoners presenting particularly acute control problems, and allocation to and from these units is arranged by the Special Units Selection Committee (SUSC). SUSC is comprised of senior headquarters staff and senior staff from the special units. Referrals for allocation to a special unit are received on a form from the governor of the establishment currently holding the prisoner, and are accompanied by contributions from the prisoner's personal officer, the medical officer, the governor, psychologist, probation officer and wing manager. Once allocated to a special unit, each prisoner is reviewed by SUSC after 10 weeks, and at three- to six-month intervals thereafter. SUSC then becomes responsible for transferring the prisoner out of the unit, and for planning his subsequent prison career. Although this procedure was not that recommended by the Control Review Committee (CRC), the Research Advisory Group (RAG) expressed its approval.[14] It would certainly seem that, by the time an individual inmate has come to the attention of SUSC, any further decisions concerning allocation will be made on the basis of very wide consultation with expert professionals, if not directly with the inmate. Some concern has, however, been expressed over the question of the prisoner's consent to transfer to a special unit.

The issue arises from the nature of the regimes within the units. Where the regime is therapeutic there is an argument for requiring the prisoner's consent, both because a therapeutic regime is unlikely to be effective in the absence of the prisoner's consent, and because it might be thought unacceptable to force treatment on an unwilling prisoner. In general, however, RAG did not wish to recommend that consent for transfer be required, nor that the prisoner should have the opportunity to transfer out after 10 weeks on request; but RAG did state that no medical nor specialist therapies should be given without consent. Only one member of the group, an independent academic, disagreed. He felt that, in the case of C Wing at Parkhurst, the regime was of such a therapeutic nature that no prisoner should be required to remain there after 10 weeks without his consent.[15] The question of consent to treatment and the extent to which it may be overridden is a vexed and much-discussed topic. The Mental Health Act 1983, Part IV, provides a specific statutory framework for the administration of treatment for mental disorder to patients detained under hospital orders, and it will be appropriate to consider the issue in more detail in that context in chapter 10.

14 *Special Units for Long-Term Prisoners: Regimes, Management and Research* (1987, London: HMSO).
15 *Ibid.* But see further discussion in J. Martin, 'Parkhurst Special Unit: Some Aspects of Management', in R. Walmsley, *Managing Difficult Prisoners: The Parkhurst Special Unit*, Home Office Research Study 122, Part III (1991, London: HMSO).

(2) Validation

As was evident in relation to transfer under CI 37/1990, there is a direct relationship between the standard of the decision making process at the application stage and demands made on the validation mechanisms. Where a decision has to be made under emergency conditions it is essential that a mechanism for full review is available immediately the emergency has passed. In general, however, the provision of extra-judicial mechanisms for the validation of internal prison decisions raises the same issues, whether the original decisions relate to transfer, or to prisoners' access to resources. Discussion of this will therefore be postponed to section **b**, below. Here attention will centre on the role of the courts.

(a) The Courts

In relation to internal prison decisions generally, court intervention at the validation stage can take a variety of forms. In the first place, as described in chapter 2, the High Court, in the exercise of its common law jurisdiction, can review the legality of the decisions reached by the prison authorities. This review can consider both the substantive legality of the decision – was the decision properly within the powers of the decision maker? – and the procedures adopted in reaching the decision. However, in the exercise of this review jurisdiction the court cannot replace the challenged decision with its own preferred decision even if it finds illegality. Instead it can choose in its discretion between a number of remedies, including a declaration to state the precise legal position, *certiorari* to quash the impugned decision, and *mandamus* to order the authority to decide according to law. In addition to these public law powers, the court can also intervene in order to protect any rights in the prisoner recognised by private law. Typically, the prisoner will allege that the actions of the authorities have infringed his or her private law rights and will claim damages for that infringement.

In 1974/75 Williams spent 180 days in the control unit at Wakefield Prison. He subsequently alleged that the unit had been set up and operated in breach of rule 43, and that consequently his detention within the unit was unlawful. He sought damages in private law for false imprisonment from the Home Office, and a declaration that the Home Office had acted unlawfully in setting up and operating the control unit.[16] Among other issues, the case raised questions concerning the process of decision making under rule 43. The court considered that rule 43 provided sufficient authority for the removal of prisoners from association and into a control unit, but in Williams' case it found that rule 43(2) had not been complied with. The rule, as it was then drafted, stated that the authority given to the board of visitors or the Secretary of State to extend segregation beyond 24 hours 'shall be for a period not exceeding one month, but may be renewed from month to month', which, to Tudor Evans J, suggested that the 'renewing authority should at least look at

16 *Williams* v. *Home Office (No. 2)* [1981] All ER 1211.

what had happened in the preceding month'.[17] Williams' segregation was not discussed nor considered by the relevant authorities from 20 August 1974 to 4 February 1975. This clear breach of the Prison Rules was, however, insufficient, on Tudor Evans' reasoning, to render Williams' detention in the control unit unlawful. In the first place, Tudor Evans argued that section 12 provided sufficient authority for a prisoner's imprisonment, and no subsequent change in the conditions could render that imprisonment unlawful in the tortious sense. Secondly, he adopted the established judicial approach to the Prison Rules by denying that they provide any private law rights in prisoners.

Almost a decade later, the operation of rule 43 again came under judicial scrutiny. In July 1988, under the provisions of CI 10/1974, Christopher Hague was transferred from Parkhurst to segregation in Wormwood Scrubs, from the Isle of Wight to London. On this occasion the action was brought primarily in public law by way of an application for judicial review, since the prisoner sought to challenge both the substantive legality of the relevant Circular Instruction and the procedural propriety of his transfer. He did, however, further seek damages in private law for breach of statutory duty and false imprisonment. The Court of Appeal, as already described, upheld Mr Hague's claim with regard to the substantive legality of the Circular Instruction: it was *ultra vires* the Prison Rules in two respects.[18] Procedurally, however, Hague's transfer and segregation were regarded as quite adequate according to the court's interpretation of the requirements of the common law.

On the basis of the finding of substantive *ultra vires*, Hague was granted a declaration. The court rejected the government's argument that, since the prisoner could complain to both the board of visitors and the Secretary of State concerning the decision of a governor, the High Court's review jurisdiction should be confined to reviewing the legality of those second-stage decisions, and it insisted that it had jurisdiction directly to review the legality of the governor's decision. However, although it was prepared to issue a declaration, the court refused to grant *certiorari* to quash the decision. Taylor LJ stressed the need for the courts to approach the excercise of their discretion with regard to remedies with great caution. He felt that, on the facts, Hague had suffered no injustice and it was therefore unnecessary to quash the decision. In a subsequent appeal to the House of Lords these findings were unaffected, but the prisoner's claim for damages for breach of statutory duty and false imprisonment were rejected (see below).[19] Thus, with regard to its public law jurisdiction, the court provided some mechanism for the independent validation of both the substance and the procedure of CI 10/1974. In relation to substance it upheld the prisoner's claim, although it was restrictive in its choice of remedy, while in relation to procedure the court failed to intervene.

Although *Hague* represents the most authoritative judicial pronouncement

17 *Ibid.*, p. 1231.
18 *Supra*, n. 9. The role of the Court of Appeal in the formulation of the 1990 policy was discussed in the previous chapter.
19 *Hague* v. *Deputy Governor of Parkhurst Prison* [1991] 3 All ER 733.

to date concerning rule 43 in particular and transfer in general, three earlier decisions had touched on the question of transfer. In a case in 1985 involving the transfer of a prisoner out of a mother and baby unit, the court held that the governor was under a duty to act fairly. On the facts, however, the governor had complied with that common law duty, since he had taken all reasonable steps to inform the prisoner and to seek her response.[20] In *McAvoy*, a category A remand prisoner challenged his transfer from London to Winchester Prison on the ground that insufficient consideration had been given to his 'right' under the Prison Rules to lay and legal visits.[21] His claim was successful in so far as the Divisional Court recognised that the Secretary of State's power to transfer arising from section 12 was subject to review by the High Court, and that in making the transfer decision the Secretary of State must consider the obligations contained within the Prison Rules. On the facts of *McAvoy*, however, once the Secretary of State affirmed that he had operational and security reasons for the transfer, the Divisional Court declined to inquire further:

in my view it is undesirable, if not impossible, for this court to examine operational reasons for a decision made under [section 12]; and to examine security reasons made under that section could, in my view, be dangerous and contrary to the policy of that particular statutory provision.[22]

Thus the court declared itself prepared in principle to review the legality of the Secretary of State's internal decision and, in particular, to ensure that the Prison Rules were accorded sufficient priority, but showed itself entirely unwilling to examine the validity of the Secretary of State's reasoning. It could not in any real sense be said to have provided an effective validation mechanism. The court was similarly unwilling to quash the Secretary of State's decision in a case involving his refusal to transfer an Irish prisoner to Northern Ireland under the power granted by section 26(1), Criminal Justice Act 1961.[23]

The discussion here has concentrated on the court's use of public law in the validation of transfer decisions. The role of private law will be considered below. With regard to public law as a means of achieving independent validation, two main issues emerge. In the first place, *Hague* has established beyond doubt that the courts are prepared to countenance judicial review in the area of prison policy application in relation not only to disciplinary decisions (*Leech*[24]) but also to managerial decisions concerning segregation and transfer. It remains to be seen whether this willingness will extend to the review of decisions concerning security categorisation and initial allocation.

20 *R* v. *Home Secretary, ex p. Hickling* (1985) *The Times*, 7 November.
21 *R* v. *Home Secretary, ex p. McAvoy* [1984] 3 All ER 417.
22 *Ibid.*, p. 423.
23 *R* v. *Secretary of State for the Home Department, ex p. McComb* [1991] COD 415. The case involved a challenge to both the policy contained in the CI involved, and its application in that particular case. Neither challenge was successful, although the policy on the transfer of prisoners to Northern Ireland has recently been relaxed.
24 *Leech* v. *Deputy Governor of Parkhurst Prison* [1988] AC 533.

Further, the Court of Appeal in *Hague*, guided by the House of Lords in *Leech*, held that the courts should not be restricted to reviewing the decisions of the second-stage bodies providing internal means of redress to the prisoner. Thus the courts, recognising the limitations of the internal review mechanisms, have offered the possibility of direct independent validation by way of judicial review.

However, while in theory, at least, such a development should further the demands of full process by providing an independent adjudicatory method of review, and thereby providing an effective means of checking the true authority of the challenged decisions, the courts seem reluctant to match their assumption of jurisdiction with any obvious enthusiasm for providing the prisoner with an effective remedy. In *McAvoy* the question of remedies was never reached, since the Divisional Court refused even to question the reasoning of the Secretary of State. While in *Hague*, having established substantive *ultra vires*, Taylor LJ laid considerable emphasis on the discretionary nature of public law remedies. The prison administration, it seems, can be assured that, although the courts have assumed jurisdiction, they will remain most circumspect in the way in which they exercise it:

Considerations of public policy may well arise in relation to prison management which would not arise elsewhere. The need to maintain good order and discipline and the need to make speedy decisions often in an emergency are important considerations in the special context of prison management. I would agree therefore . . . that the court should approach the exercise of discretion with great caution. The well-known proposition that managers should be left to manage applies a fortiori in regard to prisons, save where a clear case is made out for relief ex debito justitiae.[25]

In the event, the declarations issued by the Court of Appeal in *Hague* were apparently instrumental in the reform of the relevant Circular Instruction (see above), and to that extent, in the words of Lord Bridge in the House of Lords, confirm

the view that the availability of judicial review as a means of questioning the legality of action purportedly taken in pursuance of the Prison Rules is a beneficial and necessary jurisdiction which cannot properly be circumscribed by considerations of policy or expediency in relation to prison administration.[26]

However, by virtue of the sparsity of legislative involvement, such clear cases of *ultra vires* are likely to be rare: where there are no express legislative boundaries, prisoners will have difficulty persuading courts that they have been over-stepped. Further, Lord Bridge goes on to assert that, although the 'considerations of policy or expediency' should not affect the availability of judicial review, they can properly 'come into play when the court has to consider, as a matter of discretion, how the [review] jurisdiction should be exercised'.[27] The cumulative effect of the absence of statutory requirements, and the discretionary nature of public law remedies, is greatly to reduce the

25 [1990] 3 All ER 687, p. 701.
26 [1991] 3 All ER 733, p. 737.
27 *Ibid.*

ability of judicial review either to check the strict validity of any application of internal prison policy, or to provide an effective remedy when invalidity is established.

The second point to emerge from the cases relates to the nature of the procedural requirements imposed by the common law. In this regard, as described in the previous chapter, the judgment of Taylor LJ did little to further the pursuit of full process. The Court of Appeal refused to recognise any right to a hearing, either before the initial segregation or after the first 24 hours, and held that the prisoner had no right to be given the reasons for his segregation or transfer even after the event. In relation to policy formulation, this represented a missed opportunity to impose appropriate procedural regulation.

The formal structure of rule 43 applications may be administrative rather than adjudicatory in the true sense, but the procedures adopted should be those based on adjudication. Whether judicial intervention would have been the appropriate mechanism for the introduction of such procedures in the context of rule 43 is discussed elsewhere, but whatever the outcome of such speculation, restrictive cases such as *Hague*[28] throw an interesting light on the reviewing court's ability in practice to provide effective validation of the processes of prison decision making. When interpreted restrictively, the requirements of the common law duty to act fairly are unlikely to make any real demands on the internal decision makers. The courts typically allow the direct costs of the additional processes advocated by the prisoner to outweigh any likely reduction in error costs or additional process benefits that might flow from their imposition. Thus, in *Hague* for example, once the giving of reasons was presented by the authorities as time-consuming and difficult, the court allowed that cost to outweigh any increases in accuracy flowing from the obligation to give reasons, and any benefits in terms of issue resolution.[29]

(b) Access to Resources

(1) Application

Only limited data are available concerning the process of routine decision making within prisons in relation to such questions as the allocation of work and accommodation and the granting of privileges. As has been described, such decisions are taken against the background of Standing Orders and Circular Instructions, and it would appear that, despite the considerable discretion vested in the Secretary of State and governors by the Prison Act and the Prison Rules, the process of administrative rule making ensures that, by the time individual application decisions are taken within individual establishments, those decisions are highly structured. Ditchfield argues that the 'bureaucratic-lawful' model has become the dominant model of prison

28 In addition to *Hague* see, particularly, *Payne* v. *Lord Harris* [1981] 1 WLR 754. The judgment of the Court of Appeal in the latter case was quoted by Taylor LJ in *Hague*.

29 Against the background of such judicial reasoning, the decision in *R* v. *Parole Board ex p. Wilson* [1992] 2 All ER 576 is all the more significant. See chapter 8.

management.[30] This model is characterised by a reliance on centrally ordained rules and procedures, and by the accountability and limited autonomy of individual establishments. Its growth, according to Ditchfield, has been facilitated in the United Kingdom, not only by the strengthening of the power of central management, but also by an increase in the ability of inmates to maintain outside contacts, and thus to be aware of conditions elsewhere. Ditchfield also suggests that both the increased use of judicial review and the application of the requirements of the European Convention have meant that ordinary constitutional principles must now be applied to the treatment of prisoners. Whatever its origins, however, the bureaucratic-lawful model is extremely influential within prisons and generates certain expectations on the part of inmates. If decisions are to be structured according to predetermined rules, prisoners will expect those rules to be followed, and will feel resentment if they are not.

In practice the precise identity of the individual or body responsible for resource allocation decisions will vary depending on the subject matter. In relation to work allocation, for example, a work allocation or labour board is typically appointed in each establishment, with responsibility for the 'hiring and firing' of inmates, whereas an inmate's application to have a pocket calculator, technically a privilege, would be dealt with in the first instance by the wing manager. In the case of both work allocation boards and applications to the wing manager, the procedures followed vary from establishment to establishment. In some establishments, according to the Chief Inspector's report, inmates applied to wing managers in person at specific times of day, while in others an 'applications slip' was filled out and passed to the wing manager.[31] In either case the application and action taken in response were briefly recorded in a register. The wing manager would sometimes, but not invariably, discuss the application with the inmate to establish further details, and in some establishments the inmate was required to fill out specifically designed forms depending on the nature of the request. In relation to the work allocation boards, Genders and Player describes how, despite local variations in composition and procedure, the basic task remains the same.[32] The boards are notified of all vacancies on the work parties, and are responsible for allocating each sentenced prisoner to an appropriate job. According to the Prison Service, a new prisoner will have the opportunity to express his or her preferences, and 'in better establishments will be encouraged to do so'.[33] The boards also deal with inmates' requests to change jobs, and supervisors' requests to have unsatisfactory inmates sacked.

Although administrative rules and guidelines closely govern the decisions of first-line actors such as the wing managers and the work allocation boards, some discretion will inevitably remain. Sometimes the presence of a residual

30 J. Ditchfield, *Control in Prisons: A Review of the Literature*, Home Office Research Study 118 (1990, London: HMSO), pp. 146–52.
31 HMCIP, *A Review of Prisoners' Complaints* (1987, London: Home Office).
32 E. Genders and E. Player, *Race Relations in Prisons* (1989, Oxford: Oxford University Press).
33 Prison Service, *Evidence to the Woolf Inquiry, Phase 2* (1990, London: Home Office), part 5, p. 18.

discretion will be deliberate, but occasionally it may arise from ambiguities within the rules. Indeed, the Chief Inspector reports that staff can find difficulty in interpreting the rules.[34] Further, even specific rules and guidance can always be circumvented. The evidence of Genders and Player in relation to work allocation suggests that even detailed formal procedures can be bypassed or manipulated by individual decision makers. In their study of race relations in prison, Genders and Player found convincing evidence of racial discrimination in the allocation of work within prisons, despite CI 56/1983, which required all governors to ensure that

all jobs, tasks, training courses, and activities generally are at all times – so far as it is practicable and sensible – distributed broadly in proportion to the ethnic mix of the population.[35]

Genders and Player found no evidence that the allocation boards themselves were conspiring in a policy of discrimination, quite the contrary. However, they concluded that a

number of overt and covert means were employed by supervisors which, in practice, circumvented the formal procedures and allowed them to exercise their discretion in the selection of their workforce.[36]

For example, the formal procedures required that before an inmate was sacked he be first suspended from the job while his case was considered by the board in the light of a written statement of reasons for the suspension. However, some supervisors were said to avoid these procedures successfully by adopting such tactics as the initiation of disciplinary proceedings against individuals for minor and commonly condoned offences, or the regular failure to unlock individuals for work. In this way ethnic minority inmates could be arbitrarily removed from certain work parties, despite the presence of procedural safeguards.

McDermott and King describe a similar practice in relation to cell searching. Except in the high-security prisons, or where there has been specific information, the searching of cells becomes routine: 'the act of searching may be no more than a reassertion by staff that the cell is not private territory'.[37] In such circumstances the rules will not be enforced to the letter, and some unofficial licence will normally be given. If, however, a prisoner 'winds up' an officer, that normal licence will be denied. In one such case the beginnings of a home-made tattoo gun, to which a blind eye would normally have been turned, was confiscated from a disrespectful prisoner. Rather than charge the

---

34 *Supra*, n. 31.
35 Race Relations policy has been further developed within the Prison Service since the date of the research. *Report of the Work of the Prison Service, April 1990 – March 1991* (1991, Cm 1724, London: HMSO), pp. 32–3, describes work on the development of race relations training and the production of a new manual in April 1991. The Prison Service Race Relations Policy Statement is also reproduced in the report, at Appendix 9.
36 *Supra*, n. 32, p. 128.
37 K. McDermott and R. King, 'Mind Games: Where the Action is in Prisons' (1988) 28 Brit. Jo. Crim. 357, p. 366.

prisoner formally, however, the officers decided to 'have a quiet word with the Education Officer. That will mean he's thrown off education and sent back to the shops. That will mean he won't get daily use of the gym to lift weights either.'[38] The officers could achieve their ends more effectively outside the rules than within them, and the normal practice of low enforcement gave them the necessary flexibility.

Further, despite the influence of the bureaucratic-lawful model, the discretionary status afforded to 'privileges' under existing legislation can give rise to discrepancies in treatment between establishments. The reports of inspections conducted by the Chief Inspector provide ample evidence of discrepancies in relation to such issues as meal times, time out of cell, and association.[39] Such discrepancies, whatever their cause, inevitably give rise to resentment. The Woolf Report records the case of a prisoner who was refused permission to keep a box of tissues in his cell. He had apparently been allowed to do so in his previous prison, and the refusal to allow him a similiar 'privilege' led to a dispute with a prison officer which in turn led to the prisoner's segregation, and was ultimately a factor in the disturbances which followed.[40] The prisoner was obviously unable to accept the difference in treatment between the two prisons, and in the light of the bureaucratic-lawful model of management his expectation of conformity to a common standard is quite understandable. In the event, management's failure to meet the expectation had serious consequences for control.

Whatever the background to that particular case, however, there will always be differences in treatment, from prison to prison, from inmate to inmate, or from day to day. Many of these discrepancies could no doubt be avoided by improved management, more flexible working systems and a better distribution of resources but, however detailed the standards, honourable the decision makers, and equitable the resource allocation, some variations will continue to occur. The incidents leading to Christopher Hague's transfer under CI 10/1974 arose from the cancellation at short notice of evening exercise. Hague was held in Gartree Prison, from which, in 1987, two prisoners had escaped by helicopter from the exercise yard. As a result of the escape, security was tightened up generally, and evening exercise for category A prisoners was deliberately made unpredictable. The variation that annoyed Hague, therefore, was not the direct result of inadequate resources nor discriminatory manipulation, but sprang from a considered response to the demands of security.

Thus some variations from the norm are inevitable, and of equal inevitability perhaps, in a bureaucratic-lawful world, are the feelings of resentment that they engender. That this resentment can lead in turn to problems of control is well illustrated by the tissue incident, Hague's transfer to

38 *Ibid.*, p. 368.
39 *Report of H.M. Chief Inspector of Prisons January 1990–March 1991* (1991, London: HMSO), ch. III, for example, summarises the findings of the inspections for that year and draws interesting comparisons between establishments.
40 *Supra*, n. 4, pp. 375–6.

Wormwood Scrubs, and the research of McDermott and King, and is fully appreciated by the Woolf Report.[41] According to the arguments being offered in this book, this resentment could be reduced, and the variations rendered more acceptable, by the more frequent involvement of prisoners in the process of internal decision making, and a greater willingness to explain the reasoning behind apparently arbitrary decisions. At a fundamental level, a decision taken with the full participation of all those involved is more authoritative and worthy of respect than one taken in secret by an individual. More pragmatically, prisoners are more likely to accept a decision if they have been consulted and if they understand the reasoning behind it. To this extent the emphasis placed by the Woolf Report on the need both for greater consultation with prisoners and for a widespread obligation to give reasons is greatly to be welcomed. With regard to reasons, the Report stressed the vulnerability of prisoners to arbitrary decisions and emphasised the importance of reason giving, not just in relation to issues which are of 'central significance in the life of a prisoner', such as transfer or parole, but also in relation to 'any decision which materially and adversely affects' the prisoner.[42] It must be hoped that the government will act on its positive response expressed in the White Paper.[43]

While the giving of reasons is essential to any acceptable system of decision making, the participation of interested parties before the decision is made is arguably even more fundamental to full process. The participation of prisoners in decision making within prisons raises some very difficult issues. Notions of full process would clearly require their true participation in all decisions affecting them. In practice, however, such a proposal is unworkable. While some types of decision should be amenable to the participation of prisoners, there are others which, realistically, could never be so. In an attempt to distinguish between different types of decision for these purposes it is useful to return to the two basic duties of prison management: to maintain security and to maintain control or, more appropriately, order.

In the previous chapter it was suggested that a prisoner should at least retain all rights that are not necessarily removed by the requirements of either security or control. A similar position may be adopted with regard to participation. In chapter 3 it was claimed that the full participation of interested parties is essential for a decision to be authoritative. In the prison context it may be necessary to amend that claim: the full participation of interested parties is essential for a decision to be authoritative, provided that participation would prejudice neither security nor control/order. In some cases the operation of the proviso would be uncontroversial. At Gartree Prison in 1987, for example, there could have been no question of allowing category A prisoners fully to participate in the timing of exercise. The security implications were all too obvious. In relation to control or order particularly, however, the issues are often less clear.

41 McDermott and King, *supra*, n. 37, p. 370, describe an occasion when inconsistency between
    landing officers over the distribution of wing newspapers nearly led to violence.
42 *Supra*, n. 4, p. 413.
43 *Supra*, n. 5, p. 77.

In response to calls for greater participation the authorities typically stress the absolute need for governors to govern and for staff, rather than prisoners, to exercise the necessary discretion. Fears are also expressed concerning the ease with which powerful groups of prisoners can dominate any representative structure.[44] These are significant reasons for caution, but a number of points should be made.

In the first place, although the final responsibility for the daily running of the prison must lie with the governor, it is necessary to remember that, just as imprisonment should not imply the removal of more rights than is absolutely necessary, so it should only imply the removal of those responsibilities that are absolutely necessary. Management has to run a safe and secure establishment within the resources available to it, but this should not mean that all decisions be taken from prisoners.[45] The decision whether or not to cancel a chapel service because of threatened disruption might properly be taken by the governor with no consultation with the prisoners. On the other hand, the timing and content of meals, or the principles governing work allocation, might well be determined in consultation between management and prisoners. Secondly, participation in a decision does not necessarily mean *control* of that decision. Management might be expected to consult the prisoners and to respond to their suggestions, but the ultimate decision would still lie with management. Thirdly, while the dangers of intimidation and domination by powerful groups are particularly acute within prisons, they are not unique to that environment. If representative committees are too vulnerable to domination, then more direct methods of consultation could be tried in smaller groups. The important step is for prison management generally to accept the need for participation. Despite their imprisonment, prisoners remain responsible for their lives, and are entitled to participate in the decisions which effect them to the extent that that participation is compatible with the demands of security and control.[46]

(2) Validation

There are several channels through which an inmate may challenge internal application decisions. Essentially these include: internal procedures such as applications to the governor and to the area manager; requests to external non-judicial bodies including boards of visitors, Members of Parliament and the Parliamentary Commissioner for Administration; and, finally, the inmate may apply to courts, both domestic and European. In addition to the resolution of individual grievances and disputes, however, processes of validation include mechanisms designed to monitor the decisions of first-line decision makers. Some mechanisms, such as Her Majesty's Chief Inspector of Prisons and the European Commission on the Prevention of Torture, are

44 *Ibid.*, pp. 409–11.
45 There is evidence that greater participation helps to reduce violence: D. Cooke, 'Violence in Prisons: The Influence of Regime Factors' (1991) 30 *Howard Jo. of Crim. Jus.* 95.
46 In this regard it is encouraging to note the emphasis placed on the participation of prisoners in the consultation document *Prisoners' Compacts* (1992, London: Prison Service).

exclusively concerned with monitoring, while others, the boards of visitors for example, possess both a monitoring and a complaints investigation role.

(a) The Governor and Headquarters

(i) Individual Complaints

In September 1990 the system for dealing internally with prisoners' complaints and applications was revised. Thus most of the published data relating to the operation of the system in practice relate to procedures the details of which have now changed. The system for directly petitioning the Secretary of State, for example, has been abandoned. Nevertheless it will be useful to mention some findings of the earlier research since they illustrate the difficulties that can easily arise with an internal system of validation.

In the first place, evidence gathered by Austin and Ditchfield and by the Chief Inspector suggests that inmates, particularly those in training prisons, were broadly satisfied with the management of applications at wing and governor level, although many experienced some difficulty if they wished to see the number one governor.[47] The volume of these complaints was high. In its evidence to the Woolf Inquiry the Prison Service explained that a large local prison might deal with 10,000 applications and complaints a year at wing level, and 700 governor's applications.[48] With regard to petitioning the Secretary of State, however, dissatisfaction was widespread.[49] Inmates objected to the system that allowed reports to be attached to their petitions without their having the opportunity to comment, and they were generally unimpressed by the lack of reasoned responses.[50] Many establishment staff were also critical of the system, but some felt that the inmates' preference for the wing procedures might be related to the fact that a high proportion of wing applications were granted, in contrast to the tiny proportion of successful petitions to the Secretary of State.[51]

Whatever the precise grounds for the dissatisfaction, however, the evidence suggests that the pre-1990 system of petitions to the Secretary of State was a wholly inadequate means of validation. Indeed, it is revealing to note that even the House of Lords had reservations with regard to the efficacy of Secretary of State petitions. In *Leech*, Lord Bridge suggests that, if faced with a dispute of fact between a prisoner and a governor, any civil servant investigating on behalf of the Secretary of State 'is likely simply to accept the governor's account'.[52]

---

47 See, particularly, HMCIP, *supra*, n. 31, and J. Ditchfield and C. Austin, *Grievance Procedures in Prisons*, Home Office Research Study 91 (1986, London: HMSO).
48 Prison Service, *supra*, n. 33, p. 66.
49 According to the Prison Service, the Secretary of State received approximately 15,000 petitions from prisoners each year – *supra*, n. 33.
50 HMCIP, *supra*, n. 31.
51 According to Austin and Ditchfield, *supra*, n. 47, only six of the 120 petitions in their sample were granted.
52 *Leech* v. *Deputy Governor of Parkhurst Prison* [1988] AC 533.

In September 1990 the new procedures came into operation, implemented by a new Prison Rule 8, a new Circular Instruction, CI 34/1990, and an amendment to Standing Order 5C. Rule 8 now states:

(1) A request or complaint to the governor or Board of Visitors relating to a prisoner's imprisonment shall be made orally or in writing to the prisoner.
(2) On every day the governor shall hear any requests and complaints that are made to him under paragraph (1) above.
(3) A written request or complaint under paragraph (1) above may be made in confidence.

The petition to the Secretary of State has been abandoned and, although there are still reserved topics which must be dealt with by headquarters, the new system encourages the resolution of more complaints at establishment level. Under the new procedures prisoners are encouraged to seek formal resolution of their complaint. There is a system of oral applications at both wing level and to the governor, although the guidance to prisoners makes it clear that there is no automatic right to see the number one governor. Alternatively, a prisoner may make a formal written request or complaint, to which he or she should receive a reasoned reply within seven days; an appeal can then be made to headquarters, usually to the area manager. Any complaint relating to the Prison Rules and Circular Instructions, or to any reserved subjects, such as parole, adjudications, category A prisoners or life-sentence prisoners, should go directly to headquarters.

This system marks an improvement on the old by removing the petitions to the Secretary of State and increasing the role of the estabishments in the first instance, by attempting to reduce delays through the introduction of time limits, and by insisting that prisoners receive reasoned replies. It has also introduced a system of 'confidential access', enabling the prisoner to write in a sealed envelope to the number one governor, to the chair of the board of visitors, or to the area manager. However, as the Woolf Report pointed out, the advice given to prisoners was misleading, since the system does not guarantee confidentiality, and the complaint could often be shown to the person about whom it was made.

Following this criticism the government has undertaken to make it clear to prisoners that complaints against staff will be shown to the person concerned. While this clarification might help to avoid any misunderstanding on the part of the prisoners, the more fundamental point remains that rule 8(3) states that a complaint may be made in confidence. At the very least this must imply that a complaint made in confidence will be shown to no one, other than the recipient, without the specific consent of the complainant.

In the case of complaints against staff, fair process demands that the member of staff involved be given notice of the complaint, subject to a proviso similar to that advocated in relation to the provision to the prisoner of an explanation for transfer under CI 37/1990: namely that the provision of information is compatible with the safety of the complainant. However, the need to reveal the complaint to the staff member, and the possible implications, must be discussed with the complainant before revelation, and consent must be obtained before the matter is taken further. The investigation of complaints against staff in an environment such as a prison is an extremely delicate exercise, but one which must be tackled if a system of validation is to be effective in any real sense. The damage which can flow from a failure in this respect will be discussed further in relation to special hospitals.

(ii) Monitoring

Since 1984 the Prison Service has been improving its internal monitoring systems. All individual governors have a management contract with their area manager which is based on the objectives of the Service, set each year by the Prisons Board, and which should match the performance expected of the establishment to the resources available. There are also two monitoring systems which are said to make the Service more accountable: the regime monitoring system, and the staff planning and reporting system. As a mechanism for overseeing the level of facilities available to prisoners, the regime monitoring system should be the more significant. This is designed to measure the time spent by prisoners on different activities and, when fully operational, it should be able to provide a clear picture of the level of facilities provided at all prison establishments. However, experience suggests that the data generated by regime monitoring to date have not been sufficiently specific to indicate the precise facilities enjoyed by any particular prisoner, or group of prisoners. As a means of improving the standard of data collection, without making undue demands on resources, and of encouraging greater participation by prisoners, Morgan has suggested that the data be collected by the prisoners themselves.[53] In any event, comprehensive and accurate data on the real levels of service provided in each establishment are essential for any adequate monitoring, and they must be both produced and publicised.

(iii) The Private Sector

The development of private prisons has introduced a new form of 'internal' standard setting and monitoring, and a new structure of responsibility. Under section 85 of the Criminal Justice Act 1991 each 'contracted out' prison must have a 'director' who is appointed by the contractor, and a 'controller' who is a civil servant appointed by the Secretary of State. The director acts effectively as the governor, and possesses most of the powers vested in governors by the 1952 Act and the Prison Rules. Unlike a governor, however, the director cannot deal with disciplinary charges and, except in cases of urgency, cannot order segregation, or temporary confinement, or any other special restraint – section 85(3), Criminal Justice Act 1991. The controller, being a civil servant not employed by the contractor, has a general duty to 'keep under review' the running of the prison and to report to the Secretary of State, and also the specific duty to investigate any allegations made against prison custody officers performing custodial duties at the prison – section 85(4). The

53 See Prison Service (1991), *supra*, n. 35, p. 53, for an account of the systems. And see R. Morgan, 'Regime Monitoring with Prisoners' (1992) Prison Report 8.

controller thus acts both as a monitor and as an investigator of individual grievances. In addition, he or she is responsible for initial application decisions in relation to matters such as segregation (rule 43), temporary confinement (rule 45), restraint (rule 46), and disciplinary matters (rules 48–50 and 56).[54]

Conditions within private prisons are a matter of contract. Regime standards are set in the operating contract agreed between the contractor and the Home Office, and compliance with those standards is monitored by the controller of the establishment. If the standards are not met, financial penalties will be incurred under the contract. The Criminal Justice Act 1991 and the contracts, in combination, therefore, are designed to provide a clear structure for the setting up and monitoring of standards within private prisons. As far as standard setting is concerned, however, it is a structure from which the general public is largely excluded. Nevertheless, it was evident from the tender documents issued prior to the awarding of the contract for the Wolds that the regime within that establishment was to be significantly better than that found in most state-run prisons, and it is now clear from the accounts of those who have visited the Wolds that this high standard has in practice been met, at least initially.[55] Cells contain a duvet, curtains, a wardrobe, a lavatory, and hot and cold water, and prisoners are given keys so that they may come and go as they please during the day. The contract with Group 4, the operating company, also requires the provision of a wide range of activities outside the cell, including six hours of education each week, and six hours using the gym.

The contractual imposition of such standards adds strength to the argument that the introduction of private prisons will provide the necessary incentive to encourage the improvement of standards throughout all prisons.[56] If the private sector can be expected to meet high standards, so can the public sector. To some extent this argument may have substance. The Prison Service's own model regime for remand institutions is clearly based on the specifications for the Wolds.[57] Nevertheless, as Morgan has pointed out, the Home Office is likely to take many years to meet such standards within its own establishments.[58] Establishments such as the Wolds, he argues, cannot be directly compared to state-run prisons. The private sector is operating in significantly more favourable circumstances and, since the financial components of their contracts remain confidential, it is not possible to make precise comparisons in terms of efficiency.

---

54 Section 86, Criminal Justice Act 1991, and rule 98A Prison Rules, inserted by Prison (Amendment) Rules 1992 SI 1992/514.

55 *Tender Documents for the Operating Contracts of Wolds Remand Prison* (1991, London: Home Office), schedule 2 and 3. And see *The Independent*, 25 March 1992, for an account of conditions inside the Wolds.

56 M. Taylor and K. Pease, 'Private Prisons and Penal Purpose', in R. Matthews (ed.), *Privatizing Criminal Justice* (1989, London: Sage), ch. 8.

57 *Model regime for Local Prisons and Remand Centres* (1991, London: HM Prison Service).

58 R. Morgan, 'Prisons Accountability Revisited', paper presented at a *Public Law* seminar, London, June 1992.

(b) Boards of Visitors

(i) Individual Complaints
The boards of visitors provide the best known and most readily accessible means of 'external' challenge to internal prison decisions. The 1952 Act requires the Secretary of State to appoint a board of visitors for every prison, now including private prisons, and to make rules to require members 'to pay frequent visits to the prison and hear complaints which may be made by the prisoners and to report to the Secretary of State any matter which they consider it expedient to report', section 6. Accordingly, the Prison Rules require board members to 'hear any complaint or request which a prisoner wishes to make to them', rule 95(1). However, the boards are given no power to enforce their decisions; they are merely required to 'direct the attention of the governor to any matter which calls for his attention, and shall report to the Secretary of State any matter which they consider it expedient to report' – rule 94(3).[59]

The procedures adopted apparently vary widely between boards. According to research reported in 1984 by Maguire and Vagg, some boards required prisoners to make formal applications via prison staff, and only heard formally entered complaints at their monthly meetings.[60] Other boards held regular clinics for complaints, while still others encouraged prisoners to present complaints informally to members during their routine visits to the prison. Despite provision in the rules to enable prisoners to meet members out of sight and hearing of officers, many boards regularly conducted interviews in the presence of staff. Further, Maguire and Vagg found that very few boards provided the prisoners with a written response informing them of the outcome of their complaint.

In addition to these essentially procedural problems, research points to certain more fundamental difficulties. It is apparent that the inmates are sceptical of the independence of the boards, and that the boards themselves seldom uphold prisoners' complaints or achieve concrete results. Much has been written concerning the membership of the boards of visitors, their often close relationship with the governor, and the difficulties they faced in both providing a channel for prisoners' complaints and acting as adjudicator when serious disciplinary charges were brought against a prisoner.[61] More specifically, Maguire points to the boards' tendency to concentrate on conformity with regulations.[62] If the relevant regulations have been followed by the staff, the boards are generally satisfied and do not consider it appropriate to question the administrative rules. Further, Maguire reports that the boards'

59 Boards do, however, have the power to suspend any officer 'in any case of urgent necessity' pending the decision of the Secretary of State, rule 94(4).
60 M. Maguire and J. Vagg, *supra*, n. 3.
61 See, for example, J. Martin, *Boards of Visitors of Penal Institutions* (The Jellicoe Report) (1975, London: Barry Rose), and M. Maguire and J. Vagg, 'Who are the Prison watchdogs? The Membership and Appointment of Boards of Visitors' (1983) Crim. LR 238.
62 M. Maguire, 'Prisoners' Grievances: The Role of the Boards of Visitors', in M. Maguire, J. Vagg and R. Morgan (eds), *Accountability and Prisons* (1985, London: Tavistock), ch. 9.

inclination to accept the managerial interpretation of any disputed fact or opinion, and their identification with custodial goals rather than individual prisoner's rights, leads to a reluctance ever to challenge staff decisions in cases where the regulations leave considerable scope for discretion. Without doubt such attitudes inhibit the boards' ability to provide an independent and effective mechanism for the airing of grievances.

However, the investigation of complaints within an hierarchical institution such as a prison requires considerable skill and perseverance, and it should be acknowledged that the boards are required to operate against a background of limited powers. They have no formal powers of enforcement, and are therefore reliant on the Secretary of State: the very individual who bears ultimate responsibility for the services they criticise. Further, while the Prison Rules guarantee them 'access to the records of the prison', rule 96(3), no direct obligation is imposed on staff to answer the board's questions. In the context of disciplinary adjudications, the issue of compelling staff witnesses was regarded as met by the fact that 'an officer of the prison may be required by the governor, as part of his duties, to appear as a witness'.[63] The extension of such an argument to the investigation of complaints, while justifiable in law, would require, particularly in face of reluctance on the part of the governor, a level of determination which research suggests is rarely present in the boards.

Under the 1990 procedures a prisoner may still apply to the board at any time but, according to the guidance given to prisoners, the board will normally expect the prisoners to have raised the complaint internally. The boards' powers remain the same, but the government has issued a manual explaining their role and setting out the procedures they should follow. The Woolf Report saw the boards as possessing a twofold role with regard to complaints. In the first place, the board could help the prisoner to use the internal complaints mechanism, and secondly, if appropriate, the board could investigate the matter itself and forward a report to whichever tier within the internal system was relevant. The Woolf Report felt there should be no expectation that the prisoner would already have raised the complaint internally.

With regard to the contradictions within the boards' role, the government finally accepted that boards should no longer have a disciplinary function, and since April 1992 they have been relieved of their disciplinary role. This is a major step and, despite the government's insistence that the boards remain involved in authorising continuations of segregation under rule 43, should greatly enhance the boards' independence in the eyes of the inmates. However, as an independent mechanism for the resolution of grievances, the boards are still inadequately empowered: although they possess rights of access, they have neither direct powers of enforcement nor the power to compel evidence. The significance of these shortcomings could of course be reduced by the introduction of a complaints adjudicator (see below).

---

63 *Manual on the Conduct of Adjudications in Prison Department Establishments* (1989, London: Home Office), para. 5.10.

(ii) Monitoring

The watchdog role of the board of visitors, however, does not stop at the investigation of individual complaints. They also play a part in monitoring the general conditions prevailing within their establishments. According to the 1991 White Paper, the government is now committed to strengthening this aspect of the boards' role.[64] It has emphasised the boards' right of access to the Secretary of State, and their right to publish annual reports. Without doubt, boards of visitors do have a vital role in monitoring conditions within prison, and in some cases have managed, through their annual reports, successfully to draw attention to poor conditions. The report of the Bixton board of visitors for 1990, for example, added to the concern about conditions at Brixton by emphasising the persistent overcrowding and the high incidence of suicide: four prisoners committed suicide while in the prison that year, and two others who attempted to do so later died in hospital.[65] However, boards as a whole have expressed dissatisfaction at the level of support they receive from the Prison Service. Annual reports apparently go unanswered.[66] The board at Pentonville Prison complained that it had submitted its annual report in March 1990. It was not acknowledged until July, and the response, when it finally came, failed to deal specifically with the points raised.[67] Critical reports warning of the danger of suicide at Feltham Young Offenders Institution in 1991 and 1992 also failed to inspire change (see below). The Prison Service, it seems, has some way to go if it is to fulfil the pledges in the White Paper.

Under the present system the watchdog role of the boards of visitors has two main aspects. In the first place, the boards are part of the mechanism for the airing and investigation of individual complaints. To an extent their ability to perform this role has been enhanced by the removal of their disciplinary function. However, as an independent mechanism for the resolution of grievances, they remain underpowered. Secondly, the boards are expected to monitor conditions more generally. At present their ability effectively to perform this aspect of their role would appear to be largely dependent on the reactions of the Prison Service to any criticisms they might make. They are also expected, currently, to monitor conditions without the benefit of a baseline. With the eventual introduction of minimum standards this, at least, will change.

(c) Members of Parliament and the Parliamentary Commissioner

A further independent channel for the airing of grievances is provided by Members of Parliament and the Parliamentary Commissioner. Inmates may write to MPs or to the Commissioner, subject only to routine censorship where such exists. Of the two, MPs would appear to be the more significant, in

64 *Supra*, n. 5, pp. 94–5.
65 *H.M.P. Brixton*, Report by the Board of Visitors (1990, London: Home Office).
66 *Board of Visitors Co-ordinating Committee Annual Report 1990–91* (1991, London: Home Office).
67 *H.M. Prison Pentonville: Report of a Short Inspection by H.M. Chief Inspectorate of Prisons* (1991, London: Home Office).

numerical terms at least. The Prison Service estimates that approximately 3,000 complaints are made to MPs each year.[68] The Commissioner has jurisdiction to pursue complaints of maladministration against the Prison Service, and has considerable investigative powers. However, he has no formal powers of enforcement and is limited to the investigation of maladministration. Indeed, since the volume of cases received from prisoners has remained relatively small, it is widely accepted that the Commissioner has not and is not, as presently constituted, ever likely to provide an effective mechanism for the pursuit of individual grievances within prison.[69]

(d) Independent Complaints Adjudicator

On the basis of the above account, whatever the extent of the recent improvements to the internal complaints system, there would at present appear to be no truly effective independent mechanism for reviewing prisoners' complaints. This gap has led to consistent pressure for the creation of a prisons ombudsman or independent complaints adjudicator. The internal working party which was set up to consider the complaints procedures prior to the recent reforms, however, concluded that an independent complaints investigator would cost between £0.8m and £2.2m a year, with an additional cost of between £0.3m and £1.2m to the department in responding to the investigator's inquiries.[70] The report concluded that the new internal arrangements should be introduced and established first, before any further thought be given to an investigator. Unsurprisingly perhaps, this conclusion was immediately acceptable to ministers. In contrast, the Woolf Report took a refreshingly uncompromising position on the need for an independent element:

the presence of an independent element within the grievance procedure is more than just an "optional extra". The case for some form of independent person or body to consider grievances is incontrovertible. There is no possibility of the present system satisfactorily meeting this point, even once it has bedded down. A system without an independent element is not a system which accords with proper standards of justice.[71]

The Woolf Report recommended the introduction of a complaints adjudicator as a final avenue of appeal. The adjudicator should be a senior lawyer appointed by the Secretary of State. In relation to complaints, he or she should 'recommend, advise and conciliate at the final stage of the procedure'. He or she would report annually to the Secretary of State, who would submit the report to Parliament. The adjudicator would receive appeals from prisoners on complaints which had completed the internal stages and had received a negative but reasoned response. Although the adjudicator would be concerned not only with the way in which the complaint had been investigated internally,

68 For a general discussion of the complaints jurisdiction of MPs, see R. Rawlings, 'The M.P.s Complaints Service' (1990) 53 Mod. LR 22 and 149.
69 See P. Burkinshaw, 'An Ombudsman for Prisoners', in Maguire *et al.*, *supra*, n. 62, ch. 11.
70 *Prisoners' Complaints and Grievance Procedures* (1989, London: Home Office).
71 *Supra*, n. 4, p. 419.

but also with its merits, he or she would not have executive powers, and would have to rely on reporting to the relevant tier. In the final event the adjudicator could report to the Secretary of State. The Report makes no reference to vesting the adjudicator with specific investigative powers, although it is clear that the adjudicator could be expected to visit the establishment and interview the relevant parties. In response the government has published a consultation document setting out its proposals for the introduction of an 'Independent Complaints Adjudicator for Prisons'.[72]

The proposals contained in the consultation document broadly follow the Woolf recommendations. An adjudicator is envisaged who would both have jurisdiction with regard to ordinary complaints, and act as an appellate body in relation to governor's disciplinary awards. However, since the government does not anticipate the introduction of primary legislation in the immediate future, the adjudicator's powers in relation to disciplinary matters will be restricted to reviewing governors' decisions, both on their merits and on their procedural adequacy, on the basis of the documentation available, and to recommending the use of the Home Secretary's powers under the Prison Rules to quash disciplinary findings and to remit and mitigate punishments. The adjudicator's proposed role in relation to discipline will be discussed below, in chapter 7, but it is relevant here to raise some issues with regard to his or her role in the hearing of complaints.

In the first place, neither Woolf nor the consultation document envisage vesting the adjudicator with formal powers to compel evidence, and this omission could prove unfortunate. If a prisoner's complaint against a member of staff has not been resolved internally to the prisoner's satisfaction, the adjudicator might be faced with a conflict of evidence, the resolution of which would require extensive investigation. Any reluctance on the part of either prisoners or staff to give evidence or to produce documents might easily sabotage such an investigation. The adjudicator must therefore be seen to have the necessary powers. It is not anticipated that they would be used very often, nor that formal hearings with the full panoply of legal representation would be the norm. Indeed, adversarial adjudication might not be the ideal procedure for establishing the truth in any event. Rather, the argument is that, without formal powers, the adjudicator's investigation would be vulnerable to sabotage, and his or her effectiveness reduced. The adjudicator needs to possess the powers from the outset, it is not sufficient that he or she should be able to seek them from the Secretary of State in specific cases, nor is it appropriate that he or she should have to rely on the Director General to demand the co-operation of Prison Service personnel. Either solution would compromise the independence of the adjudicator's role.

Secondly, under neither the Woolf proposals nor the consultation document would the adjudicator be given executive powers. Presumably the possession of such powers would conflict with the traditional notion of ministerial responsibility. Within a structure which regards the Secretary of State as

72 *An Independent Complaints Adjudicator for Prisons: A Consultation Paper* (1992, London: HM Prison Service).

ultimately responsible for the running of the prison system, the adjudicator could not possess executive powers and retain his or her independence of the Secretary of State. To be effective, therefore, the adjudicator must have some alternative mechanism for enforcing decisions. Both Woolf and the government envisage a system of reports and responses from the Prison Service, and ultimately from the Secretary of State. The possibilities of fixed time limits (Woolf) or targets (the government) within which the responses should be made are also mentioned.

In the vast majority of cases, no doubt, such a system would prove effective, particularly if strict time limits are imposed and adhered to. For the exceptional case, more might be required. This further element necessary for the adjudicator to be fully effective might come from the courts, in the form of judicial review of the Secretary of State's refusal to follow the recommendations of the adjudicator. Alternatively, or additionally, it could come from the public. The adjudicator should be expected to publish his or her reports and the responses received in all cases where he or she remained dissatisfied with the outcome achieved, subject to the requirements of the complainant's privacy and the specific demands of security. This publication could be general, or it could be made directly to Parliament by way of the Home Affairs Select Committee, for example. The latter option would have to be seen as distinct from any obligation that the adjudicator might have to publish an annual report to Parliament via the Secretary of State. It would, in effect, be a mechanism for sharpening the impact of ministerial responsibility.

The reservations concerning the possession of simple executive powers by the adjudicator suggest that he or she would not be the ideal person to provide the necessary validation in relation to transfer under CI 37/1990, where the validator should ideally be empowered to order the prisoner's return to his original establishment.[73] In the circumstances surrounding such transfers, the preferred solution might be to impose on the area manager for the receiving establishment the duty to review the transfer decision at the request of the prisoner. The area manager would be obliged to offer the prisoner a hearing, and to disclose all the evidence supporting the transfer, subject only to specific waiver, and would have the authority to order the return of the prisoner to his original prison. The decision of the area manager would in turn be subject to expedited review by the adjudicator.

Thirdly, unlike the Woolf Report, the government has proposed a number of restrictions on the subject areas concerning which the adjudicator should receive complaints. Most significantly, it has suggested that the adjudicator

should be excluded from considering the *merits* of some decisions relating to Category A prisoners. These might include issues of categorisation, allocation, transfer and approved visitors.[74]

---

73 *Supra*, p. 115. The position of the adjudicator in relation to disciplinary awards is discussed in chapter 7.

74 *Supra*, n. 72, pp. 5–6.

It is hard to find any valid justification for such an exclusion, which seems merely to reflect a worrying lack of confidence in the adjudicator before he or she has even been appointed. It can only be hoped that the suggestion will be dropped when the system is finally implemented. Further, although the clinical judgement of doctors often manages to achieve immunity from challenge, in the present circumstances where the Prison Medical Service remains outside the NHS, it is particularly important that prisoners have access to an effective channel through which to complain about the medical services provided for them.

Finally, though the complaints adjudicator would certainly improve the effectiveness of the independent element in the resolution of individual complaints, there is no indication that he or she would possess a general monitoring role. Indeed, the Woolf Report makes it quite clear that the adjudicator's role should be limited to the resolution of individual complaints.

(e) Her Majesty's Chief Inspector of Prisons

The office of Her Majesty's Chief Inspector of Prisons constitutes the primary external monitor of the Prison Service. Section 5A of the 1952 Act provides for the Crown to appoint a Chief Inspector. Prior to the insertion of section 5A into the Act in 1982, there had been a system of inspection within the Prison Department, but the reports had remained confidential.[75] The absence of independent inspection was regularly criticised and, following the recommendations of the May Inquiry, the post of Her Majesty's Chief Inspector of Prisons was created outside the Prison Department, but housed within the Home Office and reporting to the Home Secretary.[76] The Chief Inspector has no executive powers, and can merely inspect and report to the Secretary of State. It was therefore assumed at the outset that the degree of influence exercised by Chief Inspector would depend in large part on the respect with which he or she was regarded both within and without the Prison Service. During the first ten years the Inspectorate has undertaken a programme of both full and short inspections of individual establishments, has conducted thematic reviews of specific topics such as prisoners' complaints and suicide and self-harm, has reported on specific issues referred to him by the Secretary of State, such as the Brixton escapes in 1991, and has produced annual reports

75 The insertion of section 5A was made by section 57(1) Criminal Justice Act 1982, although the Inspectorate was actually in existence from January 1981. See R. Morgan, 'Her Majesty's Inspectorate of Prisons', in Maguire *et al.*, *supra*, n. 62, ch. 7, for an account of the early years of the inspectorate.

76 *Committee of Inquiry into the UK Prison Services* (The May Report) (1979, Cmnd 7673, London: HMSO). Earlier criticism had come from the House of Commons Expenditure Committee, *Fifteenth Report of the Expenditure Committee: The Reduction of Pressure on the Prison System* (1978, London: HMSO). For an account of the early, pre-twentieth century inspectors, see S. McConville, *A History of Early Prison Administration 1750–1877* (1981, London: Routledge and Kegal Paul).

which have been laid before Parliament. And, over the years, his influence and public profile have increased.

Under section 5A, the principal duty of the Chief Inspector is to inspect or arrange for the inspection of Prison Service establishments in England and Wales, and to report on them to the Home Secretary, having regard in particular to the treatment of prisoners and conditions within these establishments. During the 15-month period covered by the Annual Report for January 1990 to March 1991, 24 full inspections were conducted, each lasting for at least four-and-a-half days.[77] The inspections are conducted by one of two core teams, each of which includes prison governors seconded to the Inspectorate and can be augmented by other specialists in relevant fields, such as health and safety, psychiatry and AIDS. Thus, while the inspection teams cannot be said to be entirely independent of the Prison Service, containing within their number individuals who will return to direct employment within that Service, they can claim expertise.

Inevitably each inspection can obtain only a 'snap-shot' view of life in the subject establishment and, although some short-notice and unannounced visits are made, in the majority of cases the authorities will have been given considerable notice of the visit. Nevertheless, since many of the factors which attract the Chief Inspector's attention, such as the state of the buildings, the provision of sanitation and the standard of overall hygiene, are not susceptible to cosmetic manipulation prior to the visit, the inspection teams can obtain a reasonably accurate picture, and, to judge from the tenor of some of their reports, are not afraid to voice harsh criticism. After each inspection the Inspectorate submits a report and detailed recommendations to the Home Secretary. The decision to publish then rests with the Secretary of State, but the practice has been to publish the reports of full inspections together with the government's response. Although in recent years many of these reports have achieved wide coverage in the media, there is still no adequate mechanism for monitoring compliance with all the detailed recommendations contained within them.[78] In some cases it is evident that strong recommendations from the Chief Inspector are ignored. The report of an inspection conducted at Feltham Young Offenders' Institution in 1988, for example, was highly critical of the regime there, and presented a quantity of detailed recommendations. However, according to the report of a subsequent inspection in 1992, little had changed for the majority of inmates.[79] Two inmates committed suicide in 1991, and two in the first three months of 1992.

While a full assessment of the impact of the Inspectorate since 1981 would require systematic research, it is evident, merely from an examination of press reports in recent years, that the Chief Inspector has focused public attention on prison conditions with considerable success. The views of the Chief Inspector on prison sanitation, for example, and suicide and self-harm in

77 *Supra*, n. 39.
78 *Ibid.*, p.2.
79 HMCIP, *Feltham Y.O.I.* (1988 and 1992, London: Home Office).

prisons, achieve wide press coverage, as do his more devastating reports on individual establishments: Brixton, Feltham and Dartmoor, for example. To that extent, the Inspectorate has served most effectively to inform public debate regarding the state of prisons in England and Wales, and, whatever the limits on its ability to achieve change, the Inspectorate does provide an expert, if not fully independent, means of monitoring a range of aspects of prison life. It remains to be seen how far the role of the Inspectorate will change with the introduction of agency status and a code of standards.

(f) The European Convention for the Prevention of Torture and Inhuman or Degrading Treatment

The European Convention for the Prevention of Torture establishes a committee of individuals who can visit any place within the jurisdiction of a party to the Convention where people are deprived of their liberty by a public authority.[80] The committee's main purpose is to seek, through co-operation and persuasion, improvements in the conditions of those detained; it has no judicial authority to 'find' breaches of the Convention. In making its assessments of national provisions it draws on a variety of international guidelines, but has not to date published any guidelines of its own. Before visiting any state the committee receives a list of places where people are detained, and identifies the establishments it intends to visit. The committee may seek the help of outside experts, and can interview in private anyone who is detained. The ultimate report is made to the state authorities, and the committee may publish a statement if the state refuses to introduce the necessary improvements.

In 1990 the committee visited five prisons and five police stations in the UK, including the psychiatric wing at Brixton. While it found no incidents of ill-treatment, it considered the overcrowding and sanitation in three establishments so outrageous as to amount to 'inhuman and degrading treatment'. In 1991 the government allowed publication of the committee's report and published its own response.[81] While the government denied that the conditions found amounted to 'inhuman and degrading' treatment, it has promised improvements.

Thus, despite the absence of clear, internationally agreed standards, by providing independent experts with access to custodial establishments, the Torture Convention does create a structure for monitoring prison regimes within signatory states, something which was never adequately provided for by the European Convention on Human Rights. To date, three domestic governments – Austria, Denmark and the United Kingdom – have at least responded to the resulting reports by both agreeing to their publication and

---

80 (1987) 9 EHRR 161. The Convention was ratified by the UK in 1988, and came into force in 1989.

81 Both the *Report to the United Kingdom Government on the Visit to the United Kingdom by the European Committee for the Prevention of Torture and Inhuman or Degrading Treatment or Punishment* (1991) and the *Response of the United Kingdom Government* (1991) are available from the Home Office.

promising certain improvements. However, the development of the necessary mechanisms to monitor state action in response to reports is still in its early stages, and much will depend on the strength of these mechanisms.[82] Further, the efficacy of the structure as a whole is inevitably limited by the small number of establishments the committee can visit, and is significantly dependent on the quality of the information available from independent sources.

(g) Inquiries

In the previous chapter the role of the Woolf Inquiry in the process of policy formulation was discussed. However, many inquiries, like Woolf itself, have a dual role: they are set up both to investigate a particular incident or series of incidents and to make recommendations in the light of their findings: to act as *post hoc* validators as well as policy formulators. The role of inquiries at the validation stage is discussed further in chapter 11, in the context of special hospitals, but certain specific issues should be mentioned here.

Inquiries come in many forms, as will be seen below. They can be entirely independent of the responsible authorities, and set up as a result of public concern about a specific feature of prison life. In March 1992, for example, the Howard League established an inquiry chaired by Anthony Scrivener QC into the series of suicides at Feltham. Such inquiries possess no formal investigative powers, but depend for their existence upon some non-governmental agency having the necessary resources to service them. Secondly, by virtue of section 5A of the 1952 Act, the Secretary of State can ask the Chief Inspector to investigate a particular aspect or incident, as he did in the case of the Brixton escapes in 1991. In that case some of the Chief Inspector's findings were withheld for security reasons.[83] Thirdly, the Secretary of State can appoint an individual or team of individuals, either as a departmental inquiry, when they possess no powers to compel witnesses, or as a statutory inquiry under the Tribunals and Inquiries Act 1921. The Woolf Inquiry was established in April 1990 as a departmental inquiry. The Secretary of State indicated that he would be prepared to consider establishing the inquiry under the 1921 Act if it were thought necessary, but in the event Lord Justice Woolf 'received full co-operation from all those with a contribution to make and never found that [he] needed to ask for statutory powers'.[84]

The investigation of the 1990 riots themselves was conducted at Stage I of the Woolf Inquiry, and presented the Inquiry with significant problems in its attempt to establish the true history of events. The riots, the longest in English penal history, had received extensive coverage from the media, and conse-

---

82 For a useful account of the record of the Convention to date see M. Evans and R. Morgan, 'The European Convention for the Prevention of Torture: Operational Practice' (1992) 41 ICLQ 590.

83 *Inquiry by H.M. Chief Inspector of Prisons into the Escape of Two Category A Prisoners from H.M. Prison Brixton on 7 July 1991* (1991, London: Home Office).

84 *Supra*, n. 4, p. 28.

quently the Woolf Inquiry itself attracted considerable attention. The prisoners who had been involved were scattered between other prison establishments and police stations throughout the country; many were reluctant to give evidence, either from a fear of reprisals or from a fear of self-incrimination: one man had died following the riots, and 147 members of staff, together with 47 inmates at Strangeways, had received injuries, and as a result a number of inmates were facing criminal charges.

Against this background the Woolf Inquiry team had to obtain sufficient evidence from the inmates to enable them to build up an accurate picture of events. Morgan describes the strategies adopted by the Inquiry, and the compromises that had to be made between procedural fairness and the need to establish 'broad public legitimacy for the Inquiry.'[85] In the event, although much evidence was taken at public hearings, none of those inmates who had been particularly prominent was called to give evidence. The danger of compromising the course of a criminal trial was considered too great. Such prisoners were, however, interviewed by one of the Inquiry's assessors. Other prisoners who wished to give evidence in private were permitted to do so, but were open to cross-examination by the other represented parties.[86] Thus the Inquiry sought to satisfy the conflicting demands made of it, and to provide the broad inquisitorial structure favoured in chapter 4 for the most complex decision making at the validation stage. An assessment of how far it succeeded in this latter endeavour requires research beyond the scope of this book, but the proper role for such a structure is considered further in chapter 11.

(h) Courts

Finally, the role of judicial supervision of internal decisions relating broadly to the allocation of resources should be considered. As was the case in relation to transfer decisions, court intervention can take a variety of forms, but in practice the legal structure as interpreted by the courts permits of little judicial oversight. The House of Lords has now confirmed that no rights are created in private law by the Prison Rules.[87] Thus the legislation creates no additional special rights in prisoners which are susceptible to direct enforcement through a private law action for breach of statutory duty. Until *Hague* the House of Lords had not directly considered the question whether a breach of the Prison Rules gave rise to a private law claim for breach of statutory duty, although earlier cases in the courts below had concluded that it could not.[88] In *Hague* the point was argued in full in relation to rule 43, the provisions of which had not been met by the authorities. Typically the question whether or not non-compliance with a particular statutory provision can give rise to a private law claim for breach of statutory duty is determined by reference to the intentions of the legislature: did Parliament intend individuals to possess a right to

85 R. Morgan, 'Woolf: In Retrospect and Prospect' (1991) 54 Mod. LR 713.
86 *Supra*, n. 4, pp. 34–5.
87 *Hague* v. *Deputy Governor of Parkhurst Prison* [1991] 3 All ER 733.
88 *Arbon* v. *Anderson* [1943] K.B. 252 and *Becker* v. *Home Office* [1972] 2 QB 407.

damages if a particular statutory requirement was not met?[89] In answering that question the courts will often have little clear evidence to guide them. In the earlier cases of *Arbon* v. *Anderson*, and *Becker* v. *The Home Office*, the courts had taken the view that there was nothing in the Prison Act to indicate an intention to create rights in individuals:

the real question which falls to be determined is whether it is intended by the statute to confer an individual right. I am clearly of the opinion that neither the Prison Act [1898] nor the rules were intended to confer any such right.[90]

And, according to Lord Denning, 'the Prison Rules are regulatory directions only. Even if they are not observed, they do not give rise to a cause of action.'[91]

In *Hague* the prisoner sought to avoid a similar conclusion by arguing that, where an individual is injured by the breach of a statutory duty for which the statute offers no specific remedy, that person is entitled to claim damages by way of breach of statutory duty if he or she belongs to a class which the duty was designed to protect and the damage suffered was of a kind against which the statute was intended to offer protection. Such an argument, if accepted, would have directed more precisely the court's inquiry as to the intentions of the legislature: does the plaintiff belong to the class the statute was designed to protect? Did the alleged breach cause injury of the type against which the statute was designed to offer protection? The House of Lords, however, would not accept that approach:

it must always be a matter for consideration whether the legislature intended that private law rights of action should be conferred upon individuals in respect of breaches of the relevant statutory provision. The fact that a particular provision was intended to protect certain individuals is not of itself sufficient to confer private law rights of action upon them, something more is required to show that the legislature intended such conferment.[92]

The wide judicial discretion implicit in the more general inquiry was therefore reasserted. In the event, two of their lordships examined the intentions of the legislature and, while agreeing that Hague had no cause of action, reached rather different interpretations of those intentions. Lord Jauncey was of the opinion that neither section 47 of the Prison Act, which empowers the Secretary of State to make rules, nor any other provision of the Act, was intended to confer the power to create private law rights in the event of breaches of those rules. Lord Bridge was less general in his approach. He felt that the power conferred by section 47 was very wide, particularly with reference to the 'treatment' of prisoners, and that the Secretary of State could issue rules under that section which would create private law rights in prisoners. In the opinion of Lord Bridge, if the Secretary of State were to do so he would not be acting *ultra vires* the Prison Act. The intentions of the

89 *Cutler* v. *Wandsworth Stadium Ltd* [1949] 1 All ER 544.
90 *Arbon* v. *Anderson, supra*, n. 88, per Lord Goddard at p. 254.
91 *Becker* v. *Home Office, supra*, n. 88, at p. 418.
92 *Supra*, n. 87, p. 750.

legislature, it would seem, lie squarely in the eye of the beholder. On the primary point at issue, however, Lord Bridge and Lord Jauncey were agreed: rule 43 was not intended to give rise to a claim for breach of statutory duty. As Lord Bridge unambiguously expresses it,

where the power has been exercised in good faith, albeit that the procedure followed in authorising its exercise was not in conformity with r 43(2), it is inconceivable that the legislature intended to confer a cause of action on the segregated prisoner.[93]

In the light of these judicial views, the prisoner's desire to direct the House's inquiry away from the unconstrained consideration of Parliamentary intent is entirely understandable. That it failed may represent a genuine rejection of the argument on its legal merits, or it may indicate a reluctance to impose an additional burden on the prison authorities by introducing a means for the judicial enforcement of the Prison Rules at the suit of individual prisoners. Lord Bridge's view of the purpose of rule 43 certainly suggests little sympathy for the segregated prisoner: the rule, according to his lordship, is designed to provide 'an obviously necessary power to segregate prisoners who are liable for any reason to disturb the orderly conduct of the prison generally'.[94]

Whatever the underlying basis for the court's attitude, however, it is clear that a breach of statutory duty action based on non-compliance with the Prison Rules will fail in the absence of a clear indication in the Prison Rules (Lord Bridge) or the Prison Act (Lord Jauncey) to create rights in prisoners. Similarly, it is now clear that a prisoner cannot pursue a claim for false imprisonment with regard to the conditions suffered while in prison. In *Williams* the prisoner segregated under rule 43 in breach of rule 43(2) sought a remedy, not in breach of statutory duty, but in false imprisonment.[95] He argued that his further segregation within the prison was unlawful and amounted to false imprisonment. Tudor Evans J dismissed the claim, holding that the sentence of the court and section 12 of the Prison Act were sufficient to provide lawful authority for the imprisonment, and that no subsequent change in conditions could render that imprisonment unlawful. Following that decision, the question of false imprisonment within lawful detention was considered in a number of cases without any marked consistency in approach.[96] Eventually the issue was raised before the House of Lords in *Hague* and the associated case of *Weldon* v. *The Home Office*, and the central question has finally been resolved. The sentence of the court together with section 12 provide sufficient authority for the detention of the prisoner 'in any prison', and once in prison the prisoner retains no residual liberty *vis-à-vis* the governor. The subsequent segregation of a prisoner in breach of the Prison Rules does not therefore amount to false imprisonment. To regard it as doing so would, according to Lord Bridge 'be, in

93 *Ibid.*, p. 742.
94 *Ibid.*
95 *Williams* v. *Home Office* [1981] 1 All ER 1211.
96 See, for example, *R* v. *Commissioner of Police of the Metropolis, ex p. Nahar* (1983) *The Times*, 28 May; *R* v. *Gartree Prison board of Visitors, ex p. Sears* (1985) *The Times*, 20 March; and *Middleweek* v. *Chief Constable of the Merseyside Police* (1985) [1990] 3 All ER 662.

effect, to confer on him under a different legal label a cause of action for breach of statutory duty under the rules'.[97] Further, the detention of a prisoner in intolerable conditions would not, as had been suggested in earlier cases, amount to false imprisonment. However, the House of Lords did recognise that a prisoner who is lawfully in prison could nevertheless suffer false imprisonment at the hands of a fellow prisoner or a prisoner officer acting in bad faith.

In the course of the argument before the House of Lords a number nineteenth-century cases were cited in support of the prisoners' claim, but their relevance was denied by the House on the grounds that the early cases were concerned with a very different statutory structure. Nineteenth-century prison legislation was considerably more detailed in its regulation of the nature of imprisonment than is the 1952 Act, and prisoners were subjected under it to significantly different regimes depending on their classification. In such a statutory context there were specific requirements for the courts to police. Both the Court of Appeal and the House of Lords in *Hague* emphasised the difference between the detail of the nineteenth-century legislation and the broad power vested in the Secretary of State by section 12(1) of the 1952 Act to confine a prisoner in any prison.

In a situation where wide discretion is granted to the authorities and no statutory definition of imprisonment is provided, the courts are given little encouragement to intervene. Thus the lack of Parliamentary involvement in the formulation of current penal policy not only indicates the absence of formal democratic participation, but also inhibits the potential of the courts to provide effective validation. The generosity of section 12, the silence of the 1952 Act on the question of private rights, and the absence of any specific intention to protect prisoners in the Prison Rules, have combined to deny prisoners access to either false imprisonment or breach of statutory duty as a means of challenging internal prison decisions.

The denial of both breach of statutory duty and false imprisonment does not mean, however, that the prisoner is left without any remedy against the prison authorities in private law. The courts have recognised that the authorities owe a general common law duty of care to prisoners in their custody, and that a prisoner may claim damages in negligence for any injury suffered as a result of a breach of that duty.[98] In appropriate cases a prisoner could also sue for damages in assault. So, in theory at least, a prisoner who suffers injury as a result of the conditions of his or her imprisonment can claim damages in negligence against the authorities, provided he or she can establish a breach of the authority's duty of care. Further, the courts have recognised that the Home Office owes prisoners a duty to provide them with a reasonable degree of protection against the violence of other prisoners.

In practice, however, as cases such as *Egerton* suggest, it may not prove easy to establish the breach of such a duty.[99] In that case a prisoner who had recently

97 *Supra*, n. 87, p. 744.
98 *Ellis* v. *Home Office* [1953] 2 QB 135.
99 *Egerton* v. *Home Office* (1978) Crim. LR 494.

been on rule 43 for his own protection was beaten up by other prisoners in the canvas shop. The court agreed that the Home Office owed him a duty of care, but held that there had been no breach of that duty, despite the fact that none of the staff on duty in the canvas shop at the time were aware of Egerton's history. In the more recent case of *H* v. *Home Office*, however, a prisoner whose previous record for sex offences was revealed to fellow prisoners through negligence on the part of the authorities was awarded £50 damages when he was subsequently assaulted.[100] The assault was found to be a direct consequence of the authorities' negligence. Following the assault the prisoner was placed on rule 43 at his own request and, at first instance, was awarded further damages for the consquent reduction in his quality of life. This element of the award was overturned by the Court of Appeal, which held that, in the absence of 'intolerable conditions', damages could not be awarded in negligence for segregation under rule 43. Any other conclusion, according to the court, would have been contrary to the policy established in *Hague*.

A number of the activities which take place in prisons are regulated, when they occur elsewhere, by specific regulatory schemes which either employ the courts as the final means of enforcement or provide individuals with special claims to compensation. Many of these schemes are statutory, but in relation to prisons their impact is often greatly reduced. With regard to application and enforcement, as has already been explained, the doctrine of Crown immunity can be employed to exempt prison premises from inspection by the normal regulatory bodies. The Food Safety Act 1991 has removed this exemption as it applies to prison kitchens, but the authorities will still be formally exempt from prosecution. With regard to compensation, the courts have denied that the Factory Act, creating statutory rights in employees, applies to prison workshops, and have further refused to recognise the common law relationship of master and servant.[101] They have thus denied both statutory and special common law protection to prisoners injured in prison workshops. Prisoners injured at work in prison have to rely on the general common law duty of care. A prisoner's access to the courts as a means of independent validation in these circumstances is therefore restricted in a way that appears hard to justify, and would certainly seem to have little to do with either security or control. People are not sent to prison in order to suffer inferior hygiene, nor in order to find it more difficult to receive compensation for industrial injury. Yet in practice these are the implications of imprisonment, and a willingness on the part of the Home Office either to comply with an enforcement notice or to offer *ex gratia* sums by way of compensation does nothing to alter that fact.

In view of the generally privileged position enjoyed by the prison authorities, as just described, the decision in *Alexander* v. *Home Office* is particularly welcome. A West Indian prisoner brought an action under the

---

100 (1992) *The Independent*, 6 May.
101 *Pullen* v. *The Prison Commissioners* [1957] 1 WLR 1186, and *Davis* v. *The Prison Commissioners* (1963) *The Times*, 21 November, respectively. The Home Office does have a duty to train prisoners adequately in the use of machinery, a duty that derives from the 'neighbour principle', *Ferguson* v. *Home Office* (1977) *The Times*, 8 October.

Race Relations Act, alleging that he had been refused certain jobs within the prison on racial grounds.[102] The County Court held that the Act did apply in such a situation, and the prisoner was ultimately awarded £55 in compensation. Thus, if *Alexander* is followed, with regard to racial discrimination at least, prison management decisions are subject to the same degree of regulation and court supervision as applies outside the prison system.

Prison management decisions with regard to the prisoner's access to resources are also potentially subject to court supervision by way of the public law principles of judicial review. In the first place, although the House of Lords has now confirmed that a deterioration in prison conditions cannot amount to the tort of false imprisonment, the House did reaffirm that a decision to hold a prisoner in intolerable conditions could be subject to judicial review.[103] What might amount to intolerable conditions is not, however, clear. In a now discredited judgment relating to false imprisonment, Lord Ackner used the examples of serious flooding or a fractured gas pipe,[104] and it is perhaps reassuring that Lord Bridge, in *Hague*, regarded these colourful suggestions as too extreme to offer much useful guidance.[105] Nevertheless, decided cases give no clear indication as to what conditions might be regarded as so intolerable that any decision to subject a prisoner to them would be unreasonable and hence unlawful. Indeed, the attitude of the judiciary to such issues in the past does not suggest that the threshold of tolerability will be set very high.

Secondly, although it is now clear that the private law will provide no means of direct enforcement of the Prison Rules by way of an action for breach of statutory duty, the courts have accepted that section 4(2) of the 1952 Act imposes a public law duty on the Secretary of State to ensure compliance with the obligations contained in both the Prison Rules and the Act.[106] It is therefore theoretically possible for a prisoner to challenge the Secretary of State's failure to ensure compliance, thus providing the possibility of judicial challenge to a decision denying access to resources guaranteed by the Act or Rules. However, many of the Prison Rules are expressed in such a way as to leave considerable discretion in the authorities: a prisoner who is unable to work due to the closure of prison workshops, for example, will find little support from rule 28, which states merely that a

convicted prisoner shall be required to do useful work for not more than ten hours a day, and arrangements shall be made to allow prisoners to work, where possible, outside the cells and in association with one another.

It is consequently extremely hard to establish any unreasonable refusal to ensure compliance. As was seen in *McAvoy*, the prison transfer case, the courts show little enthusiasm for challenging the exercise of discretion by the Secretary of State.[107] In that case the Divisional Court accepted in principle

102 [1988] 2 WLR 1017.
103 *Supra*, n. 87.
104 *Middleweek*, *supra*, n. 96.
105 *Supra*, n. 87, p. 746.
106 *R* v. *Deputy Governor of Camphill Prison, ex p. King* [1984] 3 All ER 897.
107 *Supra*, n. 21.

the Secretary of State must take into account the obligations imposed by the Prison Rules when exercising his discretion under the Act, but was loath to police the degree of consideration given to the requirements of the Prison Rules, and was reluctant to inquire into the Secretary of State's operational and security reasons for his decision. It will be interesting to see how the courts interpret the Secretary of State's role with regard to the performance of privately run prisons and, in particular, whether they are prepared to oversee the fulfilment by the controller of his or her duty to 'keep under review, and to report to the Secretary of State on the running of the prison by or on behalf of the director' – section 85(4)(a) of the Criminal Justice Act 1991.

Finally, there is the possibility that the courts might recognise a legitimate expectation in a prisoner to a certain resource. In his report, Lord Justice Woolf criticised the practice of referring to a prisoner's 'privileges'. According to the Woolf Report, although a prisoner has no 'legal personal right' to be provided with privileges, the Prison Service can be under a public law duty to provide them: a duty enforceable through judicial review.[108] In the previous paragraph the readiness of the courts to enforce such a duty where operational reasons for non-compliance are provided by the authorities was doubted, but it may be that if the courts were to recognise a prisoner's legitimate expectation to certain privileges they might be prepared to offer procedural, if not directly substantive, protection to that expectation. According to the relevant case law, a legitimate expectation can be created by a general statement of policy, by a specific undertaking, or by past practice.[109] So the courts might feel that a prisoner who had customarily enjoyed a certain privilege had a legitimate expectation with regard to it, which they would be prepared to protect through the imposition of procedural safeguards.

The possible development of such an approach by the courts is likely to become increasingly significant when the code of standards and the prisoners' compacts are eventually introduced, and possibly with the introduction of more privately-run prisons. On the assumption that no directly enforceable rights will be created by the code or by the compacts, the prisoner will gain no additional private law rights in reflection of his or her additional dependence. Instead, whatever the precise form adopted by the code, the most the prisoner is likely to obtain are expectations attracting public law protection. Similarly, a prisoner in a private prison may be able to claim a legitimate expectation in relation to the conditions imposed on the operator through the latter's contract with the Home Office.

In either situation, the level of effective oversight provided by the courts will depend in large part on the attitude of the judiciary to the recognition of legitimate expectations in prisoners. If the courts are prepared to insist that legitimate expectations be met unless the authorities have an overwhelming justification for not doing so, and to inquire energetically into the nature of

108 *Supra*, n. 4. pp. 374–8.
109 *Attorney General of Hong Kong* v. *Ng Yuen Shiu* [1983] 2 AC 629. For further discussion see chapter 3.

that justification, then public law may begin to provide a truly effective mechanism for checking the true authority of policy application decisions within prison.

7
Prison Discipline

Of all the areas of custodial decision making the formal prison disciplinary system has attracted the most judicial attention, the vast proportion of which has concerned matters of process. The need for some form of internal disciplinary system within prisons seems to have been generally accepted by the majority of those who have commented on the issue since the Second World War. Indeed, with reference to the basic objective of imprisonment – segregation from society – it can be argued that some enforceable internal code of conduct is required, not only to achieve segregation itself, but also to ensure that those segregated are detained in safe and humane conditions. The questions concerning the appropriate scope of such a code, its degree of formality, and its precise relationship to the ordinary criminal law are, however, far more controversial.

Over the last 20 years the prison disciplinary system has been the focus of considerable interest, not only on the part of the judiciary, both domestic and European, but also on the part of independent inquiries and government-appointed committees. Indeed, the government has recently introduced major structural change. However, the legislative basis for the present system remains section 47 of the 1952 Act, and the Prison Rules as amended in 1989 and 1992. The details of this system will be considered below, but first it is relevant to consider briefly the decision making process from which it has emerged.

(a) Policy Formulation

While for many the pace of change has been too slow, it is clear that the system has changed quite significantly since the early 1970s. To date, however, these changes have been achieved without recourse to primary legislation. The mechanics of full Parliamentary democracy have not been disturbed. Indeed, since the primary legislation with regard to prison discipline is merely enabling, and most generously so, it would appear that Parliament never intended to become too closely involved.

The 1952 Act empowers the Secretary of State to make rules for the 'discipline and control' of prisoners – section 47(1) – with the stipulation merely that the rules 'make provision for ensuring that a person who is charged with any offence under the rules shall be given a proper opportunity of representing his case' – section 47(2). The process of change has therefore been concerned with the amendment of the Prison Rules, and the administrative guidance of various forms issued under them – the Circular Instructions, Standing Orders and the Manual on the Conduct of Adjudications – and has been a process in which the courts have played a major role. The domestic courts, constrained by their constitutional position, have limited their intervention to ensuring the procedural adequacy and strict legality of disciplinary adjudications, while the European Court and Commission of Human Rights have at least addressed the nature of the adjudicatory structure itself.

(1) 1970–1990

In the mid-1970s, prior to judicial intervention, the system was subject to little outside scrutiny or control. Traditionally, the system and its procedures, which effectively date from 1899, were taken from the military model of the commanding officer maintaining discipline among his troops.[1] The 1964 Prison Rules laid down a list of disciplinary offences, classifying some as 'graver', and some as 'especially grave'. These offences, several of which mirrored ordinary criminal offences, ranged from mutiny and gross personal violence to being 'idle, careless or negligent at work' and repeatedly making 'groundless complaints'. They were heard, according to their gravity, by either the governor, the board of visitors or, very occasionally, an officer of the Secretary of State. Provision was also made for reference to the police with a view to criminal prosecution in appropriate cases. In practice, the vast majority of disciplinary charges were heard by governors, an average of 95 per cent of all offences.[2] An average of 5 per cent were therefore heard by the boards of visitors, with a very small figure, 90 in 1989, being processed by the ordinary courts. The punishments or awards available depended on the identity of the adjudicator and the gravity of the offence, and ranged from stoppage of earnings and loss of privileges, to cellular confinement for up to 56 days and, for 'especially grave' offences prior to 1989, unlimited loss of remission. Loss of remission (LOR) was (and in its new guise, additional days, still is) the most controversial of the awards since it amounts to the deprivation of liberty.[3] A prisoner could expect the remission of one-third of his sentence

---

1 E. Fitzgerald, 'Prison Discipline and the Courts', in M. Maguire, J. Vagg and R. Morgan (eds), *Accountability and Prisons: Opening up a Closed World* (1985, London: Tavistock), ch. 2, provides an account of the evolution of the system prior to 1970.

2 *Statistics of Offences against Prison Discipline and Punishments in England and Wales 1989* (1990, Cm 1236, London: HMSO).

3 Section 42, Criminal Justice Act 1991 makes provision for additional days to be awarded for disciplinary offences in the place of LOR, remission having been abolished by the Act.

unless that 'privilege' was removed through a disciplinary award. Under the old rules the governor was limited to awards of 28 days' LOR, and the boards of visitors were limited to 180 days for each graver offence; only in the case of the especially grave offences was the period for a single offence unlimited. Since an award of LOR was not itself subject to remission, a loss of 180 days was equivalent to a sentence of 270 days, or 9 months. One of the applicants in *St Germain* had originally been awarded 720 days for his part in the Hull Prison riots of 1976.[4]

By the mid-1970s a number of criticisms were emerging which allowed significant punishments, including loss of liberty, to be imposed by prison governors and boards of visitors with apparently few procedural safeguards. Neither the governors nor the boards had any professional legal expertise, nor did they possess 'ostensible independence'. The governor was clearly an internal figure for the daily management of the prison, while any formal independence on the part of the boards was often compromised, in the eyes of the prisoners, by virtue of the boards' close relationship with prison management. Further, the boards were required to perform two, arguably incompatible, roles as watchdog and as disciplinary tribunal. With regard to procedure, the 1964 Prison Rules stipulate merely that 'at any inquiry into a charge against a prisoner he shall be given a full opportunity of hearing what is alleged against him and of presenting his own case' (rule 49). No mention was made in the rules of witnesses, cross-examination, legal representation, nor burden and standard of proof, and no mention was made of review by, or appeal to, the courts, although a prisoner could petition the Home Secretary to remit or mitigate an award.

In 1975, against such a background, Lord Denning was able to refer to the military analogy and to deny a prisoner any access to legal representation.[5] The primary necessity, as in the armed forces, was to act speedily. However, despite Lord Denning, pressure for change was growing. In 1975 the independent Jellicoe Committee recommended reforms including, particularly, the removal of the boards of visitors' adjudicatory role.[6] The recommendation was repeated in a slightly different form by a Justice report in 1983.[7]

1978, however, marked the true turning point as far as the courts were concerned. In that year the Court of Appeal abandoned its traditional non-interventionist approach and opened board of visitor adjudications to the scrutiny of the reviewing courts. *St Germain* has been heralded as a landmark decision in the development of the courts' approach to prisoners' rights. The prisoners involved had all received substantial disciplinary awards, including the loss of long periods of remission, for offences arising out of the Hull Prison riots of 1976. Their claims for *certiorari* to quash the board's decision for breach of natural justice were rejected by the Divisional Court, on the grounds that

4 *R* v. *Board of Visitors Hull Prison, ex p. St Germain* [1979] QB 425.
5 *Fraser* v. *Mudge* [1975] 3 All ER 78.
6 *Board of Visitors of Penal Institutions* (The Jellicoe Report) (1975, London: Barry Rose).
7 *Justice in Prison* (1983, London: Justice).

certiorari did not lie against the decision of a board of visitors.[8] The Court of Appeal reversed this decision, holding that the common law rules of natural justice did apply, and that boards, in their disciplinary role, were subject to *certiorari*.[9] They were performing a judicial or quasi-judicial function and although LOR did not strictly concern a prisoner's legal rights, it did significantly affect his liberty and privileges, and thus fell within the ambit of Lord Reid's speech in *Ridge* v. *Baldwin*.[10] The case was accordingly remitted to the Divisional Court to decide whether, on the merits, a breach of natural justice had occurred.[11]

So the crucial point was established: board of visitor adjudications were subject to the rules of natural justice, and *certiorari* lay to ensure compliance with those rules. The courts were apparently prepared to enforce certain minimum standards of procedural propriety on the boards. From the judgments in the Court of Appeal, however, it is clear that their lordships did not consider it appropriate to extend the notion of judicial intervention too far, even with regard to strictly procedural matters. Waller LJ emphasised that many 'administrative' decisions, concerning transfer or security categorisation, for example, would not be subject to judicial review despite the serious consequences that might follow for individual prisoners. More specifically, Megaw LJ was persuaded that, while judicial review might lie to quash a board's adjudication for lack of procedural propriety, it would not be available in the case of a governor's award. Shaw LJ was unable to make such a clear distinction.

In the years immediately folowing the Court of Appeal's decision, and the subsequent finding by the Divisional Court that the requirements of natural justice had been breached, the *St Germain* case acted as both a force for change with regard to the boards' procedures, and as a brake on the pressure for reform of the structure. On the one hand, further cases of judicial review followed and the boards of visitors were made more aware of the procedural requirements of the common law with, it can only be assumed, some improvement in their procedural standards.[12] On the other hand, the May Committee of Inquiry, which considered the whole question of the disciplinary structure, including the respective roles of the boards of visitors and the criminal courts, was able to conclude on balance that a sufficient case for change had not been made out:

> the recent court decisions have substantially clarified the position and, in conjunction with recent advice from the Home Office on the conduct of adjudications, will ensure that adjudications overall are properly and fairly carried out.[13]

8 *R.* v. *Board of Visitors Hull Prison, ex p. St Germain* [1978] QB 678.
9 *Supra*, n. 4.
10 [1964] AC 40.
11 *R* v. *Board of Visitors Hull Prison, ex p. St Germain (No. 2)* [1979] 1 WLR 1401.
12 See Fitzgerald, *supra*, n. 1, for an account of the relevant case law.
13 *Report of the Committee of Inquiry into the UK Prison Services* (The May Report) (1979, Cmnd 7673, London: HMSO), paras 5.91–5.104.

The introduction of procedural regulation, it seemed, had rendered structural and more fundamental change unnecessary. The boards retained their dual role, and the disciplinary system continued to operate with little reference to the criminal courts.

In 1982 a new source of pressure emerged which threatened finally to challenge the structure itself. Campbell, a prisoner, was convicted by a board of visitors of the especially grave offence of mutiny and gross personal violence to an officer, and was awarded 570 days LOR. He complained that the award had been made in violation of article 6 of the European Convention guaranteeing him a fair hearing. The European Commission on Human Rights concluded that article 6 did apply to such a disciplinary adjudication, and that the United Kingdom procedure failed to comply in several aspects. Most significantly, the commission advised that the board of visitors was not an independent tribunal for the purposes of Article 6(1):

despite the obligation on them to act judicially, the commission does not consider that a Board of Visitors satisfies the additional requirement of possessing the necessary institutional independence of prison administration. Its members are appointed for limited periods by the Home Secretary, the Minister in charge of the prison administration, and its other functions are such as to bring it into day-to-day contact with the officials of the prison in such a way as to identify it with the administration of the prison.[14]

Further, the hearing was procedurally inadequate under article 6 in that it did not take place in public, judgment was not pronounced publicly, and Campbell was given neither legal advice before it nor legal representation at it.

Clearly such conclusions, if confirmed by the European Court, would have had significant consequences for both the structure and the procedure of the prison disciplinary process, and in 1983 the Home Secretary announced his decision to establish a departmental committee to examine the prison disciplinary system in all its aspects. But, before the Prior Committee was finally constituted in 1984, the domestic courts had intervened again, meeting one at least of the European Commission's reservations with regard to procedure. In November 1983 the Divisional Court gave its judgment in *Tarrant*,[15] to date one of the most significant successors to *St Germain*. The board of visitors at Albany Prison had refused Tarrant the opportunity to acquire legal representation for the adjudication of a charge of mutiny against him. On an application for judicial review of that refusal, the Divisional Court held that, although a prisoner had no right to legal representation, the board did have the discretion to allow representation, both legal and lay. The principle of legal representation was thus introduced, albeit at the discretion of the adjudicating board, and Webster J set out the considerations which he felt should govern the exercise of that discretion:

(1) the seriousness of the charge and the potential penalty,

---

14 *Campbell and Fell* v. *United Kingdom* [1983] 5 EHRR 207, at p. 216.
15 *R* v. *Secretary of State for the Home Department, ex p. Tarrant* [1985] 1 QB 251.

(2) whether points of law are likely to arise,

(3) the capacity of a particular prisoner to present his own case,

(4) the difficulties experienced by a prisoner in attempting to prepare his defence while awaiting adjudication,

(5) the need for reasonable speed, and

(6) the need for fairness between prisoners, and between prisoners and prison officers.

The introduction of legal representation was seen as immensely significant by most interested bodies, warmly welcomed by some and feared by others. In their memo of evidence to the Prior Committee, the Home Office described *Tarrant* as 'potentially the most significant and far reaching of the decisions which the Divisional Court has made in this field', confirming the need for a review of the disciplinary system. The memo goes on to state:

there is no doubt that many boards have viewed the introduction of lawyers with considerable misgivings. The Prison Department had always argued that the inquisitorial nature of the adjudications made legal representation unnecessary and inappropriate; the legal representatives were likely to seek to import technical and legal points for which the disciplinary system was not designed and with which boards would find it difficult to cope; and that cases were likely to take much longer to resolve . . . The Committee will doubtless assess the effect of legal representation.[16]

Finally, before the Prior Committee reported, the European Court gave judgment in *Campbell and Fell*, and its conclusions on the disciplinary structure were significantly less critical than those of the European Commission.[17] It agreed with the Commission that article 6 applied to disciplinary adjudications, at least in so far as the especially grave offences carrying unlimited LOR were concerned, and it agreed that both the lack of access to either legal advice or representation and the board's failure to publicise its judgement constituted breaches of the article. However, the Court concluded that adjudication did not have to be public and, most importantly, the boards of visitors were sufficiently independent to meet the requirements of article 6. The Court considered that the boards were independent of both the excecutive and prison management and that, although their dual function caused prisoners to regard them as closely associated with the latter, that perception alone was insufficient to establish a lack of independence under the European Convention.

The report of the Prior Committee was published in October 1985.[18] It emphasised the need for fundamental change: the piecemeal reforms which had followed the various court judgments were insufficient, structural change was required. The Prior Report recognised the need for a disciplinary system within prisons, and accepted that there must be some overlap between the disciplinary system and the criminal courts. In the Committee's view it would be inappropriate to require all technically criminal activity to be referred to

16 *Report of the Committee on the Prison Disciplinary System* (The Prior Report) (1985, Cmnd 9641, London: HMSO), vol. 2, p. 44.

17 [1985] 7 EHRR 165.

18 *Supra*, n. 16, vols 1 and 2.

the regular courts, and they understood this view to be echoed by the European Court. The committee also accepted the retention of LOR as a disciplinary sanction. In an impoverished prison system where privileges were scarce, loss of remission was the only truly serious sanction. The report recommended that 120 days be the maximum for any single offence. However, in light of the retention of LOR, the committee stressed the need for professional, 'impartial, fair and independent' adjudicators.[19] It therefore recommended the introduction of an independent prison disciplinary tribunal to hear the more serious charges in place of the boards, and a right of appeal to an appeals tribunal. Finally, after much consideration, the committee decided against recommending a right to legal representation, and endorsed the *Tarrant* discretionary approach, governed by Webster J's criteria.

Initially, ministerial reaction to Prior seemed favourable, then contrary rumours began to circulate until, in September 1986, the Home Secretary announced that the Prior proposals were to be rejected and a White Paper issued. The White Paper retained the Prior notion of an independent tribunal, but rejected the idea of legally qualified chairs and of an appeal tribunal, relying instead on petitions to the Secretary of State and judicial review.[20] Financial considerations and an alleged shortage of appropriately qualified lawyers appeared to lie behind the government's change of heart. The White Paper met a hostile reaction, but ultimately even its proposals proved too radical. In September 1987 the minister responsible for prisons announced that the new disciplinary tribunals were not to be introduced, as 'no consensus' on the need for change had been reached. Instead the government was to devise methods of improving the disciplinary system short of structural change.

As commentators have pointed out, the alleged lack of consensus is hard to maintain in light of the support for change expressed by the Law Society, the Magistrates' Association, the Prison Officers' Association, pressure groups and academics,[21] and it can only be assumed that the government saw no immediate need to incur additional expenditure. No acute problems were being caused by the current system, which was relatively cheap to run, the challenge from Europe had been neutralised, and even the problems anticipated following the *Tarrant* decision had failed to materialise.

The government's promised measures finally appeared in April 1989, but in the interim two further cases were decided influencing the ultimate form of those measures. In *Leech* the House of Lords overturned a previous Court of Appeal decision and, supporting Shaw LJ in *St Germain*, held that, since no legal distinction could be made between governors' adjudications and those of the boards, governors' adjudications were equally open to judicial review.[22] In *Hone* the House of Lords held that neither the common law nor the European

19 *Supra*, n. 16, vol. 1, para. 5.60.
20 *The Prison Disciplinary System in England and Wales* (1986, Cmnd 9920, London: HMSO).
21 R. Light and K. Matfield, 'Prison Disciplinary Hearings: The Failure of Reform' (1988) 27 Howard Jo. of Crim. Jus. 266.
22 *Leech* v. *Deputy Governor of Parkhurst Prison* [1988] AC 533.

Convention established a *right* to legal representation for a prisoner facing a disciplinary charge equivalent to a criminal offence.[23]

The April 1989 reforms were achieved by way of amendments to the Prison Rules and relevant Standing Orders, and the publication of a new manual on the conduct of adjudications.[24] The amended rules provided a new list of disciplinary offences and abandoned the categories of graver and especially grave offences. Once an initial inquiry into the charge had been made, the governor was simply empowered to refer it to the board if the governor considered that his sanctioning powers were likely to be inadequate. Rule 50 specified the punishments available to the governor, including 28 days' LOR; while, in accordance with Prior's suggested limit, rule 51 enabled the boards to impose up to 120 days' LOR for a single charge. The Secretary of State retained his power to intervene, rule 51(4), and no specific right of appeal was introduced, although the Secretary of State was empowered to quash a disciplinary finding and to remit or mitigate an award (rule 56). Finally, as an experiment, magistrates' clerks were introduced into certain establishments to clerk board adjudications.

Despite all the consultations, discussions and pressures for change, therefore, the government decided to retain the basic structure of the prison disciplinary system. No independent, legally qualified panel was established, and the system remained internal, with a jurisdiction overlapping that of the criminal courts. The boards of visitors retained their two roles, loss of remission remained the central sanction, and no right to legal representation was introduced. However, in the years since 1970 important reforms had been achieved, and of those many sprang directly from court action: the introduction of judicial supervision as a means of external validation (*St Germain*), for example, the recognition of a board's discretion to allow reprsentation (*Tarrant*), and a general tightening up of procedures. Others emerged from a combination of committee recommendations and court judgments. The introduction of magistrates' clerks, for example, was perhaps seen as a convenient way of making suffcent legal expertise available to encourage compliance with the requirements of the common law without resort to the expensive professionally qualified tribunals urged by Prior. Similarly, the abolition of unlimited LOR and the introduction of the limits recommended by Prior, while not demanded by *Campbell and Fell*, was surely influenced by a desire to minimise the impact of article 6. By contrast, Prior's proposals for the introduction of a new independent element which could claim no support from the European Court were not accepted by the government.

The significance of the part played by court decisions in the formulation of government policy up to 1990 raises some important issues. In the first place it raises the question of rule making by adjudication. The argument in previous chapters has emphasised the desirability of procedural intervention on the

23 *R* v. *Board of Visitors Maze Prison, ex p. Hone* [1988] AC 379.
24 The Prison Rules were amended by SI 1989/330. The arrangements for reference to the criminal courts were set out in Standing Order 3 D, and the *Manual on the Conduct of Adjudications in Prison Department Establishments* (1989, London: HM Prison Service) was published.

part of the courts, even in the face of legislative silence.[25] The formulation of procedural regulation by the judiciary has thus been encouraged. However, in light of the experience of prison discipline some reservations must be expressed. The endorsement given to positive judicial intervention must be reserved for intervention involving the imposition of appropriate procedural requirements: requirements which are facilitative of the full reflection of the public interest. When the judiciary resiles from the requirements of full process, as arguably was the case in *Tarrant* where full process would have demanded a *right* to legal representation, serious doubts emerge. It will be argued in chapter 12 that the adversarial adjudicatory structure adopted by the High Court is not the ideal forum for the formulation of substantive policy. The experience of *Tarrant* would suggest that it can be equally inappropriate for the formulation of process regulation. When the Divisional Court declares principles to govern procedures before boards of visitors or, more particularly, when it devises specific criteria to govern the grant of representation, it is doing so against the background of very narrow participation, and with little direct experience of the problems at issue. The judicial tendency to accept the arguments of the authorities based on direct cost and administrative convenience, has already been mentioned in relation to Taylor LJ's approach in *Hague* to the prisoner's right to reasons.[26] In a one-to-one adversarial adjudicatory contest it is hard for the prisoner to mount sufficient evidence to outweigh the powerfully presented arguments of prison management. Arguably, the position of the European Court is rather different: that body can be seen as specifically and 'democratically' vested with the task of overseeing compliance with internationally recognised standards of human rights, as interpreted by the Court itself. It is not devising detailed rules, merely declaring principles with which domestic law must comply.[27]

Secondly, there is the question of the overall effect of court intervention in the years up to 1990. While court intervention certainly achieved procedural improvements, the basic structure of the disciplinary system remained unchanged. Fundamental reform of that structure is now underway, but it remains relevant to ask whether the piecemeal procedural reforms inspired by judicial intervention actually served to delay the implementation of more radical change. Constrained by their constitutional position the domestic courts would have been unlikely to assert the pressure necessary to achieve structural change. But, perhaps if they had not intervened to impose some procedural standards on the adjudicators, the European Court would have taken a more robust view in *Campbell and Fell*, forcing the government to act. Whatever the implications to be drawn from the past, however, the government has now acceded to structural change.

---

25 See the discussion in chapters 3 and 5.
26 *R* v. *Deputy Governor Parkhurst Prison, ex p. Hague* [1990] 3 All ER 687, and see the discussion in chapter 6.
27 See chapter 9.

(2) 1990–1992

For the prison disciplinary system the Woolf Report has at last provided the necessary spark to ignite real change.[28] As has been described in earlier chapters, the Report placed considerable emphasis on the need to treat prisoners with justice and, in furtherance of its basic desire to improve standards of justice within prison, it recommended radical reform of the disciplinary system. The Report gave two principal reasons for its view that boards of visitors should cease to undertake disciplinary adjudication. In the first place, Woolf considered that the disciplinary role was incompatible with the watchdog role and, secondly, the inquiry team felt that it was not reasonable to expect the boards 'to exercise the procedural safeguards which are necessary'.[29] The inquiry team was clearly influenced by the evidence presented to a public seminar by one of the clerks involved in the magistrates' courts experiments referred to above.[30] This evidence consisted of the result of a questionnaire administered to the clerks, and it supported the view that a close, arguably too close, relationship existed between the boards and prison staff, and that boards used less care in awarding loss of remission than magistrates would use in imposing imprisonment.

Although the Woolf Report recommended the abolition of the boards of visitors' disciplinary role, it did not advocate the creation of a specialised independent tribunal along the lines of the Prior Report. Instead it went back to 'basic principles' and considered the role of disciplinary proceedings within prisons. It was clearly impressed by the frequency with which LOR was awarded. The Prison Department had calculated that the amount of remission forfeited in 1988 amounted to the equivalent of between 600 and 700 from the annual average prison population, 'an astonishing extra burden' according to the Woolf Report. In the view of the Report:

if penalties equivalent to quite long prison sentences are required, then it is more satisfactory that they should be awarded by a court. That would allow a trial which provides the full safeguards of the criminal law. Penalties of this length can only be justified by an infraction of the criminal law and not by a breach of disciplinary rules.[31]

The Report accordingly drew a distinction between disciplinary proceedings and criminal proceedings. According to the Report, disciplinary proceedings are necessary for the maintenance of order within the prison, and the level of penalty and degree of formality should be appropriate to that limited objective. Criminal proceedings should be used 'to protect the public interest in enforcing and preserving public law and order'.[32] The penalties here might appropriately be higher, but the safeguards should be greater. The

28 *Prison Disturbances April 1990* (The Woolf Report) (1991, Cm 1456, London: HMSO).
29 *Ibid.*, p. 425.
30 M. Heap, 'Adjudications in Prison Department Establishments Qualified Clerks Pilot Scheme: The Experience of the Clerks and Co-ordinators' (1990), evidence presented to the Woolf Inquiry.
31 *Supra*, n. 28, p. 427.
32 *Ibid.*

Woolf Report was thus making an express connection between the penalties at stake and the degree of procedural protection required.

In the Woolf Inquiry's view, the disciplinary objective could be met adequately by the level of penalties available to the governor. All disciplinary charges should therefore be brought before the governor, and the disciplinary jurisdiction of the board of visitors should be abolished. In the recognition of the need to match the gravity of the sanction and the formality of the proceedings, the Report recommended that more senior governors should be used when significant penalties were anticipated. The Woolf Report recognised, as did Prior before it, that loss of remission, or additional days, would have to continue to be available, but it felt 28 days was sufficient for disciplinary offences. Graver offences involving serious breaches of the criminal law should be referred to the normal channels and prosecuted through the ordinary criminal courts. The Woolf Inquiry was confident that such a recommendation was feasible since it calculated that there should be less than 700 offences per year which would fall outside the governor's sanctioning powers. It based this calculation on the fact that from April to December 1989 there were 1,723 awards of over 28 days' LOR, of which 1,200 related to absconding or failing to return from home leave: offences which in Woolf's view were clearly disciplinary in nature and should never have attracted penalties in excess of 28 days.

The Woolf recommendations mirrored the situation in Scotland and had much to recommend them in terms of both principle and practicality. They were simple and involved the creation of no extra adjudicatory mechanism. They also accorded well with the properly limited objectives of an internal disciplinary system. The Prison Service's duty to segregate prisoners from the rest of society must carry with it the power to enforce the rules required to effect that segregation safely. The disciplinary system provides it with the means to do so, but it should not be extended to become an internal mechanism for enforcing the general criminal law. Woolf's proposals significantly reduce the penalties available for infractions dealt with as disciplinary offences, and quite properly reserve for the criminal process the application of more severe sanctions. There may be strong arguments for curtailing further the sactions available to the internal disciplinary system, but the Woolf recommendations must be applauded for recognising the limits of the disciplinary role and for placing the enforcement of the criminal law, even within prisons, in the hands of the ordinary criminal courts. Further, the recommendations evolved through a relatively open process of debate. The prison disciplinary system and the role of the boards of visitors were discussed at a public seminar, and the final recommendations can be said to reflect much of the tenor of that debate. The government's positive response to the main thrust of the Woolf recommendations with regard to the disciplinary system is therefore much to be welcomed.

Boards of visitors finally lost their disciplinary function in April 1992. Late in 1991 the Prison Service had circulated draft proposals and guidelines for the referral of charges to the police, and by April 1992 the Prison Rules had been amended and the necessary changes made to Standing Orders.[33] All disciplinary charges are now heard by the governors, who may award a maximum of 28 additional days,[34] and all criminal offences deemed worthy of higher penalties are referred to the police for prosecution through the normal channels. Many minor infractions which may constitute both criminal and disciplinary offences will still be dealt with internally as disciplinary offences, but the penalties will be limited. In all other cases criminal acts by prisoners will be processed through the criminal courts. Thus, through the mere amendment to the Prison Rules and the issuing of new administrative guidance, the long-established and controversial disciplinary role of the boards of visitors has been abolished. The arguments of the Woolf Report, carefully designed to minimise the financial and administrative implications of change, finally persuaded the government to reform the fundamentally unacceptable structure of prison discipline.

(b) Application Decisions

Most of the published material relating to disciplinary adjudications concerns hearings before boards of visitors. It is not, therefore, directly relevant to the new system. However, some general points can usefully be taken from it. Further, the Manual on the Conduct of Adjudications, published in 1989, which provides the most detailed guidance on procedures, was designed to apply to both boards and governors, and thus continues to apply to the new system, with the necessary amendments.

Prior to the departmental and judicial interest in the procedure at disciplinary adjudications in the late 1970s, hearings could be most intimidating for the prisoner. At a board of visitors hearing the accused inmate would stand opposite the panel, flanked on either side by a prison officer standing at close quarters facing the accused, between him and the panel. Procedural safeguards were rudimentary. During the 1980s, however, although certain deficiencies persisted to the end, the procedures before boards of visitors were significantly improved. For example, the physical arrangements for the hearings were modified. In general, all parties were seated, and the 1989 Manual discouraged the above practice of 'eye-balling' by the escorting officers, stating 'it is possible that this practice could constitute grounds for judical review'.[35] It remained the case, however, that the procedural standards demanded of boards of visitors were lower than those required of Magistrates' Courts, although in terms of loss of liberty the sanctioning powers of the boards were potentially greater. Under the 1992 system the sanctions available for breaches of discipline are obviously much reduced but, since prisoners are still vulnerable to loss of liberty, the procedural obligations on

33 Prison (Amendment) Rule 1992, SI 1992/514.
34 See section 42, Criminal Justice Act, *supra*, n. 3, for the replacement of LOR with additional days.
35 *Supra*, n. 24, para. 4.10.

the disciplinary system must remain high. A number of specific points which caused concern in relation to board of visitors hearings should be mentioned, and their continuing relevance to the new system considered.

(1) The Allocation of Charges

Under the Prison Rules as amended in 1989 the governor had to inquire into every charge initially, and had then to decide whether to proceed with a full hearing himself or to refer the charge to the board of visitors. The governor had the power to refer the charge to the board if he felt that his own sanctioning powers would be inadequate 'having regard to the nature and circumstances of the offence' – rule 51(1). The Woolf Inquiry clearly believed, on the basis of its own investigations and the data supplied by the magistrate's clerk referred to above, that this system for reference to the boards unduly influenced the boards' sentencing practice. Most boards felt obliged to impose a penalty in excess of the governor's maximum of 28 days. This conclusion is reinforced by the full findings of the research into the magistrates' clerks experiment.[36] For a sentencing body to have felt constrained in this way on the basis of the governor's preliminary assessment of gravity was clearly unacceptable. The governor would have formed his decision to refer without a full hearing of the facts, and might himself have been following an injustifiably rigid policy. Indeed, Morgan and Jones describe the practice, apparently common to most prisons, of governors referring to boards all charges relating to a failure to return from home leave, irrespective of individual seriousness.[37] It is to be hoped that no similarly automatic assumptions will evolve in relation to the sanctions imposed by the various grades of governors under the new system.

(2) Independence

In chapter 4 impartiality was described as one of the traditional principles of fair procedure, and was said to be one of the essential characteristics of adjudication. It demands both an absence of partiality on the part of decision makers, and their independence.[38] A partial decision maker is one who possesses a predisposition to one outcome rather than another. Such a predisposition can arise from personal interest in an outcome, from preconceived conclusions of fact, or from personal feelings either for or against a particular party. The independence required by the principle includes the absence of control by interested parties and the absence of any potentially conflicting function in the decision maker. The significance of the principle is formally recognised in article 6 of the European Convention, which guarantees

36 R. Morgan and H. Jones, 'Prison Discipline: The case for Implementing Woolf' (1991) 31 Brit. J of Crimin. 280.

37 *Ibid.* Morgan and Jones describe how the governor in one establishment amended his referral practice to make it more sensitive to the gravity of the individual case after the board of visitors imposed penalties of less than 28 days in two such cases.

38 M. Bayles, *Procedural Justice* (1990, Dordrecht: Kluwer Academic Publishers), ch. 2.

the right to a hearing before an independent and impartial tribunal in the determination of civil rights and obligations or of any criminal charge. In the ordinary criminal sphere, both the Magistrates' and the Crown Courts, appointed formally by the Lord Chancellor, are regarded as institutionally independent of the prosecuting authorities. In the context of prison discipline neither the governor nor, in the past, the boards can be said to possess that quality.

Although the European Court in *Campbell and Fell* failed to condemn the boards' lack of independence, the Prior Committee, placing considerable emphasis on the perceptions of those involved, urged the replacement of the boards with a more ostensibly independent body. The Woolf Inquiry was similarly impressed by the evidence of the boards' perceived partiality and their lack of independence. The Report cites both the evidence produced for the Prior Committee, which found that 'inmates clearly believed that the adjudicatory system was heavily biased and that the inclination of both governors and board members was to believe staff, rather than them' and the subsequent research by Magurie and Vagg which reported the prisoners' belief that boards' adjudications were controlled 'behind the scenes.[39] The survey conducted among magistrates' clerks also reported that the over-whelming majority of clerks involved felt there was a closeness between board members and staff.[40] In some establishments, apparently, there were informal meetings between board members and prison staff before the hearings. This perceived partiality and obvious lack of independence was one of the main criticisms made of the disciplinary role of the boards and, on that ground alone, the removal of the boards from the disciplinary system is to be welcomed. However, the questions of independence and partiality remain relevant even within the new system.

Plainly, a prison governor cannot possess independence as defined above. While he should not be controlled by any of the parties involved in the disciplinary charge, he will typically be required to fulfil roles with regard to the prisoner that might conflict with his disciplinary function. He might, for example, be involved in preparing reports relating to the prisoner's parole or transfer. With regard to partiality, it was suggested in an earlier chapter that within a relatively static administrative structure, such as a prison, where the parties and the decision maker are well-known to one another, it might be difficult to avoid some prejudgement of fact. Further, whatever steps are taken to create a distance between the adjudicating governor and the reporting officer, the governor will appear predisposed to believe the officer rather than the prisoner, even if this is not the case, and this appearance will only be enhanced if the prisoner either finds the reporting officer with the governor on his arrival at the hearing, or leaves them together on his departure.[41] Thus,

39 The research is considered by the Woolf Report, *supra*, n. 28, at pp. 424–6. See also M. Maguire and J. Vagg, *The Watchdog Role of Boards of Visitors* (1984, London: Home Office).
40 *Supra*, n. 30.
41 The Manual, *supra*, n. 24, para. 8.34 recognised the importance of ensuring that the governor and all other members of staff left the room prior to the prisoner, before the board of visitors

although adjudication might seem to be the most appropriate decision making structure for the determination of a disciplinary charge, it may be that a prison governor cannot 'adjudicate' in the strict sense of the term.

The case for adjudication in the disciplinary context rests on the existence of a dispute between identifiable parties which requires determination according to pre-ordained rules. Nevertheless, it may be that once the need for a disciplinary structure within prison is recognised, the practicalities are such as to render true adjudication infeasible. A disciplinary system is necessary, it is said, in order safely to achieve the segregation of prisoners. It is designed to provide prison management with a formal mechanism for the enforcement of the rules necessary to maintain peace and security within prisons. Almost by definition, therefore, prison management in the form of the governor must have ready access to it, and the introduction of a truly impartial adjudicator for the initial determination of every charge might significantly diminish the effectiveness of the system.

According to the method of evaluating procedures discussed in chapter 4, a calculation should be made of the costs of impartial adjudication, discounted by the ability of adjudication to reduce error and moral costs, and its further ability to promote process benefits. It may be that the costs of true adjudication in terms of delay and complexity would be such as to destroy the credibility of the system, and thus to encourage the growth of informal disciplinary mechanisms. Such costs might effectively outweigh the benefits of adjudication where the penalties at stake are modest. On this basis it would be possible to justify the continued involvement of governors in disciplinary hearings despite their lack of independence and impartiality, provided the penalties, and thus the potential error and moral costs, are low. However, the present system allows for a maximum of 28 additional days' loss of liberty, and arguably any penalty involving loss of liberty carries with it such potentially serious error and moral costs (even when, as here, it is subject to restoration by the governor or the Secretary of State – rule 56) as to outweigh any additional costs involved in the insistence on truly impartial adjudication. According to such a view, where loss of liberty is involved, impartial adjudication must be available from the outset, on the assumption that it is better equipped to reduce error and moral cost and to promote process benefits. On this argument, the new structure still fails to meet the requirements of full process at the application stage and, given the government's continued reliance on loss of liberty as a penalty for disciplinary offences, is likely to remain deficient for the foreseeable future. In such circumstances the provision of a truly effective mechanism for independent validation becomes particularly important. It is interesting to note, however, that in a contracted out prison, where the controller rather than the director is responsible for hearing disciplinary charges, a greater degree of independence is achieved.[42]

---

considered its verdict. The same care must surely be taken in the case of governors' hearings. See also the facts of *R* v. *Governor of H.M. Prison Pentonville, ex p. Watkins* [1992] COD 329.

42 Section 86 Criminal Justice Act 1991, and rule 98A, Prison Rules, inserted by Prison (Amendment) Rules 1992, SI 1992, SI 1992/514.

(3) Inquisitorial Hearings

The Weiler Report (1975) stressed the inquisitorial role of adjudicators within the prison disciplinary system, emphasising the obligation of the adjudicators to probe the facts and assess the credibility of witnesses.[43] This inquisitorial model is further endorsed by the 1989 Manual, and was clearly understood by board members to be the prevailing model.[44] Indeed, some board members had worried that the introduction of magistrates' clerks, who were accustomed to adversarial proceedings, would inhibit the inquisitorial approach. In the event, the research conducted by Morgan and Jones suggests that boards of visitors hearings were never particularly inquisitorial.[45] The research examined the records of cases involving drug possession and found that, of 14 findings of guilt in the period to the introduction of magistrates' clerks, only one showed that evidence had been offered or inquiry made concerning the quantity of drugs found. In the period when magistrates' clerks were involved the comparable figures were 4 out of 15. The research also involved the observation of hearings, and concluded that only half of the hearings were adequately inquisitorial, with another quarter being adequately inquisitorial only because the magistrates' clerk prompted inquiries.

Whatever the practice of the boards might have been in the past, however, it is relevant to consider which model should appropriately be adopted by the governors under the new system. As explained in chapter 4, the adversarial and inquisitorial models are not exclusive to true independent adjudication: administrative decision making can be adversarial or inquisitorial in character. With regard to board hearings, the magistrates' clerks themselves felt that both the adversarial and the inquisitorial approach were equally valid provided they were properly conducted.[46] However, it was suggested earlier that the inquisitorial approach might be more appropriate than the adversarial for the discovery of fact and, on that basis, it would be the preferred model for governors to maintain within the new structure. Most contested cases will presumably involve a dispute of fact; while, in the case of guilty pleas, the governor, being under a duty to satisfy himself that the charge is made out, must question the alleged facts.[47] In the light of the evidence emerging of the lack of inquisitorial vigour on the part of boards of visitors, however, it will be necessary to establish some mechanism for insuring that governors properly fulful their inquisitorial function.

43 *Report of the Working Party on Adjudication Procedures in Prisons* (The Weiler Report) (1975, London: HMSO).
44 D. Cornwell, 'Sharpening the Watchdog's Teeth' (1990) 29 Howard Jo. of Crim. Jus. 261.
45 *Supra*, n. 36.
46 Heap, *supra*, n. 30.
47 Manual, *supra*, n. 24, paras 2.16 and 6.1.

(4) Standard of Proof

The 1989 Manual makes it quite clear that a finding of guilt can only be reached where an 'adjudicator' is satisfied beyond reasonable doubt.[48] It is the standard of proof required of the criminal courts but, as the Weiler Report emphasised in 1975, in the inquisitorial context of a disciplinary hearing, the 'responsibility to establish what happened and why goes further than that of a criminal court which determines guilt or innocence on the basis of evidence put before it by the prosecution and the defence'.[49] In other words, the standard of proof may be the same as in the criminal courts, but the 'burden' of proof will rest with neither the reporting officer nor the prisoner: it is the governor's responsibility to satisfy himself or herself. In order to encourage compliance with this strict requirement it is necessary to demand a detailed record of the hearing, indicating not only the findings of fact themselves but the evidence relied upon in reaching them.[50]

(5) Representation

When facing a criminal charge in either the Crown Court or the Magistrates' Court the accused has the right to legal representation.[51] When facing a disciplinary charge for conduct constituting a criminal offence, however, under the old system the prisoner had merely the right to require the board of visitors to consider its discretion to allow representation according to the *Tarrant* criteria. In practice this discretionary system, despite the early fears of the Prison Department, meant that very few prisoners were represented.[52] Morgan and Jones cite 33 and 50 as the number of prisoners granted legal representation in 1988 and 1989 respectively, although there is apparently some doubt about these figures.[53] The arguments used to support this discretionary system included: the claim that it would be inappropriate in the interests of providing an efficient and speedy system to impose the full procedural requirements of a criminal trial; the fact the the duty to act fairly as recognised by the court does not include a right to legal representation; the claim that most disciplinary charges are straightforward, that legal expertise is unnecessary, and that legal representation would lead to delay and increased confrontation, and, finally, that the cost of widespread legal representation would be out of proportion to its benefits.[54] There was also the argument, familiar from the discussion of the magistrates' clerks experiment, that the

48 *Ibid.* para. 6.1. 'Adjudicator' is not being used here in the technical sense.
49 The excerpt is quoted by the Manual, *supra*, n. 24, para. 1.5.
50 See the Manual, *supra*, n. 24, paras 8.4 and 8.37, for the governor's current duty to record.
51 *Supra*, n. 23, p. 391.
52 Where representation was refused the courts were not eager to quash that refusal. See *R* v. *Board of Visitors H.M. Remand Centre Risley, ex p. Draper* [1988] CoD 64; *R* v. *Board of Visitors Long Lartin and Parkhurst, ex p. Cunningham* [1988] COD 148; and *R* v. *Board of Visitors H.M. Prison Parkhurst, ex p. Norney* [1990] COD 133.
53 *Supra*, n. 36.
54 The arguments are fully rehearsed in the Prior Report, *supra*, n. 20.

introduction of legal representation would inhibit the inquisitorial nature of the proceedings'.

Until the recent reforms these arguments carried the day. The Prior Committee, with some reservations, decided against recommending a right to legal representation, and the House of Lords rejected the claim, based partly on the European Convention, that all prisoners facing a disciplinary charge equivalent to a criminal offence were entitled to legal representation.[55] Under the new system the issue has, to a certain extent, been resolved. All serious cases will now be prosecuted in the criminal courts, where the ordinary rights to legal representation will apply. There remains, however, the question of the governors' hearings at which, for the time being at least, it is still possible to award loss of liberty, in the form of additional days, for disciplinary infractions, some of which are equivalent to criminal offences. It is clear that the Woolf Report did not envisage a right to legal representation before governors: 'given the domestic nature of these proceedings, we do not propose that prisoners should have a *right* of legal representation at these proceedings'.[56] Instead the Report recommended that there should be a discretion to allow the prisoner to bring with him either another prisoner, or a lawyer, or a prison officer, and this has been reflected in the revised section of the Manual dealing with representation which was issued in 1992. While such a solution might be appropriate in the case of domestic proceedings involving minor penalities, governor's hearings, as suggested above, have powers far in excess of most domestic bodies. The loss of 28 days' liberty is not a minor penalty, even when it is imposed on a person already in prison, and it should not be available to domestic disciplinary proceedings of any sort. However, since in response to the demands of practical politics it is available, its application should be restricted to disciplinary charges which amount to criminal behaviour, and should never be imposed unless legal representation is available if the prisoner so wishes.

(6) Disclosure of Evidence, Witnesses etc.

The 1989 Manual, which was directly influenced by the views of the High Court in a series of judicial review applications, is relatively detailed in questions of disclosure and the calling of witnesses. Before the hearing the accused, or his representative, should be given access to all statements and other written material which is to be entered in evidence. A medical report can, however, be withheld from the accused at the discretion of its author.[57] Facilities for interviewing witnesses, and lists of potential witnesses, should also be made available. Contrary to the recommendations of the Prior Committee, the boards of visitors had no power to compel witnesses, although

55 *Supra*, n. 23, and see V. Treacy, 'Prisoners' Rights Submerged in Semantics' (1989) 28 Howard Jo. of Crim. Jus. 27.
56 *Supra*, n. 28, pp. 430–1.
57 However, see the provisions of the Access to Health Records Act 1990, discussed further in chapter 10.

an officer could and still can be compelled by the governor to appear as part of his duties. The acceptance of hearsay evidence is discouraged, save in exceptional circumstances, and considerable emphasis is placed by the Manual on the accused's right to call witnesses.

'Adjudicators' are advised to take special care to follow the principles laid down by the court, and are warned that failure to call the witnesses requested by the accused has led to more remissions by the Secretary of State, and to more adverse Divisional Court judgments, than any other single ground. Among the inadequate reasons for a refusal to call witnesses the Manual mentions: administrative convenience and the belief that there is already ample evidence against the accused, *St Germain (No. 2)*,[58] and the successful persuasion of the inmate that no witness he called would be believed, *Mealy*.[59] However, it is clear that even prior to 1992 the courts were prepared to grant the boards some discretion in the matter. In *Norney* the board's refusal to adjourn to enable the prisoner to call two witnesses from Northern Ireland was upheld although their evidence was directly relevant. Written statements from the two had, in the event, been considered instead.[60] It remains to be seen how assiduously the courts will require governors to call witnesses when requested to do so.

(c) Validation

(1) Extra-judicial mechanisms

Extra-judicial validation must include mechanisms for the *post hoc* review of disciplinary decisions, but should not be exclusively concerned with such mechanisms. Throughout the discussion of application decisions, reference was made to the need in future to ensure widespread compliance with process requirements, in the light of the sometimes inadequate record of past boards. To this end it is essential that the necessary process requirements are specified in advance with as much precision as possible, and that governors are required to keep detailed records, both of the evidence and their reasons. It is therefore encouraging to note the duty imposed on governors to keep a full record of the proceedings on Form 256, and particularly the requirement to record the evidence relied upon, the reasons for any refusal to call witnesses and the reasons for the specific punishments awarded.[61] However, from past evidence it would appear that the mere existence of such a duty is not enough. A rigorous policing of the record is required to ensure, for example, that sentencing assumptions similar to those described above do not re-emerge, that the governors keep a proper distance between themselves and the reporting officers, and that they adequately fulfil their inquisitorial role. The clear

---

58 *Supra*, n. 11.

59 *R* v. *Board of Visitors of Gartree Prison, ex p. Mealy* [1981] *The Times*, 14 November.

60 *Supra*, n. 52.

61 See, *supra*, n. 24, para 8.4, for the use of Form 256, and see para. 5.11 for the need to record reasons relating to witnesses.

specification of the required procedures in this way, coupled with rigorously policed record keeping, should itself help to improve standards, but where additional *post hoc* review is required it should also facilitate that review.

Under the structure introduced in 1989 there was no independent appeal against a disciplinary decision, although the prisoner could apply to the area manager, who could exercise the powers of the Secretary of State to quash a finding of guilt, or to remit or mitigate any punishment, rule 56(1). In practice the tests applied by the area managers related to the procedure of the hearing rather than to its merits, at least to the extent to which it is possible to separate the two.[62] There was no true appeal on the facts, and no rehearing of cases. The Woolf Report recommended that this system continue, but that the area manager be given the power to rehear cases, and also to award compensation if a prisoner was wrongfully deprived of pay.[63] The Report also considered that the system should be supplemented by an independent element, and recommended that the complaints adjudicator be given an appellate role with regard to disciplinary hearings.

Following the Woolf Report, the Prison Service published a consultation document in March 1992, setting out proposals for an independent complaints adjudicator for prisons. As explained in chapter 6, in the absence of new primary legislation, the powers of this adjudicator are necessarily limited to those which can be achieved within the structure of the 1952 Act. With no new primary legislation proposed immediately, the government has once again adopted an informal, administrative approach to policy formulation and has bypassed Parliamentary debate. According to the consultation document the adjudicator is to have jurisdiction to consider both the procedure and the merits of governors' disciplinary hearings, but will not, for the present, have the power to rehear cases. That power, according to the document, 'is a statutory function of the Home Secretary, who cannot delegate it to [the adjudicator]'.[64] In the absence of a rehearing the adjudicator will be expected to judge disciplinary appeals on the basis of the documents available, supplemented where necessary by interviews. The adjudicator will not, however, possess the power to act on his or her findings directly. Until new primary legislation is introduced, the adjudicator will be formally empowered merely to recommend the use of the Secretary of State's powers under the Prison Rules to quash findings, and to remit or mitigate punishments. However, the consultation document expects 'almost all recommendations on disciplinary appeals to be implemented unless it was felt that a precedent was being set that was wrong in law'.[65]

62 *An Independent Complaints Adjudicator for Prisons: A Consultation Paper* (1992, London: HM Prison Service), p. 11.

63 *Supra*, n. 28, p. 429.

64 *Supra*, n. 62, p. 12. There is, however, some ambiguity here. Paragraph 14.423 of the Woolf Report, *supra*, n. 28, seems to imply that the Secretary of State had no such power under the pre-1992 structure. If he did have such a power it must presumably have emanated from rule 56, in which case it might be susceptible to some alteration through an amendment to the Prison Rules, but an alteration which involved the delegation of such a power to a non-statutory body might be thought to step outside the proper limits of secondary legislation.

65 *Supra*, n. 62, p. 13.

Thus, prompted by Woolf, the government has recognised the need for an independent element in the disciplinary process. The Woolf Report emphasised the particular importance of independence where loss of liberty is involved, and the government appears finally to have accepted that argument. However, while the demands of full process might, when the penalties are relatively light, be satisfied with the presence of independence merely at the validation stage; when the penalties involve additional loss of liberty, as is still the case in prison discipline, independence should also be present at the application stage. That the loss of liberty involved can be restored at the discretion of the governor does not reduce the significance of its initial imposition. Finally, while the details of the new structure have yet to be finalised, it is clear that the government is not prepared to follow Woolf to the letter. Neither the area manager nor the adjudicator is to have the power to rehear the case, and the decision making powers of both will be formally limited to making recommendations to the Secretary of State. The new 'adjudicator', although independent, will not therefore have the necessary powers to impose his or her decisions that are associated with true adjudication.

(2) The Courts

Under the new system the courts will fulfil an appellate role with regard to disciplinary offences prosecuted as crimes in the criminal courts. Such cases will be subject to the usual appellate system within the criminal court structure. Disciplinary charges heard by the governors, however, will not be subject to appeal to the courts but will continue to be subject to the High Court's review jurisdiction. In 1988, as described above, the House of Lords accepted that the disciplinary decisions of governors should be subject to judicial review and thus directly subject to the public law principles of legality, including the duty to act fairly.[66] However, the decision in *Leech* to allow judicial review was influenced by their lordships' opinion that the right to petition the Secretary of State provided an inadequate remedy for a prisoner who felt he had been unfairly treated at a governor's hearing. Thus, if the courts are satisfied as to the adequacy of the new independent complaints adjudicator, it seems likely that they will be reluctant to allow an application for judicial review under the new system until a reference to that adjudicator has been completed. It is also possible the courts will expect less procedural stringency from the governors than was eventually demanded of the boards.

Following *St Germain* the High Court intervened regularly to impose procedural standards on boards of visitors. As described above, many of these interventions concerned the admissibility of evidence and the calling of witnesses and, while the standards set might not have met the strict standards expected of the criminal courts, they did mark a significant improvement. Further, and perhaps more significantly, the decisions of the High Court

66 *Supra*, n. 22, and see *Ex p. Watkins, supra*, n. 41.

influenced the internal guidance given to the boards in the form of the 1989 Manual. Earlier in this chapter doubts were raised as to the propriety of adjudication being used as a means of procedural policy formulation, and the case of *Tarrant* was used as an example. These doubts remain. The High Court, when adjudicating individual disputes, should not be given the task of determining an entire evidential regime. However, the 1989 Manual provides clear evidence of the seriousness with which judicial intervention was taken by the prison authorities. An adverse finding by the High Court was definitely to be avoided, and the procedural guidance contained in the Manual appears to have been designed, at least in part, with that end in view. To that extent judicial review has provided an effective validation mechanism.

The cases following *St Germain* were not all concerned with strictly procedural issues. In *Smith* a board's award was quashed because a lesser charge was substituted for the original half-way through the hearing.[67] Of even more significance, in 1982 the High Court was prepared to challenge the board's interpretation of the offence, and this approach was upheld by the Court of Appeal in *King*.[68] Thus the court was used as a means of controlling the substantive decisions of the board by reviewing their interpretations of the offences. In 1989 the substance of the offences was revised by amendment to the Prison Rules.

(d) Conclusions

1992 marks a watershed in prison discipline. The limited role of the internal system has been recognised and the penalties significantly reduced, the boards of visitors have lost their disciplinary responsibility, and the application of the more severe penalties is now limited to criminal conduct prosecuted as such. Such developments are welcome. The existence of an internal disciplinary code is justified only in so far as it is necessary in order to enable the authorities successfully and safely to segregate prisoners, and its scope should be limited to the requirements of that role. Although criticism of the old system had been widespread throughout the 1970s and 1980s, it was the Woolf Report that provided the final pressure needed to push the government into structural reform, but once again that reform has been achieved with the minimum of Parliamentary involvement. The Prison Rules have required amendment, but interestingly, the only primary legislation to emerge in the area has been the Prison Security Act 1992, creating the offence of prison mutiny. In one important respect, however, the new system remains flawed: loss of liberty is retained as a penalty for disciplinary offences. Loss of liberty, the most severe penalty currently imposed by the English courts, should not be available to an internal disciplinary system. That it remains available within prisons is a

---

67 *R* v. *Board of Visitors Dartmoor, ex p. Smith* [1984] *The Times*, 12 July.
68 *R* v. *Board of Visitors Highpoint, ex p. McConkey* [1982] *The Times*, 23 September, upheld in *R* v. *Deputy Governor of Camphill Prison, ex p. King* [1984] 3 All ER 897.

shameful reflection of the absence of alternatives within our impoverished prison system.

While the structure of the prison disciplinary system has changed significantly, the procedure remains much as it was before, reflecting the common law requirements imposed on the boards of visitors by the reviewing courts. The procedure at the application stage is formally inquisitorial but, in the state prisons at least, is not adjudicative in the true sense, since the governor cannot be regarded as independent and there is no right to legal representation. While the absence of fully independent adjudication and a right to legal representation might be acceptable in genuinely domestic proceedings, the retention of loss of libery carries prison discipline outside the proper boundaries of such proceedings, making true independence and legal representation essential. The introduction of a right of reference to the independent 'adjudicator' does at last inject independence at the validation stage, but this 'adjudicator', it seems, will remain underpowered until primary legislation is passed.

8
Release from Prison

(a) The Structure of Release from Sentences of Imprisonment

Few determinate sentence prisoners serve their entire sentence in custody. Until October 1992, early release was achieved through either remission or parole. The new system is described below. From earliest days the Crown prerogative has provided a means whereby individual sentences might be set aside, but it was not until the first half of the nineteenth century that any systematic procedure evolved for the mitigation of sentences through the action of the administrative authorities.[1] By the mid-20th century the remission of some of a sentence of imprisonment was almost automatic, and in 1940 the maximum period of remission was set at one-third of the sentence. With the abolition of penal servitude in 1948, virtually all prisoners became eligible for what was effectively unconditional release after they had served two-thirds of their sentence. Eligibility was lost only through specific misconduct. Thus the modern system of remission developed, and remained virtually unchanged until 1987. Through a combination of the Prison Act 1952 and the Prison Rules,[2] any prisoner serving a sentence of over five days (it was originally 31 days) could expect unconditional release after the expiry of two-thirds of his sentence. Such remission was not technically a legal right, but could be forfeited only as a consequence of a disciplinary award.[3] In 1987 the minimum qualifying period (MQP) was reduced from two thirds to one-half for those serving 12 months or less. Under the Criminal Justice Act 1991, remission in its original form was finally abolished.

Parole, although arguably sharing the same nineteenth-century origins as remission, differed significantly from the latter. In the first place, it was not an

---

1 A brief but useful history of remission and parole is provided in *The Parole System in England and Wales* (The Carlisle Report) (1988, Cm 532, London: HMSO), ch. 1.
2 SI 1964/388.
3 The status of remission was discussed in *R* v. *Board of Visitor Hull Prison, ex p. St Germain* [1978] QB 678.

automatic expectation, but lay at the discretion of the executive. Secondly, release on parole was conditional, the parolee being under supervision and subject, in the last resort, to recall until the date when he would otherwise have been released on remission. Recall could be effected by the Home Secretary alone if there was insufficient time to consult (section 62 Criminal Justice Act 1967). Discretionary early release is still available under the new system for those serving four years or more. Parole was introduced by the Criminal Justice Act 1967, which empowered the Secretary of State, on the recommendation of the Parole Board, to release on licence any determinate sentence prisoner who had served one-third of his or her sentence, or 12 months, or other specified MQP, whichever was the longer. The Criminal Justice Act 1982, section 33, empowered the Secretary of State to reduce the MQP by order and, with effect from June 1984, the original 12 month period stipulated in the 1967 Act was reduced to six months.

Under the pre-1992 structure, prisoners serving life sentences were also eligible for release on licence by the Home Secretary acting on the advice of the Parole Board, with the additional requirements of consultation with the Lord Chief Justice and the trial judge, if available.[4] In the case of lifers, however, no minimum qualifying period was specified, thus placing the initial decision to refer to the Parole Board in the discretion of the executive. Under that structure, procedures to determine the date of first review evolved painfully in the years following 1983, and are described below. Under the new system a statutory distinction is made between mandatory and discretionary life sentences.

Thus, until 1992 three distinct systems existed for the early release of prisoners. The old structure for the forfeiture of remission has already been discussed in the context of prison discipline. This chapter is primarily concerned with the parole system, and its modern counterpart, and the release on licence of life-sentence prisoners. Both of these systems have been the subject of recent review and reform, and the evolution of present policy will be examined before the process for individual application decisions is considered. Early release from fixed-term sentences will be taken first. The release of life-sentence prisoners is dealt with at **e** below.

(b) Early Release, Fixed Term: Policy Formulation

(1) The Criminal Justice Act 1967

While the notion of conditional release dates back to the mid-nineteenth century, in the form of 'ticket of leave' for transportees, the modern system of parole was not introduced in the UK until 1967. Unlike many major penal reforms, as the Carlisle Committee point out, parole did not emerge from the deliberations of a Royal Commission, advisory council or departmental committee. Its origins were far more modest.[5] In 1964 a Labour Party study

4 Section 61, Criminal Justice Act 1967.
5 In addition to the Carlisle Report, *supra*, n. 1, for discussion of the evolution of parole, see N.

group produced a report, 'Crime: A Challenge to Us All', which recommended setting up a Parole Board to select prisoners for early release. During the Parliamentary debates on the Murder (Abolition of Death Penalty) Bill, an amendment was moved in the House of Lords to give the Home Secretary power to release on licence prisoners serving long, determinate sentences. The government's reaction was to promise to publish shortly its own proposals. These duly appeared in a White Paper in 1965, and were largely reflected in the 1967 Criminal Justice Act.[6]

During the passage of the 1967 Act there was wide all-party acceptance of the basic idea of selective early release on licence. The controversy centred rather on the decision structure provided for making the selection. This general acceptance of discretionary early release, and the lack of challenge to its underlying concept, has led some, including the Carlisle Committee, to conclude that its introduction was a largely pragmatic reaction to managerial problems within prisons, such as overcrowding and the maintenance of internal discipline: 'parole seems to have been conceived for primarily political and pragmatic reasons rather than as a result of any substantial exercise in penological thinking'.[7] It was introduced as part of a package which included the suspended sentence and had the common theme of 'keeping out of prison those who need not be there', according to the then Home Secretary, Roy Jenkins. Neil Morgan, however, suggests that the origins of parole should not be seen in exclusively managerial terms.[8] He argues that the 1964 report which established parole within Labour Party penal policy was an ideological document grounded in a belief in rehabilitation. He points out that the White Paper that followed predated the significant rise in the prison population of 1966/67, and, in fact, justified parole on rehabilitative grounds, asserting that a 'considerable number of long-term prisoners reach a recognisable peak in their training at which they may respond to generous treatment, but after which, if kept in prison, they may go down hill'.[9] Whatever the precise mix of motives lying behind the introduction of parole, it emerged with relatively little controversy at a time when there was both 'a strong liberal consensus of informed penal thought' in the UK in favour of rehabilitation,[10] and a widespread concern over prison overcrowding.

As mentioned above, however, more controversy attached to the process for the selection of parolees. The government had originally proposed placing full discretion with the Home Secretary. This met opposition from the Conservative Party and the judiciary, who were reluctant to see so much power transferred to the executive. The Parole Board, assisted by the local review

Morgan, 'The Shaping of Parole in England and Wales' (1983) Crim. LR 137, and K. Bottomley, 'Dilemmas of Parole in a Penal Crisis' (1984) 23 Howard Jo. of Crim. Jus. 24.

6 *The Adult Offender* (1965, Cmnd 2852, London: HMSO).

7 *Supra*, n. 1, p. 7.

8 *Supra*, n. 5.

9 *Supra*, n. 6, para. 5.

10 A. E. Bottoms and R. H. Preston (eds), *The Coming Penal Crisis* (1980, Edinburgh: Scottish Academic Press) p. 1.

committees (LRCs), was established to advise the Home Secretary, and the Home Secretary was empowered to release only on the recommendation of the Board. However, no statutory criteria for parole were provided, nor was any formal adjudicatory procedure imposed. The scheme was designed as a predominantly administrative process where the Home Secretary, advised by an independent panel of experts, would grant the privilege of early release under supervision to selected prisoners. The independent experts on the Parole Board had a crucial role in so far as the Home Secretary could not act without them but, as subsequent events have proved, the real power still lay with the executive.

(2) 1976–1983

Long before parole was established in the UK, selective early release was general in both state and federal jurisdictions in the United States. By the early 1970s, however, criticism of the various US schemes was growing. In 1976 indeterminate sentencing was abandoned in Maine, and by 1984 ten other states had followed suit. In this country, by contrast, support for parole was maintained throughout the 1970s by both of the main political parties, and in 1977 for the first time parole was granted to more than 50 per cent of those applying. Dissatisfaction was beginning to grow, however, even here. Within the academic community particularly, concerns were expressed with regard to both the procedures for the granting of parole and the fundamental concept of selective release itself.[11] Whatever the pragmatic reasons for the introduction of parole, the underlying concept was justified on the basis that treatment and training within prison could help to change people. As penological thinking in the early 1970s began to reject this rehabilitative ideal, so the basis for selective release by executive discretion collapsed. Parole was seen as a hidden and unaccountable system through which prisoners were resentenced by the executive. Belief in the existence of a 'peak' in training dwindled, to say nothing of the parole system's ability to recognise such a peak. Indeed, some regarded parole merely as a device for the maintenance of control within prisons.[12]

Ten years after the introduction of parole the Home Office set up an internal review of the sytem, the findings of which were published in 1981.[13] The review rejected the criticisms of the system, both substantive and procedural, but proposed a new structure for the automatic early release of those sentenced to between six months and three years. This proposal, described as 'another penological "leap in the dark" ... grounded on no clear principles and

11 See K. Hawkins, 'Parole Procedure: an Alternative Approach' (1973) 13 Brit. J. of Crimin. 6, for the arguments relating to procedure. See R. Hood, *Tolerance and the Tariff* (1974, London: NACRO) for the case against discretionary release itself. In response to Hood, see N. Walker, 'Release by Executive Discretion: A Defence' (1975) Crim. LR 540, and the rejoinder by Hood, 'The Case against Executive Control over Time in Custody' (1975) Crim. LR 545.

12 M. Fitzgerald and J. Sim, *British Prisons* (1979, Oxford: Basil Blackwell).

13 *Review of Parole in England and Wales* (1981, London: Home Office).

attractive only to those wishing to bring about an immediate reduction in the prison population', was abandoned by the government following an 'ignoble retreat' in the face of judicial opposition.[14] The problem of prison overcrowding was, however, addressed again in the Criminal Justice Act 1982, which provided both for the reduction in the MQP for parole (section 33), and for the release of certain categories of prisoner up to six months early (section 32).

(3) The 1983 Initiatives

Whatever its conceptual and procedural shortcomings the parole system survived into the 1980s with little official criticism. In the face of ever-worsening prison overcrowding it was a means whereby a significant proportion of prisoners could be released early under the supervision of the Probation Service. The Home Secretary's speech at the 1983 Conservative Party Conference, however, shattered the official peace. Leon Brittan announced the introduction of two significant changes in the operation of parole. The first, which caused the most public reaction at the time, was achieved simply through ministerial decision. As a response to what he saw as growing public concern over both the rise in violent crime and the apparent gap between the sentence and the time actually served, Brittan announced his intention to use his discretion to insure that certain long-term prisoners did not benefit from parole. Prisoners serving sentences of over five years, for offences of violence or drug trafficking, were to be granted parole only in exceptional circumstances, or where a short period of release under supervision was desirable, while certain categories of murderer would in future serve at least 20 years in custody. By contrast, the second change unveiled in the speech was a liberalising measure. Brittan announced his intention to use his powers under section 33 of the 1982 Act to reduce the MQP to six months. This was achieved by statutory instrument, coming into effect in June 1984.[15]

The changes concerning long-term prisoners caused considerable outrage from criminal justice practitioners and commentators of all persuasions, including the National Association of Probation Officers, the Prison Governors and the Prison Officers' Association.[16] One member of the Parole Board resigned. In the first place, the use of the Conservative Party conference as the forum for the announcement of the changes served to reinforce the view that these changes were grounded in political expediency rather than considered penal theory. Secondly, there was no consultation with the Parole Board prior to the announcement. The policy was merely presented as a *fait accompli*, emphasising the powerful role of the executive in the parole system. Thirdly, the policy was to be retrospective, and would apply to prisoners sentenced many years previously, who might reasonably have regarded themselves as close to release. Finally, the introduction of a policy which categorised prisoners solely according to the length of their sentence and the

14 Bottomley, *supra*, n. 5, p. 27.
15 SI 1983/1958.
16 See 'Penal Policy File No. 14' (1984) 23 Howard Jo. of Crim. Jus. 119–20.

nature of their offence was thought to run counter to the whole notion of parole.

Thus, a far reaching change in policy was announced by the Secretary of State at a political gathering. There had been no prior public debate, nor any consultation with the statutory body most directly concerned. It was not until after the Conservative Party conference that the Home Secretary met the general purposes committee of the Parole Board to discuss the implementation of the policy. It was then agreed that the Parole Board would continue to see the cases of prisoners from the restricted categories in order to determine whether special circumstances existed. In November 1983, in response to a Parliamentary question, the Home Secretary set out the new arrangements for both long fixed-term prisoners and lifers.[17] It was a clear example of rule making by ministerial decision in the absence of any real public or expert participation.

In 1984 two life-sentence and two fixed-term prisoners sought to challenge the policy by way of judicial review.[18] It was clear that the structure of the 1967 Act provided the Secretary of State with very wide powers to shape the parole system, and the prisoners had, therefore, to rely on the common law principles of judicial review to challenge the way in which he had exercised those powers. By the time the case had reached the House of Lords, the prisoners' argument had centred on two main claims: first that the Home Secretary's failure to consult the Parole Board amounted to a fundamental defect in the decision making process, and secondly, that the policy itself was unlawful. With regard to consultation, Forbes J at first instance was prepared to hold that, despite the absence of any statutory requirement, no reasonable Home Secretary could fail to consult the Parole Board prior to the formulation of such an important new policy.[19] In the House of Lords, however, Lord Scarman thought otherwise. He held that the failure to consult was not unlawful since the Home Secretary had taken into account the demands of deterrence, retribution and public confidence, all of which were relevant considerations. The prisoners' more general claim that the policy itself was unlawful was equally unsuccessful in the House of Lords. Lord Scarman held that only if Brittan's policy constituted a refusal to consider prisoners within the specified categories would it be unlawful, and this it did not do. It was quite lawful for the Home Secretary to consider the demands of deterrence, retribution and public confidence and, in the light of those demands, to limit the consideration given to the category cases.

Arguably, the *Findlay* case provides a depressingly good example of the UK courts' attitude to the process of administrative policy formulation. In chapters 2 and 3 the nature of the principles applied to the regulation of process by the common law were considered and, in theory at least, it might be thought that through the principles of substantive legality, the rule against the

17 Parl. Debs., 1982–3, vol. 49; Written Answers, 30 November 1983, cols 506–7.
18 *Re Findlay* [1985] AC 318.
19 See the judgment of Donaldson MR in the Court of Appeal *Findlay* v. *Secretary of State* [1984] All ER 801, p. 810.

fettering of discretion, and the requirements of a fair hearing the common law was equipped to regulate respectively, the formulation, substance and application of administrative policy. An examination of the *Findlay* judgment, however, suggests otherwise.

In the first place, the insistence that a policy must be 'lawful' develops a distinctly hollow ring in the context of *Findlay*. In the Court of Appeal, Browne-Wilkinson LJ argued that the consideration of prisoners according to categories based on length of sentence and nature of offence was unlawful because it ignored one of the fundamental principles of parole: the individul assessment of prisoners.[20] It did not become lawful merely because it was influenced by the perceived demands of deterrence, retribution and public confidence. While many of those familiar with the ideas behind parole might agree with Browne-Wilkinson, at least in theory, Lord Scarman, in the House of Lords, did not. For him the policy was lawful simply because it was based on the relevant considerations of deterrence, retribution and public confidence, and it purported to provide for the exceptional case. While this argument scarcely seems to answer Browne-Wilkinson's point concerning the fundamental basis of parole, it was sufficient to carry the Lord's, and the policy was upheld. That two senior judges can differ as to the purpose of a statutory scheme and, consequently, as to the interpretation of lawfulness, can come as no surprise, but it should illustrate the poverty of the guidance provided to administrators by broadly stated standards such as lawfulness.

Findlay also provides an interesting commentary on the common law's stipulation that administrative policies must not be so rigid as to fetter the exercise of discretion, and must accordingly cater for the exceptional case.[21] The two appellants who were serving life sentences had both been transferred to open prison in the expectation of fairly imminent release. On the day of the Conservative Party conference in 1983 they were transferred back to closed conditions and, in the light of the new policy, could not then anticipate release before 1989 and 1993 respectively. The Home Office never alleged that the return to closed conditions was related to the appellants' behaviour and, indeed, the court seemed to accept that it resulted exclusively from the change in policy. Neither the Court of Appeal nor the House of Lords, however, could accept that the transfer to open conditions, with all its implications, constituted 'exceptional circumstances'.

On the basis of *Findlay* alone, little confidence can be placed on the ability of the common law to influence the quality of administrative rules through the principles relating to the content and application of those rules. Unfortunately this failure is exacerbated by the court's reluctance to become directly involved in the process of rule formulation itself by, for example, recognising a common law duty to consult third parties where there is no such requirement in the legislation. If the Secretary of State had been required to consult the Parole Board before formulating his new policies in 1983, perhaps the worst effects of those policies, subsequently described as 'flawed in principle and

20 *Ibid.* pp. 819–24.
21 See *British Oxygen Co Ltd* v. *Board of Trade* [1971] AC 610.

harmful in practice',[22] might have been avoided. Admittedly, the 1967 Act left the Secretary of State with considerable power to shape the system, but in terms of rational policy making, to say nothing of full process, it would appear quite inexplicable that the Secretary of State was not required to consult the one expert body in the field before introducing significant changes to the system. Forbes J alone was prepared to regard the failure to consult as unreasonable: by any reasonable standards, he must have been right.

In sum, the introduction of Brittan's restrictive policy in 1983 not only provides a vivid examples of rule making by ministerial decision, unsullied by either public debate or expert consultation; it also illustrates the inability of the common law to impose any requirement on the decision maker that might lead to the adoption of any improvements in the decision making process. It is thus particularly unfortunate that the new provisions under the Criminal Justice Act 1991 impose no express duty on the Secretary of State to consult the Parole Board prior to issuing directions 'as to the matters to be taken into account by it', section 32(6) (see below).

Ironically, perhaps, it was not the reverberations following the introduction of Brittan's restrictive new policy in 1983 that led finally to the proposed restructuring of the parole system; but the other, more liberal, reform of 1983: the reduction of the MQP to six months. With effect from July 1984 prisoners became eligible for parole after they had served one-third, or six months, of their sentence, whichever was the longer. This meant that, in practice, prisoners serving sentences of about $10\frac{1}{2}$ months became eligible, whereas previously the minimum sentence eligible for parole was about $19\frac{1}{2}$ months. Inevitably this led to a huge increase in workload, most of which was carried by the LRCs: in 1983 only 265 prisoners serving less than two years were considered for parole, in 1986 the figure was 10,603.[23]

At an administrative level the difficulties presented by the increase were considerable, and from the outset the approval rate was high, running at about 75–80 per cent of all section 33 cases, and giving rise to considerable judicial disquiet. In 1985 the Lord Chief Justice formally drew to the Secretary of State's attention the mounting concern. The main problem lay in the nullifying effect of section 33 on the distinctions between sentences within the 9–18-month range.[24] To an extent the administrative difficulties were eased through the efforts of an internal Home Office working group, but it was clear that the judicial concerns raised more fundamental issues. The Conservative Party manifesto for the 1987 general election contained an undertaking to institute a review of the parole system, and in July the Carlisle Committee was set up 'To examine the operation of the parole scheme in England and Wales, its relationship with the current arrangements for remission, time spent in custody on remand, and . . . to make recommendations.'

---

22 The Carlisle Report, *supra*, n. 1, para. 190.
23 *Ibid.*, para. 39.
24 *Ibid.*, paras 34–40, provides a clear account of the concern generated by the reduction in MQP.

(4) The Criteria for Parole

Before moving on to consider the Carlisle Committee and its aftermath, it is necessary to refer to the question of the criteria for parole. The 1967 Act, as has been described, provided no statement of the purposes of parole nor any criteria to govern parole decisions. In 1975 the Home Secretary issued a statement designed to encourage a wider granting of parole and, following consultation with the Parole Board, issued guidelines to the LRCs concerning selection for parole. The factors to be considered were: the nature of the original offence, criminal and other history, behaviour and response to imprisonment, medical considerations, home circumstances and employment prospects on release, and prospects of co-operation with supervision. The Parole Board accepted those guidelines as relevant also to their work, and published them together with the 1975 Home Secretary's statement in every subsequent Annual Report.[25] With hindsight these criteria have been interpreted as placing a major emphasis on the assessment of risk, particularly on the risk of the prisoner re-offending in the period during which he or she would otherwise have been in prison.[26] Following the introduction of Leon Brittan's restrictive policy in relation to long-term prisoners, the criteria had to be revised by the Board and, from 1983, the revised criteria together with the 1983 statement to the House by Brittan were published annually.[27]

Thus the criteria, whatever their merits, and the operational aims of the parole system evolving from them, were devised and refined through a combination of ministerial and administrative decision making.[28] There was no direct Parliamentary involvement, nor any major exercise in consultation, although the criteria and accompanying statements were published annually. The original statutory scheme left the purpose of parole unstated, and the minister and the Parole Board merely filled the resulting vacuum.

(5) The Carlisle Committee and the Government Reaction

Against this background, the first wide-ranging inquiry into the system of parole was established. The membership of the Carlisle Committee, while appointed by the Home Secretary, was independent of the Home Office. The Committee invited and received evidence from a wide variety of groups and individuals, and eventually published its report in November 1988. In substance it recommended the retention of selective early release for prisoners serving long sentences, over four years, and its abolition for those serving

25 The criteria were first published in the *Report of the Parole Board 1975* (1976, London: Home Office), appendix 4.
26 Bottomley, *supra*, n. 5.
27 See *Report of the Parole Board for 1983* (1984, London: Home Office), Part III, for the publication of Brittan's statement, *supra*, n. 17, and the amended criteria. The restricted policy was finally abandoned in June 1992, see Parl. Debs., 1992–3, vol. 210, Written Answers, 29 June 1992, col. 384.
28 Further adjustments to procedure were required to take account of the influx of section 33 cases. See *Report of Parole Board 1986* (1987, London: Home Office), Appendix I.

shorter sentences. Those serving four years or less would be released automatically, subject to disciplinary awards, after serving 50 per cent of their sentence, and would be subject to supervision in the community up to the 75 per cent point. Those serving over four years would be eligible for parole after 50 per cent, and, if released, would be subject to supervision up to the 75 per cent point. If they were not granted parole they would be released after two-thirds of their sentence.

The Carlisle Committee was highly critical of both the parole decision making process, as will be discussed below, and the Secretary of State's 1983 policy intervention, and made several important recommendations, including the abolition of the Secretary of State's role in individual decisions. According to the Committee, the Parole Board should have power to reach binding decisions in all cases, and should be governed by legislatively prescribed criteria (paragraph 324). While the Committee felt the Parole Board should be free to draw up its own guidelines, it emphasised that those guidelines would have to be consistent with the statutory criteria. The Committee was clearly of the view that parole decisions should be based on an evaluation of the risks of an offender committing a further serious offence during the period on parole, as against the benefits accruing to both the prisoner and the public from a period of supervision following release (paragraph 322).

The Committee's report received a somewhat muted response from the government initially.[29] The Parole Board, on the other hand, was generally supportive, save in relation to some of the recommendations concerning the decision making process (see below) and the criteria for parole.[30] In relation to the criteria, the Board was keen to urge greater specificity, it felt the Committee's recommendations, based simply on risk of re-offending, were too limited. In the Board's view, statute should state whether the presumption was to be in favour of release in the absence of specific reasons, or in favour of further detention in the absence of a case for release:

> it would certainly be helpful if Parliament were to say that parole should be granted unless good reasons are shown why this should not be; or that parole should not be granted unless the prisoner has shown that, on balance, he has earned it . . . Either way, the extent of risk must be set out by statute.[31]

In February 1990 the government finally published a White Paper, *Crime, Justice and Protecting the Public*, which accepted, with some amendment, the basic early release structure recommended by Carlisle, although the Secretary of State was to retain his role in individual decision making for longer-term prisoners.[32] The White Paper also accepted the need for 'clear and published' criteria for parole, but did not expressly commit the government to a statutory statement. Neither did it commit itself as to the nature of the Parole Board's inquiries, it merely confirmed that 'the decision whether to allow parole

29 Parl. Debs., HL 1988–89, vol. 507, Earl Ferris, 12 May 1989, cols 899–904.
30 *Report of the Parole Board 1988* (1989, London: Home Office).
31 *Ibid.*, para. 7.
32 Cm 965 (London: HMSO).

should be based first and foremost on considerations of the risk of serious harm to the public', and, after elaborating its intentions, concluded that its proposed criteria would be 'sufficiently stringent to replace the present restricted policy on parole for those sentenced to more than 5 years'.[33] Perhaps with the Brittan initiative in mind, it also proposed that the Secretary of State should have the power to give policy directions to the Parole Board.

(6) The Criminal Justice Act 1991

With regard to the release of fixed-term prisoners, the 1991 Act replaces remission and parole with a new structure for early release. A distinction is made between short- and long-term prisoners: the former are those serving a sentence of less than four years, and the latter are those serving four years or more. In the case of short-term prisoners, the Secretary of State is under a duty to release after half the sentence has been served, section 33(1). The release is unconditional if the sentence is for less than 12 months, while it will be on licence if the sentence is for 12 months or more. In the case of long-term prisoners the Secretary of State has the *power* to release on licence after half the sentence has been served, provided he is recommended to do so by the Parole Board, section 35(1). If the prisoner is still in prison after two-thirds of the sentence has been served the Secretary of State has a *duty* to release on licence, section 33(2). While on licence both short- and long-term prisoners may be made subject to conditions. In the case of long-term prisoners, and where applicable in the case of short-term prisoners, release becomes unconditional after three-quarters of the sentence has expired (section 37). While on licence, long-term prisoners remain subject to recall by the Secretary of State, either on the recommendation of the Board, or, in the case of those sentenced to seven years or more, by the Secretary of State acting on his own where he considers it inexpedient to wait for the Parole Board's decision (section 39).[34] The procedures to be followed by the Parole Board in fulfilling its various tasks are left to specification by rules, section 32(5), the substance of which is considered below.

Thus, under the 1991 Act, discretionary early release is applicable to a significantly smaller number of prisoners. The LRCs have been abolished, and it is anticipated that the Parole Board will be dealing with a greatly reduced case load.[35] The scheme is essentially that envisaged by the Carlisle Committee, but there are some significant distinctions, and a number of points should be emphasised. In the first place, although the Secretary of State has,

33 *Ibid.*, paras 6.21–6.23.
34 Acting under the powers provided by section 50 of the 1991 Act, the Secretary of State has, by statutory instrument, reduced his role under section 39 with regard to the recall of long-term prisoners serving less than seven years. The Secretary of State must now recall such prisoners if recommended to do so by the Parole Board, but may not recall them without the Board's recommendation: The Parole Board (Transfer of Functions) Order 1992, SI 1992/1829.
35 Although the scheme will apply to all prisoners sentenced after 1 October 1992, there will

by statutory instrument, relinquished his role with regard to prisoners sentenced to under seven years, his role with regard to the release and recall of longer-term prisoners is retained.[36] This insistence on the retention of the Secretary of State's role in individual cases is unfortunate, and is discussed further in **c** below.

Secondly, despite the recommendations of the Carlisle Report, the 1991 Act itself does not directly specify the criteria for early release in any detail. Instead s.32(6) empowers the Secretary of State to give directions to the Parole Board 'as to the matters to be take into account by it in discharging any functions under [Part II]', and requires the Secretary of State to have particular regard to

(a) the need to protect the public from serious harm from offenders; and (b) the desirability of preventing the commission by them of further offences and of securing their rehabilitation.

Such a provision, while representing an improvement on the total silence provided by the 1967 legislation, and reflecting the substantive issues emphasised by Carlisle, can hardly be seen as a comprehensive statutory statement of the criteria to be applied to release decisions. The absence of such a statement is unfortunate since a full legislative explanation of the criteria, which, formally at least, can be taken as an expression of the full public interest, is essential as a standard against which to judge all subsequent policy formulation and application decisions. Under section 32 the bare principles only are specified, leaving further clarification to be provided by ministerial direction. In theory the directly accountable Secretary of State is an entirely appropriate person to act as the initiator of policy, and section 32 serves formally to delegate to him that function: there is no conflict between the demands of full process and the issuing of directions by the minister *per se*. Nevertheless, in a sensitive area of policy directly affecting the liberty of the individual, particular care must be taken to ensure that policy is formulated in the full reflection of the public interest. Ideally the forum for such decision making should be Parliament itself but, if Parliament sees fit to delegate, it should not only provide clear statutory guidance as to substance, but should also impose specific procedural obligations on the Secretary of State to ensure that the directions evolve through an open process of consultation, during which the government must be required to justify the position it proposes to adopt. Section 32(6) provides no such procedural stipulations and it seems unlikely, judging from the judicial attitude in *Findlay*, that the courts will agree to intervene to remedy the omission.

In August 1992, following consultation with the Parole Board, the Secretary of State wrote to the chairman enclosing the policy directions which the Board should take into account when considering the release and recall of prisoners.[37]

remain a dwindling population to be dealt with under the old system. The LRCs will therefore remain in place long enough to process the transitional arrangements.

36 SI 1992/1829, *supra*, n. 34, issued under section 50. The role of executive discretion is further discussed in relation to life sentences and in the context of hospital orders in chapter 12.

37 *Directions for Release and Recall* (1992, London: Home Office). The *Report of the Parole Board 1991* (1992, London: Home Office), para. 22, makes reference to consultation.

These directions emphasise first the factors specified in section 32(6) and state that each case must be considered on its individual merits. They then require that, before recommending release, the Board should be satisfied that a) the longer period of supervision provided by parole is likely to reduce the risk of further imprisonable offences, b) the offender has shown by his attitude in custody a readiness to address his offending and has made positive progress in doing so, and c) the resettlement plan will help secure the offender's rehabilitation. The obligation is thus on the Board to satisfy itself, but unless it is so satisfied the presumption lies against release. On the question of risk assessment, the directions merely state that a small risk of violent offending is to be treated as more serious than a larger risk of non-violent offending. The implications arising from the substance of these directions coupled with the new procedural rules will be considered further below.

(7) Conclusions: Policy Formulation

The absence of formal public debate in the form of commissions or inquiries which characterised the early formulation of parole policy, culminating perhaps in the 1983 initiative, has given way in recent years to a more familiar system of independent review and recommendations. While it remains to be seen precisely what impact the recent reforms will have on individual release decisions, it is clear that the opportunity for open debate provided by the Carlisle Committee, for example, served to crystallise some of the major issues emerging from the operation of the original parole scheme, and many of the Committee's resulting recommendations have subsequently found reflection in the 1991 Act.

However, the new Act still leaves considerable policy making power in the hands of the Secretary of State and, while this delegation might be acceptable in principle, it is most unfortunate that little attempt has been made to regulate the process through which the Secretary of State is to fulfil his policy making role. While a duty to consult the Parole Board is imposed on the Secretary of State before he exercises his power under section 50 to extend the powers of the Board in certain ways, no such requirement is imposed on the crucial policy making powers granted by section 32. It is also significant that the Act empowers the Secretary of State to issue procedural rules but does not require those rules to be presented as a statutory instrument. Thus even the most cursory and formal Parliamentary scrutiny of the kind which had been applied to the old procedures relating to the LRCs has been abandoned.[38] The important issues of disclosure to the prisoner and the duty of the Parole Board to give reasons have been left to administrative decision making, with no express requirements to consult interested parties, or even to inform Parliament.[39]

38 The rules applying to the LRCs, although not very detailed, were at least contained in delegated legislation: The LRC Rules 1967, SI 1967/1462.
39 The administrative rules have emerged as rules and CIs.

Finally, the limited role of the court in the process of parole policy formulation should be emphasised. The litigation following Brittan's 1983 initiative starkly illustrates the limitations of the court, both as an evaluator of the substantive validity of administrative policies and as a regulator of the process whereby those policies are formulated. However, in certain areas the court's refusal to intervene has itself had important policy implications. It can be argued, particularly in relation to procedural issues, that when the courts decline to impose common law obligations on decision makers they are, in a negative sense, making policy. As will be seen below, in 1981 the Court of Appeal declined to recognise an obligation on the Parole Board to afford a hearing or give reasons: a 'policy' choice that had a wide and enduring influence on parole decision making procedures.[40]

(c) Application Decisions: Fixed-term Sentences

Up until 1992, and even under the new system, the process of parole decision making in England and Wales was, and remains, largely a paper exercise. Under the old system the main actors were: the local review committees (LRCs), the Parole Board, the parole unit, and the Secretary of State. Every prison establishment containing eligible inmates had to have an LRC.[41] The members were nominated by the governor and appointed by the Secretary of State. The Parole Board, by contrast, has always been a national body. Its members are appointed by the Secretary of State and must include a judge, a psychiatrist, a probation officer and a criminologist or penologist.[42] Originally the Board had 16 members but, by 1990, had grown to approximately 70. The parole unit within the Prison Department of the Home Office manages the parole system and, under the old system authorised each individual grant of parole on behalf of the Secretary of State. Only a small proportion of the most sensitive cases were referred to either a junior minister or to the Secretary of State.

For fixed-term prisoners the pre-1992 process began when the governor identified them as eligible for parole and prepared the papers prior to reference to the LRC. In theory all cases were referred in sufficient time to ensure that all prisoners knew the outcome at least three weeks before the due date. In practice the delays were such that 'quite a number [of prisoners] hear nothing until they have gone past their date'.[43] Each case was considered by a panel of LRC members. The prisoner could make written representations, and would be interviewed by one of the panel members. The interview was not meant to be an assessment, but rather to provide an opportunity for the prisoner to put

40 *Payne* v. *Lord Harris* [1981] 1 WLR 754.
41 Section 59, Criminal Justice Act 1967 and SI 1967/1462, *supra*, n. 38.
42 Originally the composition of the Parole Board was governed by the Criminal Justice Act 1967, section 59 and schedule 2; it is now covered by section 31 and schedule 5 of the Criminal Justice Act 1991.
43 *Supra*, n. 1, para. 121.

forward his case. The LRC member's account of the interview was then attached to the dossier together with any written submissions from the prisoner. The dossier would also include: a statement of prison history; an assessment by prison staff, including a medical report if relevant; a record of any prison offences; a report by the Probation Service; a home circumstances report; details of any previous convictions, and a police report of the present offence.

According to the Carlisle Committee, LRC panel meetings lasted from about one to three hours, at which anything from six to ten cases were considered. Officially, the same criteria were used as those applied by the Parole Board, but the Carlisle Committee observed 'considerable diversity of approach and a good deal of confusion over the test to be applied'.[44] The LRC's recommendation was then recorded on a standard form and, although the LRCs were encouraged to explain their reasoning, very little space was provided for them to do so. It is clear, however, that the vast majority of recommendations were unanimous: an exercise completed for the Carlisle Committee on the 1986 figures showed that all but 3.5 per cent of LRC decisions were unanimous.

Following consideration by the LRC, all papers were sent to the parole unit. Release could be ordered directly without reference to the Parole Board in the case of some positive recommendations, by virtue of section 35 of the Criminal Justice Act 1972. All other positive recommendations had to go to the Board. Negative recommendations in section 33 cases rarely went to the Board, but longer-term cases did go, either if the negative decision was by bare majority of the LRC, or if the prisoner's reconviction prediction score (RPS) was good. The RPS is a measure of statistical probability of reconviction within two years, and is calculated on the basis of 18 variables relating to the prisoner's criminal and social background. The use of such statistical techniques in relation to the assessment of risk in individual cases is discussed further in chapter 12.

About 32 per cent of cases reviewed by the LRCs came before the Parole Board and were considered by panels, typically consisting of four members. The Board considered the same papers as were available to the LRC, with some occasional additions: an RPS might be added, for example, or a recent police report. Each meeting lasted between three and four hours, the papers having been circulated in advance, and considered about 28 cases. Some cases were disposed of in a matter of minutes while others took up to half an hour. Special panels with a reduced case load were convened to consider life-sentence cases. Like the LRCs, the Board panels usually reached unanimous decisions. During two weeks in October 1987 all but 7 per cent of the 325 cases considered were decided unanimously.[45] At the meetings, panel members had a list of the six criteria and would record which criteria formed the basis of any decision not to recommend release.

44 *Ibid.*, para. 126.
45 *Ibid.*, para. 134.

After consideration by the Parole Board the papers were returned to the Parole Unit. All positive recommendations were then screened to ascertain whether there was any danger of public criticism, or any conflict with normal policy. A handful of sensitive cases would then be identified for reference to ministers. All other positive recommendations were authorised without further scrutiny. In a tiny number of cases annually, usually within single figures, the Secretary of State turned down the Board's positive recommendation. According to Wasik and Pease, there is some evidence in the case of fixed-term prisoners that the ministerial veto was used more frequently in electorally sensitive years, and more frequently by Tory Home Secretaries than by their Labour counterparts.[46] Within anything up to three months after the start of proceedings, or even longer if the case had been referred to the minister, the prisoner was informed of the outcome. A negative outcome was conveyed on a standard form. The prisoner was merely told that his or her case had been given full and sympathetic consideration, but that parole had not been authorised. No reasons were given.

A prisoner granted parole was released on licence, and was therefore subject to recall. Under the 1967 Act recall could be ordered by the Secretary of State acting on the advice of the Parole Board, or in urgent cases by the Secretary of State acting on his own (section 62). In all urgent cases, and in any other where the prisoner so requested, the case had to be referred to the Board, and if it ordered immediate release, the prisoner had to be so released, section 62(5). The prisoner was also entitled to be given reasons for his recall, section 62(3). Similar provisions are included in the 1991 Act, section 39 of which provides for the recall of long-term and life-sentence prisoners.

There is little empirical data available in this country concerning the way in which parole decisions are reached in practice. Keith Hawkins, drawing on research conducted in the United States, emphasises the importance attached to the idea of 'time from crime': had the prisoner been in custody long enough to reflect the gravity of the offence?[47] In responding to that question, the individual Board members would assess the prisoner's level of 'wickedness', but, as Hawkins remarks, individual members could easily interpret factual evidence in different ways. The importance of 'time for crime', or in this country the demands of the tariff, was also stressed by Maguire, Pinter and Collis in their study of the review of lifers prior to the 1983 changes.[48] Analysing the decisions reached on lifers between 1977/8, Maguire *et al.* discovered a marked consensus between the professionals involved in assessing individual cases, and emphasised the significance of the role played by the secretariat responsible for compiling the dossiers. The preference for consensus matches

---

46 M. Wasik and K. Pease, 'The Parole Veto and Party Politics' (1986) Crim. LR 379. In 1991 the Home Secretary rejected 13 recommendations for release in relation to fixed-term prisoners (the figure had been 36 in 1990) and 12 in relation to life sentences – *supra*, n. 37.

47 K. Hawkins, 'Assessing Evil' (1983) 23 Brit. Jo. of Crimin. 101.

48 M. Maguire, F. Pinter and C. Collis, 'Dangerousness and the Tariff' (1984) 24 Brit. Jo. of Crimin. 250.

the 'strong momentum towards consensus' within both the LRCs and the Parole Board, discovered more recently by the Carlisle Committee.

This brief account of the pre-1992 procedures applying to the application of parole policy to individual fixed-term prisoners, reveals the old arrangements as falling far short of those required by full process in a number of respects. In the first place, as has already been explained, there existed no formal statutory criteria to guide the decisions of any of the actors involved, and there is evidence that those 'informal' guidelines which did exist were not always fully understood. The Parole Board's plea for clear statutory guidance is particularly revealing here since it does no more than reflect the minimum demands of full process. It is clear that the Board regarded both the pre-1992 criteria and Carlisle's own proposals as insufficiently specific. It was the Board's view that, if it were to be given executive powers to release prisoners, the criteria to be applied to those decisions would have to be articulated with far greater precision, particularly with regard to the nature of the initial presumption.[49]

Secondly, under the original procedures, the prisoner's participation in the process was limited to the right to make written representations and to meet one member of the LRC. The prisoner had no right to the disclosure of the written material on which the Parole Board reached its decision, no right of direct access to the Board, and achieved no reasons for the final decision. Admittedly, in formal terms the Board's role was advisory only, but it was nevertheless required to assess each case, and any notion of full process would have demanded the prisoner's full participation, particularly since the prisoner was, and still is, entirely excluded from participation in the process of ministerial review.

Finally, the role of the Secretary of State served simply to compound the problems. It is hard to find any convincing justification for the involvement of a senior political figure in individual decisions of this nature, where political self interest will almost invariably point against release. The public interest must of course be represented, but private consideration by a politically vulnerable member of the government does not provide an appropriate means of ensuring the full reflection of the public interest. A decision making structure which required the open application of clearly articulated criteria, and before which the Secretary of State was entitled to be represented in individual cases, would be more appropriate.

These decision making procedures were severely criticised in the Carlisle Report, which recommended: full disclosure of reports to the prisoner; the development of 'parole counsellors' to help prisoners with their submissions to the board; an obligation on the Board to give their reasons for the refusal of parole, and a right in the prisoner to complain to the chairman of the Board.[50] On the question of an oral hearing, the Carlisle Committee was divided. A minority were of the view that in cases where, after consideration of the papers,

49 See *supra*, n. 30, for the Parole Board's response to Carlisle's proposals. That response was reproduced in the 1989 Annual Report following the 1990 White Paper, *Report of the Parole Board 1989* (1990, London: Home Office), para. 11.
50 The Carlisle Committee's proposals with regard to procedures are contained in *supra*, n. 1, ch. 8.

the board was inclined to refuse parole, the prisoner should be entitled to an oral hearing. The majority, however, for largely financial and logistical reasons, felt that a paper hearing following disclosure would be sufficient. The Parole Board's initial response to these proposals was mixed and cautious.[51] They expressed the familiar fears that disclosure would result in less candid reporting, and that the giving of reasons would be difficult in practice and would lead to challenge from disappointed prisoners. It was therefore encouraging that the White Paper, recognising the potential of greater openness to improve the quality of decision making, committed the government to 'moving towards disclosing reports made to the board and the board giving reasons for its decision'.[52] On the other hand, the White Paper joined the majority of the Carlisle Committee in rejecting an oral hearing.

As was described above, the 1991 Act leaves the specification of procedures to the Secretary of State. Section 32(5) empowers him to issue rules 'with respect to the proceedings of the board'. These procedures have now been supplied by way of Circular Instruction, CI 26/1992, and will apply to the discretionary conditional release of all prisoners sentenced from October 1992 to fixed terms of four years or over.[53] The review process will remain a largely paper exercise but some significant improvements have been introduced. The parole dossier will be disclosed to the prisoner, although the governor may recommend to the chairman of the Parole Board that certain items be withheld in the interests of national security, for the prevention of disorder or crime, for the protection of information received in confidence, or if it is felt necessary to withhold information on medical grounds. A panel member will visit the holding establishment and interview the prisoner, the panels will be required to give reasons for their decisions, whether they be negative or positive, and to assist them in this a list of factors which should be taken into account are given in the 1992 directions, reproduced in C1 26/1992. Thus, while there are still no oral hearings, prisoners will be better informed and thus better able to make representations to the panels. Nevertheless some reservations remain concerning the operation of the criteria for parole contained in the 1992 directions.

As described above, these directions place considerable emphasis on the risk of re-offending, and require the Parole Board to balance the risk of re-offending during the period when the offender would otherwise have been in custody against the benefit to be derived from supervision. There is, however, no guidance on the level of acceptable risk, beyond the stipulation that the risk of violence is to be regarded as more serious than the risk of non-violent offending. In practice, no doubt, a variety of factors will be taken into account in reaching individual decisions and some panels will be more risk-averse than others, but the absence of clear guidance in the directions reflects the difficulties inherent in using risk assessment as a guide to early release. Indeed the Carlisle Committee itself attracted some criticism for giving insufficient consideration to the assessment of risk. Adverse comparisons were drawn

51 *Supra*, n. 30, paras 9–11.
52 *Supra*, n. 32, para. 6.26.
53 CI 26/1992, 'Criminal Justice Act: The Discretionary Conditional Release Scheme'.

between the efforts being made in Canada to develop sophisticated statistical analyses of risk and the relative lack of rigour with which the issue is tackled in this country.[54]

The directions in CI 26/1992 also require the Parole Board, before recommending parole, to be satisfied that 'the offender has shown by his attitude and behaviour in custody that he is willing to address his offending and has made positive efforts and progress in doing so'. Strictly, the stipulation would seem to require evidence of positive improvement. It will no longer be sufficient for the panel to be assured that the prisoner has kept out of trouble. The prison reports in the dossier will therefore take on a far greater significance, and it is to be hoped that the panels will be prepared to challenge inadequate reports in order to uncover any positive evidence that might exist, rather than merely to accept silence as indicating an absence of 'positive efforts'. The stipulation will also question the true 'voluntariness' of any participation in treatment programmes which purport to address offending. The problem of 'coerced' consent is considered further in the context of special hospitals.

(d) Validation Decisions: Fixed-term Prisoners

(1) Internal

As is generally the case at the validation stage, the ability of an individual prisoner effectively to question a parole decision, whether before an internal or an external validator, will be greatly dependent on his or her knowledge of the criteria governing the particular decision and the grounds on which it was based. In these respects, therefore, some improvements have been achieved by the 1992 innovations. Prisoners will have access to the dossiers and will be informed of the reasons for the panel decision. It is not clear how far they are to have access to the criteria contained in the 1992 directions but it is to be hoped that these will at least be available in prison libraries and published in the annual reports of the Parole Board. The wide dissemination of the criteria would also enable the interested public more generally to understand and monitor the decisions of the Board. The mechanisms available for the internal validation of parole decisions at the instigation of individual prisoners are not, however, extensive and relate primarily to procedural issues.

According to CI 26/1992, on receipt of the Parole Board decision a prisoner has the right under the requests and complaints procedure to write to the chairman of the Parole Board and/or to the parole unit. However, a further review will only be authorised in exceptional cases where there has been a change of circumstance, or where the Parole Board was not aware of some information which would have affected the decision, or where procedural

54 See, particularly, N. Polvi and K. Pease, 'Parole and its Problems: a Canadian–English Comparison' (1991) 30 Howard Jo. of Crim. Jus. 218. The attitude of the courts to these problems is considered below in the context of life sentences. The issue is also discussed in chapter 12.

errors have occurred. With particular regard to details contained in the dossier it is apparent from the Circular that there will be an attempt to resolve any dispute locally if possible. As will be seen below, the position with regard to the discretionary lifer panels is more formal. There the relevant rules empower the individual panels to issue directions concerning the service of documents, for example, and disclosure, and specifically vest the chairman of the Parole Board with an appellate role.[55] Finally, since the Parole Board is itself an independent body, it is not envisaged that the proposed complaints adjudicator will have any jurisdiction over parole decisions.

In addition to the resolution of individual complaints, internal validation mechanisms may also perform a general monitoring role. In this respect the parole unit receives all panel decisions and inspects them for compliance with the directions.

(2) The Courts

In the main, the courts have played a very limited role in the review of either the procedure or substance of parole decision making in the case of fixed-term prisoners. The vast proportion of judiciary activity has related to life sentences, and is considered below. *Re Findlay* was an exception in so far as it concerned policy with regard to both life and fixed-term sentences; but, as already described, the courts in that case proved most respectful of the executive.[56] However, although the process of release from fixed-term sentences had seldom been the object of direct judicial scrutiny, up until the 1992 reforms the attitude of the Parole Board to its procedural obligations in general was greatly influenced by the case of Roger Payne, a mandatory life-sentence prisoner.[57]

Roger Payne was convicted of murder in 1968 and sentenced to life imprisonment. His application for release on licence was refused and he sought a declaration that, among other things, he was entitled to be told the reasons for the refusal. Much of the argument in the Court of Appeal centred on the precise nature of the statutory requirements, and considerable significance was attached to the fact that, while the giving of reasons was obligatory in the context of recall, there was no such requirement in the case of a refusal by the Parole Board to recommend release. Whatever the statutory obligations, however, the court recognised that the common law principles of natural justice were potentially available as a supplement. In deciding to make no use of them in the context of parole, the judges resorted to a wide variety of arguments, some more convincing than others. Shaw LJ was plainly troubled by the fact that 'a prisoner might find in being told the reasons for a refusal a specious and insincere means of creating a totally misleading impression by his conduct thereafter'[58] – do not reveal the rules for fear they might be

55 See rule 9, The Parole Board Rules (1992).
56 *Supra*, n. 18.
57 *Payne* v. *Lord Harris* [1981] 2 All ER 842.
58 *Ibid.*, p.850.

manipulated. But finally, as Denning LJ freely admitted, it was a question of policy: 'what does public policy demand as best to be done? To give reasons or to withhold them?'.[59] Their lordships were ultimately unanimous in believing that the weight of argument was against the giving of reasons. Parole was a privilege, the Parole Board was an expert and advisory body which should not be required to provide reasons. Indeed, any obligation to do so would hamper its work, provide ammunition for litigious prisoners, and inhibit the production of candid reports.

A number of points should be made. In the first place, the influence exercised by the *Payne* case over both the attitude of subsequent courts and the practice of the Parole Board supports the conclusion of the previous chapter that adjudication occurring at the validation stage can in practice, for better or ill, fulfil a major policy making role. Secondly, influential though it might be, individual court adjudication is not the appropriate forum for policy formulation. Although Denning's bare reference to public policy is quite in keeping with the aims of full process as understood here, the evidence available to the Court of Appeal when identifying the requirements of public policy falls far short of that which would be demanded by any attempt to reflect the broad public interest as required by full process.

Finally, the efficacy of a mechanism for validation is dependent on the standards that mechanism seeks to enforce. Arguably, the narrow attitude towards procedural fairness adopted by the Court of Appeal in *Payne* significantly reduced the efficacy of subsequent reviewing courts charged with the task of assessing the adequacy of discharge procedures.[60] *Payne* successfully froze the attitude of subsequent reviewing courts for over a decade.[61] It remains to be seen whether the courts will concern themselves with the procedures provided under the new system, and whether the change of heart with regard to lifers, represented by *Wilson*, will be reflected in the context of fixed-term release.[62] Although the panels operating under the new system will, for example, be under no statutory duty to provide reasons, CI 26/1992 requiring them to do so should certainly create a legitimate expectation on the part of the parole applicant, and it will be interesting to see how far the courts will be prepared to police the fulfilment of that expectation by ensuring that the reasons given are adequate.

In the absence of statutory release criteria, any attempt to challenge the substance of a parole decision under the 1967 Act was unlikely to succeed, and indeed such challenges were rare and limited to cases involving life sentences (see below). The introduction of statutory criteria by the 1991 Act is unlikely

59 *Ibid.*, p. 846.
60 See the discussion of *Hague* in chapter 6.
61 See, for example, Stuart-Smith LJ's statement in *R* v. *Parole Board, ex p. Bradley* [1990] 1 WLR 134, at p. 150: 'We acknowledge that there is much force in the argument that reasons and reports should be made available to those who are considered for parole . . . But, unless we can distinguish *Payne's* case, which we cannot, it is not open to us to embark upon the public policy considerations of whether natural justice requires disclosure of reports and reasons.'
62 *R* v. *Parole Board, ex p. Wilson* [1992] 2 All ER 576. See below.

to change things greatly. Section 32(6) is addressed to the Secretary of State when issuing directions, and is thus not directly applicable to panel decisions. The directions in CI 26/1992 themselves, although providing a list of factors which should be taken into account by Parole Board panels in their consideration of fixed-term cases, give no indication of the weight to be attached to each factor, nor do they provide any guidance as to levels of acceptable risk. Thus, while the courts may be able to challenge the exclusion of a listed factor from consideration, it will be very difficult for them to question the weight attached to each factor in an individual case, or to challenge a panel's judgment as to either the level or the acceptability of any risk.

(e) Release from Life Sentences

(1) Policy Formulation

As in the case of the discretionary release of fixed-term prisoners, the structure for the release of prisoners from life sentences has recently undergone major review and reform. In relation to life sentences, the power of executive release has a long history. Even before legislative intervention, the executive has possessed the power, originally through the prerogative, to release life-sentence prisoners.[63] In 1965 the Murder (Abolition of the Death Penalty) Act required the Home Secretary to consult the Lord Chief Justice and the trial judge, if still available, before releasing a prisoner sentenced to life for murder. The 1967 Criminal Justice Act extended to all life sentences the obligation to consult, and introduced the additional requirement that the Home Secretary only release when recommended to do so by the Parole Board. To an extent, therefore, the release on licence of lifers was incorporated within the parole structure, but there was a crucial difference: in the case of lifers there was no MQP specified in the legislation, the date of first review by the Parole Board was technically within the discretion of the Home Secretary.

Originally, all life-sentence cases were referred to the LRC not later than seven years into the sentence.[64] In 1973, in order to involve the Parole Board at an earlier stage, a joint committee of the Parole Board and the Home Office was created to consider all cases at the three to four-year point in order to fix a date either for first review or for reassessment by the joint committee. In 1983 the whole system was reorganised in light of Brittan's policy initiative. Brittan declared his intention to exercise his discretion as Home Secretary so that murderers of police or prison officers, terrorist murderers, sexual or sadistic murderers of children, and murderers by firearms in the course of robbery could usually expect to serve at least 20 years in custody. The joint committee was disbanded, and the Home Secretary arranged to consult the judiciary, three or four years after trial, in order to gain their views of the period

---

63 S. McCabe, 'The Powers and Purposes of the Parole Board' (1985) Crim. LR 489.

64 See *Report of the Select Committee on Murder and Life Imprisonment* HL Paper 78–1 (1989, London: HMSO), part 8, for an excellent account of the evolution of the pre-1992 system for the release of life-sentence prisoners.

necessary to satisfy the demands of retribution and deterrence, the tariff period. The system was to apply to all life sentences whether mandatory – imposed for murder – or discretionary.[65]

As was seen above, the overall policy behind Brittan's initiative survived the challenge mounted in the *Findlay* case. The amended system for establishing the tariff, and thus the date for the first review of a discretionary life sentence, was, however, criticised by the courts. In *Ex p. Handscomb* the Divisional Court felt that the tariff period for discretionary lifers should be fixed with reference to the judicial view, and held that it was unreasonable of the Secretary of State to delay for three to four years before consulting the judges: he should do so immediately after the trial.[66] Following this decision, the system was amended to enable the trial judge to write to the Home Secretary via the Lord Chief Justice immediately after the trial to convey his view of the period necessary to satisfy retribution and deterrence. A junior minister on behalf of the Home Secretary then, in accordance with those views, fixed the tariff period, which itself determined the date of first review. With the benefit of evidence sought by the House of Lords Select Committee on Murder and Life Imprisonment it became clear that, in practice, the Home Secretary regarded himself as bound by the judicial view of the tariff in discretionary life sentences, but not so bound in the case of mandatory sentences.[67] In the months between April and September 1988 the Home Secretary set a higher tariff than that indicated by the judiciary in 63 out of 106 mandatory sentences referred to him.

So by the mid-1980s a system for the release of life-sentence prisoners had evolved which, while based essentially on the 1967 statutory structure, was fashioned in terms of its detail by ministerial decision constrained by court intervention. The main difference between the resulting structure and that applying to fixed-term prisoners lay in the mechanism for determining the date of first review by the LRC. In this regard there was a significant distinction in practice between mandatory and discretionary lifers. For the discretionary lifers the crucial tariff period from which the first review date was calculated was set on the basis of advice from the presumed experts in the field: the judiciary, one at least of whom, the trial judge, would have heard the evidence. But it was not set in open court and was not subject to appeal. For the mandatory lifer, on the other hand, the judicial view, however inadequately acquired and communicated, was merely advisory. His tariff period was in the gift of a junior minister.

The Secretary of State was also responsible for the recall of life-sentence prisoners. Normally, as described above, recall would only be ordered by the Secretary of State on the advice of the Parole Board, but in urgent cases he had the power to act on his own, section 62(2). In all urgent cases, and in any Parole Board recall, where the prisoner so requested, the case had to be referred to the Board, and if it recommended immediate release the prisoner

65 Parl. Debs., 1984–5, vol. 76, Written Answers, 1 April 1985, col. 443.
66 *R* v. *Secretary of State for the Home Dept, ex p. Handscomb* (1987) 86 Crim. Ap. R 59.
67 *Supra*, n. 64, paras 154–6.

had to be so released. It was the only circumstance under the pre-1992 structure where the Parole Board had more than advisory powers.

In the years following the *Handscomb* decision the structure for the release and recall of life-sentence prisoners, both discretionary and to a lesser extent mandatory, has come under increasing pressure from a number of sources, and has been the subject of recent statutory reform. The structure for the release and recall of discretionary life-sentence prisoners will be considered first.

(a) Discretionary Life Sentences

In so far as discretionary life sentences are concerned, the prevalence of executive discretion with regard to both release and recall has now been successfully challenged before the European Court of Human Rights (ECHR). In 1981 the ECHR held that articles 5(1) and 5(4) of the European Convention guaranteed a mentally disordered offender compulsorily detained under a restricted hospital order regular access to a 'court' to determine the lawfulness of his detention.[68] In 1987 these principles were applied to a prisoner serving a discretionary life sentence who had been released and recalled on several occasion.[69] Weeks' life sentence had originally been imposed for the purposes of social protection because of his mental instability and potential dangerousness. His offence was relatively trivial. Mental instability and dangerousness are conditions which are susceptible to change over time, and Weeks was thus entitled, under the European Convention, to test their validity before a 'court'. According to the ECHR, Weeks' right of access to the Parole Board and his ability to seek judicial review were insufficient to meet this requirement. While the Parole Board was sufficiently independent and impartial to constitute a 'court', it had insufficient power and could only order release immediately after recall. Procedurally, it also fell far short of what was required of a court. Further, the control offered by the reviewing court was insufficient to meet the requirements of article 5(4) since the grounds for judicial review were too narrow fully to confront the question of the 'lawfulness' of the detention: whether the detention 'was consistent with and therefore justified by the objectives of the indeterminate sentence imposed'.

Given a generous interpretation, this judgment of the ECHR carried broad implications for the release structure for all discretionary life-sentence prisoners held after the expiry of their tariff period. Such prisoners have, by definition, served the period necessary to fulfil the requirements of retribution and deterrence, and their continued detention can only be justified in terms of social protection. The government, however, chose to take no action, presumably hoping that *Weeks* was special to its facts.

At the time of the *Weeks* decision, domestic pressure for change was also mounting, and in July 1988, with support from all political parties, a House of Lords Select Committee was set up to consider the crime of murder, the

---

68 *X* v. *United Kingdom* (1981) 4 EHRR 181.
69 *Weeks* v. *United Kingdom* (1988) 10 EHRR 293.

penalty it should attract, and 'the working arrangement for reaching decisions on the release of those serving sentences for murder'. The select committee reported in 1989 and, while its report concluded that the life sentence should remain available for murder, it recommended that it should no longer be mandatory.[70] The report envisaged its use in two situations: where there was a degree of uncertainty, arising from the prisoner's mental condition, as to the risk he would present if released at the end of a determinate sentence; and where a particularly outrageous murder had occurred. In either case the judge would specify in open court the period he considered appropriate to satisfy the requirements of retribution and deterrence – the penal sanction. The period would be appealable by either side, but not subject to revision by the executive. On the expiry of the penal sanction, release would depend on the degree of risk presented by the offender. The committee recommended that the release decision by taken by a specially constituted tribunal. It should have all the characteristics of a court under the European Convention, including, most particularly, independence of the executive. All relevant documents should be disclosed to the prisoner, who would have the right to appear and to be represented. Release would still be on licence, but recall would be subject to the approval of the tribunal.[71]

Although the government made reference to the Select Committee's report in the 1990 White Paper, its considered response was overtaken by a further judgment of the ECHR.[72] The decision in *Thynne, Wilson and Gunnell* v. *The United Kingdom* makes it clear that the principles expressed in *Weeks* cannot be restricted to the facts of that case alone.[73] According to *Thynne, Wilson and Gunnell*, the requirements of article 5(4) apply to all discretionary life-sentence prisoners who are detained, on the basis of their mental instability and dangerousness, after the expiry of the punitive, or tariff, period of their sentence. While the ECHR accepted that it might be hard to distinguish the punitive from the protective element in a discretionary life sentence, it felt that, at some point, however heinous the offence, the punitive element must expire, leaving the continued detention to be justified solely on the grounds of the prisoner's potential dangerousness. A person's capacity to be dangerous must change over time and thus, on the principles of *Weeks*, anyone detained solely on the grounds of their dangerousness must be entitled regularly to challenge the lawfulness of that detention before a court.

When the Criminal Justice Bill was first published in November 1990 no concessions were made to the ECHR ruling: the government presumably felt no urgency attached to its obligation to comply. Following widespread revolt in the House of Lords over the retention of the mandatory life sentence for murder, however, the government, by way of compromise at the report stage of

---

70 *Supra*, n. 64.
71 For discussion of these aspects of the report, see G. Richardson, 'The Select Committee and the Sentencing Structure for Murder' (1990) Howard J. of Crim. J. 300.
72 White Paper, *supra*, n. 32, ch. 6.
73 *Thynne, Wilson and Gunnell* v. *United Kingdom* (1991) 13 EHRR 666.

the bill, finally introduced provisions to enable the Parole Board to order the release of discretionary life-sentence prisoners.

Section 34 of the Criminal Justice Act 1991 empowers the Parole Board to direct the release of a discretionary life-sentence prisoner if the Secretary of State has referred the case to the Parole Board, and it is satisfied 'that it is no longer necessary for the protection of the public that the prisoner should be confined', section 34(4)(b). For the purposes of section 34, a discretionary life-sentence prisoner is one whose sentence is imposed for a violent or sexual offence for which the sentence is not fixed by law, and the sentencing court has ordered that section 34 apply once the prisoner has served 'the relevant part' of his sentence. 'The relevant part' of the sentence shall be that period that the court considers appropriate in view of the seriousness of the offence, and shall be specified in the order of the court. A discretionary life-sentence prisoner may require the Secretary of State to refer his case to the Board once he has served the relevant part of his sentence, and at two-year periods thereafter. After release, a life-sentence prisoner is on licence, and so subject to recall, 'until his death', section 37(3). Thus the new scheme provides for the specification of the relevant (or tariff) period by the trial judge, and empowers the Parole Board to release the prisoner after the expiry of that period: there is no executive veto. The release is on licence, and may be subject to such conditions as the Secretary of State specifies 'in accordance with recommendations of the board', section 37(5). The baldness of the statutory provisions themselves testifies to the speed with which they were introduced to the bill following pressure from the House of Lords. They came into force in October 1992, and on 31 August rules were made specifying the procedures to be followed by the Parole Board when hearing discretionary cases, both for initial release and on reference after recall.[74] The content of these rules is considered at 2 below but, although it is too early to comment on the details of the scheme, some preliminary points may be made.

In the first place, it is clear from the provisions of section 34 that it was designed to provide the minimum necessary to fulfil the requirements of the *Thynne, Wilson and Gunnell* judgment. It is limited to discretionary lifers who are so identified by the court. Mandatory life sentences, which the government was so determined to retain for murder, are not included. It is also possible under the section to envisage the imposition of a life sentence, for an offence for which it is not mandatory, in a case where the trial judge does not order the application of section 34. In such a case the release of the prisoner presumably remains in the gift of the Home Secretary, and in the terms of the European Convention must be justified on punitive rather than social protective grounds. However, for the discretionary lifer under section 34 the tariff (or relevant part) is now to be specified in open court and will be subject to appeal, a significant improvement on the old post-*Handscomb* procedure. The Act also introduced transitional arrangements under which all of the more than 500 prisoners serving discretionary life sentences imposed before October 1992 were issued with certificates specifying their tariff dates.[75] In 300 to 350 of these

74 The Parole Board Rules 1992.
75 For the transitional arrangements see sch. 12, para. 9, Criminal Justice Act 1991. In *R* v.

cases the tariff date had passed by 1 October 1992, and they thus became eligible for a hearing under section 34.

Secondly, it is unfortunate that the 1991 Act neither gave any guidance on the content of the procedural rules to be applied to the discretionary lifer panels, nor required those rules to be promulgated as a statutory instrument.[76] They are administrative rules only. Thirdly, it is most regrettable that the government has followed the pattern adopted by the Mental Health Act 1983, and has required the Parole Board to be 'satisfied that it is no longer necessary for the protection of the public that the prisoner should be confined'. Such statutory wording effectively creates a presumption against release which must be rebutted. Indeed, as will be seen in chapter 12, a similar provision in the 1983 Act has been interpreted in practice as requiring the patient seeking discharge to satisfy the Mental Health Review Tribunal that he is no longer a danger. In the context of a discretionary life sentence the presumption should be in favour of release unless the case for further detention is made out to the satisfaction of the Parole Board. It should not be up to the prisoner, who will have served the appropriate tariff period, to establish that no grounds exist to justify his or her continued detention. The implications of the wording of section 34(4)(b) for the procedures to be adopted by the discretionary lifer panels is discussed below.

Finally, the stipulation that the Parole Board must be 'satisfied that it is no longer necessary for the protection of the public that the prisoner should be confined', implies that the public must be protected from some potential harm at the hands of the prisoner. However, the section gives no clear guidance to the Board as to what is required, either in terms of the degree of likelihood of the harm occurring or of the gravity of the harm itself. Further guidance must be provided; it should not be left to the reviewing courts on an incremental basis to formulate this important aspect of policy.[77]

(b) Mandatory Life Sentences

The position with regard to mandatory life sentences remains much as it was in 1987, being largely unchanged by the 1991 Act. A tariff period is set by the Secretary of State in consultation with the judiciary, and the date of first review by the Parole Board is fixed with refernce to this period. On review, the Parole Board then decides whether or not to recommend release, and if it does so recommend the Secretary of State retains the final power of decision (section 35). Following the judgment in *Handscomb*, the Secretary of State

---

Secretary of State for Home Dept, ex p. Walsh [1992] *The Independent* May 8, the Court of Appeal confirmed that a discretionary lifer sentenced prior to October 1992 was entitled to know the length of his tariff period.

76 See, by way of contrast, the Mental Health Tribunal Rules 1983, SI 1983/942.

77 The difficulties encountered by a reviewing court when attempting to articulate levels of risk are well-illustrated by the *Bradley* case, *supra*, n. 61. The issue is discussed further below. See the criticism levelled at the Carlisle Committee with regard to its treatment of the assessment of risk, *supra*, n. 54.

consults the judiciary immediately after the trial as to their views on the appropriate tariff period but, as the figures listed above at page 195 indicate, he has never regarded himself as bound by those views. That he is not bound in law was confirmed by the Court of Appeal in *Ex p. Doody and others*, where Lord Justice Glidewell held that the Secretary of State was free to depart from the views of the judiciary in mandatory cases if he had good reason for doing so.[78] On the other hand the Court of Appeal did confirm that a mandatory life-sentence prisoner should be informed of the judicial view of his tariff, and of any comments made by the judges which might influence the Secretary of State's decision, and should be allowed to make representations in writing to the Secretary of State prior to the setting of his tariff. With regard to this aspect of the judgment, however, a stay has been granted pending appeal to the House of Lords.

The European litigation which eventually forced change on the structure for the release of discretionary life sentences did not directly affect mandatory life sentences. The reasoning behind the ECHR's judgment on the application of article 5(4) to discretionary life sentences and hospital orders cannot be directly applied to the mandatory life sentence for murder if the official justification for that sentence is maintained: the requirements of deterrence and retribution are not factors which change over time in the case of a single prisoner. However, the mandatory system is now facing direct challenge in Europe, and it remains to be seen for how long international pressure for change can be deflected. In the mean time the government retains executive control over the release of murderers, and it can only be hoped that the actual operation of this fundamentally indefensible system will be in some way ameliorated by the influence of the changes imposed on the release of discretionary lifers. Indeed in December 1992 the Home Secretary announced that, from April 1993, mandatory life-sentence prisoners will be given access to their parole dossiers, and will be given the reasons for the Parole Board's decision and for any negative decision of the Secretary of State.[79]

(c) Conclusions

The process of policy formulation in relation to lifers over recent years has been characterised by a marked reluctance to act on the part of government. No steps towards reform were taken following the challenge from Europe in 1987, nor after the House of Lords Select Committee Report in 1990. Even after the unambiguous ruling from the ECHR in 1990, nothing was done until the government's hand was forced by opposition within the House of Lords,

---

78 *R* v. *Secretary of State for the Home Dept, ex p. Doody and others* [1992] *The Times*, 8 May.

79 In *R* v. *Secretary of State ex p. Creamer* (1992) *The Independent*, 23 October, a mandatory lifer failed to persuade the High Court to follow *Wilson* (see below) and to order disclosure and reasons despite *Payne*, but Rose LJ sent a strong message to the Court of Appeal indicating that he considered it was now time to reverse the earlier decision. It seems that the Secretary of State has now acted to pre-empt direct pressure from the courts.

and even then only the minimum reforms necessary to comply with the European requirements were introduced.

Within this reluctant progress towards change, the important role played by the House of Lords in its legislative capacity is of considerable interest. It is clear that the members of the House of Lords, whose familiarity with the issues had been enhanced by the Select Committee, and who contain within their number a group of high-ranking judges, took a very different view of the public interest from that taken by the directly elected and tightly disciplined members of the House of Commons. The implications to be drawn from this in terms of full process in relation to policy formulation are considerable, and must go far beyond the scope of this study. However, it is evident that, while the 'public' interest reflected by the House of Commons will typically be dictated by the interests of the government of the day, the politically less constrained membership of the House of Lords can range more freely. Whether this alone provides a sufficient argument for the retention of a second House must be considered elsewhere, but it certainly illustrates with depressing clarity the very limited ability of the House of Commons to carry its consideration of the public interest beyond the demands of daily politics.

Whatever the influences at play within the formulation process, however, the statutory provisions that have emerged have done so without the benefit of any considered release strategy beyond the need to comply with the European requirements. As a result the provisions leave many issues unresolved. Some have been dealt with by the procedural rules issued by the Secretary of State, others will inevitably require resolution through the courts, while the whole question of mandatory life sentences still awaits reform. Such a formulation process falls far short of the fully participatory ideal. In the first place, Parliamentary discussion of the revised structure has been limited. The provisions themselves were introduced at the report stage of the bill, and the necessary procedural rules have been issued, with no formal period of consultation, by way of administrative rules rather than statutory instruments. Secondly, if any clear guidance is to be given to the discretionary lifer panels with regard to the criteria for release, the test contained in section 34 will require amplification. Unfortunately, the domestic courts acting as adjudicators in particular cases are not the appropriate forum for the provision of this amplification in relation to such a complex area of substantive policy. Quite apart from the absence of public participation and consultation, the courts are not equipped to perform such a task. The case of *Bradley*,[80] which is discussed further below, illustrates the difficulties faced by courts when required to formulate a generally applicable test in a highly complex area with inadequate statutory guidance.

(2) Application Decisions

Under the old structure the procedures adopted by the Parole Board for the

---

80 *Supra*, n. 61.

application of release policy to individual lifers' cases, whether discretionary or mandatory, were broadly similar to those adopted in relation to fixed-term prisoners, and have been described in that context. Before the Secretary of State the prisoner had no procedural rights. Further, the restrictive attitude to procedural fairness adopted in relation to the Parole Board's procedures for deciding its initial recommendation were extended to its role with regard to recall. The 1967 Act stipulated that the recalled prisoner be given reasons for the recall and be allowed to make representation in writing to the Parole Board, section 62(3). Gunnell, a recalled life-sentence prisoner, sought to challenge the process of his recall. He argued that he was entitled to a written statement of reasons and a hearing before the Parole Board, involving at the very least the disclosure of police and medical reports. He was unsuccessful before both the Divisional Court and the Court of Appeal.[81] Neither court was prepared to read into the statutory requirements more than was absolutely necessary. The circumstances of the case were such, the court felt, that the prisoner must have understood the reasons, and the statute did not specifically require a written statement to be given. Neither did the statute demand an oral hearing or full disclosure of adverse reports.

The new structure for the release of discretionary life-sentence prisoners under section 34 of the 1991 Act, and for the review of their recall (section 39), was introduced specifically to comply with the requirements of the European Convention, and the content of the procedural rules issued in 1992 must presumably have been designed with that end in view. While sections 34 and 39(5) refer merely to the powers of the Board to order release, the rules make it clear that individual cases will be dealt with by panels of three Parole Board members, including one judge who shall act as chair. Such a body, having executive powers, should be regarded as sufficiently independent to constitute a 'court' under the European Convention. Indeed, the new panels would seem to be truly adjudicatory in structure, although formally there might be no dispute between indentifiable parties, as required by the classic definition of adjudication.[82]

Under the 1992 rules the precise details of the procedure are left to the discretion of the chair of each panel, but certain important stipulations are made. Specific information and reports must be submitted to the Board by the Secretary of State prior to the hearing and, subject to an exception on the grounds of adverse affect to the health or welfare of the prisoners or others, the submitted reports and information must be disclosed to the prisoner (rule 5). The prisoner may be legally represented at the hearing (rule 6), and legal aid is available. The prisoner may apply to the panel chair for permission to call witnesses, and any refusal of such permission must be accompanied by reasons (rule 7). The decisions of individual panel chairs on such issues as disclosure are subject to appeal to the chairman of the Parole Board (rule 9). The prisoner may also put questions to any witnesses at the hearing, rule 13(3).

81   *R* v. *Secretary of State for the Home Dept. ex p. Gunnell* [1984] Crim. LR 170 DC and [1985] Crim. LR 105 AC.
82   See the discussion in chapter 4.

And, finally, the panel's decision must be communicated to the prisoner in writing with reasons (rule 15).

Such a procedure marks a considerable advance on the old, non-participatory, Board decisions. However, the provision for non-disclosure of reports to the prisoner would seem unjustifiably wide, particularly in view of the Court of Appeal's strong support for disclosure in *Wilson*, and it is therefore to be hoped that the courts will not regard the wording of rule 9 as ousting their jurisdiction to review the appellate decisions of the Parole Board chairman on this issue.[83] Finally, the new hearings might attract criticism on the ground that they are not public (rule 12).[84] While the privacy imposed by the rules in this context was perhaps inspired by the logistical difficulties involved in holding public hearings within high-security establishments, the more fundamental difficulties involved in achieving appropriate public participation in such sensitive decision making are discussed further in relation to Mental Health Review Tribunals.

As was described above, before releasing a prisoner, section 34(4)(b) requires the Parole Board to be satisfied 'that it is no longer necessary for the protection of the public that the prisoner should be confined'. The presumption is thus against release: unless the Board is satisfied otherwise the prisoner will remain detained. Such a presumption, in the context of individual liberty, places a significant obligation on the Board to takes steps to satisfy itself if it is to reach decisions that fully reflect the public interest. In early chapters it has been suggested that, although an inquisitorial model of decision making might be preferred where facts are in issue, adversarial adjudication might be better suited to decisions, such as those before the Board's which turn on opinion. In the light of the wording of section 34(4)(b), however, any such initial preference must be overborne. Boards cannot rely on the ability of the individual prisoner to provide the evidence necessary to oust the initial presumption in favour of continued detention. They must, in other words, be encouraged to become actively inquisitorial. The Boards must themselves challenge the evidence of the Secretary of State in favour of continued detention and must help to seek out any evidence in favour of release. On their face, the procedural rules place no such obligations on the Boards, and it thus seems likely that the Parole Board's willingness to pursue the demands of full process will greatly depend on the attitude adopted by the individual panel chairs, and on the assiduity with which their reasoning is policed. Predictive assessment of the type demanded by section 34(4)(b) present individual

---

83 *Ex p. Wilson, supra*, n. 62. Rule 9, Parole Board Rules 1992 stipulates that the decision of the Parole Board chairman 'shall be final'. For the court's attitude to such ouster clauses, see H. W. R. Wade, *Administrative Law* 6th. edn (1988, Oxford: Oxford University Press), ch. 19.

84 Neither *Weeks* nor *Thynne, Wilson and Gunnell* stipulates that article 5(4) requires a public hearing, although rule 21, Mental Health Review Tribunal Rules 1983, SI 1983/942, allows the patient to request a public hearing. Further, even article 6, which guarantees a fair and public hearing in the determination of civil rights and obligations, has been interpreted in *Campbell and Fell* v. *United Kingdom* (1985) 7 EHRR 165, as permitting the exclusion of press and public from prison disciplinary hearings.

decision makers with particular difficulties. The general issues raised are discussed in more detail in the context of Mental Health Review Tribunals.

The secrecy and lack of participation that characterised the release decision itself was also evident in relation to the process of setting the tariff. As far as discretionary lifers are concerned, as has been described above, this has all changed. The relevant period is now specified in court and is appealable, but it remains to be seen on the basis of what evidence it will be set, and how far the prisoner will be allowed to participate in the decision making.[85] For mandatory lifers the position remains much as it was before, although, subject to the impending appeal, they may soon be told the judicial view, and may be permitted to make representations to the Secretary of State.[86] Finally, it should be noted that the 1991 Act makes no provision for the conversion of a release on licence to an absolute release, although it does provide for the cancellation of conditions by the Secretary of State 'in accordance with recommendations of the board', section 37(5).

At the time of writing, subject to the eventual outcome of *Ex p. Doody*, the structure for the release of mandatory life- sentence prisoners remains as it was prior to October 1992. However, from April 1993 the dossier will be disclosed to the prisoner and reasons will be given.

(3) Validation Decisions

The question of internal validation was dealt with in relation to fixed-term prisoners. The discussion here will concentrate on the courts.

(a) Courts

Since the mid-1980s the High Court has become increasingly involved in determining applications for judicial review of different aspects of the structure for the release of life-sentence prisoners. However, as suggested above in the context of fixed-term release, there are significant limits imposed on the courts' ability to act as an effective mechanism for independent validation. Constitutionally they can only comment on the formal legality of the decision in question, judging that legality either by reference to the express words of the empowering statute or by reference to the principles of the common law. In order to understand better the courts' performance in relation to the release of lifers it will be useful to distinguish between those cases which have involved essentially procedural issues and those that have examined the application of the release criteria themselves.

---

85 See A. Ashworth, *Sentencing and Criminal Justice* (1992, London: Weidenfeld and Nicolson), ch. 11, for a discussion of the factual basis on which sentencing decisions are reached.
86 *Ex p. Doody, supra*, n. 78.

(i) Procedures

Over the last ten years the processes immediately surrounding the release and recall of life-sentence prisoners have been subjected to much judicial scrutiny, the flavour of which has recently changed significantly. Initially the courts displayed a marked reluctance to develop the requirements of the common law. The considerable influence exercised by the restrictive Court of Appeal decision in *Payne*, involving a mandatory life sentence, has already been mentioned. In *Gunnell* the Court of Appeal, finding support from *Payne*, refused to use the common law to supplement the bare statutory requirements relating to the recall of a discretionary life-sentence prisoner released on licence.[87] The prisoner was entitled to the statutory procedures and no more. Similarly, in *Bradley*, a case involving another discretionary sentence, the Divisional Court regarded itself as bound by *Payne*, and both refused to recognise a right to the disclosure of the reports on which the release decision was made, and denied the prisoner any right to reasons for the decision of the Parole Board.[88] While it was technically open to the *Bradley* and *Gunnell* courts to distinguish *Payne*, on the ground that Payne's sentence was mandatory and the others were discretionary, it is perhaps unsurprising that they refused to do so. Arguably, in both *Gunnell* and *Bradley* the court was adopting a constitutionally correct position. In *Gunnell* it refused to ask more of the decision maker than was demanded by Parliament, while the court in *Bradley* refused to tinker with the orthodoxy as expressed in *Payne*, and referred the issue to Parliament. In the words of Stuart-Smith LJ,

unless we can distinguish *Payne's* case, which we cannot, it is not open to us to embark upon the public policy considerations of whether natural justice requires disclosure of reports and reasons. This is a matter for Parliament.[89]

In January 1992 Benjamin Wilson, a 76-year-old man serving a discretionary life sentence for buggery, and one of the successful applicants before the ECHR in *Thynne, Wilson and Gunnell*, sought a declaration that the material before the Parole Board relating to his case should be disclosed to him. Although, if he had not already been released, his review by the Parole Board would eventually be covered by the transitional arrangements coming into force in October 1992, his review in early 1992 was still conducted under the old arrangements. In the Court of Appeal an impressive catalogue of factors in favour of disclosure was presented, ranging from the procedures required of Mental Health Review Tribunals to the decision of the ECHR and the subsequent enactment of the 1991 Act, the combined force of which led Taylor LJ to declare:

For my part, unless otherwise bound by authority, I would unhesitatingly hold that fairness does require disclosure to the appellant of the reports to be presented to the parole board on the current review.[90]

87 *Supra*, n. 81.
88 *Supra*, n. 61.
89 *Ibid.*, p. 150.
90 *Supra*, n. 62, p. 584.

However, potentially binding authority in the shape of *Payne* and *Gunnell* did exist, and much of the judgment of the Court of Appeal is concerned with justifying departure from it. Eventually Taylor LJ accepted the liberty of the subject as sufficient justification, and gave judgment in favour of the prisoner. Thus, after over a decade, the stranglehold of *Payne* was broken. The policy and simple fairness arguments in favour of disclosure were so strong that the Court of Appeal was prepared to find a reason to depart from previous authority. It remains to be seen how far the example of *Wilson* will be followed: whether the general attitude towards procedural fairness by Taylor LJ in that case will be extended to the release of mandatory lifers or fixed-term prisoners, or even to more internal decisions, such as transfer under CI 37/1990.

In relation to the role of courts as validators more generally, however, *Wilson* provides an interesting commentary. Exceptionally perhaps, counsel for the prisoner in that case was able to provide strong arguments in favour of disclosure which went far beyond the interests of the individual applicant. He was, for example, able to quote the recommendations of the Carlisle Committee and the House of Lords Select Committee, and to mention the presence of disclosure in the context of Mental Health Review Tribunals, and the decision of the ECHR that the Parole Board procedures did not comply with the requirements of article 5(4). The Court of Appeal, despite being formally engaged in the adjudication of an individual dispute, was thus able to take broader policy issues into account in reaching its conclusion on the facts before it. Further, by providing a full account of the impact of *Payne*, Taylor's judgment clearly illustrates the difficulties posed by the doctrine of precedent to any subsequent court wishing to depart from an earlier, much endorsed, decision. Whether the Court of Appeal would have possessed the necessary resolve in the absence of the impending legislative changes can never be known.

In relation to the process of tariff setting, the court has occasionally intervened to impose certain standards on a procedure that has evolved essentially through ministerial practice. In the first place, the *Handscomb* court was quite prepared to be critical.[91] In the court's opinion the practice of delaying consultation with the judiciary was unreasonable and therefore unlawful, and the process was altered accordingly. The court was using the broad principles of the common law to condemn an administrative process, and in doing so succeeded in inducing change. More recently in *Ex p. Doody and others* the Court of Appeal has declared that a mandatory life-sentence prisoner is entitled to know the judicial view of the tariff and to be shown any judicial comments that might influence the Secretary of State. This decision of the Court of Appeal is considerably more favourable to procedural intervention than was the decision at first instance,[92] and it is possible that it is reflecting the attitude of *Wilson*. However, the court has still denied the prisoner any absolute right to

91 *Supra*, n. 66.
92 *Supra*, n. 78, for the Court of Appeal. See [1991] *The Independent*, 31 January, for the Divisional Court.

reasons, although the Secretary of State will be expected to justify any tariff he sets which is radically different from that recommended by the judiciary.

(ii) Release Criteria
In addition to the oversight of procedural issues, the courts can, to a limited extent, review the application of the release criteria themselves. On an application for judicial review of the Secretary of State's refusal to order release, for example, the High Court can review the legality of the decision. The court must determine whether the decision was reasonable, whether it was taken on proper grounds, and whether irrelevant considerations were taken into account. These principles of judicial review are, however, notoriously flexible. As explained earlier, Lords Scarman and Browne-Wilkinson took two completely different views of the legality of Brittan's policy in *Findlay*. Further, by refusing, in the same case, to regard the two lifers who were returned to closed conditions as exceptional, and thus entitled under well-established legal doctrine to special consideration, Lord Scarman illustrated the ease with which a seemingly straightforward legal principle can be moulded to fit the perceived demands of policy. According to legal principle, a public official who develops a policy to guide the exercise of his or her discretion must be prepared to take account of exceptional cases,[93] but, in the prison context at least, the judicial interpretation of 'exceptional' seems unlikely to be generous to prisoners.

On the basis of *Findlay* alone, it might be thought that the courts will invariably interpret the flexible principles of review in favour of the authorities. If this were the case, the validation provided by the courts would be of little value. However, in some more recent cases the courts have been prepared to adopt interpretations which have left the authorities vulnerable to challenge. In *Benson* the Divisional Court held that the Secretary of State had misdirected himself in refusing to release a discretionary lifer despite positive recommendations by the Parole Board on three occasions.[94] Although the Secretary of State was not obliged to accept the Board's estimate of risk, the court held that in reaching his own decision on the point he appeared to have taken irrelevant considerations into account. Two incidents in the prisoner's past, which did not relate to his continuing dangerousness, had apparently influenced the Secretary of State, and were thus irrelevant considerations in law.

In slightly different circumstances in *Ex p. Cox*, the Divisional Court was also prepared to overturn the Secretary of State's decision.[95] The case involved a mandatory lifer who had been released on licence and subsequently recalled following his arrest and charge on an offence of violence. The charge was subsequently dropped and the prisoner was given a provisional release date. Prior to that date he pleaded guilty to the possession of cannabis and the fraudulent use of a tax disc, and the Secretary of State cancelled his release.

93 *Supra*, n. 21.
94 *R* v. *Secretary of State for the Home Dept. ex p. Benson* [1988] *The Independent*, 16 November.
95 *R* v. *Secretary of State for the Home Dept. ex p. Cox* [1991] *The Independent*, 8 October.

The court held that the test which should have been applied by the Secretary of State was dangerousness and, although there was no evidence that the Secretary of State had not considered that test, his conclusion on the facts was perverse. The cancellation of the release date was unreasonable and therefore unlawful. Certainly this case illustrates a willingness on the part of the court to question the grounds for the Secretary of State's decision, and suggests that the courts can provide effective independent validation in certain cases.[96] However, while the *Cox* court provided an effective challenge after the event, it refused to find that the Secretary of State had been under a common law duty to consult the Parole Board prior to his decision. As the court itself recognised, prior consultation with the Parole Board might have prevented the impugned decision being made, and plainly in terms of full process such consultation would be essential. The common law, therefore, missed yet another opportunity (this time in relation to the application of policy) to impose a basic process requirement which could greatly improve the quality of decision making.

While *Benson* and *Cox* concerned the exercise of discretion by the Secretary of State, *Ex p. Bradley* involved a challenge to the Parole Board. Bradley, a discretionary life-sentence prisoner, sought to challenge the Parole Board's refusal to recommend his release on licence. The court pointed to the criteria adopted by sentencing courts when deciding to impose a discretionary life sentence, the relevant aspects of which it summarised as 'the perception of grave future risk amounting to an actual likelihood of dangerousness',[97] and argued that the test adopted by the Parole Board when advising the Secretary of State on release could be 'less favourable to the prisoner', at least in so far as likelihood was concerned. The court concluded that, once lawfully imposed, the life sentence 'justifies the prisoner's continued detention, even although the risk as ultimately perceived is substantially less than an actual probability of his seriously re-offending upon release'.[98] The court recognised that this left the level of risk required 'wholly undefined', but conceded that the longer the prisoner had remained in prison after the expiry of the tariff period the clearer must be the Board's perception of the risk of re-offending. Interestingly, in *Wilson* the prisoner sought to argue that the *Bradley* court had, in fact, conceded that the relative weights to be accorded to the potential dangers from release and the injury to the prisoner from prolonged detention after the expiry of the tariff should be adjusted over time in favour of the prisoner, but this interpretation was rejected by the Court of Appeal.[99] On the facts of the case, the court in *Bradley* held that the Parole Board's refusal was reasonable and, more specifically, that they were not obliged to follow the expert psychiatric

---

96 It is perhaps significant that Popplewell J., who decided *Cox*, was a member of the Carlisle Committee and thus particularly familiar with the criticisms of the discretionary nature of parole. However, a similarly interventionist approach has been taken more recently by Watkins LJ and May J in *R* v. *Secretary of State, ex p. Georghiades* [1992] *The Times*, 3 June.

97 *Supra*, n. 61, p. 145.

98 *Ibid.*, p. 146.

99 *Supra*, n. 62.

advice submitted to them. The case now endorsed by *Wilson*, provides an interesting illustration of the problems involved in any attempt to specify the levels of risk required, and thus emphasises the difficulties faced by any attempt to provide effective validation of decisions concerning prediction and risk.

Conclusions

The discretionary conditional release of prisoners which was first introduced in 1967 was fundamentally reformed with effect from October 1992. On both occasions Parliamentary debate focused primarily on the shape of the scheme and the structure of parole decision making. With regard to the 1967 legislation particularly, little thought was given to the underlying purposes of discretionary release, and in consequence the Act contained no criteria to guide the release decision. In the years between 1967 and 1992 the gaps left by the legislative framework were filled by administrative rules and guidance, and by ministerial decision, most notably that of Leon Brittan in 1983, the formulation of which lacked even the most basic requirements of full process.

In a welcome development, the reforms to the structure of release for fixed-term prisoners contained in the Criminal Justice Act 1991 were initiated by an independent committee chaired by Carlisle, and had thus been the subject of quite wide and informed debate. The new provisions for the release of discretionary life-sentence prisoners, by contrast, were introduced at short notice in response to pressure from both the ECHR and the House of Lords. In relation to both schemes, however, the 1991 Act left significant areas of policy to the discretion of the Secretary of State, merely empowering him to issue rules and directions relating to both procedure and substance, with no requirements as to consultation, and no stipulation that such rules be introduced by way of statutory instrument. Such an approach not only fails to meet essential process requirements with regard to policy formulation, but also, by failing to provide adequate guidance as to either procedure or the criteria for release itself, presents difficulties at both the application and the validation stages of implementation.

In the years up to 1992, although some 'criteria' for release emerged and were published annually, the parole decision remained secret and unaccountable, with the prisoner almost entirely excluded from the process. The ultimate decision rested with the Secretary of State. Although certain procedural problems persist, the 1992 scheme has introduced considerable improvements with regard to fixed-term prisoners and discretionary lifers. However, for both sets of prisoner the statutory criteria for release remain inadequate. Risk of re-offending is clearly to be the dominant factor, but no indication is given in the Act as to how that risk is to be assessed. In the case of fixed-term prisoners the issue is addressed in slightly more detail in the 1992 directions, contained in CI 26/1992, but even there the guidance leaves much to the discretion of individual panels. As far as discretionary lifers are concerned, section 34 merely identifies the protection of the public as the governing factor and requires that the panel be satisfied of the absence of need to detain before directing release. In view of such a test and the presumption in favour of continued detention that it implies, it is essential that the discretionary lifer panels develop a strong inquisitorial approach to their decision making. The structure for mandatory life-sentence prisoners, as described above, has yet to be affected by the reforms of 1992 and remains unacceptable and indefensible. It must be only a matter of time before the government takes the necessary steps.

Although some provision is made for the internal validation of the procedures of parole decision making, judicial review by the High Court provides the main mechanism through which independent validation is commonly sought. By assessing the legal validity of a parole decision, judicial review has the potential to examine both its substantive and its procedural propriety. However, the absence of any statutory criteria from the 1967 Act and the dearth of procedural requirements severely limited its ability to do either. With regard to procedural matters the important influence of the Court of Appeal's restrictive attitude to the requirements of the common law in *Payne* was emphasised, and it was suggested that the reflection of such an attitude had significantly reduced the court's ability to provide effective validation. In the face of increasingly strong arguments of both policy and fairness a change of heart was finally achieved in *Wilson*, but it remains to be seen how far the spirit of that decision will be extended. Under the new scheme the first testing ground is likely to be provided by the mandatory lifers, although the courts will also have to decide how far to intervene either to enforce or to extend the procedural rules relating to both fixed-term prisoners and discretionary lifers.

Finally, the judgment in *Bradley* starkly illustrates the difficulties facing any court when attempting to review the Parole Board's assessment of risk, and although some additional clarification has been introduced by the 1991 Act and the 1992 directions as regards fixed-term prisoners, the scope for judicial challenge is still very limited. That the early release of an individual should depend on the application of a test which is not susceptible to effective independent validation is itself cause for concern. However, the position with regard to discretionary lifers is arguably even more unsatisfactory in this regard. The test employed by section 34 leaves extensive discretion in the hands of individual panels, and the only real scope for effective validation is likely to lie in the assiduous policing of the panels' obligation to provide reasons. The problems arising from the various approaches to risk assessment are discussed further in chapter 12 in the context of Mental Health Review Tribunals.

Part III
Patients

9
Mentally Disordered Offenders

Mentally disordered offenders are primarily catered for through the provisions of the Mental Health Act 1983 (the 1983 Act), and it is with the structure provided by that Act that this chapter and the subsequent three chapters are mainly concerned. However, a significant proportion of 'mentally disordered offenders' never find their way into the Mental Health Act structure, and an account that confined itself to the provisions of that Act would provide a very partial view of the experience of mental disorder within the custodial system. This chapter is divided into three main sections. Firstly, an outline of the main provisions of the 1983 Act, of relevance to the mentally disordered offender, is given. Secondly, a brief account is provided of the formulation of mental health policy and facilities. Thirdly, the mechanisms available for identifying those requiring hospital care are considered. The process of decision making within special hospitals and the question of discharge from hospital are dealt with in subsequent chapters.

(a) The Statutory Scheme

The Mental Health Act 1983 provides the legal structure for the compulsory detention and treatment in hospital of those suffering from mental disorder.[1] In Part III it deals specifically with those concerned in criminal proceedings or under sentence, and provides a variety of mechanisms whereby 'offender patients' can be accommodated within the general structure of the 1983 Act. For present purposes the most relevant provisions are found in sections 37, 41, 47 and 49. Section 37 enables a hospital order to be imposed by either a Crown Court or a Magistrates' Court after conviction for an offence punishable by imprisonment, provided certain conditions are fulfilled. The court must be satisfied on the evidence of two doctors that the offender is suffering from mental illness, psychopathic disorder, mental impairment or severe mental impairment to a nature or degree which makes it appropriate for him or her to

1 For a full account of the law relating to mental disorder see L. Gostin, *Mental Health Services: Law and Practice* (1986, London: Shaw).

be detained in a hospital for medical treatment. In the case of psychopathic disorder or mental impairment such treatment must be likely to alleviate or prevent a deterioration in the condition. The court must also be of the opinion that a hospital order is the most appropriate way of dealing with the person, and must be satisfied that a bed will be available within 28 days of making the order. Section 41 enables a Crown Court to impose restrictions on such an order where it deems it necessary to do so in order to protect the public from serious harm.[2]

A section 37 patient is detained in hospital in essentially the same position as a non-offender patient compulsorily detained for treatment under section 3 of the 1983 Act. The order lasts initially for six months and, after a first renewal for six months, is renewable for additional periods of 12 months by the hospital managers on the provision of a report by the responsible medical officer (rmo). The patient may be discharged by his rmo, the hospital managers or the Mental Health Review Tribunal, and while in hospital his rmo is responsible for such issues as transfer and leave.

By contrast, a patient placed under section 41 restrictions is more closely controlled by the Home Office. The imposition of a restriction order means that, unless the restrictions are time-limited, the detention lasts indefinitely, no renewal is required, and the patient can only be discharged by the Mental Health Review Tribunal or the Home Secretary. Discharge can be either conditional or unconditional. If conditional, the patient remains liable to recall. Further, questions such as leave and transfer are made dependent on the consent of the Home Secretary. Consequently patients under a restriction order are typically held in hospitals for which the Secretary of State for Health is ultimately responsible, while responsibility for their discharge or transfer rests with the Secretary of State for the Home Department or the tribunal. This spreading of responsibility reflects the ambiguity of the offender/patient's position.

Thus the Mental Health Act 1983 provides for the indefinite detention in hospital and the compulsory treatment of a convicted offender (see below). The choice of such a non-penal disposal is ostensibly justified by the offender's mental disorder and need for treatment, and the decision is taken in open court on the basis of expert advice from at least two doctors.[3] Further, on the grounds of social protection, additional restrictions may be placed on the transfer and discharge of the offender patient, thus emphasising the indeterminate nature of the disposal. In 1988, 151 patients were admitted to hospital under restriction orders and, on 31 December 1988, 1,874 such patients were detained in hospital.[4]

---

2 See *Birch* (1989) Crim. LR 296 where the court provides a lengthy discussion of the criteria for the imposition of a restriction order under s. 41 and the implications flowing from such an order. The court emphasises that it is not bound to follow medical evidence on the question of restrictions. For a discussion of the relevant principles see A. Ashworth, *Sentencing and Criminal Justice* (1992, London: Weidenfeld and Nicolson), ch. 11.

3 On the role of expert witnesses see R. McGee, J. D. Atcheson and B. C. L. Orchard, 'Psychiatrists, Lawyers and the Adversarial System', in S. J. Hucker, C. D. Webster and M. H. Ben-Aron, *Mental Disorder and Criminal Responsibility* (1981, Toronto: Butterworths).

4 Home Office Statistical Bulletin 16/90.

Sections 47 and 49 provide a similar structure for offenders initially sentenced to imprisonment, whether fixed-term or life. Section 47 enables the Home Secretary to transfer a sentenced prisoner to hospital if he is satisfied, on the evidence of two doctors, that the prisoner is suffering from the relevant mental disorders to a nature or degree which makes it appropriate for him to be detained in hospital for medical treatment. Section 49 enables the Home Secretary to impose special restrictions similar to those available under section 41.

Provisions are also made for those awaiting trial or sentence. A person awaiting trial for an offence punishable by imprisonment may be remanded in hospital by the Crown Court, or in certain circumstances by a Magistrates' Court, to enable a report on his mental condition to be provided (section 35), or such a person may be remanded by the Crown Court to hospital for treatment (section 36). A person already remanded in prison may be transferred to hospital under section 48 in certain fairly restricted circumstances. Finally, section 38 enables the trial court, after conviction, to impose an interim hospital order of up to six months to enable the patient to be assessed for a full hospital order.

In many respects the position of offender patients detained in hospital under any of the above provisions is similar to that of those detained under the civil detention powers provided by sections 2 and 3 of the Act. Most significantly, all the above patients, apart from those remanded for report under section 35, are subject to the consent provisions contained in Part IV of the Act. As will be seen below, the 1983 Act introduced an entirely new system to govern the question of the compulsory treatment of detained patients.

Treatments for mental disorder are effectively divided into three categories: those requiring the patient's consent *and* an independent second opinion, those requiring the patient's consent *or* a second opinion, and those requiring *neither* consent *nor* a second opinion. Into the first category fall specialised treatments such as brain surgery and the surgical implantation of hormones. These cannot be given to a patient, whether they are detained under the Act or not, unless the patient consents and an independent panel of three, including a doctor, certifies the validity of the consent and the doctor certifies the appropriateness of the treatment (section 57). Treatments in the second category include the administration of drugs after three months, and electro-convulsive therapy. Here, if a detained patient does not consent, the treatment can still be given provided it is certified by an independent doctor (section 58).

Any other treatment for mental disorder can be given to a detained patient without his consent, under the direction of the RMO (section 63). Special provisions apply to urgent treatment (section 62). Where a patient is not detained under the Act no treatment may be given without his or her consent except under the common law principles of necessity. Section 57 is the only provision within Part IV of the Act which applies to informal patients – those who are not detained – and, rather than providing for treatment in the absence of consent, it imposes requirements in addition to the patient's consent.

Under the provisions of the Criminal Procedure (Insanity) Act 1964, accused people found unfit to plead and those found not guilty by reason of insanity used to be treated as if they were subject to a restriction order under sections 37 and 41 of the 1983 Act. The Criminal Procedure (Insanity and Unfitness to Plead) Act 1991 has now amended the 1964 Act. Those found unfit to plead and found, following a trial of the facts, to have done the act charged, may now, provided the charge is not murder, receive a wider range of disposals, including not only a hospital order, but also a guardianship order, a supervision and treatment order, or an absolute discharge. A similar extension of the available disposals is applied to those found not guilty by reason of insanity, again provided the charge is not murder.

(b) Policy Formulation

This section is concerned with the process through which the policies relating to the treatment of mentally disordered offenders have evolved.

(1) The Mental Health Act 1983

The Mental Health Act 1983 introduced significant reforms to the legislative framework for the treatment of mental disorder, and a great amount has been written about its evolution.[5] Typically it has been seen to represent the reassertion of legalism over the medical model provided by the previous Mental Health Act of 1959 and its predecessor, the Mental Treatment Act 1930. The medical model, which emphasises the value of psychiatric treatment, favours the placing of considerable discretion in the hands of the medical profession to enable the relevant specialists to treat those in need. Legalism, on the other hand, while recognising the value of psychiatry, stresses the need to impose limits on the exercise of professional power. The 1959 Act had been introduced during a period of optimism following a number of significant advances in psychiatric care, and was seen as an attempt to facilitate access to mental health services and to remove some of the old formalistic restrictions. Indeed, at the time it was widely expected that the next reform would move steadily in the same direction.[6] In the event, the 1983 Act performed an about-turn. In many respects it strengthened the safeguards available to patients and increased the controls on psychiatric discretion and, according to some, 'restored formal legal safeguards to a central place in mental health legislation'.[7]

---

5 See, especially, C. Unsworth, *The Politics of Mental Health Legislation* (1987, Oxford: Oxford University Press); P. Bean, *Compulsory Admissions to Mental Hospitals* (1980, London: Wiley) and *Mental Disorder and Legal Control* (1986, Cambridge: Cambridge University Press); and P. Fennell, 'Law and Psychiatry: the Legal Constitution of the Psychiatric System' (1986) 13 Jo. of Law and Soc. 35.

6 Unsworth, *supra*, n. 5, p. 315.

7 Unsworth, *supra*, n. 5, p. 316. But see J. Peay, *Tribunals on Trial* (1989, Oxford: Oxford University Press).

It is not appropriate here to pursue the debate concerning the politics of mental health in any detail. It is necesssary merely to outline some of the main features of the process leading up to the introduction of the 1983 Act. From the early 1970s a number of governmental committees addressed the question of the reform of mental health legislation in general, and the 1959 Act in particular. In the first place, the position of the mentally disordered offender in prison, hospital and the community was considered by a committee set up by the Home Secretary in 1972, under the chairmanship of Lord Butler. Following the Interim Report in 1974, the committee's final, and still influential, Report was published in 1975.[8] In January 1976 the government announced its intention to review the 1959 Act, and to that end, set up an inter-departmental committee representing the Department of Health and Social Services, the Home Office, the Lord Chancellor's Department and the Welsh Office. The committee's initial suggestions were set out in a consul-tative document,[9] and comments were invited from interested bodies and individuals. On the basis of this consultative exercise, in 1978 the government published a White Paper setting out its proposals for reform.[10] A general election leading to a change of government intervened, and a new White Paper was published in 1981.[11] Eventually the Mental Health (Amendment) Act 1982 was passed, and finally consolidated in the Mental Health Act 1983.

Those who have studied the history of this reform have commonly attributed considerable significance to the contribution of a particular pressure group, the National Association for Mental Health (MIND).[12] By the early 1970s the optimism of the 1950s had been replaced by a growing scepticism towards the achievements of psychiatry. In particular the vulnerability of psychiatric patients, and their relative powerlessness were recognised.[13] In sympathy with this trend, MIND became the main proponent of what has been termed the 'new legalism', to distinguish it from the rather sterile legalism of the late nineteenth and early twentieth centuries.[14] The thrust of this new legalism was based on the 'ideology of entitlement'. Patients were to be entitled to the psychiatric care which they needed, in the least restrictive setting, and were to be free of all derogations of liberty not demanded by some legitimate social objective. In 1975 MIND published its proposals for reform in relation to non-offender patients, and placed them before the inter-departmental committee.[15] MIND's proposals on the question

8 *Interim Report of the Committee on Mentally Abnormal Offenders* (1974, Cmnd 5698, London: HMSO). For the full report see *Report of the Committee on Mentally Abnormal Offenders* (The Butler Report) (1975, Cmnd 6244, London: HMSO).
9 *The Review of the Mental Health Act 1959* (1976, London: DHSS).
10 *The Review of the Mental Health Act 1959* (1978, Cmnd 7320, London: HMSO).
11 *Reform of Mental Health Legislation* (1981, Cmnd 8405, London: HMSO).
12 Unsworth, *supra*, n. 5, chapter 10; Bean (1986), *supra*, n. 5, ch. 10; and N. Rose, 'Unreasonable Rights: Mental Illness and the Limits of the Law' (1985) Jo. of Law and Soc. 199.
13 *Report of the Committee of Inquiry into Allegation of Ill-Treatment of Patients and other Irregularities at the Ely Hospital Cardiff* (1969, Cmnd 3975, London: HMSO).
14 Fennell, *Supra*, n. 5, p. 39.
15 L. Gostin, *A Human Condition*, vol. 1 (1975, London: MIND).

of offender patients were published in 1977, and considered by the committee before the submission of its final recommendations.[16] MIND, of course, was not the only non-governmental participant in the debate. The various professional bodies were powerfully represented. The Royal College of Psychiatrists produced a review of the Mental Health Act 1959 which was also before the inter-departmental committee in 1975, and it remained closely involved throughout.

From the first appearance of the consultative document in 1976 to the final form of the 1982 Amendment Act, the reforms underwent many adjustments and alterations. There were significant differences between the White Papers of 1978 and 1981, and the Amendment Bill itself suffered approximately 200 alterations in the course of its Parliamentary passage.[17] Much of the debate, of course, concerned issues which were not of primary relevance to mentally disordered offenders, but some idea of the bargaining involved can be gleaned from a brief examination of the history of the consent provisions.

The requirements relating to consent to treatment represent one of the most significant innovations introduced by the reforms. The 1959 legislation had made no express provision with regard to the need or otherwise for the consent of a detained patient prior to treatment for mental disorder. The Department of Health had taken the view that the 1959 Act gave implied authority to the rmo to treat if necessary without the consent of the patient. However, the legal accuracy of this advice was being questioned, and the Royal College, MIND and the Butler Committee all called for clarification of the position. It was thus clear from the outset that some legislative statement was required, but its precise substance remained the subject of considerable controversy.

The Royal College suggested a code of practice which would require consultation with the next of kin and an independent consultant in cases where the detained patient was either unwilling or unable to consent. The final decision would, however, remain with the rmo. By contrast, MIND advocated arbitration by an independent committee, containing non-medical members. Despite opposition from the psychiatric establishment the 1978 White Paper favoured multi-disciplinary panels, and recommended that treatment should not be imposed without the endorsement of such a panel:

much, but not all, medical opinion was against the introduction of multi-disciplinary panels, but it is hoped that, in light of the widespread support for them, the medical profession will feel able to go along with this proposal.[18]

However, such panels were never established. Following the general election the new government proposed a system which was more in line with the views of the psychiatric profession, and which ultimately emerged as Part IV of the 1983 Act. For most forms of medical treatment for mental disorder a detained patient can be treated without his consent, provided an independent doctor agrees. The decision to impose treatment has been left primarily in the

16 White Paper 1978, *supra*, n. 10, p. vi.
17 See Unsworth, *supra*, n. 5, p. 325.
18 White Paper 1978, *supra*, n. 10, p. 76.

hands of the doctors. Despite their success in defeating the multi-disciplinary panels, however, the medical profession had to concede certain points. Under section 58, in contrast to the Royal College's proposals, the independent doctor has the right of veto, and can override the rmo. The independent doctor is also required to consult a nurse and one other professional concerned with the patient's care, who must be neither a doctor nor a nurse. The inclusion of the 'second professional' was particularly unpopular, representing a direct incursion into the clinical preserve. In a letter to the Special Standing Committee on the 1982 Amendment Act, Dr Hamilton and Dr Unwin of Broadmoor Special Hospital wrote:

we are firmly against any proposal that the independent psychiatrist should be required to consult any other professional person than a registered nurse concerned with the patient's treatment.[19]

As will be seen below, this particular aspect of Part IV continues to give rise to difficulties in practice.

This brief look at the history of the consent provisions helps to illustrate the process of consultation and compromise that seems to have characterised the formulation of the reforms. The professional bodies, particularly the Royal College, exercised an obvious influence, but so did MIND. Even if the claim by Larry Gostin,[20] MIND's legal director at the time – that approximately two-thirds of the changes introduced by the 1982 Amendment Act derived from MIND's proposals – is slightly inflated, it is clear that MIND's campaign was very influential.[21] It was powerfully stated and well-timed during the early rounds of policy formulation, and assiduously sustained throughout the Parliamentary stages of the 1982 Amendment Act.

The significant contributions of these various interest groups, whether professional or 'independent', might be seen as an example of effective public participation in the process of policy formulation. On the other hand, MIND's success and the influence of the Royal College may merely serve to support the claim that participatory procedures designed to facilitate interest representation tend to assist the powerful and articulate.[22] MIND was a well-established pressure group with some influential political support which was able to achieve wide circulation for its proposals, while the Royal College represented the interests of a significant professional body. Nevertheless, it would seem that the process of policy formulation prior to the 1982/83 reforms was genuinely participatory, even if the main participants were powerful and articulate. The relevant government departments took evidence and listened,

19 Quoted in Bean 1986, *supra*, n. 5, p. 145. See Parl. Debs, Special Standing Committee, 22nd sitting, 29 June 1982, col. 812.
20 L. Gostin, 'Contemporary Social Historical Perspectives on Mental Health Reform' (1983) 10 Jo. of Law and Soc. p. 47.
21 See, particularly, Fennell, *supra*, n. 5, and Unsworth, *supra*, n. 5, ch. 10.
22 See chapter 4 for further discussion of interest representation. For the role of pressure groups more generally, see W. Grant, *Pressure Groups, Politics and Democracy in Britain* (1989, London: Philip Allan), and C. Harlow and R. Rawlings, *Pressure Through Law* (1992, London: Routledge).

and in some cases accepted proposals carrying significant resource implications. Admittedly a number of the more costly proposals accepted in the 1978 White Paper were dropped in 1981, and the majority of the eventual reforms involved few additional resources. Nevertheless, the second opinion system, the creation of the Mental Health Act Commission (see below), and the extension of rights of access to Mental Health Review Tribunals, all involved additional outlay. In the sphere of prison policy making it is hard, certainly prior to the Woolf Inquiry, to find examples of such apparently effective participation from non-governmental bodies.

Before leaving the history of the 1983 reforms, one further feature must be mentioned. Under the 1959 Act, restriction order patients could only be discharged with the consent of the Home Secretary. In those cases the Mental Health Review Tribunal was purely advisory. In addition, in the case of particularly dangerous patients, the Home Secretary sought the advice of the Aarvold (or Advisory) Board on the question of public safety.[23] The Butler Committee considered it appropriate that the Secretary of State remain responsible for the discharge decision and recommended greater use of the Aarvold Board.[24] MIND, in an attempt to reduce indeterminacy, recommended the stipulation of a penal element in restriction orders, after the expiry of which the restrictions would lapse.[25]

The 1978 White Paper made no proposals to alter the relative roles of the tribunal, the Aarvold Board and the Secretary of State. However, during the consultative period prior to the 1982 Amendment Bill, MIND was pursuing the issue before the European Court of Human Rights, and in 1981 the ECHR published its judgment in *X* v. *United Kingdom*.[26] The issue is considered in further detail in a later chapter, but essentially, as explained in chapter 12, the ECHR decided that the existing procedures for the discharge of restricted patients were in breach of article 5(4). The European Convention requires access to to a 'court' to determine the lawfulness of a patient's detention, and the Home Secretary, advised by the Mental Health Review Tribunal, did not constitute a 'court' under article 5(4). The government was therefore forced to act. At the time of the 1981 White Paper it was still considering its reaction, and eventually introduced its proposals as amendments to the 1982 Amendment Bill in the House of Lords.[27] Mental Health Review Tribunals were given the power to discharge restricted patients without the consent of the Home Secretary. As will be argued below, these provisions constitute the barest minimum required to comply with the European Convention but, inadequate as they may be in certain respects, it is almost inconceivable that any changes involving the diminution of the Home Secretary's discretion would have been

---

23 For further discussion see chapter 12.
24 *Supra*, n. 8, ch. 4 (II).
25 L. Gostin, *A Human Condition*, vol. 2 (1977, London: MIND).
26 (1981) 4 EHHR 181.
27 HL Debs 426, cols 756–63, 25 January 1982. See Unsworth, *supra*, n. 5, p. 340 for further discussion.

introduced in the absence of the intense political pressure imposed by the direct intervention of the European Court of Human Rights.

(2) The Code of Practice

Section 118 of the 1983 Act requires the Secretary of State to prepare, and from time to time revise, a Code of Practice. The legislative statement of policy contained in the 1983 Act was therefore to be formally supplemented but it was never envisaged that the Code would be legally binding. Rather it was to be a statement of good practice for professionals working in the field, recommending principles and procedures to govern the exercise of their various powers and duties under the 1983 Act. As such it might provide evidence of good practice but would not itself be directly enforceable at law.

The growing reliance on codes of practice as a regulatory tool has caused concern among some commentators.[28] Codes of practice are often a feature of self-regulation, where a self-regulatory body, such as the Advertising Standards Authority and the Press Complaints Commission, issues a code of practice to its constituents. They also occur within public regulatory schemes. The Secretary of State or other relevant agency is required by statute to produce a code of practice: the codes published under the Police and Criminal Evidence Act provide such an example. At a formal constitutional level this may cause concern if the device is seen as an attempt to 'legislate by the back-door', particularly if there is some ambiguity as to the precise status of the code's requirements. In the case of the Mental Health Act 1983, however, it would appear entirely appropriate to supplement the bare legislative requirements with a statement of good professional practice, and to entrust the formulation of that statement to a body more expert than Parliament. In terms of expertise alone, Parliament cannot be regarded as the ideal decision maker in this context. However, even if the selection of an extra-Parliamentary decision maker is indicated on grounds of expertise, great care is still required to ensure that that decision maker is sufficiently accountable, and that the procedures adopted during the process of policy formulation are such as to encourage the broad reflection of the public interest.

The idea of a code of practice appears in the 1981 White Paper, together with the proposed creation of a Mental Health Act Commission. The idea of a commission was initially inspired by a proposal in the Boynton Committee Report on Rampton Special Hospital, and a suggestion from the Royal College that an equivalent to the Scottish Mental Welfare Commission be created for England and Wales.[29] Wherever the idea originated, however, the Commission

28 For the general debate, see G. Ganz, *Quasi-Legislation* (1987, London: Sweet and Maxwell); R. Baldwin and J. Houghton, 'Circular Arguments; The Status and Legitimacy of Administrative Rules' (1986) *Public Law* 239, and C. Crawford, 'Complaints Codes and Ombudsmen in Local Government' (1988) *Public Law* 246.

29 *Report of the Review of Rampton Hospital* (1980, Cmnd 8073, London: HMSO) and 'Mental Health Act Commissions: The Recommendations of the Royal College of Psychiatrists' (1981, London: Royal College of Psychiatrists).

as finally proposed seems to have been designed primarily as a means of introducing an independent element into the consent provisions that would be acceptable to the psychiatric profession. In the event the Mental Health Act Commission was created as a special health authority by the 1982 Amendment Act, and continues under section 121 of the 1983 Act. It is a body of approximately 90 part-time members, including psychiatrics, psychologists, nurses, social workers and lawyers, and, whatever the debates preceding its creation, now sees its primary task as the protection of the interests of detained patients. Its statutory functions include the discharge of the Secretary of State's duty under section 120(1) to

keep under review the exercise of the powers and the discharge of the duties conferred or imposed by this Act so far as relating to the detention of patients or to patients liable to be detained under this Act,

and the appointment of second-opinion doctors for the purposes of the consent to treatment provisions.

In the 1981 White Paper it was assumed that the Commission would draw up the Code of Practice.[30] A similar assumption was made during the committee stage of the 1982 Amendment Bill.[31] The 1983 Act itself, however, imposes no such duty. The task is given directly to the Secretary of State who 'shall consult such bodies as appear to him to be concerned' – section 118(3). The only other procedural requirements imposed are an obligation to publish the Code before Parliament, subject to negative resolution. The latter requirement was included as a result of an amendment at the committee stage, and reflects a desire to provide Parliament with an opportunity for comment. An attempt to write the Commission back into the drafting process was made in 1983 by regulations requiring it to perform on behalf of the Secretary of State the function of submitting proposals as to the contents of the Code.[32] Acting on the strength of that regulation, the Commission set about producing a draft Code which was submitted to the Secretary of State in 1985. The draft did not find favour with the professional bodies, particularly the Royal College, and in 1987 what is now the Department of Health produced its own draft without further consultation with the Commission. In the sometimes acrimonious discussions that followed between the Department and the Commission it became apparent that the Commission's role was advisory at best, and that even the duty of submitting proposals imposed on it by the regulations had been queried by the Joint Select Committee on Statutory Instruments as possibly *ultra vires* the 1983 Act.[33] Eventually a working party, of which the Commission's vice chair was a member, was established by the Department to produce a final draft code. After further informal consultation

30 White Paper 1981, *supra*, n. 11, para. 38.
31 Special Standing Committee, Mental Health Amendment Bill, 16th sitting, 17 June 1982, col. 608.
32 SI 1983/892, reg. 3(2)(d), made under s.11, National Health Services Act 1977.
33 Joint Select Committee on Statutory Instruments, Minutes of Evidence, 1 November 1983.

the Code of Practice was laid before Parliament and, following debate in the House of Lords, was finally published in 1990.

Thus more than seven years passed before a Code of Practice ultimately emerged – seven years of confusion. The Act and the regulations had been insufficiently precise in their allocation of responsibility for formulating the Code's and in their imposition of duties to consult. The whole history of the Code evolution illustrates a lack of rigour which is perhaps characteristic of the attitude towards administrative rule making in this country. At the very least, the principles of full process would demand the precise identification of a subsidiary rule maker who was appropriately qualified in terms of expertise and accountability, and the imposition of full and specific duties to inform, consult and respond. Since the initial publication of the Code, the Mental Health Act Commission has been asked by the Secretary of State to monitor its implementation and to advise ministers from time to time of any changes it judges to be appropriate.[34] Perhaps the process of revision will prove more satisfactory than the process of initial drafting. In the continued absence of formal consultation requirements, however, much will depend on 'good will'.

On questions of substance, certain aspects of the Code's requirements have already attracted criticism from those working in the field, but whatever the merits of such criticism, it is clear that the existence of the Code has assisted the Commission in its task of keeping under review 'the exercise of the powers and the discharge of the duties imposed' by the 1983 Act. However, the Code is very general in terms, and should not be likened to the code of minimum standards proposed for the Prison Service. It provides a guide to professional standards rather than a statement of a patient's entitlements, and as such forms a useful bench-mark for those concerned with the maintenance of standards in psychiatric hospitals, for which the Prison Service at present has no equivalent. In theory it should be particularly useful in relation to the special hospitals where many offender patients are housed and which, in the past, have tended to become rather isolated from developments within ordinary National Health Service hospitals; but, as will be seen below, its full potential in this respect has yet to be realised.

(3) Preliminary Conclusion – Policy Formulation

The process of policy formulation prior to the reforms of 1982/83 was characterised by a significant degree of openness and interest group participation. Despite the endeavours of MIND, however, it is evident that the influence of the psychiatric lobby was powerful enough to ensure the survival of 'professional dominance', particularly with regard to compulsory treatment.[35] Whether this fact alone is sufficient to suggest that the policy maker was able to reflect only a partial interpretation of the public interest is beyond

34 Mental Health Act Commission (MHAC), *Fourth Biennial Report 1989–1991* (1991, London: HMSO), p. 35.
35 See Bean 1986, *supra*, n. 5, ch. 6, where he develops the notion of professional dominance in relation to mentally disordered offenders.

the scope of the present discussion; but it does indicate the considerable influence exercised by articulate and well-resourced interest groups, and thus serves to illustrate the need to facilitate wide participation and to encourage contributions from those less willing to volunteer.

It is also interesting to note the significant part played by the ECHR in forcing reform of the discharge process. Elsewhere reservations are expressed as to the use of the adjudicatory structure for the purposes of policy formulation. Arguably, these reservations do not apply with such force to the role of the ECHR. The ECHR is monitoring compliance with an agreed policy, the European Convention, and is doing so in the light of international practice. Admittedly the Convention is open to a variety of interpretations, but in selecting the 'correct' interpretations the ECHR is not confined to the arguments presented by two conflicting parties. Further, in this context as in the context of life sentences, the ECHR does not formulate domestic policy when it declares UK practice to be in breach of the Convention; it merely indicates the limits placed on that policy by international law. The ECHR, just as the Court of Appeal in *Hague*, is policing legislative boundaries.[36] The selection of the precise means of achieving compliance is left to the UK Parliament.

Finally, while the notion of a Code of Practice might be welcomed, the process surrounding its creation was sadly deficient. Parent legislation must properly identify the subsidiary rule maker, in the light of the requirements of both expertise and accountability, and must specify the procedures to be followed, particularly with regard to consultation and openness.

(4) The Evolution of Facilities

The greatest concentration of offender patients in England and Wales is to be found in the three special hospitals: Rampton, Broadmoor and Ashworth. In March 1991 these three hospitals provided 1,769 places between them, the vast majority of which were taken by offender patients.[37] Carstairs State Hospital provides similar facilities in Scotland. The special hospitals were formally constituted by section 97 of the 1959 Act, replaced by section 4 of the National Health Service Act 1977, which requires the Secretary of State to provide special hospitals 'for patients subject to detention', who 'require treatment under conditions of special security on account of their dangerous, violent or criminal propensities'. The special hospitals were placed under the direct management of the Secretary of State for Health, and on his behalf their overall management was undertaken by the office committee within the Department of Health and Social Security.[38]

36 *R* v. *Deputy Governor of Parkhurst Prison, ex p. Hague* [1990] 3 All ER 687. The issue is discussed in the prison context in chapter 5, and is also considered in relation to hospitals in chapter 12.
37 Report of the Hospital Group (1991, London: DoH/Home Office), para. 2.5. It should be noted that there are patients in special hospitals who are detained under section 3 of the 1983 Act, which does not require a court hearing.
38 For the history of the special hospitals see N. Walker and S. McCabe, *Crime and Insanity in*

Since 1977 there have been a number of changes in the management structure of special hospitals. Finally, in October 1989, following a critical report on Broadmoor by the Health Advisory Service, management of the special hospital service was transferred from the Department of Health (as the DHSS had become) to a new special health authority, the Special Hospital Service Authority (SHSA).[39] The Department of Health retains merely a residual role and 'will be concerned with strategic policy and priority setting'.[40] It was recognised that the old structure of management through the Department was unsatisfactory, leading to the 'administration' of the special hospitals, rather than to their 'management'. The new system is intended to bring the management structure more closely in line with that operating within the National Health Service. Initially the SHSA was given very general management functions, but these were later amplified and extended to include the role of managers under the 1983 Act.[41] The SHSA has thus acquired specific powers in relation to detained patients under the Act. In addition, Hospital Advisory Committees have been established as sub-committees of the SHSA to perform the Authority's statutory duties as manager under the 1983 Act and various other non-statutory, advisory functions.

The role of the SHSA will be further considered below in relation to particular areas of decision making. It is relevant to note, however, that the need to retain the special hospital system at all in its present form is now a matter of some debate. Although the future of special hospitals in general was strictly outside the terms of reference of the Inquiry into Complaints about Ashworth Hospital (the Ashworth Inquiry), in his letter to the Secretary of State accompanying the Report the inquiry chairman questioned 'the need for the special hospitals within contemporary forensic psychiatric services', thus paving the way for a fundamental review of services.[42]

Offender patients do not all require the security provided by the special hospitals, but as local psychiatric units abandoned locked wards in favour of an 'open door' policy, alternative secure accommodation became less readily available, and the movement of patients on from special hospitals became more difficult. It is a well-documented problem, but its practical solution remains elusive.[43] In 1974 the Butler Committee published an interim report

England (1973, Edinburgh: Edinburgh University Press), and J. Hamilton, 'The Special Hospitals', in L. Gostin (ed.), *Secure Provisions* (1985, London: Tavistock), ch. 3.

39 Health Advisory Service Report, *Broadmoor Hospital* (1988, London: DHSS). The SHSA was set up as a special health authority under s. 11, National Health Services Act 1977: Special Hospital Service Authority (Establishment and Constitution) Order 1989, SI 1989/948.

40 *S.H.S.A: Starting Afresh* (1989, London: DoH).

41 The Special Hospital Service Authority (Functions and Membership) Regulations, SI 1989/949, amended by SHSA (Functions and Membership) Amendment Regulations 1989, SI 1989/1611.

42 *Report of the Committee of Inquiry into Complaints about Ashworth Hospital* (The Ashworth Report) (1992, Cm 2028-1, London: HMSO), p. vi. Following publication of the report a departmental committee, the High Security Working Group, has been set up, which will consider the provision of services for patients in need of secure accommodation.

43 E. Parker, 'The Development of Secure Provision', in L. Gostin, *supra*, n. 38, ch. 1.

stressing the urgency of providing regional secure units (RSUs), where patients requiring medium levels of security could be accommodated nearer to their homes.[44] Eventually special revenue allocations were made to the Regional Health Authorities, but still progress was slow. By 1984 all Regions had plans for permanent secure accommodation of some kind, and by early 1991 all but one of the fourteen Regions had an RSU in operation.

However, by January 1991 only 600 beds were available within these units, although a target of 1,000 had originally been set in 1974. This progress has been described as 'unacceptably slow' by a report published in November 1991 by an inter-departmental working group,[45] and indeed the record seems hard to justify. If patients are to be moved out of special hospitals as soon as they no longer require maximum levels of security then the provision of medium-secure beds must be improved. However, since RSUs generally only accept patients for relatively short periods of up to two years, local health authorities must also provide local secure accommodation for those requiring long-term care.[46] The paucity of secure accommodation of all kinds outside the special hospitals is thought to have contributed to the number of mentally disordered people within the prison system, and the government is currently reviewing the provision of health and social services for mentally disordered offenders through an inter-departmental working group chaired by Dr Reed.[47] With the provision of treatment from the health and social services at a premium it is particularly important to establish precisely how a mentally disordered 'offender' is identified, and thus diverted from a penal disposal.

(c) The Identification of Offenders in Need of Hospital Treatment

According to a Home Office Circular Instruction published in 1990,

it is government policy that, wherever possible, mentally disordered persons should receive care and treatment from the health and social services. Where there is sufficient evidence, in accordance with the principles of the Code for Crown Prosecutors, to show that a mentally disordered person has committed an offence, careful consideration should be given to whether prosecution is required in the public interest. It is desirable that alternatives to prosecution . . . should be considered first before deciding that prosecution is necessary.[48]

Despite this policy, the levels of mental disorder within the prison population remain high. In its report for 1989–90 the Prison Service recorded

44 *Supra*, n. 8.
45 *Supra*, n. 37, para. 5.24.
46 *Ibid.*, section 5.
47 The Review of Health and Social Services for Mentally Disordered Offenders and Others Requiring Similar Services.
48 CI 66/1990. See J. Gunn, 'The Role of Psychiatry in Prisons and "the Right to Punishment" ', in M. Roth and R. Bluglass (eds), *Psychiatry, Human Rights and the Law* (1985, Cambridge: Cambridge University Press), for an account of the development of Home Office policy.

that 141 sentenced prisoners were considered to meet the criteria for transfer to hospital under the Mental Health Act 1983.[49] However, an independent survey conducted in 1988–89 found that 37 per cent of the sentenced male population suffered from some broadly defined psychiatric disorder; while 2 per cent, or approximately 730 men at any one time, suffered from psychoses.[50] It further found that 3 per cent of the sentenced male population, or approximately 1,100 men at any one time, were suitable for transfer to hospital, a figure significantly in excess of that recorded by the Prison Service.

On the basis of such data, it is evident that a large number of mentally disorded people are not being diverted from the penal system. It is important, therefore, to examine the current procedures available for identification and diversion. At the beginning of this chapter the choice of a hospital in preference to a penal disposal was said to be grounded primarily on the perceived need for treatment, with the need for social protection providing a subsidiary reason in some cases. In the case of convicted offenders and those found unfit to plead, the selection of a hospital disposal carries with it the possibility of compulsory treatment and indeterminate detention. While the selection of the mentally disordered for special consideration in this way may be open to question,[51] such a selection is authorised by current legislation and carries with it important implications for both the individual offender and society more broadly. It is therefore essential that the selection be made as accurately as possible and in the true reflection of the purposes underlying the existing provisions. The objective should not be diversion at all costs, but rather diversion in all *appropriate* cases. Some mentally disordered offenders might properly remain within the prison system to receive treatment voluntarily in specialist units while serving fixed terms of imprisonment.[52]

A brief account of all the formal stages at which diversion can occur will be given first, and then particular attention will be paid to the procedures available for the diversion of mentally disordered prisoners once they have arrived in prison, whether on remand or after sentence.

(1) The Police

Many 'offenders' may never enter the criminal justice system, but may be referred straight to hospital, either by members of the public or the police. Section 136 of the Mental Health Act 1983 gives a police constable the power

49 *Report of the Work of the Prison Service 1989–90* (1990, Cm 1302, London: HMSO), app. 5. The comparable figure for the remand population was 149.
50 For a full report of the survey see J. Gunn, T. Maden and M. Swinton, *Mentally Disordered Prisoners* (1991, London: Home Office).
51 The issue is taken up below, but see the discussion in: Bean 1986, *supra*, n. 5, ch. 6; Gunn, *supra*, n. 48; and N. Morris, *Madness and the Criminal Law* (1982, Chicago: University of Chicago Press).
52 See Gunn, *supra*, n. 48, and the report of the Prison Advisory Group (1991, London: DoH/Home Office). Treatment in specialised prisons such as Grendon can be effective: J. Gunn, G. Robertson, S. Dell and C. Way, *Psychiatric Aspects of Imprisonment* (1978, London: Academic Press); and E. Genders and E. Player, *Grendon: A Study of a Therapeutic Community within the Prison System* (1989, Oxford: Oxford University Press).

to remove to a place of safety a person who 'appears to him to be suffering from mental disorder and to be in immediate need of care and control'. The person removed may be detained in the place of safety for up to 72 hours in order to enable him to be assessed by a doctor and a social worker, and in order to facilitate the 'making of any necessary arrangements for his treatment or care'. In this way a number of people are diverted to hospital without any further involvement in the criminal justice system.[53]

In some cases, however, where it appears that a mentally disordered person may have committed an offence, the police will have to consider whether any formal action is necessary. In deciding this issue the police should consider whether a caution would be appropriate. However, if the decision to charge is taken, the police must bear in mind that the mentally disordered suspect 'has the same right as other suspects to bail after charge'.[54] It has been suggested that the police may 'feel more than usually inhibited from granting bail if the suspect is homeless, or because they doubt he will understand the obligation to attend court if he is released'.[55]

The ability of the police to reach fully considered decisions at any of the above stages will be largely dependent on the standard of the information and expertise available to them, and on the level of health and social service provision available to support the suspect within the community. These issues, as mentioned above, are currently the subject of a review by an inter-departmental committee. They are not, however, of central relevance here, where the concern is primarily with custodial decision making. Nevertheless, it must be assumed that the more proficient the criminal justice system becomes at identifying and diverting the mentally disordered at the earliest possible point, the fewer mentally disordered offenders will inappropriately enter the penal system.

(2) Prosecution

Similar issues arise with regard to the Crown Prosecution Service (CPS) and the decision to prosecute. Once the decision to charge is taken by the police, the papers are referred to the CPS which 'will review the sufficiency of the evidence and consider carefully whether or not the public interest requires a prosecution in accordance with the Code for Crown Prosecutors'.[56] This Code lists a number of factors, including mental disorder, which if present in a case indicate that criminal proceedings may not be in the public interest. More specifically, CI 66/1990 emphasises the need for the CPS to assess the likely impact of prosecution on the suspect's mental disorder, and to consider discontinuance of proceedings where the adverse effects are likely to outweigh the 'interests of justice'. Where no adverse affect is likely from prosecution, 'the

53 For an account of police practice see E. Rassaby and A. Roberts, *Psychiatric Referrals from the Police* (1986, London: MIND).
54 CI 66/1990, para. 4v.
55 Report of the Community Advisory Group (1991, London: DoH/Home Office) para. 2.21.
56 CI 66/1990, para. 6.

Crown Prosecutor will take account of the public interest in attempting to ensure that the offence will not be repeated as well as having regard to the welfare of the person in question'.[57]

As was the case in relation to the police, the quality of CPS decision making will be greatly dependent on the quality of the information it has before it. If a policy of diversion is to be properly pursued, decisions in individual cases must be made on the basis of the best possible information. In practice much of the information typically before the CPS comes from the police, and is concerned primarily with details of the offence rather than the suspect's circumstances. In view of this deficiency a Public Interest Case Assessment project was set up in 1990 by the Probation Service, originally in Inner London, but subsequently extended to other centres, in an attempt to improve and extend the nature of the information available to the CPS.[58]

(3) Magistrates' and Crown Courts

Both Magistrates' and Crown Courts have various powers to divert mentally disordered people from the penal system, both while awaiting trial and after conviction. CI 66/1990 declares that 'a mentally disordered person should never be remanded to prison simply to receive medical treatment or assessment' (paragraph 7). Residence at a hospital, or specialised bail hostel, or attendance at an out-patients' clinic, for example, may be imposed as a condition of bail, although the mentally disordered person cannot be compelled to comply with treatment.[59] Further, section 35 of the Mental Health Act 1983 provides courts with the power to remand an accused person in hospital for a report on his or her mental condition. Acting on medical evidence that the person is suffering from mental illness, psychopathic disorder, severe mental impairment or mental impairment, a Magistrates' Court may use such powers in relation to a person convicted of an imprisonable offence, or any person charged with such an offence provided the court is satisfied that the accused person did the act or made the omission charged. Acting on similar medical evidence, the Crown Court may use the power in relation to any person awaiting trial or sentence for an imprisonable offence. The power was designed to give effect to a recommendation in the Butler Report that the courts should have the option of remanding an accused person to hospital for the preparation of a psychiatric report. It was not designed as an alternative to bail but as an alternative to a remand in prison, and is exercisable only where the court 'is of the opinion that it would be impracticable for a report on [the person's] mental condition to be made if he were remanded on bail', section 35(3)(b).

In addition to the powers available to remand on conditional bail and to

---

57 *Ibid.*

58 Community Advisory Group, *supra*, n. 55, para. 2.25, and see N. Stone, *Public Interest Case Assessments* (1989, London: Vera Institute of Justice).

59 Bail Act 1976, s. 3 and sch. 1, and Magistrates' Courts Act 1980, s. 30.

remand to hospital for a report, section 36 of the Mental Health Act enables the Crown Court to remand to hospital for treatment. The court must be satisfied on the evidence of two medical practitioners that the accused is suffering from mental illness or severe mental impairment of a nature or degree which makes it appropriate for him to be detained in hospital for medical treatment. Unlike a person remanded to hospital under section 35, the person remanded under section 36 is subject to the compulsory treatment powers in Part IV of the 1983 Act.

Despite the powers available under the Mental Health Act, however, and despite the flexibility provided by the grant of conditional bail, there is evidence to suggest that the courts are still remanding mentally disordered people to prison for primarily psychiatric and social reasons.[60] Indeed, it is clear that relatively little use has been made of the powers to remand to hospital. Approximately 300 people are remanded to hospital each year under the Mental Health Act, compared to the approximately 6,000 who are remanded to prison for medical reports.[61] In light of the increased awareness of the problems of remand prisoners, and the government's declared policy in favour of diversion, it is to be hoped that an extension of the schemes providing specialist psychiatric assessment currently operating in certain courts will encourage courts to use health or social service provision in preference to penal remands in appropriate cases. However, if the inappropriate use of prison remands is to cease, there may also be a case for restraining the courts' power to remand to prison solely for medical reports. Thus the Prison Advisory Group, reporting to the inter-departmental committee, has recommended a review 'with a view to amendment or repeal' of the relevant powers in the Bail Act 1976 and the Magistrates' Court Act 1980.[62]

Once a mentally disordered person has been convicted of an offence the court may be able to impose one of a number of non-penal disposals. Of these non-penal options two involve detention in hospital and are therefore of direct relevance here. In the circumstances described above, at section **a**, courts may impose a hospital order under section 37 where the offender has been convicted of an offence punishable with imprisonment. The Crown Court is further empowered to impose restrictions under section 41, where it appears necessary for the protection of the public from serious harm. The implications arising from the imposition of such restrictions have already been described. Finally, section 38 enables both Magistrates' and Crown Courts to impose an interim hospital order to enable the offender's reaction to hospital to be evaluated before any final disposal is made. The order, with renewal, can last for a maximum of six months.

60 S. Dell, A. Grounds, K. James and G. Robertson, *Mentally Disordered Remand Prisoners* (1991, London: Home Office, unpublished).

61 See Dell *et al.*, *supra*, n. 62, for the use of the Mental Health Act 1983, and Gunn, *supra*, n. 48, where he argues that the success of the 1983 Act must depend on the resources made available.

3 Prison Advisory Group, *supra*, n. 52, para. 3.3.

(4) Prisons

While in prison, whether on remand or following a sentence of imprisonment, offenders can only be transferred to the hospital system by the Secretary of State under sections 48 and 47 respectively, or, in the case of remand prisoners, by the trial court following conviction and the imposition of a non-penal disposal. Section 47, which deals with the transfer of sentenced prisoners, requires the certification by two doctors that the prisoner is suffering from mental illness, psychopathic disorder, severe mental impairment or mental impairment to a nature or degree that makes it appropriate to detain him in hospital for medical treatment. In addition a suitable placement must be identified, and the Secretary of State must agree the move should take place 'having regard to the public interest and all the circumstances'. Section 48, dealing with remand prisoners, imposes similar requirements but restricts transfer to those suffering from mental illness and severe mental impairment, and to those in urgent need of medical treatment. Prisoners transferred under section 47 are placed in much the same position as offenders given hospital orders under section 37, and by virtue of section 49 can have restrictions imposed upon them similar to those imposed by section 41. The process surrounding the ultimate discharge of such prisoner/patients is discussed in chapter 12.

(5) The Process of Diversion from Prison

(a) The Remand Population

From the above description it would appear that three main options are available for the diversion of mentally disordered remand prisoners from the prison system. In the first place, the assessment services can recommend a non-custodial disposal to the sentencing court, neither imprisonment nor a hospital order; secondly, a hospital order under section 37 can be recommended, and finally, a remand prisoner can be transferred under section 48. Many mentally disordered people remanded in prison will not meet the statutory criteria for detention under the Mental Health Act, nor will they necessarily require a custodial sentence from the court. They would therefore appear suitable for the first, non-custodial, option. However, recent research has confirmed that, despite being urged to the contrary, those involved in the medical assessment of remand prisoners tend to think primarily in terms of in-patient care, a tendency which may result in the inappropriate use of compulsory treatment and indeterminate detention.'[63]

Research into the practice at three prisons with large remand populations has provided an interesting insight into the process of assessment and diversion in relation to the second option, the imposition of a hospital order.[64] In the first place, the research highlights the problem of delay. Since section 37

63 Dell *et al.*, *supra*, n. 60, and see the recommendations of the Prison Advisory Group, *supra*, n. 52, p. 6.
64 Dell *et al.*, *supra*, n. 60.

requires the court to be satisfied on the evidence of two doctors, patients who were to be assessed with a view to a hospital order recommendation had to be seen by a second psychiatrist. This second assessment could often take time to arrange, and so lead to further remands.

The data from Brixton indicate that, regardless of offence type, the men who were referred to an outside consultant and accepted spent longer in custody on remand than those who were not so referred.[65] Indeed, it was evident at Holloway that the prison doctors were only too aware of the penalty, in terms of extra custody on remand, that prisoners would pay if referred to outside consultants.[66] Delay could also occur between the making of a hospital order and the admission of the patient to the hospital, despite the fact that the hospital would already have guaranteed a bed. The first type of delay, that resulting from the need to arrange assessments, starkly indicates the practical implications of remanding mentally disordered people to prison in the first place. In order to ensure that their ultimate disposal is to hospital rather than back to prison, they are detained longer in prison before trial than their less disordered colleagues. The existence of delays after the imposition of the order by the court suggests that the receiving hospitals are affording insufficient priority to patients who are already in custody, albeit unsuitable custody.

A process of identification and diversion which itself creates delays leading to longer periods of prison custody cannot be acceptable. The recommendations of the Prison Advisory Group, which are designed both to reduce the number of prison remands in the first place and to speed up the process of assessment where remand in prison cannot be avoided, are therefore to be welcomed. According to these latter recommendations, the Prison Medical Service would have to assess all prisoners for whom there is evidence of mental disorder immediately on admission to prison, and would have to assess all other prisoners within 24 hours of admission. The Prison Advisory Group also stressed the need for health authorities to respond promptly to requests from the Prison Service for second assessments, and the need for the Prison Service to display greater flexibility in arranging assessments by outside consultants.[67]

In addition to problems of delay, the research also suggests that a number of potentially eligible prisoners are never referred to a second doctor because of problems within the Prison Medical Service itself. The research illustrates the 'pivotal role of prison doctors' in the whole assessment process, and stresses the need to ensure continuity of care for the mentally disordered remanded in prison. Some effective quality control mechanism is evidently required.[68] However, the data from Brixton, at least, suggest that those who are referred are treated favourably by the NHS consultants. There was no evidence of discrimination against offender patients.[69] In the light of the findings of this

---

65 *Ibid.*, p. 20.

66 *Ibid.*, p. 26.

67 Prison Advisory Group, *supra*, n. 52, ch. 3.

68 The question of the provision of medical services within prisons is discussed further in chapter 5.

69 Such discrimination was discussed in J. Cheadle and J. Ditchfield, *Sentenced Mentally Ill Offenders*

research it will be interesting to observe the impact of the requirements of section 4 of the Criminal Justice Act 1991. This section imposes an obligation on the sentencing court to obtain and consider a medical report before passing a custodial sentence on an offender who 'is or appears to be mentally disordered', and further requires the court to consider the likely effect of a custodial sentence on the mental disorder.

Transfer to hospital under section 48, the third option for the diversion of mentally disordered remand prisoners, is apparently little used, although its use increased markedly between 1978 and 1988. In 1978 nine prisoners were transferred with restrictions before sentence, compared to 82 in 1988.[70] Section 48 stipulates that the potential transferee be in 'urgent need' of medical treatment, and the research indicates that this requirement is interpreted very strictly by the Prison Medical Service. In the light of the delays surrounding the diversion of the mentally ill prisoner via a section 37 order imposed at trial, however, it is perhaps particularly unfortunate that any such restriction should be placed on the transfer power. Indeed, the Prison Advisory Group has recommended that the provisions of section 48 be relaxed, and be widened to include psychopathic disorder and mental impairment.[71] Great care will be needed, however, to ensure that inappropriate transfers are not made. The prison authorities must not be encouraged to see transfer to hospital as a convenient way of dealing with disruptive remand prisoners.

(b) The Sentenced Population

The Secretary of State has the power to transfer sentenced prisoners under section 47 of the Mental Health Act. Once more the effective exercise of this power is in part dependent on the ability of the prison medical service to identify mental disorder. However, there is also concern at the delay that can occur once the need for transfer is recognised within the prison. A study of patients transferred to Broadmoor found that it took on average eight to nine months from the initial medical recommendation to effect a transfer, although a more recent inter-departmental report suggests that some improvements have been achieved.[72] Again it seems that difficulties arise through a combination of lack of suitable resources and poor liaison between prisons and local psychiatric services. However, as was the case with the remand population, the number of sentenced prisoners transferred to hospital has risen: 41 were transferred with restrictions in 1978 compared to 94 in 1988.[73]

(1982, London: Home Office Research and Planning Unit), and J. Coid, 'Mentally Abnormal Prisoners on Remand: 1. Accepted or Rejected by the N.H.S.' (1988), 296 BMJ 1779.
70 Home Office Statistical Bulletin, Issue 16/90.
71 Prison Advisory Group, *supra*, n. 52, para, 3.11.
72 A. Grounds, 'The Transfer of Sentenced Prisoners to Hospital 1960–83: A study in One Special Hospital' (1991) 31 Brit. Jo. of Crimin. 54; and see *Report of Interdepartmental Working Group of Home Office and DHSS Officials on Mentally Disturbed Offenders in the Prison System in England and Wales* (1987, London: DoH).
73 Home Office, *supra*, n. 70. According to the *Report of the Work of the Prison Service 1989–90* (1990,

From a slightly different perspective, concern is sometimes expressed about the practice of transferring a prisoner very late in his or her sentence.[74] When this occurs in the case of a fixed-term prisoner, that person is effectively made subject to further indeterminate detention, often in a special hospital, just at the point when he or she could have expected release from prison. In the prisoner/patient's eyes the sentence is suddenly extended through medical and executive action. There is no third-party involvement in the process as is the case for civil detention under the Mental Health Act, nor is there an order of the court as required for the imposition of a section 37 hospital order.

(6) Conclusions – Identification and Diversion

Present legislative policy provides for the diversion of mentally disordered offenders from the penal system to the hospital system. In relation to those susceptible to a custodial disposal of either sort, the selection of the hospital option is ostensibly based on the individual's need for, and susceptibility to, treatment for mental disorder, and carries with it vulnerability to compulsory treatment and indeterminate detention. It is therefore essential that the identification process be as accurate as possible throughout the criminal justice system. In the first place, it is appropriate to keep the less serious offenders suffering mental disorder out of the penal system altogether. Secondly, from among those offenders requiring detention it is important that those in need of treatment in hospital be identified and diverted as soon as possible; but, as the issue of transfer to hospital late in a prisoner's sentence suggests, it is possible that diversion can be used in circumstances where the offender's need for treatment is not the primary motivation. It is essential that diversion be properly limited to those in real need of treatment for mental disorder. Diversion must not be used as a means of achieving the indeterminate preventive detention of those for whom there is no realistic prospect of treatment. If such detention is deemed necessary it must be expressly authorised in primary legislation.

The issue of preventive detention is discussed further in chapter 12, but it is relevant to mention briefly here the question of psychopathy. Personality disorder, or in legal terminology, psychopathy, is a condition which is hard both to define and to diagnose, but which at its most extreme is often regarded as unsusceptible to treatment in any curative sense.[75] At present the most that is likely to be achieved is the provision of skills to enable the sufferer to cope with the consequences of the disorder. In the face of such medical pessimism

London: HMSO), a record 230 prisoners, including both sentenced and remand, were transferred in 1989. This would include those transferred without restrictions.
74 MHAC, *supra*, n. 34, p. 41.
75 For general discussion of the issue, see M. Roth, 'Modern Neurology and Psychiatry and the Problem of Criminal Responsibility', in S. Hucker, C. Webster and M. Ben-Aron (eds), *Mental Disorder and Criminal Responsibility* (1981, Toronto: Butterworths); and see H. Prins, *Dangerous Behaviour, the Law and Mental Disorder* (1986, London: Tavistock), ch. 5, where he describes the

the inclusion of psychopathy in a disposal designed to provide treatment in hospital is open to question.[76] Indeed, the Butler Report considered that certain psychopathically disordered offenders should be treated in the penal rather than the hospital system, and when the 1983 Act finally emerged it contained some recognition of the dilemmas involved. Psychopathy is defined in section 1(2) as

a persistent disorder or disability of mind (whether or not including significant impairment of intelligence) which results in abnormally aggressive or seriously irresponsible conduct on the part of the person concerned.

Section 1(3) goes on to explain that no one is to be regarded as mentally disordered under the Act 'by reason only of promiscuity or other immoral conduct, sexual deviancy or dependence on alcohol or drugs'. There is therefore an attempt in the legislation to confine the scope of psychopathy: it cannot be established merely on the evidence of sexual deviancy or drug abuse. A further important constraint is added by sections 3, 37 and 47, which introduce the notion of treatability. A person suffering from psychopathy disorder may not be admitted to hospital for treatment, nor transferred from prison to hospital, unless the treatment in hospital 'is likely to alleviate or prevent a deterioration of his condition'.

Despite these legislative attempts to restrict the susceptibility of 'psychopaths' to compulsory detention and treatment under the 1983 Act, doubts remain as to the propriety of their inclusion within the ambit of the Act at all. In 1986 a joint Home Office/Department of Health working group looked at the position of psychopathic offenders and produced a consultation document.[77] However, the initiative was dropped and, although professional psychiatric opinion remains divided on the nature of the ideal provision for personality disordered offenders, the suspicion lingers that their retention within the terms of the Mental Health Act is motivated as much by a desire to provide for social protection via indeterminate hospital detention as it is by any real expectation of effecting their treatment.[78] It is therefore encouraging to note that the position of psychopathy is again under review by the interdepartmental working group chaired by Dr Reed mentioned above.

While the phenomenon of psychopathy raises questions about the propriety of compulsory treatment and detention in hospital with particular clarity, those questions are not unique to psychopathy, and should be borne in

evolution of 'psychopathy', its main identifying features, and the means available for the management of 'essential' psychopaths.

76 S. Dell and G. Robertson, *Sentenced to Hospital: Offenders in Broadmoor*, (1988, Oxford: Oxford University Press).

77 See J. Peay, 'Offenders Suffering from Psychopathic Disorder: the Rise and Demise of a Consultation Document' (1988) 28 Brit. Jo. of Crimin. 67, where she discussed the background to the consultation document and its fate.

78 The numbers of patients admitted to hospital under restrictions who are diagnosed as psychopathic have remained remarkably constant – 46 in 1978 compared to 58 in 1988 – although there have been fluctuations in between – 26 in 1979 and 63 in 1986, see Home Office, *supra*, n. 70.

mind whenever diversion to the hospital system is under consideration. Detention in hospital under the Mental Health Act, carrying with it susceptibility to compulsory treatment, must be justified in every case with reference to the individual's mental disorder and need for treatment. Where restrictions are imposed, hospital detention must further be justified with reference to the need to protect society from serious harm.

10
Decision Making within Special Hospitals: Application Decisions

This chapter is concerned with the process of policy application in relation to the management and care of offender patients within special hospitals. The discussion will focus on special hospitals because it is within special hospitals that the greatest concentration of offender patients is still to be found, and it is typically within a special hospital that an offender patient, particularly if under a restriction order, will pass the majority of his or her period in detention. In the course of the discussion in this chapter and the next it will become clear that there are some interesting similarities as well as dissimilarities between the decision making processes operating within special hospitals and prisons. The discussion in this chapter will concentrate on application decisions relating both to consent to treatment and to the imposition of other restrictions on a patient's freedom of choice.

(a) Consent to Treatment

(1) Autonomy, Participation and Consent

As was seen earlier, the imposition of a hospital order by the sentencing court, or the use of a transfer direction by the Secretary of State, is justified ostensibly in terms of the need to treat the offender. The way in which decisions about treatment are made is therefore of particular significance. Under the present legislative scheme, Parliament has approved the imposition of treatment for mental disorder on mentally disordered offenders in hospital despite the absence of consent on the part of the offender patient, provided the safeguards introduced by Part IV of the 1983 Act are met. It is necessary to examine the nature and implementation of these safeguards.

Unsworth describes Part IV as the 'high-water mark of legalism in the Act'.[1] It transforms what was essentially a matter of medical ethics policed, if at all, by private litigation, into a public law procedure overseen by the Mental Health Act Commission rather than the courts.[2] In the case of electro-

1 C. Unsworth, *The Politics of Mental Health Legislation* (1987, Oxford: Oxford University Press), p. 324.
2 P. Fennell, 'Law and Psychiatry: the Legal Constitution of the Psychiatric System' (1986) 13 Jo. of Law and Soc. 35.

convulsive therapy and drugs, if the responsible medical officer (rmo) is not satisfied that a detained patient is consenting, another doctor appointed by the Commission (the second-opinion doctor) must certify that, despite the absence of consent, the treatment should be given 'having regard to the likelihood of its alleviating or preventing a deterioration in his condition', section 58(3)(b). In the case of psycho-surgery and 'the surgical implantation of hormones for the purpose of reducing male sex drive',[3] a more exacting procedure is required. Such treatments cannot be given without both the patient's consent, certified by an approved panel of three people, and certification by an appointed doctor that the treatment should be given (section 57).

As was seen in the previous chapter, these provisions, particularly those introduced by section 57 which apply to all patients, not just those who are detained under the 1983 Act, met considerable opposition from within the psychiatric profession, and in some quarters that opposition persists. The introduction of independent oversight into an area that had previously been a matter of individual professional judgement was unlikely to go unchallenged, even if the oversight was merely a matter of peer review. But, arguably, the sensitivity of the consent provisions springs from more than injured professional dignity.

The question of consent to medical treatment can be seen to contain at least two potentially conflicting principles: autonomy and beneficence.[4] In moral philosophy, personal autonomy implies personal self-governance, or the capacity to govern yourself with adequate understanding while remaining free from the controlling interference of others and from personal limitations that prevent choice.[5] Beneficence, on the other hand, contains a number of elements linked by the common theme of promoting the welfare of others. In the medical context those elements include the prescriptions to avoid inflicting harm, to prevent harm, to remove harm, and to promote good. Faden and Beauchamp believe that autonomy is the single most important principle in the context of consent, but that in certain circumstances beneficence, coupled occasionally with justice, may override it.[6]

In the debate about consent, lawyers typically are seen as emphasising the autonomy of the patient, while psychiatrists, acting in the patient's best interests, place greater weight on beneficence.[7] Faden and Beauchamp suggest that the lawyers' interest in autonomy is pragmatic. The patient may be granted the right to give or withhold consent, but the lawyer's focus remains on the doctor, who retains ultimate legal responsibility. Whatever the precise nature of the lawyers' professional interest, however, it is clear that any

3 SI 1983/893, rule 16.
4 R. Faden and T. Beauchamp, *A History and Theory of Informed Consent* (1986, New York: Oxford University Press), ch. 1.
5 *Ibid.*, p. 8, and see I. Berlin, *Four Essays on Liberty* (1969, Oxford: Oxford University Press).
6 *Ibid.*, ch. 1.
7 See P. Bean, *Mental Disorder and Legal Control*, (1986, Cambridge: Cambridge University Press),

attempt, through the regulation of consent, to interfere with the relative weights attached by clinicians to beneficence and autonomy was bound to encounter opposition.

The provisions of Part IV of the 1983 Act certainly allow for the supremacy of beneficence where the second-opinion doctor certifies the treatment under section 58 despite lack of consent. The extent to which those provisions also increase the weight accorded to autonomy, and thus the relevance of the patient's participation, is more difficult to determine. Before pursuing this issue further by examining the operation of the provisions in practice, however, it is necessary to emphasise the close relationship between the question of consent and the notion of full process, and to consider briefly the meaning of consent within the psychiatric context.

The extent to which practical significance attaches to the presence or absence of the patient's consent to treatment raises questions of process central to the concerns of this book. It is being contended here that the true participation of all those involved in a decision is an essential requirement of full process, and thus an essential component of the legitimate exercise of public power. It is important here to distinguish between participation and control. A system which accepts a patient's right to reject treatment, and is accordingly prepared to withhold treatment in the absence of the patient's consent, would enable the patient not only to participate in the treatment decision but also to exercise a significant degree of control over it. On the other hand, a system might encourage participation by insisting that the patient's consent be sought before treatment, but might reduce the patient's control over the outcome by allowing treatment to be imposed in the absence of that consent in certain circumstances.

The value of the participation offered to the patient under a scheme of the latter type will be dependent on a number of factors, including the level of information provided to the patient and the rigour with which the treatment authorities are required to justify the imposition of treatment in the absence of consent. The legislative structure provided under section 58 falls clearly within the second category, it purports to encourage participation but does not guarantee control. A further variation is provided by section 57, which requires the patient's participation, but denies the patient control by authorising the withholding of treatment despite the patient's desire for it. Before considering the value of the participation afforded to patients in practice under Part IV of the Act, however, some thought must be given to the notion of consent in psychiatry.

In his discussion of consent to psychiatric treatment, Bean identifies four features of consent as he understands it: awareness, information, coercion and specificity.[8] Awareness relates to a person's capacity to consent: to be aware of themselves and their predicament. There is a link here with the distinction between autonomous persons and autonomous choices. Someone who lacks

and C. Kaufman *et al.*, 'Informed Consent and Patient Decision Making; the reasoning of Law and Psychiatry' (1981) 4 Int. Jo. of Law and Psychiatry 345.
8 *Supra*, n. 7, ch. 8.

the capacity to be entirely independent and in control may, nevertheless, be able to make an autonomous choice on a specific issue or, in other words, may be capable of full participation in certain contexts.[9] Bean feels that the recognition of fluctuations in awareness need not be the elusive preserve of psychiatry. Secondly, in order to consent to treatment the patient requires information concerning that treatment and its likely effects. Without such information 'consent', and thus participation, is meaningless. Bean emphasises the need to create an environment where the patient can ask questions, receive answers and be given time to deliberate. The absence of coercion is also central to true consent. A patient cannot be said to be consenting if her consent is obtained through threats, explicit or implied, of prolonged detention or loss of privileges. Coercion should, however, be distinguished from psychological pressure of the kind that might arise if the patient is told that her condition will deteriorate if she refuses medication.[10] Unfortunately, the distinction is not always easy to draw in practice. Finally, Bean emphasises the need to ensure the specificity of consent. Consent cannot be open-ended, it must relate to a specific treatment or course of treatment.

With these issues in mind it is necessary to consider the operation of the consent provisions in practice. The discussion will concentrate on section 58, since no special hospital patients have yet sought treatment under section 57. The requirements of Part IV were phased in over a number of months following September 1983. Once a detained patient has been receiving treatment for mental disorder for three months the rmo must seek the patient's consent and, if such consent is forthcoming, must certify accordingly.[11] If the patient is not prepared to consent to treatment, or if the rmo does not consider that the patient is capable of consenting, the rmo must call in a second-opinion doctor.

When called in, a second-opinion doctor should follow a basic procedure.[12] On arrival at the hospital the second doctor should be provided with the patient's treatment plan, detention documents and clinical case notes. The doctor should interview the patient, preferably in private, discuss the case in person with the patient's rmo, and consult a nurse and one other professional concerned with the patient's care. Where appropriate, the second doctor should also consult a wider range of professionals, supporters and relatives. In cases of initial disagreement between the rmo and the second-opinion doctor over the nature of the proposed treatment, an attempt to negotiate should be made. Proposed dose ranges can be altered or alternative drugs prescribed. If disagreement persists, however, the second-opinion doctor should record his or her reasons for refusing to certify the treatment. The second-opinion doctor

---

9 The issue of capacity is discussed in the Law Commission Consultation Paper No. 119, *Mentally Incapacitated Adults and Decision-Making: An Overview* (1991, London: HMSO).

10 J. Murphy, 'Therapy and the Problem of Autonomous Consent' (1979) 2 Int. Jo. of Law and Psychiatry 415.

11 The relevant forms on which certification must be made are contained in sch. 1 of the Mental Health (Hospital, Guardianship and Consent to Treatment) Regulations, SI 1983/893.

12 The required procedure is described in the *Code of Practice* (1990, London: HMSO), ch. 16.

is responsible for his or her own decision, which cannot be appealed to the Mental Health Act Commission.[13]

Under the statutory scheme therefore, the rmo is primarily concerned with the validity of the patient's participation, while the second-opinion doctor is concerned with both the validity of the participation and the justification for acting in the absence of consent. When the rmo certifies that the patient is both capable of consenting and has consented, he or she is essentially certifying that the patient has participated in the treatment decision and is in agreement with it. In cases where the rmo regards the patient as incapable of consenting, the second-opinion doctors has to assess the patient's capacity to consent and, if such capacity is absent, to determine whether the treatment should be given. In all cases where the second-opinion doctor regards the patient as capable yet withholding consent, he or she must determine whether the treatment should be given despite the patient's objections. While questions of capacity are related closely to participation, the certification of treatment in the absence of consent involves the issue of justification. Both aspects of the statutory scheme require further examination.

(2) The Validity of Consent – Participation in Practice

First, the question of capacity and participation. In all cases the rmo, and in the case of the possibly non-volitional patient the second-opinion doctor, must assess whether the patient is capable of understanding the nature, purpose and likely effects of the treatment, and if so, the relevant doctor must then consider whether the patient has in fact consented. The phrase 'nature, purpose and likely effects' also appears in section 57, in relation to those treatments for which both consent and certification are required, and in that context it was considered by the High Court in *Ex p. W*.[14] While the decision in that case did not turn on the interpretation of the phrase, the court appeared to suggest that, for the purposes of Part IV, consent rests not on actual understanding but merely on the patient's abstract intellectual ability to understand. Such an interpretation would have been at odds with established second-opinion practice, according to which doctors were advised to consider both the patients' intellectual capacity and their actual understanding. It would also dilute the notion of consent. In the light of further legal advice, however, the Mental Health Act Commission has not altered its interpretation of consent, and continues to advise second-opinion doctors to consider both capacity and actual understanding.[15]

The 1983 Act requires the second-opinion doctor to consult a nurse and one other professional who has been concerned with the patient's 'medical treatment', section 58(4). This obligation to consult is imposed in cases where the patient is regarded either as incapable of consenting or as withholding consent. It is not expressly required when the second doctor forms the opinion

13 MHAC, *Fourth Biennial Report 1989–1991* (1991, London: HMSO), p. 33.
14 *R v. Mental Health Act Commission ex p. W* (1988) *The Times*, 27 May.
15 MHAC, *supra*, n. 13, p. 32.

that the patient is capable and is consenting, nor is it expressly imposed on rmos. Nevertheless, the Code of Practice states that the consultees should comment on 'the proposed treatment and the patient's ability to consent to it.'[16] There is thus formal recognition of the view, expressed by Bean, that the assessment of capacity should not be the exclusive preserve of psychiatry.

In practice, however, second-opinion doctors can experience difficulties in achieving consultation with the 'third professional': the non-nurse. Sometimes, owing to the absence of a multi-disciplinary approach at the detaining hospital, such a person simply does not exist.[17] In such circumstances the second-opinion doctor should not certify the treatment. Certainly, where such gaps are found, both the doctor concerned and the Mental Health Act Commission comment adversely to the hospital, and to a considerable extent such gaps have been filled. The 1989–91 Biennial Report of the Commission suggests that the difficulties encountered by second-opinion doctors in this respect now arise primarily from poor organisation by the hospitals, not from the complete absence of the relevant personnel.[18] Thus, to some extent it can be said that a formal procedural requirement – the obligation to consult – has contributed to an improvement in the standard of decision making by forcing psychiatrists to include other disciplines, such as social work and psychology, in their decisions concerning patient care.

The level of information available to a patient was the second aspect of consent emphasised by Bean. The patient's ability fully to consent, and thus to participate, will be significantly affected by the nature and quality of the information provided by all those involved. If consent is to include not merely the intellectual capacity but also actual understanding, then the provision of adequate information is of crucial importance. At present there is some debate as to whether the requirement that the patient understand the nature, purpose and likely effect of the treatment is merely declaratory of the common law on the question of the information that must be given, or whether it requires more. The common law merely insists that the patient be given that amount of information that a reasonable body of professional opinion would give.[19] Whatever the precise relationship between the 1983 Act and the common law, however, there appears to be some agreement that the nature of the required information will vary from 'broad terms' to great detail, depending on the patient's ability to understand and the complexity and risks of the proposed treatment.[20] It is up to the doctor to ensure that adequate information has been given to enable the patient to consent.

16 *Supra*, n. 12, para. 16.35.
17 See the First, Second and Third *Biennial Reports* of the MHAC (1985, 1987 and 1989, London: HMSO), at pp. 40, 23 and 23, respectively.
18 *Supra*, n. 13, p. 32.
19 See: *Chatterton* v. *Gerson* [1981] Q.B. 432 and *Sidaway* v. *Governors of Bethlem Royal Hospital* [1985] AC 871; and, for further discussion, see P. Fennell, 'Sexual Suppressants and the Mental Health Act' (1988) Crim. LR 660, and P. Fennell, 'Inscribing Paternalism in the Law: Consent to Treatment and Mental Disorder' (1990) 17 Jo. of Law and Soc. 29.
20 See *Ex p. W, supra*, n. 14, and Mental Health Act Commission, *Third Biennial Report 1987–1989* (1989, London: HMSO), pp. 24–5.

In addition to the provision of adequate information, Bean also emphasises the importance of specificity. In order for consent to be real it must relate to a specific course of treatment: the patient must know exactly what he or she is consenting to. When the consent provisions were first introduced it was common, particularly in some special hospitals, for the treatment allegedly consented to be described in very broad terms by the rmo. The rmo might, for example, certify that the patient was consenting to 'a course of treatment'. Such certifications are now the exception, but the problem of specificity still exists. The 1983 Act itself does not deal directly with the issue, and the forms provided by statutory instrument require merely a 'description of treatment or plan of treatment'.[21] The issue is addressed with greater precision by the Code of Practice, which states that the

r.m.o. should indicate on the certificate the drugs proposed, by the classes described in the British National Formulary (indicating the dosages if they are above the B.N.F. advisory maximum limits) and the method of their administration.[22]

However, such a prescription does not necessarily impose sufficient specificity to enable true consent to occur. In the first place, under the requirements of the Code of Practice, the rmo can certify that the patient is consenting to the administration of any number of an extensive class of drugs, each one up to the advised limit. Thus, in combination, the patient is regarded as 'consenting' to a very high dose indeed. It would seem unlikely that most allegedly consenting patients are aware of this. Further problems occur where the certified doses are above the BNF limits. Here the Code of Practice, which although indicative of good practice is not directly binding in law, is slightly ambiguous in its requirements, enabling those rmos who are hostile to any interference with their clinical judgment to evade the spirit, if not the letter, of the regulations. Whatever the nature of the formal requirements, however, from the point of view of the validity of the patient's consent, the greatest practical specificity should be encouraged. A patient cannot be said to consent unless, within the limits of his or her capacity, he or she knows the precise nature of the treatment proposed.

Finally, the issue of coercion is an enduring problem in relation to consent. In practice its impact is felt early in the decision process. A patient who is 'coerced' into consenting will never be seen by a second-opinion doctor: he or she will be certified as consenting by the rmo. During routine visits to special hospitals, members of the Mental Health Act Commission discuss treatment with patients, and in the course of such discussions may conclude that the consent of a particular patient is of doubtful validity. A patient may, for example, have 'consented' to treatment because a Mental Health Review Tribunal was due and he or she did not wish to alienate the rmo at such a sensitive time by appearing uncooperative. In many such cases the commissioners will raise the issue with the patient's rmo, who will be advised to seek a second opinion, but quite frequently the patient will ask that the matter be not

21 See, *supra*, n. 11, forms 38 and 39.
22 *Supra*, n. 12, para 16.11.

mentioned to the rmo. Such requests appear typically to reflect the patient's fear that any failure to co-operate with treatment will be regarded as evidence of continuing disorder, and militate against favourable reports from the rmo. While these fears may be exaggerated, they emphasise the difficulty of assessing 'consent' against a background of indeterminate detention and within an environment such as a special hospital, where coercion is subtle and pervasive.

The statutory structure for seeking and certifying the patient's consent to treatment has led to some welcome adjustments to practice, most notably in the involvement of other professionals and in the greater specificity with which treatment plans are now presented to patients. But it is evident that the effectiveness of the system is largely dependent on the co-operation of the rmo. If the rmo certifies that the patient is capable and is consenting, the second-opinion procedure is never initiated unless the case is picked up on, for example, a Commission visit to the hospital.

This feature of the system is all too clearly illustrated by the attitude of medical staff at Broadmoor to the consent provisions when first introduced. In the first two years of the operation of Part IV, 89 second opinions were requested at Broadmoor, as opposed to 413 at Rampton, and 262 at Moss Side and Park Lane (now Ashworth).[23] The patient numbers at the three hospitals over the relevant period were 494, 590, and 562, respectively. In their second Biennial Report the Mental Health Act Commission refer to the fact that the clinical teams at Broadmoor would not consider a patient ready for discharge or transfer to a less secure hospital if the patient was not co-operating with medication. Patients were, no doubt, only too aware of this attitude, and consequently reluctant to withhold consent. Further, among certain clinical teams there was a tendency to certify that patients were consenting to 'medication', for example, or to 'a course of treatment'. As suggested above, such certifications were of no value as evidence of true consent; but, more significantly, they served in practice successfully to evade the need for a second opinion.

More recently the position at Broadmoor has improved,[24] although there are still problems with achieving universal compliance with the Code of Practice. Nevertheless, the experience of the first few years is arguably just one example of the exploitation by medical staff of a feature inherent in the system. Where detention is indeterminate and the rmo immensely influential, many patients are likely to incline towards acceptance of the rmo's proposals.[25] They will therefore be certified as consenting unless very strenuous efforts are made to neutralise the inevitable 'coercion'. In other words, from the perspective of full process, it is hard to ensure true and free participation where the patient occupies such a dependent role.

23 MHAC, *First Biennial Report 1983–5* (1985, London: HMSO), pp. 43–4.
24 MHAC, *Third Biennial Report 1987–1989* (1989, London: HMSO), p. 39.
25 The importance of the rmo is discussed further in chapter 12.

(3) Overriding the Absence of Consent

The second-opinion doctor, as explained above, also has to assess the validity of imposing treatment in the absence of consent. If a patient is either not consenting or is regarded as incapable of consent, the second-opinion doctor must determine whether the treatment should be given, 'having regard to the likelihood of its alleviating or preventing a deterioration of [the patient's] condition', section 58(3)(b). It is here, particularly in the case of a patient withholding consent, that the second doctor is being asked to balance the principles of autonomy and beneficence – in other words, to test the justification for imposing treatment in the absence of consent. In theory, at least, the second-opinion doctor should be aware of the significance of the decision that he or she is required to make. Both the guidance from the Mental Health Act Commission and the Code of Practice implicitly emphasise the relevance of autonomy, and the importance of questioning the need for the proposed treatment.[26]

In practice, however, it seems that second-opinion doctors seldom refuse to certify a course of treatment. In the period up to June 1985 certification was refused in only 4.6 per cent of cases throughout England and Wales.[27] The Commission freely admits that this represents a high level of agreement, and that further research is required to examine the reasons for it, but certain possible explanations present themselves. In the first place, as the Commission points out, it is not clear from the figures how many certifications have emerged from a process of negotiation between the rmo and the second-opinion doctor. It is possible that rmos have been prepared to agree alterations to their proposals in order to achieve approval. A revised report form enabling second-opinion doctors to record the presence of such negotiations has now been introduced by the Commission.[28] Secondly, there is the question of professional loyalty and the nature of the test itself. The second-opinion doctor is asked merely to assess whether 'the proposed treatment is reasonable in the light of the general consensus of appropriate treatment for such a condition'.[29] It is thus a review of reasonableness, rather than an appeal. Thirdly, although the second doctor is encouraged to search for less intrusive forms of treatment and to discuss the possibilities with the 'statutory consultees', it is possible that, however receptive the second doctor might be to non-drug-based options, the availability of viable alternatives is limited. Finally, it is possible that the existence of the second-opinion system has deterred rmos from proposing anything but the most orthodox treatments in the case of patients who do not consent – treatments which, given the test applied, are almost bound to receive approval.

Whatever the reasons, however, it would appear that the system of independent peer review introduced by section 58 has done little overtly to

---

26 *Code of Practice, supra,* n. 12, para. 16.37.
27 MHAC, *Second Biennial Report 1985–1987* (1987, London: HMSO), p. 22.
28 Its introduction was promised in MHAC, *supra,* n. 13, para. 6.3.d.
29 Code of Practice, *supra,* n. 12, para. 16.37.

challenge the authority of the rmo. The patient's genuine participation, short of control, is not guaranteed, and the second-opinion system seems rarely to question the rmo's assessment of the need to impose treatment in the absence of consent. Beneficence, it seems, will tend to outweigh autonomy. Perhaps this is not surprising since the crucial weighting is being performed by another psychiatrist. Certainly, many patients regard approval of the proposed treatment by the second doctor as almost inevitable and, as a consequence, their confidence in the system is minimal. It is relevant, therefore, to ask what alterations to the process might encourage a more searching system, a system better designed to ensure both the fullest participation of the patient and the most stringent examination of the justification for the imposition of treatment.

The question, to some extent, presupposes an acceptance of the demands of autonomy but, as explained above, such a position flows naturally from the whole approach to legitimate authority adopted here, and from the characteristics of full process that flow from it. Any changes to the current system would need to address the difficulty of ensuring true consent, and the need rigorously to question the justification for overriding the patient's wishes.

The second point is perhaps more readily dealt with than the first. The most obvious change to the system would be the introduction of multi-disciplinary review before a patient's lack of consent, whether volitional or non-volitional, could be overridden. Social workers, psychologists and lawyers, while appreciating the benefits to be gained from treatment, might bring with them a deeper sympathy for autonomy. The suggestion is not new, but the experience of the first few years of the compromise introduced by Part IV,[30] at least, indicates that peer review has tended merely to legitimate the professional preference for beneficence. However, such multi-disciplinary review once the absence of consent is recognised does not meet the difficulties posed by the initial assessment of consent. Here it is essential to ensure that no patient can be certified as consenting unless the treatment for which consent is sought is specified with some precision, unless the patient is given, in an accessible form, sufficient information about its nature, purpose and likely effects, and unless adequate steps are taken to guard against inevitable 'coercion'. In this respect, therefore, the Code of Practice must become significantly more stringent in its requirements, and compliance with those requirements must be assiduously monitored, as a matter of routine, by an independent body.

(b) Restrictions on a Patient's Freedom

The decisions discussed in this section concern the regulation of a patient's freedom in areas which are not directly related to the administration of treatment in the narrow sense. They are, nevertheless, decisions which impinge directly on the residual freedoms of the patient, and as such require some specific justification.

As was explained in the previous chapter, a patient is detained in hospital

---

30 See the previous chapter for the history of Part IV.

under the Mental Health Act 1983 because he or she is deemed to be in need of treatment for mental disorder, compulsorily administered if necessary. Additional restrictions relating to discharge etc. can be imposed in the case of patients from whom society is thought to require protection from serious harm. The infringements of the patients' freedoms which are expressly authorised by the Act must therefore be assumed to be justified by reference to the demands of treatment and security. The infringements flowing from the decisions considered in this section, however, are not specifically authorised by the 1983 Act, and no such assumption can therefore be made. Such infringements can only be justified if clearly required by the need to treat or to maintain security, and the internal decision making processes should be designed to ensure that they are so justified. Individuals are not compulsorily detained in hospital for any other purpose. As in the context of imprisonment, however, the need to maintain security – that is, successfully to segregate individuals from the rest of society – carries with it the need to maintain order or control within the secure environment.

(1) Seclusion

A patient is secluded when he or she is placed alone in a locked room for any period of time. The Mental Health Act 1983 empowers the hospital authorities to detain and to treat a patient held under either a hospital order or a transfer direction. It makes no mention of seclusion, which is not expressly included in the statutory definition of 'medical treatment' contained in section 145. Despite this omission, however, the Code of Practice states that seclusion does fall within the statutory definition of medical treatment, presumably by implication; but it goes on to explain that 'seclusion is not a treatment technique and should not feature as part of any treatment programme.'[31] An alternative legal approach might accept that seclusion is not contained in the notion of treatment, nor is its lawful use confined to circumstances where it is necessary in order to effect detention, and might argue instead that its legal base resides in the common law power to use reasonable force to prevent a breach of the peace. If such is the true nature of the legal authority, then the power to seclude must be restricted to significantly shorter periods than are currently employed. Whatever its precise legal status, however, the use of seclusion is both approved by the Code of Practice and widespread within special hospitals.

According to the Code of Practice, seclusion 'is the supervised confinement of a patient alone in a room which may be locked for the protection of others from significant harm'.[32] Thus, whatever its formal legal basis, the justification for seclusion must be linked ultimately to the demands of security and control. The Code makes it clear that seclusion should not be used as a punitive measure or to enforce good behaviour. Neither should it be used where there is a danger of self-injury or suicide, nor where equipment is being damaged. Its

31 *Code of Practice, supra,* n. 12, para. 18.14.
32 *Ibid.*

proper use, according to the Code is strictly limited, and must be restricted to situations where the confinement of the patient is necessary for the protection of others 'from significant harm'. The Code also insists that the use of seclusion be governed by clear policy guidelines within each hospital and, although the initial decision to seclude may be taken by a nurse, a doctor must attend immediately. The strict monitoring and review of each individual instance of seclusion is also required.

Whatever the Code of Practice may require, the actual use of seclusion in special hospitals has caused concern for some time.[33] This concern has centred on the reasons for its use, the length of time during which individual patients are secluded, and the manner in which seclusion is effected. In recent years patients in special hospitals have been secluded because of industrial action, because they present a suicide risk, or because they do not wish to associate with other patients for a period and no other provision can be made for them. There is also evidence that seclusion is used as a punishment, and the Committee of Inquiry into Complaints about Ashworth Hospital (the Ashworth Inquiry) concluded that it had been so used in the case of Sean Walton.[34] Not one of these reasons accords with the guidance provided by the Code of Practice, nor do they reflect exclusively the demands of security and control. A small number of patients have also been secluded for prolonged periods of time. According to the Mental Health Act Commission Fourth Biennial Report, 'there has been a small minority of patients [in Broadmoor] who have consistently spent more than 28 days out of each 3 month period in seclusion'.[35] Also at Broadmoor, there has been concern over the practice of stripping patients prior to seclusion. In some cases it is considered necessary to place a patient in protective clothing prior to seclusion for his or her own safety, but there is a fear that the use of protective clothing has become a matter of routine on certain wards.[36] The practice of stripping disturbed patients prior to seclusion has also been questioned by an inquiry team established to investigate the death of a patient in seclusion at Broadmoor.[37]

The Code of Practice is designed to apply equally to all hospitals, including the special hospitals. However, it is evident from the above that the practice of seclusion in the special hospitals is in breach of the Code in many significant respects. Indeed, although the SHSA appears to be committed to ultimate compliance, it would appear that compliance in practice is still some way away.[38]

33 MHAC, *supra*, n. 13, p. 21.
34 *Report of the Committee of Inquiry into Complaints about Ashworth Hospital* (The Ashworth Report) (1992, Cm 2028–1, London: HMSO), p. 57. See also MHAC, *Evidence to the Committee of Inquiry into Complaints about Ashworth Special Hospital* (1992).
35 *Supra*, n. 13, p. 23.
36 *Ibid.*
37 *Report of the Inquiry into the Circumstances Leading to the Death in Broadmoor Hospital of Mr Joseph Watts on 23 August 1988* (1989, London: SHSA).
38 MHAC, *supra*, n. 13, p. 21. The SHSA has now established a steering committee to review the use of seclusion within special hospitals.

The seclusion of a patient is an exercise of power that has a direct and significant impact on the interests of the individual. It immediately deprives the patient of any residual freedom of movement and association that he or she previously enjoyed within the normal hospital environment, and it typically involves the removal of 'privileges' such as toilet facilities and cigarettes. Because of its draconian nature, its susceptibility to abuse, and the incidence of patients dying while in seclusion, there is a case for arguing that seclusion should not continue to be used for the control of psychiatric patients.[39] Adequate staffing and skilled nursing might avoid the need for seclusion without increasing resort to the forced administration or neuroleptic medication. Nevertheless, seclusion is still employed with some frequency within the special hospitals, and it is important to consider the principles which should govern its use.

In the first place, in keeping with the notion of full process, the circumstances in which seclusion may be used must be specified with considerable precision and care, and must be open to public debate. Hospital authorities, however well-intentioned, must be required to justify the principles according to which they impose such restrictions on the freedom of individual patients. Indeed, if seclusion is to be allowed, its nature and use should be prescribed in statutory form. Secondly, the manner in which seclusion is effected must be subject to detailed regulation. Further, and arguably of even greater importance, a monitored system must be developed to ensure that a considered decision is taken on each occasion. It must ensure that the continuing need for seclusion is assessed at regular intervals and, if seclusion persists beyond a certain period, that its continued justification is judged by someone independent of the clinical team.

Unfortunately, in certain ward environments resort to seclusion can become commonplace, and the recording of reasons a matter of pure form.[40] Great care is therefore needed to check the accuracy and adequacy of the records kept. If the culture on a ward supports the use of punitive seclusion and the stripping of patients, such practices can only be prevented by the most assiduous monitoring and the continual oversight by personnel from outside the ward and, ultimately, from outside the hospital. The likely disincentive effect of such intrusive monitoring requirements can only be welcomed if it serves to reduce the incidence of seclusion, provided no alternative control technique is allowed to flourish unregulated in its place.

---

39 Since 1984 three black patients have died in seclusion in one special hospital alone: Michael Martin (1984), Joseph Watts (1988) and Orville Blackwood (1991). The first two cases are discussed in *Deadly Silence* (1991, London: Institute of Race Relations). See also the account of the death of Sean Walton in seclusion at the then Moss Side hospital, Ashworth Report, supra, n. 34. ch. X. In chapter XXII the Ashworth Report recommends the phasing-out and ultimate ending of seclusion.

40 See the findings of the Ashworth Report, *supra*, n. 34 p. 57.

(2) Discipline

Within the prison context, inmates can be bad. There is a statutory code of discipline and a formal system for the adjudication of charges and the imposition of awards and, as was suggested in chapter 7, the existence of such a code can be justified by the need to maintain security and control. Within special hospitals there is no such formal code. In prisons the authorities, when dealing with disruptive prisoners, are ostensibly presented with the choice between a formal disciplinary charge or segregation under rule 43. In special hospitals disruptive behaviour will commonly be regarded as pathological – a symptom of the patient's disorder – and will be dealt with by the clinical team in the way considered most appropriate within the context of the patient's overall treatment plan. The problem behaviour may involve anything from violence, firesetting or the possession of illicit drugs, to the collection of morbid press cuttings or the display of 'inappropriate' behaviour towards female staff members. In cases concerning drugs or firesetting, for example, the police may be called in to investigate. In nearly all cases the behaviour will be considered at a multi-disciplinary case conference and an appropriate response agreed, but occasionally some action will have to be taken immediately in order to defuse a dangerous situation. In all cases the rmo is ultimately responsible to management for the treatment of the patient.

The notion of disciplinary sanctions has no place within the official language of special hospitals, but the consequences which can flow from the discovery of inappropriate behaviour are often regarded as punitive by the patients and might include: confinement to the ward, denial of certain forms of work, removal of association with patients of the opposite sex, removal of 'parole', the freedom to move around certain parts of the hospital, cancellation of trips or transfer to the special care unit. In the case of all such consequences, the patient will suffer an immediate sanction, and may have recorded on his or her file an account of behaviour which could prejudice his or her future assessment. Patients in the one special hospital known to the author were generally aware of the consequences that might follow if they broke the rules, and were fully aware of the significant role played by the rmo.[41] Most patients were also aware of the sort of behaviour that would attract adverse consequences but, in the absence of any formal statement of rules, ambiguities could and did arise. Seclusion, when used according to the official policies, falls into a special category of response and, as already explained, should not be used punitively. However, there will inevitably be occasions when a patient believes that seclusion has been used as a punishment, and the real potential for such abuse, as suggested above, can only be controlled through rigorous monitoring.

Thus, consequences carrying significant short- and possibly long-term effects can be imposed on a patient in the exercise of 'therapeutic' judgement. While staff will attempt to establish the facts before any decision is taken, the

41 This recognition of the rmo's authority is confirmed in J. Peay, *Tribunals on Trial*, (1989, Oxford: Oxford University Press).

factfinding and decision making process adopted is likely to be one of informal discussion between the rmo and the parties involved. In such circumstances the patient will be at a significant disadvantage, and will find it hard effectively to challenge any account presented by members of staff.

A typical incident might involve allegations that a patient has been verbally or physically threatening to a member of staff. As a result the patient might be secluded immediately, and restricted to the ward for a number of days after the incident. The staff involved may claim that the patient's behaviour was unprovoked, while the patient contends that he reacted to verbal abuse from a staff member. The patient will face considerable difficulties in seeking to establish the validity of his account: he may have a history of threatening behaviour, there may be no witnesses to the incident who are prepared to come forward other than staff members, and the patient may have to confront an implied assumption on the part of his interlocutors that, as a patient, his evidence is automatically unreliable. The dismissive attitude typically displayed towards the evidence of psychiatric patients is well-documented in the Ashworth Report.[42] While it is certainly true that patients will face formidable difficulties under *any* investigative system, the informality and discretionary nature of the current system gives rise to particular concern. However, any suggestion that a more rigorous process be introduced immediately confronts the conflict between legalism and the therapeutic endeavour which is said to underlie the history of the law's involvement in the regulation of mental health care.[43]

From the point of view of special hospital staff, offenders are sent to hospital rather than to prison because they are mentally disordered and in need of treatment. From this perspective it is possible to see all subsequent 'deviance' on the part of the patient as a function of that mental disorder, and consequently as requiring treatment, not punishment. The imposition of sanctions would, therefore, be entirely inappropriate except as part of a strict behavioural treatment programme. According to such a view, the correct approach would be to identify the problem behaviour and to help the patient to work it through, either with or without the assistance of drugs. The introduction of legalistic procedures for the determination of 'guilt' and the imposition of 'sanctions' would merely disrupt the therapeutic endeavour.

There are, however, two other matters of concern to special hospital staff which may dilute the pure treatment objectives, and which, in fact, reflect the demands of control and security. In the first place, special hospital staff recognise that special hospitals, like prisons, have to provide a safe environment for both patients and staff. There may therefore be control rather than treatment reasons for taking certain action. A violently disruptive patient may need to be secluded immediately for the protection of others on the ward, or a patient's access to visitors may need to be restricted in order to prevent the

42 *Supra*, n. 34. The Ashworth Report recommends that staff receive special training on the interviewing of patient witnesses and complainants.
43 See, for example, Unsworth, *supra*, n. 1; Peay, *supra*, n. 41; and N. Rose, 'Unreasonable Rights: Mental Illness and the Limits of the Law' (1985) Jo. of Law and Soc. 199.

import of unauthorised drugs. Secondly, special hospital staff appreciate that they are performing a custodial as well as a treatment role. They are required to maintain security and thus to ensure that the public are protected from the dangerous offenders within their hospitals, while at the same time they are expected to treat those offender patients. The dilemmas presented by these potentially conflicting objectives are well-recognised, particularly in relation to discharge decisions.[44] In the present context the public protection objective may indicate a more stringent response to internal deviance than that suggested by treatment alone, and may impose an apparently overwhelming obligation to record all incidents of suspected problem behaviour, however slender the suspicion, particularly if it involves firesetting or violence.

Whatever the primary motivation of the clinical staff, however, it is important to dispel the belief that any recognition of a disciplinary code and any introduction of the accompanying process requirements would be counter-therapeutic and lead to sterile legalism. Any move towards full process should, by definition, lead to better decision making. In the first place, full process would require openness. Patients should be fully aware of what is expected of them and should know, as precisely as possible, what is prohibited and what the consequences of non-compliance will be. A closed community such as a special hospital must be expected to require adherence to certain general rules in addition to any included within an individual treatment contract devised between a patient and his or her clinical team. The formal recognition that such rules exist can hardly be regarded as anti-therapeutic, and ideally the patient should be involved in their creation, at least at ward level. A formal statement of the rules would also help to ensure that those rules and the restrictions flowing from them are fully justified.

In cases of suspected deviance from the rules every effort should be made to establish the facts. In some cases this might require the intervention of an 'adjudicator' from outside the clinical team or, in cases where serious criminal conduct is alleged, the intervention of the police. Where a member of the hospital staff is used to investigate, they should be sufficiently distanced from the ward to possess at least some of the independence of a true adjudicator. Further, such a figure should be actively inquisitorial, not only because he or she would be engaged in the investigation of facts, but also because of the need to overcome some of the difficulties faced by the patient in attempting to uncover supporting evidence. He or she would also have to be specifically trained to overcome any possible bias against believing the evidence of a patient.

Whatever the precise structure of the decision maker, however, the procedure itself should involve the fullest possible participation on the part of the patient. Once the facts are established it should be open to the clinical team to select a treatment rather than a disciplinary response, but if they do so they should explain their reasons to the patient and record them in full on the patient's clinical notes. If, in a case such as that described above, for example,

44 Peay, *supra*, n. 41, and see chapter 12.

the clinical team believe that the patient's threatening behaviour was grounded in his delusional system, a treatment response would clearly be indicated, rather than a disciplinary sanction. Finally, if doubts remain as to the relevant facts but it is still thought necessary to record the incident, the record must note the absence of conclusive evidence, and the patient must be offered the opportunity to add his account of the events.

Such an approach, arguably, would be facilitative of the treatment objective, not obstructive of it. In the first place, the patient would have access to a definitive statement of 'rules' and would know the formal limits imposed. Secondly, by encouraging the public formulation of those rules, the approach would help to ensure that the rules themselves were appropriate and, by demanding the open investigation of any alleged breach by an 'independent adjudicator', it would encourage their accurate application in individual cases. The insistence on the provision of a full explanation to patients should also help to increase the patient's confidence in the clinical team. Further, the obligation to record on the patient's notes the precise status of any suspicions would guarantee that those who have subsequently to assess the patient on the basis of the information contained in those notes could draw their own conclusions in as full a knowledge of the facts as possible. Finally, by empowering the patients to participate, the whole approach would be designed to restore to them some element of responsibility for the decisions made.

In the light of the approach here, certain recent developments in special hospital policy are greatly to be welcomed. The SHSA is currently under-taking a review of patients' basic entitlements throughout the special hospital system, and it is envisaged that any such review will have to confront the question of derogations from those entitlements, for whatever reason. Secondly, by virtue of the Access to Health Records Act 1990, patients in special hospitals, as elsewhere, now have a right of access to their health records (section 3). A health record 'consists of information relating to the physical or mental health of an individual', which 'has been made by or on behalf of a health professional in connection with the care of that individual', section 1(1)(a) and (b). Health professionals include registered medical practitioners, registered nurses, clinical psychologists and art or music therapists employed by a health service body. The 1990 Act therefore provides special hospital patients with a prima facie right of access to most of the relevant records compiled on them within the hospital, with the exception of the notes kept by social workers. However, the 1990 Act only applies to records compiled after November 1991, unless the holder of the record considers it necessary to give access to earlier records in order to make the more recent records intelligible. Further, it does not apply to any record 'which, in the opinion of the holder of the record, would disclose . . . information likely to cause serious harm to the physical or mental health of the patient or of any other individual', section 5(1)(a). If a person considers that any information given in a record to which he or she has had access is inaccurate, he or she may apply to the holder of the record for a correction to be made (section 6). The record holder must then make the necessary correction or, if not satisfied that there is an inaccuracy, record the patient's objection. Thus a special hospital patient would now appear to have both a right of access to any record kept in his clinical notes, subject to the important exception allowed by section 5(1)(a), and the right to record any objections he may have as to the accuracy of those notes.

It remains to be seen how these legislative requirements, particularly section 5(1)(a), are implemented in practice, but it is interesting to compare the internal guidance on the 1990 Act issued to prison medical staff with that issued by one special hospital. With regard to access to records compiled prior to November 1991, the prison doctors are told, on behalf of the Director of the Prison Medical Service, that she 'would expect applications for access to be granted unless there are overriding indications to the contrary', while special hospital staff are told that it is 'not necessary to disclose information recorded prior to 1 November 1991 unless it is required to make sense to [sic] any part of the record which is being disclosed'.[45] It must be hoped that this is not indicative of a generally restrictive approach to the 1990 Act within special hospitals.

(3) Contact with the Outside World

(a) Correspondence

Voluntary patients within an ordinary hospital are not subject to any special controls over their correspondence. The controls operating in the case of prisoners were discussed in chapter 5, where it was remarked that there has been a considerable reduction in censorship in recent years. Detained patients, and particularly those in special hospitals, fall into an intermediate category in this respect. Section 134 of the 1983 Act empowers the managers of a special hospital to withhold a patient's outgoing mail if they consider that the mail is likely

i) to cause distress to the person to whom it is addressed or to any other person (not being a person on the staff of the hospital); or ii) to cause danger to any person.

The managers are also empowered to withhold incoming mail from a patient

if, in the opinion of the managers of the hospital, it is necessary to do so in the interests of the safety of the patient or for the protection of other persons.

Mail to and from certain bodies and individuals is excluded from these provisions. In the exercise of these powers the special hospitals do not operate a general policy of censorship but treat each patient's case individually. In practice it is the responsibility of the rmo to decide whether a patient's mail,

45 See, respectively, DDL (91)9, HM Prison Service, and Broadmoor Hospital Policy Relating to Access to Health Service Records, HP33. The SHSA is intending to comply with the recommendation in the Ashworth Report that patients should have access to their records prior to November 1991, except in exceptional circumstances.

either outgoing or incoming, should be withheld and, if so, whether it should be withheld generally or only with regard to mail to or from certain people. The role of the Mental Health Act Commission in the review of these decisions is discussed in chapter 11.

While the restrictions imposed on a patient's right to correspond with people outside the hospital are specifically contained in the 1983 Act, and to that extent are formally justified, those imposed on correspondence between patients within the same hospital possess no such statutory pedigree. It was normal practice in one special hospital known to the author for ward staff to monitor correspondence between patients. The practice was officially justified on grounds of treatment: a patient's letters were thought to be revealing of the patient's state of mind. That such an infringement of individual privacy could occur routinely without serious challenge is indicative of an approach to patient care which rarely sees the need to question the stated demands of treatment.

(b) Visits to Patients Within Special Hospitals

There is no statutory regulation relating a patient's access to visits from outside the hospital. Until 1991 the practice was relatively liberal and patients were allowed supervised visits from friends and relations, constrained only by staffing levels and the patient's health. There was, however, a growing concern that illicit drugs might be entering the hospitals from visitors. Further, in 1991 considerable publicity was given to the escape of a convicted rapist from Broadmoor, and his receipt of a visit from a 15-year-old girl a few days after his recapture. In late 1991 a new and more restrictive visiting policy was introduced at Broadmoor. All existing visitors were required to be authorised by the patient's clinical team and to have their identities recorded so that they might be checked at each subsequent visit, while all new visitors had to apply to be included on the approved list. In addition, patients and visitors were informed that no food could be brought in for patients from the outside.[46]

Following many complaints from patients and visitors at Broadmoor the policy was reviewed internally and the prohibition on the importation of food lifted. The requirement that visitors be included on an approved list has not, however, been significantly revised. While the hospital authorities have a right to know who is on their premises, and a duty to protect patients from the attentions of unwanted visitors, as well as a right to prevent the importation of illicit drugs, doubts remain as to both the propriety and the efficacy of the approved list policy as a means of achieving these objectives. Special hospital patients have few remaining freedoms, and it is essential that any restrictions imposed beyond those expressly contained in the Act be carefully and specifically justified. With regard to the 1991 restrictions on visiting it is unclear whether their justification is to be found by reference to treatment, or

46 The policy was conveyed in letters to patients and visitors from the hospital management in November 1991.

to security, or to control. Such loose thinking on the part of management cannot be acceptable when it is employed to restrict the rights of patients.

(c) Trips Out from the Hospital

Before a patient will be considered ready for discharge or transfer from a special hospital he or she will usually have been on escorted trips from the hospital as part of a rehabilitative programme. Section 17 of the 1983 Act empowers the rmo to grant a patient leave of absence from the hospital, which may be for a matter of hours and in the custody of hospital staff, or may involve 'home' leave over the weekend. In the case of a patient who is under a restriction order or a restriction direction, the consent of the Home Secretary is required before the rmo may exercise his or her powers under section 17, an additional hurdle which is presumably justified by reference to security. Thus, under section 41(3) the rmo must obtain such consent from the Home Office before arranging for a rehabilitation trip. In practice this can cause a delay, and disagreement can emerge between the Home Office and the rmo. As will be seen in chapter 12, in cases where the Home Office adopts a more cautious approach than that advocated by the rmo, the Home Office can exercise a significant influence over the patient's chances of discharge.

Whatever the implications of the Secretary of State's involvement, however, it is required by statute. The same is not true of the additional requirements imposed by the special hospitals. At Broadmoor a patient's rmo had, until recently, to obtain the agreement of the medical director before a rehabilitation trip, or any leave of absence, was allowed. It is hard to find any legal basis for such a requirement. Sections 17 and 41 refer only to the rmo and the Secretary of State. While it might be reasonable to expect the medical director to demand to be informed of the movement of any patient from the hospital, and possibly to authorise any requests for additional staff or resources, he or she would appear to have no authority under the 1983 Act to impose any additional restrictions on the exercise by the rmo of his or her powers under section 17. The dropping of this requirement by Broadmoor following the report of an investigation conducted by two Mental Health Act Commissioners is therefore to be welcomed.[47] The involvement of the SHSA in decisions concerning the granting of leave to individual patients appears similarly to be without specific statutory foundation, and is discussed elsewhere.[48]

(4) Conclusions – Restrictions on a Patient's Freedom

The above discussion suggests that the majority of decisions concerning the imposition of additional restrictions on a patient's freedoms while in hospital

---

47 *Adjudication on AP Complaint* (1992, Nottingham: MHAC). The role of the Mental Health Act Commission in the investigation of complaints more generally is discussed in chapter 11.

48 See chapter 9 for the role of the SHSA as Mental Health Act manager, and see chapter 12 for further considerations of its role in relation to decisions concerning specific patients.

are very loosely regulated. The Mental Health Act 1983, although in many respects more detailed than its counterpart the Prison Act 1952, is designed to regulate only very specific areas of hospital decision making: the administration of medical treatment, for example, and the censorship of patients' mail. Outside those areas the SHSA and the special hospitals are largely free to create their own policies and practices. The Code of Practice applies, but it has no direct legal force, and even where it is relevant, as in the case of seclusion, it is honoured, typically, in the breach. The resulting legal vacuum is filled in practice by internal policies created by management and reflecting, inevitably, the priorities of management. The experience of the visitors' policy and the procedure for granting trips out of hospital, and the practice of monitoring internal mail, all illustrate the ease with which administrative requirements and procedural hurdles can evolve internally to impose restrictions on the freedom of patients in excess of those demanded by statute. More rigorous formal regulation is required if the importance attaching to the retention by patients of areas of personal autonomy is to be adequately reflected, and each infringement specifically justified.

It is also evident that many of the practices currently prevailing allow decisions which carry significant implications for individual patients to be taken in the exercise of therapeutic discretion on the basis of few stated criteria. More rigorous regulation of the processes whereby such decisions are reached were advocated, not as an attempt to impose the requirements of sterile legalism, but as a positive step towards the improvement of the resulting decisions. With regard to disciplinary decisions specifically, it was suggested that the introduction of greater procedural rigour would be facilitative of the therapeutic goal rather than destructive of it. The open formulation of more specific rules was urged, together with proper investigation and the full participation of the patient at the application stage. Similarly, in relation to seclusion, if it is to be retained at all, greater stringency both in the specification of the criteria for its use and in the procedures for its implementation and monitoring was demanded, in order to ensure that every use of seclusion is justified and of as short a duration as possible.

11
Decision Making within Special Hospitals: Processes of Validation

Many of the application decisions considered in the previous chapter were characterised by a lack of formal criteria and procedural rigour, and reference was made to the importance of adequate monitoring. It is now necessary to examine all the various mechanisms designed specifically to provide for validation, and to consider the role they play in the provision of *ex post* regulation of special hospital decision making. The detention of a patient in hospital is justified under the Mental Health Act 1983 by reference to the need to provide medical treatment (section 37), and, in the case of restricted patients, the need to protect the public from serious harm (section 41). As argued in the previous chapter, all restrictions imposed on a patient should therefore be justifiable ultimately by reference to either treatment or security, and the process of validation should be designed to ensure that they are so justifiable.

(a) Internal Complaints Procedures

The Hospital Complaints Procedure Act 1985 requires the Secretary of State to issue directions to health authorities requiring them to make arrangements for dealing with complaints made by or on behalf of patients. The requirement applies equally to special hospitals, but it was not until May 1989 that the Secretary of State for Health issued a policy which was widely understood to be for immediate implementation at special hospitals.[1] In the interim each special hospital had applied its own procedures. A case described in the Third Biennial Report of the Mental Health Act Commission illustrates how complaints were handled in one special hospital under the pre-1989 procedure.

A special hospital patient was confined to his ward on security grounds and denied access to activities, a management rather than a treatment-motivated decision. Staff had received information which had convinced them that he

[1] MHAC, *Fourth Biennial Report 1989–1991* (1991, London: HMSO), p. 26.

was the ringleader of a plot to riot and to take staff hostages. The patient denied the allegations and, on the advice of the Commission, complained to management in June 1988. Management requested further details, which were supplied in writing by the patient. At no stage was the patient interviewed by management, and no member of staff was designated with the responsibility of following up the complaint. The alleged conspiracy was, however, investigated and a sharpened metal bar was found in one of the wards. In September the hospital management team received a report on the security aspects of the suspected conspiracy, which concluded that there was no firm evidence against the patient, but that the possibility that he was a security risk could not be ruled out. In November the patient finally received a formal response to his complaint. This simply rehearsed the charges originally made against him, with no indication that their substance had been thoroughly examined. The patient replied, requesting an interview. The hospital administrator's response merely stated that lengthy consideration had been given to his complaint.

First, this case illustrates the difficulties that can arise from a failure fully to substantiate a 'discipinary' charge. Here the patient had been confined to his room and denied certain facilities because of his alleged involvement in a conspiracy. Staff belief in his involvement, it transpired, had been fortified by a previous incident which, similarly, had been denied by the patient and never adequately investigated by management: an edifice of suspicion can be constructed on very slender foundations. Secondly, the case highlights the inadequacies of a complaints procedure which both failed to designate an investigating officer and denied the complainant any opportunity to explain his concerns in person. In chapter 4 it was suggested that, while the demands of speed might justify resort to internal decision making modelled on adjudication, even for the resolution of disputes, true independent adjudication should be provided at the validation stage. It is clear from the above example that the complaints procedure operating within special hospitals prior to 1989 fell far short of such an ideal.

A similar but yet more devastating conclusion with regard to Ashworth can be drawn from the Mental Health Act Commission's evidence to the 1992 Ashworth Inquiry. The Commission reported 'a total lethargy in handling complaints' in the hospital between 1983 and 1989, and suggested that the lack of a proper complaints policy 'led to the appearance of complete administrative chaos and facilitated inertia'.[2] Indeed, the findings of the Ashworth Inquiry itself vividly illustrate the complete inadequacy of the system, and highlight two particular features which had a pervasive and stultifying effect on the internal investigation of complaints at the hospital.

It was the practice at Ashworth to refer all complaints alleging possible criminal acts to the police. Thus all allegations of physical abuse or the theft of patients' property would go immediately to the police, who would invariably be unable to recover the necessary evidence to bring a criminal prosecution,

2 MHAC, *Evidence to the Committee of Inquiry into Complaints about Ashworth Special Hospital* (1991), pp. 23–4.

and the matter would be dropped without further action on the part of management. Secondly, the trade union acting on behalf of the nurses at Ashworth, the Prison Officers' Association, consistently maintained that any nurse accused of a potentially criminal act was entitled to stand upon the right to silence. Management was therefore denied the co-operation of staff in a number of complaints investigations.[3]

While the 1989 special hospital complaints procedure met some of the shortcomings illustrated by the first case described above, there was still no firm requirement that the complainant be interviewed and, perhaps of even more significance in the light of the experience of the Ashworth Inquiry, the 1989 procedure made no special provision for dealing with complaints by members of staff about the standard of care afforded to patients.[4] In 1992 the SHSA finally produced a new policy for application to all special hospitals which in certain respects represents a marked improvement on anything that has gone before.[5] It locates responsibility for the initial investigation of complaints in a specific individual, it expresses a commitment to keeping the complainant fully informed throughout, and recognises the need for an interview, for representation, and for the full reporting of conclusions. It also recognises the need to provide specifically for complaints from members of staff. Finally, it accepts the need for 'investigation by an independent professional' where the complaint alleges ill-treatment, abuse or significant theft.

While these expressions of principle and intent must be welcomed, serious doubts remain. In the first place, although the need to provide representation for patients is recognised the policy gives little indication of how this should be done. Secondly, the principles expressed with regard to complaints from staff are admirable, but it is not clear how much trust will be placed by vulnerable staff in the body to which they are advised to complain, the Hospital Advisory Committee, which is constitutionally a sub-committee of the SHSA, the statutory managers of the hospital. Finally, the identity and status of the independent investigator is left unexplained. It seems that this figure, or in practice these figures, will be appointed and paid by hospital management, a fact which must call their independence into question. They will presumably have management support, which should ensure them a level of co-operation, but there seems to be no suggestion that they should have powers to compel evidence.[6] Major improvements must therefore be introduced if the 1992

---

3 *Report of the Committee of Inquiry into Complaints about Ashworth Hospital* (The Ashworth Report) (1992, Cm 2028-1, London: HMSO); see chapters X, XI and XII for an account of the investigation of complaints, and see chapters IV and XIV for discussion of the privilege against self-incrimination and the role of the police respectively.

4 The policy is discussed in MHAC, *Third Biennial Report 1987–1989* (1989, London: HMSO), p. 18.

5 *Complaints: Statement of Policy* (1992, London: SHSA), and *Complaints Procedure* (1992, London: SHSA).

6 For a discussion of the relevance of the 'privilege against self-incrimination', frequently claimed by nursing staff at Ashworth, see *supra*, n. 3, ch. IV.

complaints policy for special hospitals is to provide an adequate structure for the internal validation of hospital decision making.

Most importantly, patients must be adequately represented. A proper system of patients' advocacy must be developed in special hospitals to assist patients to participate in all the decision making structures, whether they be concerned with policy formulation, application or validation. The Ashworth Report strongly recommends the introduction of a properly funded patients' advocacy service across all three special hospitals, and it is encouraging to note that the SHSA is seriously considering the proposal.[7] Secondly, more thought must be given to the position of staff who are dissatisfied with standards in the hospital. The evidence before the Ashworth Inquiry has provided a vivid illustration, not only of the vulnerability and isolation experienced by 'whistle blowers', but also of the crucial role they can perform in initiating effective scrutiny.[8] Finally, while the policy recognises the need for independent investigation at an early stage in serious cases, the structure provided is not immediately convincing. The role of the independent element is considered further at the end of the next section.

(b) Mental Health Act Commission

(1) The Investigation of Complaints

The complaints jurisdiction of the Mental Health Act Commission is contained in section 120 of the 1983 Act. The Commission on behalf of the Secretary of State, has a duty to 'keep under review the exercise of the powers and the discharge of the duties' conferred by the Act in relation to detained patients. In addition to this general duty, the Commission has the duty, under section 120(1)(b), to investigate two categories of complaint:

(i) any complaint made by a person in respect of a matter that occurred while he was detained under this Act in a hospital ... and which he considers has not been satisfactorily dealt with by the managers of that hospital; and
(ii) any other complaint as to the exercise of the powers or the discharge of the duties conferred or imposed by this Act in respect of a person who is or has been so detained.

A number of points should be made in relation to this specific remit. Unlike the Health Service Commissioner, the Mental Health Act Commission can consider matters of clinical judgment. It is also free to look at the merits of the complaint, not just the way in which the complaint was managed internally. As will be seen, however, the Commission has no power directly to enforce its conclusions. Section 120(1)(b) provides for the investigation by the Commission of two different types of complaint. Under paragraph (i) a detained patient or ex-detained patient may complain about any 'matter that

7 *Ibid.*, ch. XIII.
8 *Ibid.*, ch. XVIII provides a shocking account of the hate mail received by members of staff who criticised existing practices. On whistle blowers within the Health Service more generally, see V. Bearshaw, *Conscientious Objectors at Work* (1981, London: Social Audit).

occurred while he was detained', but he must first have pursued the internal complaints mechanisms. Paragraph (ii), by contrast, refers to a complaint brought on behalf of a patient concerning the exercise of the powers or the discharge of the duties under the 1983 Act. There is no requirement that the internal mechanism be exhausted first, but the subject matter of the remit is more closely confined than under (i). The main problems which have arisen with regard to this remit in practice have related to complaints concerning the death of detained patients, which by definition must come within paragraph (ii) not (i); consequently they can only be investigated by the Commission if the specific complaint relates to the exercise of powers or the discharge of duties.[9] Similarly, complaints made on behalf of non-volitional patients have to be brought within the narrower remit of paragraph (ii).

In practice the Commission receives complaints from and on behalf of special hospital patients by telephone, by letter, and at routine visits to the special hospitals. Minor 'complaints' can frequently be resolved in the course of the visit, in which case they may never be recorded as a complaint. Alternatively the patient may be advised to pursue the complaint internally first, and to come back to the Commission if he or she remains dissatisfied. Once a complaint is formally adopted by the Commission it may be pursued by letter, or two commissioners may be specifically appointed to follow it up.[10] This will typically result in two commissioners visiting the patient, inspecting documents and interviewing members of staff. In the period 1 July 1989 to 30 June 1991 the Commission received 1,068 complaints from all hospitals, including special hospitals, 458 of which were pursued by two commissioners.[11] The commissioners' right of private access to patients and their records is conferred by section 120(4), and it is an offence to obstruct the exercise of these rights, section 129, but the commission has no power to require members of staff or others to answer questions or to provide evidence. The Commission is therefore limited in the extent to which it can re-open issues which turn on disputes of fact. A case in which nursing staff at a special hospital were advised by their union not to answer commissioners' questions in certain circumstances, but to offer merely a written statement, is reported in the Commission's Second Biennial Report.[12] The Commission also has no direct powers of enforcement, it can merely report to the Secretary of State, and through him, every two years, to Parliament. It can, however, pursue matters of policy with the hospital management or the SHSA and can comment on the way in which the complaint was investigated internally.

Section 121(7) gives the Mental Health Act Commission specific power to

---

9 In this respect the MHAC's remit is narrower than that of the Health Service Commissioner, who may investigate a complaint made by a patient's family or personal representative – s. 11, National Health Services Act 1977.

10 The MHAC's Complaints Policy is published at *supra*, n. 1, appendix 5.

11 *Supra*, n. 1, p. 25.

12 *Second Biennial Report 1985–1987* (1987, London: HMSO), p. 17. See also the Ashworth Report, *supra*, n. 3, ch. IV for a discussion of the question of staff witnesses.

review any decision to withhold a postal packet under section 134, and in this particular context the Commission is given the power to enforce its conclusions – section 121(8). However, with regard to the withholding of outgoing mail, the complaint has to be made by the patient, and experience suggests that patients are often insufficiently knowledgeable of their rights to formulate their suspicions into a formal complaint to the Commission. Further, there was evidence that management at Ashworth failed to take seriously the 'accidental' opening of patient's mail addressed to the bodies listed in section 134(3), with whom a patient's right to correspond is not subject to the controls in section 134(1) and (2).[13]

The case described above, at page 259, again provides a useful example to illustrate the limits of the Commission's role in practice. The patient himself complained to the Commission about the way in which he had been treated and, as it was a complaint falling clearly within paragraph (i) of section 120(1)(b), the Commission intervened after the completion of the internal investigation. Two commissioners were appointed to investigate. From the evidence they reviewed 'there were indications that the patient might have been the object of a conspiracy to get him into trouble', and the commissioners concluded that this aspect of the episode had been inadequately investigated internally.[14] Possessing neither the necessary investigative powers nor the expertise, the Commission did not feel it appropriate to investigate the matter itself, nor could it persuade the hospital management to re-open the case. After negotiations with management the patient's access to activities had been restored, but the Commission did not consider that this justified management in regarding the case as closed. Further, management refused, at that stage, to accept the Commission's contention that any patient making a complaint to management should be entitled to an interview. In effect, from the point of view of both the patient and the Commission, the case remained unresolved. The Commission could merely publicise the case in its Biennial Report, and use it as an example of the inadequacy of the internal procedures in subsequent negotiations with the Secretary of State and the SHSA.

The Commission is well aware of the limits of its own ability effectively to pursue complaints on behalf of special hospital patients. In its evidence to the Ashworth Inquiry the Commission described its experience of investigating complaints at the hospital. Many complaints related to the inappropriate and punitive use of seclusion, and to the practice of nurses of 'winding up' particular patients in order to have grounds for secluding them. When such incidents were mentioned to the Commission 'the Commission could do little but examine the records, which would give the staff's account: there was no way in which an independent assessment could be obtained'.[15] According to the Commission there was no adequate internal appeal system. An inquiry to management would be met with the response that a senior nurse had looked into it and all was in order. When the Commission was able to show that a

13 *Supra*, n. 2, pp. 25–6.
14 MHAC, *Third Biennial Report 1987–1989* (1989, London: HMSO), p. 21.
15 MHAC, *supra*, n. 2, p. 18.

procedural irregularity had occurred, management would promise that it would not happen again 'but it did'. According to the Commission's evidence, 'there was never an occasion, so far as can be recalled, when [management] admitted that a patient had been secluded wrongly or for too long'. The same general lack of success was recorded in relation to other categories of complaint as well, and led the Commission to conclude that, although it

could ameliorate some matters, and hopefully its presence and visiting also had some effect, it did not succeed in the eyes of the majority of patients in overcoming or partially remedying many of their most serious grievances.[16]

The experience of the Mental Health Act Commission in attempting to provide an effective means of independent validation in relation to decision making within special hospitals suggests that such a task is likely to be fraught with difficulty. In the first place, where the internal mechanisms are inadequate and management reluctant to investigate patients' complaints with any real vigour, the independent investigator, here in the form of the Commission, is presented with the task of seeking the evidence itself. Even in favourable circumstances such a job would impose enormous demands on the independent investigator in terms of resources, powers and expertise. In the actual circumstances prevailing in special hospitals, where management has typically been disinclined to act, and ward staff are both hostile and powerful, the independent investigator is confronted with an almost impossible task. A body such as the Commission, comprised of part-time members possessing few express powers, cannot realistically meet such demands: a conclusion which had led the Ashworth Inquiry to recommend the removal of the Commission's formal complaints investigation role under section 120.

Whatever the merits of that particular recommendation and whatever the future of the Commission, the presence of a truly independent element which is properly empowered and resourced is essential to any adequate extra-judical mechanism for the validation of internal special hospital decisions. Only a truly independent validator can possess the impartiality necessary authoritatively to resolve a dispute arising concerning the application of policy within a closed environment. However, there are strong arguments in terms of expertise, speed and the need to maintain positive relationships in the future, for seeking to resolve complaints and grievances at the most local level possible.

Provided the internal mechanism is effective and adequately monitored, independent investigation of the complaint itself might properly be restricted to the appellate stage. Thus the initial investigation of complaints should be left to the internal system, which might, as under the 1992 policy, include the involvement of a semi-independent investigator for the more serious allegations. The truly independent national body would then act primarily as a monitor of the standards of internal investigation, and to that end should possess the power to order an internal reconsideration. Its own powers of direct investigation would be reserved for the appellate stage in cases of

16 *Ibid.*, p. 2.

particular difficulty or intransigence on the part of management. Such a two-tier structure would, in most cases, be formally comprised of administrative decision making, modelled on inquisitorial adjudication at first instance, but would be backed up by the possibility of independent inquisitorial adjudication at the appellate stage.

The discussion in the previous chapter illustrated the vulnerability of special hospital patients to the discretionary judgement of hospital staff. A complaints mechanism such as that described above is essential in order to provide some means of ensuring that all such decisions are justified by reference to the reasons for the patient's detention in hospital, medical treatment and security. However, the very factor which exacerbates the patient's vulnerability – the breadth of professional discretion – makes the process of validation particularly difficult. The provision of adequate *ex post* validation by an independent body would be greatly facilitated by the introduction of better *ex ante* regulation. Some agreed statement of a patient's entitlements, for example, or the articulation of the special grounds on which a patient's visitor can be refused access, would not only help to regulate the initial decision, but would also facilitate the process of review. While it might be suggested that such a formal structure would impinge improperly on the clinical judgement of the medical staff, it should be argued in response that, if clinical judgement is too intangible to be susceptible to some degree of codification, it is an improper basis on which to restrict the freedoms of any individual.

(2) Oversight of Second-opinion Doctors

In addition to its complaints jurisdiction, the Mental Health Act Commission also, to a limited extent, oversees the activities of the second-opinion doctors appointed for the purposes of Part IV of the 1983 Act. All second-opinion doctors are appointed and 'trained' by the Commission. It is now clear that in exercising its duty to appoint second-opinion doctors the Commission is subject to the review jurisdiction of the High Court, but in fulfilling that duty it incurs no private law liability for breach of statutory duty. Further, once a second-opinion doctor is appointed, he or she is not acting as the servant or agent of the Commission, but is personally responsible for his or her own actions. Indeed, the Commission cannot act as an appellate body in relation to second-opinion doctors, and any challenge to the conclusions of such doctors must be by way of judicial review.[17]

The Commission has issued guidelines relating to the way in which second-opinion doctors should fulfil their role. The first guidelines were published as a Circular by the Department of Health and Social Security in 1984,[18] while the second were published by the Commission itself, and have been recommended to clinicians by the Code of Practice. In all cases where a second-opinion

17 MHAC, *supra*, n. 1, p. 33, and *Witham* v. *Jeffreys, Finch, Land and the Mental Health Act Commission* (1991) 11 July, unreported.
18 Circular No. DDL(84)4.

doctor has approved treatment, section 61 requires the responsible medical officer to report periodically to the Secretary of State. In practice the report is made to the Commission, which is accordingly responsible for the periodic review of all treatments certified by second-opinion doctors. In addition, as discussed in the previous chapter, commissioners examine complicance with the requirements of Part IV when they visit individual hospitals, including special hospitals. Thus the Commission, although not directly responsible for the actions of second opinion doctors, nevertheless provides the primary mechanism for overseeing the operation of the consent provisions.

(c) Health Service Commissioner

The National Health Service Reorganisation Act 1973 created two Health Service Commissioners, one for Wales and one for England. In practice the office is held by the Parliamentary Commissioner. In 1990 special hospitals were transferred from the jurisdiction of the Parliamentary Commissioner to that of the Health Service Commissioner (HSC). The HSC has jurisdiction over alleged failures to provide a service, alleged failures in a service provided, and any other action taken by or on behalf of an authority in connection with which there has been maladministration.[19] The HSC may not, however, investigate any complaint concerning the diagnosis of illness or the care or treatment of a patient which was in consequence of the exercise of clinical judgement.[20] In general, the HSC can only investigate complaints made by the patient, but he does have the discretion to accept complaints on behalf of patients where the patient has died, or for any other reason is unable to act for himself.[21] Clearly there is considerable overlap between the jurisdiction of the HSC and the Mental Health Act Commission. In matters concerning the detention of patients and the exercise of powers under the Mental Health Act 1983, however, it has been agreed that the Commission should intervene first.[22]

(d) Mental Health Review Tribunals

As will be seen in the following chapter, Mental Health Review Tribunals are primarily concerned with decisions relating to a patient's discharge. However, episodes recorded on a patient's clinical notes and subsequently seen by those assessing the patient for discharge, including the medical member of the tribunal, can have a significant impact on the attitude of the tribunal. It may fairly be assumed, for example, that if the allegations of planned riot and hostage-taking were to remain on the file of the patient discussed earlier, they

19 Section 115, National Health Services Act 1977.
20 *Ibid.*, Part II of Schedule 13.
21 *Ibid.*, s. 111.
22 MHAC, *supra*, n. 1, p. 26.

would influence subsequent assessments of that patient's likely dangerousness. Patients are well aware of this possibility and, in the absence of adequate alternatives, may consider using the tribunal hearing as a means of challenging the validity of the record. Indeed, the patient involved in the riot allegations did seek to minimise the impact of those allegations at a subsequent tribunal hearing, and called one of the commissioners involved in the investigation to give evidence to the tribunal.

In one other case known to the author, four allegations remained on the patient's notes at the time of the tribunal, and appeared likely to be central to the tribunal's deliberations. Three related to suspected attempts at fire-lighting, and one concerned a suspected assault attempt, where a pot 'fell' from a window-sill. With the agreement of the rmo, the tribunal arranged an interlocutory hearing to attempt to assess the strength of the allegations. Police officers who had been involved in earlier investigations were called and evidence was taken, even a site visit was conducted. However, in the event the tribunal was able to reach its ultimate decision without reference to the allegations, and therefore made no finding on them. It is interesting, nevertheless, that the potential significance of the allegations was sufficiently appreciated by all involved to persuade the tribunal of the need to assess their accuracy. If this practice is adopted more generally, some clarification will be required of the standard of proof to be applied by the tribunal before it can properly take such allegations into account. The role of the tribunal is discussed further in the next chapter.

Under the existing system, where allegations and suspicions can be recorded with some ease and the patients have little opportunity to challenge, it is necessary for the tribunal to provide some process of validation. However, since some considerable time might have elapsed, validation by the tribunal is not ideal. In this respect it is encouraging to note that, under the Access to Health Records Act 1990, patients now have a right of access to their medical records, and a right to seek the correction of any alleged inaccuracies and, if such correction is refused, the right to have their own reservations recorded.[23] Welcome as these developments are, however, it seems likely that, in practice, greater credence will be given to the suspicions recorded by the rmo than to the denials entered by the patient. Stricter controls are required over the making and the recording of allegations in the first place, together with a more rigorous process of internal validation.

(e) Courts

Although in recent years the courts have become more willing to oversee the decisions of the Mental Health Review Tribunals, they have yet to display much enthusiasm for the oversight of internal special hospital decisions. As

23 Sections 3 and 6, Access to Health Records Act 1990. See chapter 10 for a description of the main provisions of the Act, and for further discussion of its operation in relation to tribunals, see chapter 12.

has already been suggested, the Mental Health Act 1983 itself leaves significant areas of hospital decision making unregulated by statute, and thus does nothing to encourage judicial intervention. Further, as far as private law is concerned, there is an express statutory exclusion of judicial oversight. According to section 139 of the 1983 Act no action can be brought in relation to 'any act purporting to be done in pursuance' of the Mental Health Act, unless leave of the High Court is obtained, and either bad faith or lack of reasonable care can be established. The section does not apply to the decisions of the Secretary of State, nor to those of health authorities, but it does cover the actions of individual doctors and nurses, and it is perhaps a testament to the strength of the professional lobby that it has survived in its present form.

It is in relation to consent to treatment, where the 1983 Act is at its most specific, that the courts have been most active to date. With regard to the private law it is clear that an action for assault could lie against any member of staff at a special hospital who forcibly treated a patient in breach of the provisions of Part IV, provided the requirements of section 139 could be met. Section 139, however, does not apply to applications for judicial review,[24] and in the field of consent and the provision of treatment in general, the courts have been prepared to use the public law to provide authoritative interpretations of the Act's requirements.

At the substantive hearing in *R* v. *Hallstrom ex p. W* the Divisional Court eventually resolved an ambiguity in the Act which had been causing difficulties from the beginning. In order to ensure that their patients continued to accept medication when living in the community, some doctors were 'discharging' detained patients on leave under the provisions of section 17, on condition that they continued to accept their drugs. The patient would then be recalled to hospital for a notional period to enable the leave to be renewed, and to prevent the provisions of section 17(5) from causing the patient to cease to be liable to detention. Once the patient ceased to be liable to be detained, no requirement to accept treatment could be imposed. It was a device that could be used in relation to offender patients subject to a simple hospital order without restrictions: in the case of restriction order patients, the power to discharge conditionally rendered it unnecessary. In *Hallstrom* the court held that recall under section 17(4) could not be used in this notional way.[25] Similarly, in a rather different context the Divisional Court clarified the meaning of the 1983 Regulations. In *R* v. *Mental Health Act Commission, ex p. W* the court held that the injection of a hormone analogue did not constitute a 'surgical implantation of hormones' under regulation 16, and was not therefore covered by the section 57 procedures.[26]

In both cases there has been a dispute among practitioners about the

24 *R* v. *Hallstrom, ex p. W* [1985] 3 All ER 775.
25 *R* v. *Hallsrom, ex p. W* [1986] 2 WLR 883.
26 *R* v. *Mental Health Act Commission ex p. W* (1988) *The Times*, 27 May. For the relevant regulations see Mental Health (Hospital, Guardianship and Consent to Treatment) Regulations 1983, SI 1982/893.

meaning of the legislation and, at the very least, the court's intervention served to resolve those disputes. Two further points, however, should be mentioned. In the first place, genuine reservations may be felt over the wisdom of encouraging the courts to provide definitive interpretations of statutory requirements in highly specialised areas, and it may be instructive to consider the relevance of such reservations here.[27]

Arguably, both the cases mentioned above presented a conflict between the demands of autonomy and beneficence: in *Hallstrom* the applicant was endeavouring to assert her right to refuse treatment despite the advice of her clinician, while in *Mental Health Act Commission* the applicant wanted to receive treatment despite the reservations of the appointed panel. In both cases the court's interpretation of the relevant legislation favoured the applicant, and to that extent supported autonomy. However, to claim that such an outcome was inevitable because the courts will always favour autonomy over beneficence, and thus they should not be used as the definitive interpreters, would be to misstate the position. Even if the courts do have preference for autonomy, which is certainly open to doubt, there are strong arguments for suggesting that they are still the most appropriate bodies to provide the definitive interpretation of statutory requirements in cases where autonomy and beneficence clash. If Parliament, in the reflection of the public interest, wishes to authorise the overriding of a person's choice with regard to his or her bodily intergrity it must do so unambiguously: it cannot be taken to have done so by implication.[28] Consequently, any legislation purporting to provide such authorisation must be interpreted restrictively in cases of ambiguity. The judges' presumed preference for autonomy should not, therefore, disqualify them from determining genuinely ambiguous statutory wording when the constitutionally preferred solution would be the maintenance of a restrictive interpretation in the face of the compelling demands of beneficence. By contrast, however, where a conflict between patient autonomy and the need to protect society has been perceived, the courts have tended to adopt expansive interpretations of the statutory wording, thus favouring social protection over individual freedom. The issue is discussed further in chapter 12.

Secondly, by adopting their narrow interpretations of the statutory wording, the judges in both *Hallstrom* and the *Mental Health Act Commission* were arguably resisting the temptation to formulate policy themselves: they were merely reflecting the literal meaning of Parliament's words as they saw them. Arguably, they were doing no more than their colleagues in the Court of Appeal in *Hague*, and were merely policing the legislative boundaries of legality.[29] Whatever the validity of such a claim, by denying interference with personal autonomy on the grounds of beneficence the courts were undoubtedly placing the onus of seeking express legislative endorsement on those arguing

27 P. Craig, *Administrative Law* 2nd edn (1989, London: Sweet and Maxwell), ch. 9, and J. Beatson, 'The Scope of Judicial Review for Error of Law' (1984) 4 Oxford. Jo. of Legal Studies 22.
28 See the discussion in chapters 2, 5 and 12.
29 *R* v. *Deputy Governor of Parkhurst Prison, ex p. Hague* [1990] 3 All ER 687. See discussion in chapter 5.

for such interference. In the event, both cases, but particularly *Hallstrom*, have generated considerable public debate as to whether the law should be amended, and such a debate can only increase the likelihood of full participation in the process of policy formulation. The device declared illegal by *Hallstrom* had effectively provided doctors with a method of imposing compulsory treatment on erstwhile in-patients living in the community and thereby, it is claimed, facilitating their earlier discharge from hospital. Following the *Hallstrom* decision, many doctors believe that a proper community treatment order should be introduced to fill the resulting gap, but it has become clear in the course of the debate that other relevant professional and patient groups are more hostile to the idea.[30] Whatever the outcome, an open public debate has been generated, and the Parliamentary process will have to be used if the law is to be changed.

Apart from the question of the interpretation of the regulations, the *Mental Health Act Commission* case had additional implications, and has spawned further litigation.[31] The question of the meaning of consent has already been discussed, but it is also relevant to note that the court was prepared to comment on the procedures adopted by the appointed panel in their dealings with both the rmo and the patient. The panel was under a duty to act fairly. While the recognition of such a duty is encouraging, and would presumably be extended to the individual second-opinion doctor acting under section 58, the substance of the duty has yet to be specified.

Outside the area of consent to medical treatment the courts, to date, have played only a minor role in the validation of internal special hospital decision making. As in the prison context, the private law recognises few relevant rights in patients. However, the court has granted leave under section 139 to enable a patient to pursue negligence and false imprisonment claims arising out of a 16-day period of seclusion at Moss Side Special Hospital (now Ashworth).[32] More recently, leave has not been opposed in the case of a group of patients seeking to establish false imprisonment in relation to their seclusion by nursing staff during an industrial dispute, again at Moss Side. In the prison context, it will be recalled, the House of Lords has rejected the possibility of a false imprisonment claim by a prisoner based on the conditions of his imprisonment.[33] Nevertheless, their lordships left open the possibility of such an action succeeding against an individual prison officer who acts 'in bad faith by deliberately subjecting a prisoner to a restraint which he knows he has no authority to impose'.[34] It remains to be seen whether the Moss Side cases will be distinguishable from *Hague* on that basis. In the light of the practical difficulties confronted by those who currently attempt to monitor the use of

30 MHAC, *supra*, n. 4 and n. 1.
31 The patient involved sought damages against both the MHAC and the three-person panel, but the claim was struck out, *Witham* v. *Jeffreys, Finch, Land and the M.H.A.C.* (1991) 11 July, unreported. See, also, the report of W's trial in *The Independent*, 28 April 1992.
32 *Furber* v. *Krater* (1988) *The Times*, 21 July.
33 *Hague* v. *Dep. Gov. of Parkhurst Prison* [1991] 3 All ER 733.
34 *Ibid.*, per Lord Bridge, p. 745.

seclusion, and the widespread belief that its use is open to abuse, it would certainly be unfortunate if, on those rare occasions when the necessary evidence is available, the courts failed to provide an adequate remedy for hospital patients subjected to seclusion improperly and consciously imposed by nursing staff.

In the validation of internal special hospital decision making outside the realm of consent, the public law has proved even less active than the private law. Special hospital patients, unlike their prison counterparts, have not yet succeeded in fully exploring the potential for external review by the courts, although at the time of writing leave to apply for judicial review has been granted to a patient wishing to challenge the application of the visitors policy at Broadmoor.[35]

In principle if a generous approach is taken to recent developments, judicial review should be available to a special hospital patient whose legitimate expectations are denied in the absence of a fair hearing. Thus, if a patient who has previously enjoyed full ground parole is confined to the ward on the basis of an unsubstantiated allegation which he is given no opportunity to answer, the reviewing court might recognise a legitimate expectation and impose a duty to act fairly. In practice the reviewing courts have yet to enter this arena, indeed a patient alleging that he should not have been transferred from one special hospital to another without consultation was refused leave to apply for judicial review.[36] In another case known to the author, involving the transfer of a patient from his own room on a parole ward to the intensive care ward, the application for judicial review was withdrawn before leave was granted, when the hospital moved the patient back to his original ward. Thus a readiness to seek court intervention is present on the part of some patients and, provided the courts are prepared to recognise a legitimate expectation protected by the duty to act fairly, there is scope for the introduction of some of the basic procedural requirements of the common law once the 'correct' case is found.

In the light of the legislative vacuum within which the majority of internal hospital decisions are in practice taken, *ex post* validation by the courts of the process through which these decisions are reached is the most that can realistically be achieved within the existing framework. Patients have few substantive rights susceptible to direct enforcement, and some insistence by the courts that those seeking further to restrict a patient's freedoms be required to justify their proposed restrictions by reference to the demands of treatment and/or security would go some way towards ensuring that the wide discretion granted to the hospital authorities is exercised appropriately. However, the still predominately adversarial approach of the common law procedural principles may not be the ideal model to apply within the hospital context. The more participatory inquisitorial processes discussed in the previous chapter might be more readily achieved by the introduction of a set of practices and

35 For discussion of the policy see chapter 10. The challenge relates to the refusal by the general manager to allow a patient to receive a visit from a journalist.

36 *R* v. *Specialist Hospitals Service Authority, ex p. P* (1990) 14 May, DC, 25 May, AC (unreported).

procedures devised and agreed by those most closely involved. Such procedures could then reflect the experience of those required to operate within them, and would perhaps be regarded as more sensitive to the therapeutic setting than would a set of procedures imposed by the courts. Once accepted, such procedures could be monitored internally in the first instance, and then by some conspicuously independent extra-judicial body. The courts would be called upon rarely to act as ultimate arbiters.

(f) Coroners' Courts

The Coroners Act 1988 imposes a duty on coroners to hold an inquest where they have reasonable cause to suspect that someone 'a) has died a violent or an unnatural death; b) has died a sudden death of which the cause is unknown; or c) has died in prison . . .', section 8(1). In addition, a jury must be called where there is reason to suspect that the death occurred in prison, or in police custody, or from an industrial disease or that 'death occurred in circumstances the continuance or possible recurrence of which is prejudicial to the health or safety of the public or any section of the public', section 8(3). Thus, although there is no automatic duty to hold an inquest following the death of a special hospital patient, many inquests are held into such deaths under either section 8(1)(a) or (b), and juries will typically be called under section 8(3)(d). It is, however, important to remember the limits of the coroner's jurisdiction. The purpose of an inquest is essentially to establish the cause of death, and the Coroners' Rules specify that

the procedures and evidence at an inquest shall be directed solely to ascertaining . . . (a) who the deceased was; (b) how, when and where the deceased came by his death; (c) the particulars for the time being required by the Registration Act to be registered concerning the death.[37]

The rule then proceeds to declare that 'neither the coroner nor the jury shall express any opinion on any other matters'. Thus the investigation is narrowly focused, and the 'verdicts', or conclusions as to the death, open to the jury are quite restricted.[38] In particular, juries are no longer allowed to add riders or recommendations to their verdicts, except where explanation is necessary.[39] Thus there is a limit to the extent to which an inquest can be expected to investigate the policies and practice within a special hospital which might provide the background to the death. However, 'lack of care', which is not a verdict on its own, may be attached to a verdict such as natural causes, where it can be used to indicate 'that some other persons had at least the opportunity of rendering care . . . which would have prevented the death',[40] and can

37 The Coroners Rules, SI 1984/552, rule 36(1) and (2).
38 *Ibid.*, Schedule 4, Form 22.
39 By virtue of rule 36(2), and see *R* v. *Shrewsbury Coroners' Court, ex p. British Parachute Assoc.* (1987) 152 JP 123, and *R* v. *West London Coroner, ex p. Gray* [1987] 2 All ER 129.
40 *R* v. *Southwark Coroner, ex p. Hicks* [1987] 2 All ER 140, at 147.

therefore be used to express disapproval of the level of care provided. Similarly, the return of an open verdict in certain circumstances might indicate that the jury was not completely convinced by the authority's account of the death. The inquest into the death of a patient in Broadmoor has recently been overturned by the High Court due to the coroner's refusal to allow counsel for the patient's family to address the jury on lack of care.[41] A new inquest will accordingly be held.

Thus an inquest can provide some, albeit limited, investigation of deaths in special hospitals, and while many criticisms may be levelled at the procedures adopted by coroners, and at their relaxed attitude towards evidence and proof, the holding of an inquest does constitute an important means of validation.[42] Since 1984, inquests have been held into the deaths of at least three patients while in seclusion at Broadmoor. In each case the inquest has been followed by an independent inquiry into the circumstances of the death, whether such inquiries would have been held without the publicity generated by the inquests must remain unknown.[43]

(g) Inquiries

In addition to their role in policy formulation,[44] inquiries also have a part to play at the validation stage. Ill-treatment of the mentally disordered has been a recurring theme in the history of health care provision, and the appointment of independent inquiries has been one of the standard reactions of those in authority to allegations of abuse.[45] Typically, such allegations will surface

41 *R* v.*Her Majesty's Coroner for East Berkshire, ex p. Buckley* [1992] *The Times*, 1 December. The patient concerned was Orville Blackwood, whose death has been the subject of an independent inquiry, see below, n. 43.

42 For general accounts of the role of Coroners' Courts, see P. Knapman and M. Powers, *Thurston's Coronership Third Edition: The Law and Practice on Coroners* (1985, Chichester: Barry Rose); G. Kavanagh, *Coroners' Rules and Statutes* (1985, London: Sweet and Maxwell); P. Matthews and J. Foreman, *Jervis on the Office and Duties of Coroners* 10th edn (1986, London: Sweet and Maxwell); and Justice, *Coroners' Court in England and Wales* (1986, London: Justice). The role of inquests in the investigation of the death of patients in special hospitals is further discussed in the Ashworth Report, *supra*,n. 3.

43 See *Report to the Secretary of State for Health and Social Services concerning the Death of Michael Dean Martin at Broadmoor Hospital on 6 July 1984* (1985, London: Department of Health and Social Services), *Report of the Inquiry into the Circumstances Leading to the Death in Broadmoor Hospital of Mr Joseph Watts on 23 August 1988* (1989, London: SHSA). The report into the death of Mr Orville Blackwood is to be published in 1993. For a discussion of the deaths of Michael Martin and Joseph Watts see Institute of Race Relations, *Deadly Silence* (1991, London: Institute of Race Relations).

44 The issue is discussed in chapter 5 in relation to the formulation of prison policy, but it is relevant in the present context as well: see *Report of the Review of Rampton Hospital* (1980, Cmnd 8073, London: HMSO), and, of course, the Ashworth Report, *supra*, n. 3.

45 For an account of the use of independent inquiries in the investigation of allegations of patient abuse see K. Jones, *Lunacy, Law and Conscience, 1744–1845: The Social History of the Care of the Insane*

through the media, and an inquiry will be set up to investigate in the wake of the resulting scandal. The Boynton Inquiry into the ill-treatment of patients at Rampton special hospital was established following a television programme, 'Secret Hospital', in 1979[46] while the Ashworth Inquiry followed allegations in the *Cutting Edge* television documentary, 'A Special Hospital', transmitted in 1991. In these two examples the allegations achieved wide national publicity, but inquiries can equally be called where the publicity is less widespread, as in the case of the inquiries into the deaths in seclusion at Broadmoor referred to above.

These independent inquiries are established in the exercise of a variety of powers. The Ashworth Inquiry, for example, was set up initially by the Secretary of State for Health under no specific statutory power, while the inquiry into the death of Orville Blackwood at Broadmoor was set up by the SHSA in the exercise of their broad management function.[47] But, whatever their formal status, all inquiries share the common task of investigation as a preliminary to any powers to recommend change which might be contained in their terms of reference.[48] In the pursuit of this investigative task, inquiries will not all possess the same express powers. The Ashworth Inquiry was initially established with no formal investigative powers, but after threats from the Prison Officers' Association that their members would cease to co-operate, the inquiry team was forced to seek, and indeed was granted, statutory powers from the Secretary of State under section 125 of the Mental Health Act of 1983. The smaller inquiries appointed by local management, on the other hand, must generally rely on the support of management to ensure access to evidence and the co-operation of staff.

As investigators, these inquiries are essentially providing a mechanism for external validation, and in many cases will be established following the failure of internal mechanisms to check abuse of power on the part of hospital staff. The obvious advantages they possess are thought to include independence, publicity, and hence openness, and investigative enthusiasm, matched on occasion by formal powers. Independence, if truly present, would indeed be a major advantage.

It has been consistently argued here that independence is an essential feature of an acceptable structure at the validation stage. However, it is clear that independence is sometimes hard to achieve. The four-person team appointed to inquire into the allegations at Ashworth were all independent of the hospital and the SHSA, but they were all serving members of the Mental Health Act Commission and included both the chair and the vice chair of the

(1955, London: Routledge and Kegan Paul); J. Martin, *Hospitals in Trouble* (1984, Oxford: Basil Blackwell), and V. Beardshaw, *supra*, n. 8.

46 *Supra*, n. 44.

47 The Scottish Mental Welfare Commission has the power to set up formal inquiries – Mental Health (Scotland) Act 1984.

48 The terms of reference of the Ashworth Inquiry included investigating 'allegations of improper care and treatment at Ashworth Hospital' contained in the *Cutting Edge* programme and any

Commission. Although none had visited Ashworth as a commissioner during the relevant period, they might still be thought partial in two respects. In the first place, since the inquiry's terms of reference included a review of the 'arrangements for the handling of complaints by or on behalf of patients', the appointed team, as commissioners, might be regarded as interested parties. Secondly, they might be regarded as 'statutorily' biased towards the patients because, in their role as commissioners, they had been specifically charged with the general protection of detained patients.[49] In the event, although the independence of the team was challenged by the Prison Officers' Association, the challenge centred on allegations of personal bias on the part of the chairman, and on that basis failed.[50]

The example of the Ashworth Inquiry, however, does serve to illustrate the very real difficulties involved in identifying, in the small world of secure psychiatric provision, an individual or individuals who possess both the necessary expertise and the necessary independence to meet the full process ideal. Perhaps in reflection of such difficulties, the requirements of the common law, it seems, are sufficiently undemanding to accept something short of full independence: a fact which must endow the person responsible for selecting the investigator with some influence over the outcome.

As investigators, public inquiries have to establish fact, and in so doing have to be seen to be fair to all those involved. The steps taken by the Woolf Inquiry to achieve such fairness were considered in chapter 6. In its turn, the Ashworth Inquiry was most conscious of its obligation to appear fair, and if it carefully followed the practice of issuing 'Salmon letters' in order to warn all those who were potentially subject to criticism of the nature of that criticism. However, the Ashworth Report itself was criticial of the over legalistic way in which such letters tend to be scrutinised.[51] Public inquiries are not courts of law employing adversarial adjudication to the determination of specific disputes. As the Ashworth Report emphasised, there is no obligation on any one party to establish its case: the 'burden of proof' if such exists, rests with the inquiry team itself, which must satisfy itself of the validity of its findings. It is a strictly inquisitorial procedure. The Report also considered the standard of proof which should be applied, and rejected both of the usual tests: beyond reasonable doubt, and the balance of probabilities. It concluded that 'confidence is the acid test':

> Our view of the proper approach, therefore, is that, having examined all the relevant material, weighed and evaluated the various pieces of the material, and having paid due regard to all the surrounding circumstances that may inform the events under

other relevant allegations, reviewing the arrangements for handling complaints by or on behalf of patients, and making recommendations.

49 S. 120, Mental Health Act 1983.

50 *R* v. *Secretary of State for Health, ex p. Prison Officers Association* (1991) *The Times*, 28 May. See chapter 3 for the application of the doctrine of waiver.

51 The practice of issuing such letters originates from the *Report of the Royal Commission on Tribunals of Inquiry* (The Salmon Report) (1966, Cmnd 3121, London: HMSO). For the views of the Ashworth Inquiry see, *supra*, n. 3, ch. II.

scrutiny, we must be able to say in our Report that we are confident of having uncovered the true picture of the events under investigation.[52]

In the event the application of this standard to the incidents under inquiry is one of the most significant aspects of the final Report. Against the background of what it knew of the practices of the hospital, the inquiry team was prepared to attach weight to patients' accounts of events even if they did not accord with the accounts of staff. In the case of Sean Walton, for example, the inquiry team concluded that a particular nurse not only assaulted Sean Walton, but also failed to uphold the standards expected of a nursing assistant, acted 'disgracefully towards a patient', failed to report his own misconduct and 'persistently denied any fault on his part'. These findings were based on 'a welter of evidence . . . from a large number of patients on the ward at the time', and were adopted by the Inquiry despite 'categorical denials' from members of staff.[53] In the context of a special hospital where the internal review mechanisms had consistently failed to take the allegations of patients seriously, this recognition of the value of patient evidence was of immense importance. In the almost total absence of any real effort within the hospital properly to investigate, the introduction of an independent investigative body which was prepared to challenge official accounts and was committed to uncovering an accurate picture of events represented a real advance towards the provision of effective validation.

Public inquiries of the scale of the Ashworth Inquiry, which covered 37 days of oral hearings and 18 days of public seminars, are undeniably long, expensive and disruptive for those whose behaviour is under scrutiny. Their long-term impact on policy is also hard to assess.[54] It is still far too early to gauge the impact of the Ashworth Report on either the regime at Ashworth itself or the special hospital system in general. However, as a structure reaching beyond both adjudication and administrative decision making, public inquiries have closely resembled the wide investigative forum considered in chapter 4, and have performed a vital role in the process of validation.[55]

The Ashworth Inquiry, particularly, has drawn attention to the gross inadequacies of the regime within the hospital, has illustrated the absence of any effective mechanisms for internal review and, perhaps most significantly, has been prepared to listen to patients and to assess their evidence, not only against the denials of the staff, but also in the context of the prevailing hospital regime as it had been revealed to the inquiry. It is, however, a poor reflection on the existing mechanisms for review that it required a television exposé followed by an expensive inquiry to reveal the inadequacies of the regime.

While public inquiries may achieve true independent validation of a very

52 *Supra*, n.3, p. 14.
53 *Ibid.*, ch. X, p. 55, particularly.
54 The question is developed further in the context of the Woolf Inquiry in chapter 5.
55 The potential role for such a structure was discussed in chapter 4.

high standard, their use must be reserved for the most exceptional of circumstances. Special hospitals require an effective and permanent mechanism for review such as that described above in section **b**. the main contribution of the Ashworth Inquiry must lie in its authoritative condemnation of the existing mechanisms, and its illustration of the importance of listening to the evidence of patients.

12
Release from Hospital

As was seen in chapter 9, the allocation of any particular mentally disordered offender to a treatment rather than a penal disposal will be influenced by a variety of factors, not all of which relate to the needs of the offender. Significant consequences, however, flow from the choice. A hospital order authorises indeterminate detention and compulsory treatment in hospital. It is based not on retributive calculations but rather on a belief in both the benefits and the propriety of compulsory treatment, and in the need to protect society from potentially violent and dangerous people. The decision to discharge should therefore be determined by the presence or absence of the need to treat, and the level of risk posed by the individual patient. The assessment of such factors, however, raises immense evidential and moral difficulties which have to be confronted by those responsible for the discharge of offender patients.

Under the provisions of the Mental Health Act 1983, the Mental Health Review Tribunals, together with the Secretary of State and, in the case of non-restricted patients, the responsible medical officer (rmo) and the hospital managers, are entrusted with the unenviable task of reaching these decisions. This chapter will concentrate primarily on the tribunals.[1] The evolution of the tribunals will be described first, and then their present constitution and powers. In section c the interpretation of the discharge criteria in practice will be considered, and finally, some thought will be given to possible alternative structures.

(a) The Evolution of Mental Health Review Tribunals Prior to 1982

In 1957 the Royal Commission on the Law Relating to Mental Illness and Mental Deficiency recommended that detained patients should have the right

1 For the law relating to the discharge of patients generally, both restricted and non-restricted, see L. Gostin, *Mental Health Services: Law and Practice* (1986, London: Shaw); R. Jones, *Mental Health Act Manual* 3rd edn (1991, London: Sweet and Maxwell), and B. Hoggett, *Mental Health Law* 3rd edn (1990, London: Sweet and Maxwell).

of appeal to a local body consisting of both medical and non-medical members.[2] Such a body should provide some protection against unjustified detention. Mental Health Review Tribunals were first established under the Mental Health Act 1959. They consisted of three-person panels – a medical member, a lay member and a legal president – and were empowered, on certain grounds, to discharge detained patients, including non-restricted hospital order patients. In the case of restriction order patients, their role was purely advisory; the ultimate decision to discharge rested with the Home Secretary.

In the years following their introduction, the tribunals were the target of widespread criticism. Significant variations in practice were found across the 15 tribunal regions,[3] and it was suggested that tribunal decisions were governed more by the members' assessment of what was sensible than the statutory criteria for discharge.[4] Further, research by Peay revealed significant and influential differences in the attitude and knowledge of tribunal members.[5] As a result the constitution and powers of the tribunals were subjected to some scrutiny in the debate that led up to the reforms of 1982/3.[6] At the same time, and of greater relevance to the present theme, reform of the process for the discharge of restriction order patients was also being considered.

Following the conviction in 1972 of an ex-Broadmoor patient in relation to a multiple poisoning, the Aarvold Committee was set up to advise on the procedures for the discharge and supervision of restriction order patients. In line with the recommendations of this committee, the Special Advisory Board, consisting of a lawyer, a forensic psychiatrist and a social worker, was created to advise the Home Secretary in cases thought to require special care in assessment.[7] Any proposals involving a substantial relaxation in control over such a patient, which would of course include any tribunal recommendation to discharge or transfer, would be referred to the Board. Thus, while in the case of all restriction order patients the final decision on discharge, and indeed transfer, rested with the Home Secretary, in the case of patients deemed to be particularly dangerous and in need of special assessment the Home Secretary would draw on advice from the Advisory Board, and evidence suggests that this advice was most influential. During the mid-1970s the Home Secretary was rejecting approximately 40 per cent of tribunal recommendations in restriction order cases, but by September 1976 he had accepted the advice of the Board in all of the 24 cases referred to it.[8] It was apparent, therefore, that

2 *Report of the Royal Commission on the Law relating to Mental Illness and Mental Deficiency 1954–1957* (The Percy Report) (1957, Cmnd 169, London: HMSO).

3 C. Greenland, *Mental Illness and Civil Liberty* (1970, Birkenhead: Wilmer Bros).

4 P. Fennell, 'Mental Health Review Tribunals: A Question of Imbalance' (1977) 2 Brit. Jo. of Law and Soc. 186.

5 J. Peay, 'Mental Health Review Tribunals: A Study of Individual Approaches to Decision Making' (1980, University of Birmingham, Ph.D. thesis).

6 L. Gostin, *A Human Condition*, vol. 1 (1975, London: MIND).

7 *Report on the Review of Procedures for the Discharge and Supervision of Psychiatric Patients Subject to Special Restrictions* (The Aarvold Report) (1973, Cmnd 5191, London: HMSO).

8 L. Gostin, *A Human Condition* vol. 2 (1977, London: Mind), p. 169.

the Board, whose 'recommendations' were not subject to natural justice and judicial review,[9] was of far greater significance in the decision making process than was the open and 'judicial' tribunal. Thus, throughout the 1970s, a hidden and executive process of discharge prevailed, which remained relatively untouched by domestic criticism.

Domestic opinion, as expressed by the Butler Committee on Mentally Abnormal Offenders, was specifically in favour of the retention by the Secretary of State of the final power to discharge. The Butler Committee felt it entirely appropriate that the Home Secretary should be ultimately responsible.[10] Even MIND, in its official report, accepted the executive role, but argued for a fair hearing before the Advisory Board.[11] In the event, the final shape of the 1982 reforms was dictated by international rather than domestic pressure. As the Amendment Bill was passing through its Parliamentary stages, the European Court of Human Rights published its judgment in *X* v. *United Kingdom*,[12] a case sponsored by MIND, and the government was obliged to introduce further amendments to meet its obligations under the European Convention. The European Court held that article 5(4) guaranteed a detained patient periodic access to a 'court' to determine the substantive lawfulness as well as the procedural propriety of his or her detention in hospital. In the case of restriction order patients, neither the Secretary of State, the tribunal nor the High Court constituted a 'court' with the necessary powers. The Secretary of State was a senior member of the executive; the tribunal, while possibly sufficiently independent, had no power to discharge, and the High Court, in the exercise of its review jurisdiction, had insufficient power to question the substantive grounds for detention. The solution chosen by the government in 1982 was an extension of the powers of the Mental Health Review Tribunal, and the removal of the Secretary of State's exclusive right to discharge. The tribunal was given the power, in certain circumstances, to discharge a restriction order patient, either absolutely or conditionally.

(b) The Constitution and Powers of Mental Health Review Tribunals Under the 1983 Act

(1) The Discharge Powers of the Mental Health Review Tribunal

Under Part V of the Mental Health Act 1983 the Mental Health Review Tribunal is given real powers with regard to the discharge of all mentally disordered offenders detained under a hospital order, whether with or without restrictions. In the case of those detained under a simple section 37 hospital order the tribunal has both a duty to direct a discharge if it is satisfied as to

9 *R* v. *Secretary of State, ex p. Powell*, 21 December 1978, unreported.
10 *Report of the Committee on Mentally Abnormal Offenders* (1975, Cmnd 6244, London: HMSO), para. 7.16.
11 *Supra*, n. 8.
12 (1981) 4 EHRR 181.

certain factors, and a general discretion to discharge. According to section 72, a tribunal must discharge a patient if it is satisfied:

(1) that the patient is not suffering from any of the four specified types of mental disorder, *or*
(2) that the patient is not suffering from them to a nature or degree making it appropriate for him to be detained in hospital for treatment, *or*
(3) that the patient's detention for treatment is not necessary for his health or safety, or for the protection of others.

When acting under these provisions, a tribunal may direct a discharge on a future date – section 72(3). In deciding whether to exercise its powers of discretionary discharge, the tribunal must have regard to the likelihood of the treatment alleviating or preventing a deterioration in the condition, and, in certain circumstances, to the patient's ability to look after himself on release, section 72(2). Where a tribunal does not direct a patient's discharge it may, 'with a view to facilitating his discharge on a future date', recommend that a patient be transferred to another hospital or given leave of absence, section 72(3)(a).

The tribunal's powers in relation to restricted patients are more limited. If the tribunal is satisfied as to the matters specified in relation to non-restricted patients it must order an absolute discharge, provided it does not consider it appropriate that the patient remain liable to recall, section 73(1). If it is satisfied as to the relevant matters, but considers liability to recall appropriate, it must order a conditional discharge, section 73(2). In the case of a restricted patient, the tribunal has no general discretion to discharge, neither does it have an express power to recommend transfer. In practice, the power to order a conditional discharge is of utmost significance, not only because of the recall power, but also because of the opportunity such a discharge offers for imposing controls on the patient's behaviour in the community after release.[13] As a condition of discharge, patients are often required to live in approved accommodation, accept treatment from a specified doctor, and accept the supervision of a probation officer or social worker. Any failure by the patient to meet such conditions could lead ultimately to recall, section 73(4). Thus a conditional discharge can be used to achieve effectively the same, if not a greater, degree of control than that which might be achieved by a community treatment order if such existed. The conditions imposed must, however, be consistent with both the findings of the tribunal and the notion of discharge from hospital. Thus, while the acceptance of *out-patient* treatment as a condition of discharge might be lawful, the Divisional Court has declared a requirement of *residence* in hospital to be inconsistent with the notion of discharge and thus unlawful.[14] The conditional discharge power cannot,

13 S. Dell and G. Robertson, *Sentencing to Hospital: Offenders in Broadmoor* (1988, Oxford: Oxford University Press).
14 *Secretary of State for the Home Dept* v. *Mental Health Review Tribunal for the Merseyside Regional Health Authority* [1986] 3 All ER 233. For the question of out-patient treatment, see *Secretary of State for the Home Department* v. *Oxford Regional M.H.R.T.* [1987] 3 All ER 8, per Lord Bridge at p. 12.

therefore, be used by tribunals to achieve the transfer of a restricted patient to a less secure hospital as a detained in-patient.

At a more fundamental level, it has been argued that the imposition of a conditional discharge on a patient who the tribunal is satisfied is *not* suffering from one of the specified mental disorders is inconsistent with that negative finding. According to such an argument, a conditional discharge should only be made where the tribunal is satisfied that the patient is suffering from a mental disorder, but not to a degree making it necessary for him to be detained in hospital for medical treatment. The Court of Appeal has, however, rejected that argument, and it is clear that section 73 is to be interpreted as permitting the imposition of a conditional discharge even where the tribunal does not believe the patient to be suffering from a relevant mental disorder at the time.[15] It is also relevant to note that, while the acceptance of treatment might be properly required as a condition of discharge, the safeguards applying to the imposition of compulsory treatment under Part IV of the Act, such as regular review and the second-opinion provisions, do not apply to conditionally discharged patients.[16]

Most restriction orders are imposed without limit of time, and a conditionally discharged patient remains subject to conditions indefinitely unless those conditions are lifted by either the Secretary of State – section 42(2) – or by the tribunal, to which a conditionally discharged patient may apply every two years, section 75(2). In 1971 K was convicted of manslaughter and given a restricted hospital order without limit of time. In 1985 he was conditionally released by the tribunal, which found that he was no longer suffering from mental disorder under the Act. Six months later he assaulted two women and was sentenced to six years' imprisonment. While in prison, K applied to the tribunal to have the conditions on which he was discharged from hospital lifted. The tribunal concluded that K was still not suffering from any mental disorder, but refused to lift his conditions on the ground that he was nevertheless in need of strict supervision, and 'that supervision will still be required even after he has been released from his present sentence'. The tribunal did, however, agree to suspend the conditions for the period during which K was in prison. K applied for judicial review of the tribunal's decision, arguing that, since both the 1985 and the 1986 tribunals had agreed that he was no longer suffering from mental disorder, he was no longer a 'patient' under the Act, and was entitled to an absolute discharge. The Court of Appeal rejected this argument, preferring to interpret section 73(2) as impliedly permitting the conditional discharge of a person who is not suffering from mental disorder.[17] Admittedly, the express statutory provisions are open to various interpretations, but the interpretation adopted by the Court of Appeal effectively provides the tribunal and the detaining authorities with the power to impose conditions, including susceptibility to recall, on ex-patients in the community who are not mentally disordered.

15 *R* v. *Merseyside M.H.R.T. ex p. K* [1990] 1 All ER 694. See further below.
16 S. 56(1)(c), Mental Health Act 1983.
17 *Supra*, n. 15.

While there may be strong arguments based on social protection for providing such a power, and while the instant case involved an individual with a well-established history of alarming assaultive behaviour, nevertheless the outcome achieved by the Court of Appeal permits the application of compulsory powers to those who are not suffering from mental disorder. There can be no doubt that the power to recall which is provided by a conditional discharge is regarded as being of considerable importance, both by the psychiatric establishment and by the Secretary of State, to judge from his reluctance to grant absolute discharges to patients originally granted conditional discharges. If individuals can be 'dangerous' without being mentally disordered, it matters little in practice to those who are seen as responsible for the protection of the public that the desired controls are imposed equally on the ordered and the disordered. Nevertheless, however strong the case for compulsion might be, its extension to those who are not apparently disordered should be approved consciously and expressly by the legislature; it should not be left to the strained interpretation of the Court of Appeal in the adjudication of a particular dispute.

An interesting comparison can be made here between the interpretations adopted in and the consequences flowing from the two cases concerned with treatment and consent discussed in chapter 11, and *Ex p. K*. In the two treatment cases, which arguably involved a conflict between autonomy and beneficence, the courts adopted narrow interpretations of the legislation which favoured autonomy in preference to the more expansive interpretations favourable to beneficence. Those wishing to extend the statutory power to intervene on grounds of beneficence had therefore to seek express Parliamentary approval for such an extension: approval which they have not yet acquired. In *Ex p. K*, by contrast, where the conflict was between the freedom of the individual patient and the perceived demands of social protection, the generous interpretation of section 73(2) adopted by the Court of Appeal met the latter demands. Had the court adopted the alternative interpretation, favouring the freedom of the individual patient, those arguing for a power of recall in the absence of mental disorder would have been obliged to seek express Parliamentary approval. In the event, by adopting the interpretation favourable to those arguing for the power to interfere with the patient's freedom, the court was avoiding the need to seek express legislative authority: it was effectively formulating policy itself. Two points should be made.

In the first place, the senior judiciary are not the most appropriate policy formulators. While they are independent of the interested parties, they have no particular expertise with regard to the management of dangerous individuals. Further, while the Court of Appeal is formally accountable to the House of Lords, and both courts are accountable to Parliament, in the sense that Parliament can neutralise judicial policy formulation through the introduction of fresh legislation, the judiciary are not accountable in the broader sense mentioned in chapter 4: they are not obliged to encourage wide public participation in their decision making. Secondly, neither the adversarial adjudicatory structure adopted by the courts nor the procedures which flow from it are appropriate to the formulation of policy. Before a court, the issue for resolution is concentrated on the circumstances of a particular case, and the evidence and arguments presented are controlled by those directly affected by the outcome of that case. In *Ex p. K* only the patient, the tribunal and the Secretary of State were represented. The ability of the court to assess the wider public interest is therefore significantly restricted.

With regard to the established principles of statutory interpretation, there is a presumption that where a penal statute is open to alternative interpretations a strict construction in favour of the citizen will be adopted.[18] Further, in relation to police powers of arrest, Lord Bridge has declared 'no one doubts that a prime factor in the process of construction is a strong presumption in favour of the liberty of the innocent subject'.[19] Such a presumption, if conscientiously adhered to, would require the legislature expressly to authorise each interference with the liberty of the citizen, and thus itself to assess the public interest involved. However, in the same case Lord Bridge went on to state that 'it is clear from the authorities at least that a statute may be held to have rebutted the presumption by something falling short of clear express language'. Thus, while there may be a presumption in favour of autonomy and liberty in such cases, that presumption is vulnerable to implied rebuttal. In practice, the ease with which any such 'presumption' can be overcome in cases like *Ex p. K* allows the judiciary rather than the legislature to perform the necessary public interest assessment. Arguably, the presumption in favour of personal liberty and bodily integrity should be paramount. The courts are not the appropriate forum for the assessment of the public interest in such cases. In chapter 5, in relation to the Court of Appeal decision in *Hague* it was suggested that in reviewing the legality of substantive policy the courts should strictly police the legislative boundaries.[20] Had the court in *Ex p. K* adopted such an approach, and coupled it with a strong presumption in favour of liberty, those arguing for the interpretation favourable to social protection would have had to seek express legislative approval.

(2) The Constitution of the Tribunals

Although, as will be seen, reservations remain concerning the adequacy of the tribunals' increased powers, those powers were granted specifically to comply with the European Convention. Article 5(4), as interpreted in *X*, guarantees a detained patient regular access to a 'court' to determine the lawfulness of his continued detention. It is clear from the judgment that a 'court' under the European Convention must be independent of the executive, and must have the power to make a binding decision. It does not, however, have to be a 'court' in the traditional sense, and the Mental Health Review Tribunal, if appropriately empowered, was thought adequate to meet the requirements of the Convention. Indeed, for the purposes of the domestic law of contempt, the Mental Health Review Tribunal has been declared to be a court.[21]

18 *Tuck and Sons* v. *Priester* (1887) 19 QB 629.
19 *Wills* v. *Bowley* [1983] 1 AC 57, at p. 101.
20 *R* v. *Deputy Governor of Parkhurst Prison, ex p. Hague* [1990] 3 All ER 687.
21 *Pickering* v. *Liverpool Daily Post and Echo* [1990] 1 All ER 335.

From the government's point of view, however, there was a danger that the tribunals would not carry the confidence of the public and the judiciary.[22] They would not be regarded as sufficiently responsible to take binding discharge decisions concerning patients who had been convicted of serious criminal offences. The government, in other words, was concerned to ensure that the selected decision maker would not only possess the necessary expertise but would also appear to possess appropriate status. Of the various solutions canvassed, the government finally decided to restrict to circuit judges the legal membership of tribunals deciding restriction order cases.[23] There are, however, no specific statutory requirements. The Mental Health Act and the Tribunal Rules merely state that legal members must be appointed by the Lord Chancellor and have such 'legal expertise as the Lord Chancellor considers suitable', and that those considering restricted patients must be approved for that purpose by the Lord Chancellor.[24] Indeed, this flexibility has enabled the Lord Chancellor to designate non-circuit judges, and a number of recorders who are also QCs have been approved.

In terms of the present analysis, Mental Health Review Tribunals are now required to reach application, or more realistically in the case of unrestricted patients, validation decisions with regard to discharge. Since 1983 the structure for this decision making can be regarded as adjudicatory: the tribunal represents an independent third party empowered to resolve, according to preordained statutory criteria, an issue which is often interpreted as a dispute. It is also apparent that the choice of decision maker was governed both by considerations of expertise (hence the legal, medical and lay components of each tribunal) and by a desire to encourage confidence in the system (hence the additional concern over the presidency of panels dealing with restricted cases).

(3) The Remaining Influence of the Secretary of State

(a) Transfer and Leave of Absence

Without a doubt, the acquisition by the newly-constituted Mental Health Review Tribunals of the power to direct the discharge of restricted patients is of immense formal significance, and it is most unlikely that it would have occurred without the intervention of the European Court of Human Rights (ECHR) in *X* v. *United Kingdom*.[25] However, its significance in practice should not be overestimated. The most common route out of a special hospital is not directly to the community via a tribunal discharge, but rather via transfer to a regional secure unit, then to a local hospital, and finally into the community. With regard to transfer, the tribunal has no express power even to

22 J. Peay, *Tribunals on Trial* (1989, Oxford: Oxford University Press), p. 11.
23 *Ibid.*, pp. 14–15.
24 Sch. 2(1)(a), Mental Health Act 1983, and rule 8(3), Mental Health Review Tribunal Rules 1983, SI 1983–942.
25 *Supra*, n. 12.

make recommendations in the case of restricted patients. Indeed, section 41 stipulates that the transfer of restriction order patients between hospitals and the granting of leave of absence can only be done with the consent of the Secretary of State.

Thus, despite *X*, the Secretary of State retains final power in relation to what are, arguably, the most important decisions concerning the discharge of restricted patients, and in reaching these decisions he still relies upon advice from the Special Advisory Board in a number of individual cases. If an rmo recommends the transfer of a patient who has been referred to the Advisory Board, a member of that Board will be required to advise the Secretary of State. He or she will visit the patient, examine the case notes and advise accordingly. Such advice is apparently influential, and certainly unappealable. In addition, since 1989 it has been the practice for the Home Secretary to receive advice on the transfer and leave of absence of individual patients from the Special Hospital Services Authority (SHSA). Applications by the restricted patient's rmo will be processed by the SHSA, which will attach its own opinion before forwarding the papers to the Home Office.

As described in chapter 9, the Secretary of State for Health gave the SHSA the role of hospital manager under the 1983 Act with regard to the special hospitals. In this capacity it would be formally involved in the process of transfer by virtue of sections 19 and the regulations, but since the role of statutory manager has been specifically delegated to the Hospital Advisory Committee at each hospital, the continuing involvement of SHSA headquarters in individual decisions might require some additional justification.[26] In relation to applications for leave under section 17, as opposed to transfer, the SHSA has even less formal justification for becoming involved in individual decisions since the statutory managers have no express role under the 1983 Act. Further, the Home Secretary must not allow himself to be dictated to by any other body when exercising his powers under section 41 to grant transfer and leave of absence. He must not, therefore, allow himself to be bound by the views of the SHSA. If he does do so, he will be in breach of well-established principles of the common law, prohibiting both the fettering and the abdication of discretion.[27]

In practice, the advent of the SHSA has inserted an additional layer of advice between the patient seeking leave or transfer and the authority empowered to grant it: the Home Secretary; but, in contrast to the position

26 See rule 7, Mental Health (Hospital, Guardianship and Consent to Treatment) Regulations 1983, SI 1983/893, for the statutory role of the hospital managers in relation to transfers under section 19. The position of the Hospital Advisory Committees was described in chapter 9, and see *S.H.S.A. Review 1991* (1991, London: SHSA). On the assumption that the delegation of the functions of statutory manager by the SHSA to the Hospital Advisory Committees was both formal and lawful, the question arises whether a delegating authority can retain the power delegated, see H. Wade, *Administrative Law* 6th edn (1988, Oxford: Oxford University Press). Finally, section 123 empowers the Secretary of State to direct the transfer of a special hospital patient to another hospital whether or not the receiving hospital has agreed that a bed is available, but this power is seldom used.

27 Wade, *supra*, n. 26, ch. 11.

with the Advisory Board, the patient concerned may never see the member of the SHSA who presents this crucial advice to the Home Secretary. Arguably, the new practice provides a further example of the ease with which the restrictions already imposed on patients by the Act can be informally extended without any attempt openly to justify that extension in terms of either treatment or security.

Thus, despite *X*, important decisions upon which a restricted patient's ultimate discharge will depend are still reached by way of administrative decision making undertaken in private with few procedural safeguards. The independent adjudicatory structure introduced by the 1982 reforms has not been extended beyond the very narrowest understanding of discharge, and the Home Secretary still controls the crucial decisions which typically precede discharge. In theory, the Secretary of State's central role in the discharge of restricted patients prior to 1982 was justified on the grounds of public interest. The release of potentially dangerous mentally disordered offenders was regarded as a matter of legitimate public interest, which should not be left to the judgement of a single professional group.[28] According to this view, the responsibility for individual decisions should rest with the Secretary of State, who is responsible to the public through Parliament.

While such an argument has certain merits at a theoretical level, since it vests the decision directly in an identifiable and accountable individual, it is hard to support in practice. The Secretary of State is a politically vulnerable figure who has every incentive to act with caution. The opprobrium attaching to the discharge of a patient who subsequently rapes or kills will far outweigh any public outcry at the prolonged detention of non-dangerous patients. To leave the interpretation of the public interest to a figure whose own interests are so intimately tied up in the outcome cannot be appropriate, a fact plainly recognised by the judgment in *X*.

(b) The Mental Health Review Tribunal Hearing

In addition to his central role in transfer and leave of absence, under the 1983 structure the Home Secretary still retains both concurrent powers of discharge and a role in the tribunal process itself. With regard to the latter, the regulations provide for the Secretary of State to be informed of any application by a restricted patient, to be provided with copies of all the documents before the tribunal, to submit any other relevant information, and to be informed of the hearing date.[29] The object is clearly to enable the Secretary of State to make representations to the tribunal and to oppose the discharge if he so wishes. His role in this respect is seen as crucial: in the words of Lord Bridge, he is 'the only party capable of representing any interest the public may have in opposing an application for discharge'.[30] Indeed, if the tribunal fails to inform the Secretary

28 *Supra*, n. 10.
29 *Supra*, n. 24.
30 *Secretary of State for the Home Dept.* v. *Oxford Region M.H.R.T.* [1987] 3 All ER 8 at p. 10.

of State of the date of the hearing, that failure is likely to be regarded as sufficient to vitiate any subsequent decision.[31]

In principle, this conversion of the Secretary of State from decision maker to mere representative of the public interest is to be welcomed. The reservations attaching to the Secretary of State's exclusive power of decision making do not so strongly apply to the Secretary of State as advocate. His interpretation of the public interest may still be coloured by his own position but, in theory at least, the tribunal can take account of any such colouration. It is unfortunate, however, that the Secretary of State's participation at a tribunal tends in practice to be limited to the provision of a rule 6 statement and the appointment of counsel to cross-examine witnesses advocating discharge. The executive seldom, if ever, provides oral evidence of its own against discharge, and so is in no position to be cross-examined on its opinion.

Since 1989 the SHSA, as statutory manager, has constituted the responsible authority under the regulations, and in that capacity has been represented at certain tribunal hearings. While the SHSA has tended to take a more active part in the proceedings than the Secretary of State by, for example, providing its own witnesses; its role is very different from that performed by the Secretary of State in the guise of the Home Office. The SHSA represents one of the immediate parties, the detaining hospital, and its portrayal of the public interest must be influenced by that perspective. In theory, the Home Office, being removed from any role in the management of the detaining institution, can adopt a broader view. Thus the more active intervention of the SHSA does not obviate the need for some representation of the broader public interest, and major reservations must remain concerning the structure currently in place to provide for that representation.

(c) The Discharge of Patients Transferred from Prison

Before leaving the subject of the continuing powers of the Secretary of State, two further issues should be considered: the discharge of sentenced prisoners transferred to hospital, and the recall of conditionally discharged patients. The Secretary of State still retains significant influence in relation to the discharge of prisoners transferred to hospital under a restriction direction, by virtue of sections 47 and 49, for the period during which they would otherwise have been detained in prison. If the prisoner/patient remains in hospital after the expiry of the prison sentence, the restriction direction ceases to have effect. He will then be treated as if detained simply under section 37,[32] and the Secretary of State will cease to play any significant role in his eventual discharge. During the period in which the sentence is in force, however, the prisoner/patient can only be discharged with the agreement of the Secretary of State.

31 *Ibid.*
32 Section 41(5). It is relevant to note that in some cases the reversion to unrestricted status on the completion of the prison sentence can delay release since it removes the possibility of a conditional discharge.

There are effectively three mechanisms provided for discharge in such cases. In the first place, as is the case with ordinary restriction order patients, the Secretary of State may order a patient's absolute or conditional discharge 'if he thinks fit', section 42(2). In these circumstances, discharge is achieved under the provisions of the Mental Health Act 1983, and the Secretary of State is given no express statutory guidance as to the criteria to be used. Secondly, the tribunal may notify the Secretary of State if, using the criteria listed in section 73, it believes that either an absolute or a conditional discharge would have been appropriate had the patient been subject merely to a restriction order (section 74). The Secretary of State must then decide within 90 days whether to authorise the tribunal's conditional or unconditional discharge of the prisoner/patient. If the Secretary of State fails to provide such authorisation, the offender will be returned to prison unless the tribunal has made a recommendation under section 74(1)(b) that he should continue to be detained in hospital. Unlike sections 42 and 74, which provide for discharge under the 1983 Act, the third mechanism relies on penal release powers. Under section 50, either the rmo or the tribunal may notify the Secretary of State, either that the prisoner/patient 'no longer requires treatment in hospital for mental disorder or that no effective treatment for his disorder can be given in the hospital to which he has been removed'. Following such a notification, the Secretary of State may either order the person's return to prison or may release him from hospital under the same provisions as would have been available had he been in prison.

While the variety of discharge structures and criteria may appear daunting, at least in the case of fixed-term prisoner/patients, their restriction directions are of determinate duration. Life-sentence transferees, on the other hand, can remain subject to a restriction direction indefinitely: there is no pre-ordained point at which their sentence comes to an end. In 1985 the Home Secretary announced that he intended to release life-sentence transferees by way of section 50(1)(b) rather than through the exercise of his powers under section 42. He thus indicated a preference for the life-licence provisions of the Criminal Justice Act 1967 rather than the conditional discharge provisions of the Mental Health Act.[33] Transferred lifers would be considered by the Parole Board if referred to the Secretary of State by the tribunal after the expiry of their tariff period, and the Secretary of State would then make up his mind to release on licence, having consulted the relevant judiciary. In theory, this process could be completed without the prisoner/patient being returned to a penal institution.

Since the introduction of the Criminal Justice Act 1991, this procedure is further complicated by the creation of a statutory distinction between mandatory and discretionary life sentences. The Parole Board panel to whom a mandatory life-sentence transferee will be referred will presumably possess only advisory powers, while the discretionary transferee, if certified under

---

33 The Home Secretary does treat some life sentence prisoners who were mentally ill at the time of the offence or trial as 'technical lifers'. For such prisoner/patients the tariff date is no longer relevant, and discharge is achieved through the hospital system.

Schedule 12, paragraph 9, or if sentenced after October 1992, will be considered by a discretionary lifer panel with direct powers to release. The distinction between the two types of lifer, which has little beyond political expediency to explain it, will only cause further confusion in practice, and will result in the discharge of discretionary life-sentence transferees being considered by two similarly constituted and empowered tribunals. At the time of writing, however, the Home Office has avoided the irrational difference in treatment between mandatory and discretionary transferees, by the simple expedient of refusing to certify discretionary transferees under schedule 12 of the 1991 Act. Both types of transferred lifer continue to be treated under the pre-1992 structure.

(d) Recall

Section 42(3) of the Mental Health Act empowers the Secretary of State to recall a patient who has been conditionally discharged. No statutory criteria for recall are given:

The Secretary of State may at any time during the continuance in force of a restriction order in respect of a patient who has been conditionally discharged under subsection (2) above by warrant recall the patient to such hospital as may be specified in the warrant.

The Code of Practice, and earlier guidance from the Department of Health,[34] recognise that it will not always be necessary for the Home Secretary to exercise his formal powers of recall when a conditionally discharged patient requires hospital treatment. Such a patient may agree to attend hospital as an informal patient, or may be detained under Part II of the 1983 Act. However, if the patient is formally recalled the Home Office adopts a two-stage procedure. The person taking the patient into custody should explain that he is being recalled, and that a full explanation will be given later. As soon as possible after admission, and at least within 72 hours, the rmo should explain the reasons for the patient's recall, and should ensure that, as far as the patient's mental state allows, he understands what is happening. The patient should also be told that his case will be referred to the tribunal within a month.[35] These procedures were introduced after criticisms by the European Commission of Human Rights in *X* v. *United Kingdom*, and effectively provide for a first-tier administrative decision with access to validation by an independent adjudicator within a month. In 1985, 131 restricted patients were discharged, and within two years 24 had been recalled, while in 1986 the numbers were 94 and 13 respectively.[36]

Few data exist concerning the recall process in practice, but in the light of the absence of express statutory guidance as to the criteria for recall it is interesting to return to the case of K. In a previous section K's position was

---

34 DHSS Circular LASSA(80)7, and see *Code of Practice* (1990, London: HMSO), ch. 27.
35 Section 75(1). Although referred within a month, the case may not be heard for six months.
36 *Statistical Bulletin* 27/90 (1990, London: Home Office).

discussed in relation to the scope of the tribunal's power of conditional discharge. While on conditional discharge, K assaulted two women and was sentenced to six years' imprisonment and, despite his application to have the conditions lifted, he remained formally subject to a conditional discharge while in prison. K became eligible for release from prison on 24 October 1989. On 1 September the Secretary of State wrote to inform him that, because he could not be satisfied that K no longer presented a serious risk to public safety, he had authorised his recall to Broadmoor Hospital on the expiry of his prison sentence. K again sought to challenge this decision by way of judicial review.

On its face, K's application presented the judiciary with a classic opportunity to use its powers of validation to specify the legal boundaries of an apparently unfettered executive discretion. The familiar principles of judicial review indicate that such a discretion must be exercised in furtherance of the policy and objects of the empowering Act.[37] The common law empowers the High Court both to test the validity of executive action against the stated statutory policy and, in cases where that policy is not stated expressly but must be implied, to amplify the statutory statement. Through the exercise of its powers of validation, therefore, the High Court may also act effectively as policy formulator. According to both the Divisional Court and the Court of Appeal, the policy and objects of the 1983 Act are

to regulate the circumstances in which the liberty of persons who are mentally disordered may be restricted and, where there is conflict, to balance their interests against those of public safety.[38]

In the light of these statutory objects and the Home Secretary's obvious fears for public safety, both the Divisional Court and the Court of Appeal upheld the recall decision. As was suggested with regard to K's earlier litigation, it is easy to understand why the court might have been sympathetic to the executive. Nevertheless, it is important to note that there was clear medical evidence that K was not suffering from mental disorder under the Act, and that two successive tribunals had found that he was not so suffering. There was evidence that the Secretary of State doubted the validity of the medical opinions, but he had provided no medical reports in support of his view. He had relied instead on what was said by K's defence counsel at his trial, and on the report of a psychiatrist compiled for, but not produced at, the trial. This report concluded that, while K had 'a severe personality disorder', it could not 'be equated with a psychopathic disorder which needs or which would respond to treatment, and is not of a nature or degree which makes it appropriate for him to receive medical treatment in hospital'.[39] In other words, K was not suffering from mental disorder under the Act. In upholding the decision to recall K, therefore, the Court of Appeal was allowing the Secretary of State to return to hospital detention an ex-patient who could reasonably be regarded

37 *Padfield* v. *The Minister of Agriculture Fisheries and Food* [1968] AC 997.
38 *R* v. *Home Secretary, ex p. K* [1990] 3 All ER 562.
39 *Ibid.*, p. 567.

as dangerous, but whose mental disorder and susceptibility to treatment were in serious doubt.

The Mental Health Act is not ostensibly designed to provide preventive detention for dangerous people irrespective of their mental state, but by allowing the Secretary of State to exercise his section 42 powers to recall K to hospital in order that his mental disorder might be further assessed, the Court of Appeal was effectively allowing his preventive detention. While K had been locked up in prison he was supremely available to medical scrutiny. The Secretary of State had had ample time to arrange further psychiatric assessment before the expiry of the prison sentence and should have been required to do so. In the presence of fresh expert evidence of mental disorder under the Act, the decision to recall to hospital would have been beyond challenge; in its absence, K should have been entitled to release at the end of his sentence. In failing to require such action from the Secretary of State the Court of Appeal revealed its inadequacy as a mechanism for independent review, and at the same time permitted preventive detention at, if not beyond, the very limits of what can reasonably be implied from the wording of the 1983 Act. Once more, policy was formulated through adjudication in sensitive circumstances and in the absence of informed public debate.[40]

(4) Preliminary Conclusions: Statutory Structure

The most significant effect of the reforms following the decision in *X* v. *The United Kingdom* was the introduction of an independent adjudicatory structure for the discharge of restricted patients and for the validation of recall decisions. The procedures adopted by this adjudicatory structure will be considered further below. Outside discharge narrowly defined, however, administrative decision making still predominates, especially with regard to the transfer and leave of restricted patients and the initial decision to recall. Further, in the absence of unambiguous statutory guidance, adjudication has been used for the formulation of policy in the course of resolving individual disputes.

(c) The Discharge Criteria in Practice

Whatever view might ultimately be taken of the discharge criteria and their application in practice, there is no intention here to deny the significance of the risks involved in the decision to discharge. K's case provides a salutary illustration. In 1985, on the basis of a substantial body of uncontradicted medical evidence that he was not then suffering from any mental disorder, and assertions that he was no longer a danger to himself or to others, K, as we have already seen, was conditionally discharged by a Mental Health Review Tribunal. Within seven months he had made unprovoked and frightening attacks on two young women aged 16 and 21, both of whom were complete

40 See the earlier discussion at pp. 282–4.

strangers to him. There is nothing to suggest that the tribunal's decision was wrong on the basis of the evidence before it; the case serves merely as a reminder of the difficulties of prediction, the uncertainties surrounding definitions of mental disorder and the possible consequences of discharge. Even recognising the nature of the risks involved, however, the discharge criteria and their application in practice raise some serious questions of principle.

(1) The Statutory Criteria

In the first place, the formal wording of the criteria themselves requires further examination. A Mental Health Review Tribunal must discharge a restricted patient, whether conditionally or unconditionally, if it is satisfied as to any *one* of three states of affairs: 1) that the patient is not suffering from either of the four specified forms of mental disorder; 2) that the patient is not suffering from them to a nature or degree making it appropriate for him to be detained in hospital for medical treatment, or 3) that it is not necessary for the patient's health or safety or for the protection of others that he receive such treatment.

All three states of affairs are expressed in the negative, and in cases of uncertainty the tribunal need merely express itself as unsatisfied as to the absence of some condition: that, for example, it is not satisfied that the patient is not suffering from one of the mental disorders. To order discharge, the tribunal must be satisfied of a negative. The initial presumption thus lies *against* discharge and, in the absence of an actively inquisitorial tribunal, the patient must satisfy the tribunal either that he is not suffering, or that he is not in need of treatment in hospital, or that he is not a danger to himself or others. Any persisting uncertainty will result in the tribunal's failure to be satisfied, and thus in the patient's continued detention. In this respect, as Jill Peay argues, the criteria are 'out of keeping' with many other provisions dealing with the liberty of the individual.[41] The presumption, strictly, should be in favour of discharge, requiring the detaining authority to make out the case for continued detention: it should not be for the detainee to establish the case for release. Indeed, there is some reason to doubt whether this feature of the discharge procedure complies with the requirements of the European Convention.

Thus, although at first sight the criteria appear to be designed to ensure the discharge of all those whose detention in hospital is no longer fully justified, their actual wording encourages a cautious approach on the part of the tribunals and, arguably, an inadequate assessment of the public interest. According to Peay, this tendency towards caution is encouraged by a number of additional factors, including the very limited powers possessed by tribunals in restricted cases, and the nature of the evidence on which the tribunals are required to reach their decisions.

41 Peay, *supra*, n. 22, p. 85.

(2) The Powers of the Mental Health Review Tribunal

On the question of powers, the Mental Health Review Tribunals are presented with very little flexibility. They must either direct a discharge or leave the patient in the secure conditions of a special hospital. As was explained above, they have no power to order the intermediate solution of a transfer to a less secure hospital. Although tribunals have no express powers to recommend transfers in respect of restricted patients, they can, and do, do so. However, such recommendations have very little impact unless supported by the rmo, and may often, as described above, involve a further layer of scrutiny by the Advisory Board and by the SHSA. Under section 73(7) a tribunal may defer a direction for a conditional discharge 'until such arrangements as appear to the tribunal to be necessary for that purpose have been made to their satisfaction'. But this power to defer can only be used where the tribunal is satisfied that a discharge is appropriate. Indeed, the House of Lords has made it clear that a tribunal which has made a deferred direction under section 73(7) cannot reconsider the question whether the patient should in fact be discharged once the necessary arrangements have been made.[42] The sub-section is designed merely to enable the discharge to be delayed until the arrangements for the implementation of the conditions are made. Many tribunals, therefore, when faced with the reality of their limited powers, will incline against discharge to the community even under tight conditions, leaving the patient, perhaps inappropriately, detained in a special hospital. As the tribunals see it, they have no real choice and the discharge criteria are ripe for cautious interpretation.

A case which was decided by the tribunal shortly after the re-offending referred to in *ex p. K* illustrates the impressive flexibility of the discharge criteria.[43] In this case, seven doctors including the rmo testified that the patient was no longer suffering from a psychopathic disorder under the 1983 Act, and recommended conditional discharge. However, since the rmo admitted that it was logically impossible for him to prove that the patient's disorder was no longer present, the tribunal was quite free to declare itself 'not satisfied' that the patient was 'not suffering'. Further, the patient's behaviour at the hearing convinced the medical member of the tribunal that the disorder was of a nature and degree that required treatment in hospital, and that single opinion was sufficient to outweigh the preponderance of expert opinion to the contrary. Perhaps if the timing had been more favourable, or if the tribunal had had the option of ordering a transfer to a less secure hospital, the outcome would have been different.

A further problem relating to transfers arises from the paucity of suitable accommodation for mentally disordered offenders outside special hospitals. Many regional secure units refuse to take special hospital patients unless they are guaranteed a bed in a local hospital within 18 months to two years. Unfortunately, but perhaps understandably, many local hospitals refuse to

41 *Supra*, n. 30.
42 Peay, *supra*, n. 22, pp. 122–4.

give such guarantees. An impasse can therefore be reached even when the tribunal, rmo and Home Secretary are all agreed on a transfer. In such circumstances it is of course possible for the tribunal to find the flexible criteria met, and to direct a discharge to the community. In one case, known to the author, a man convicted of arson who had been a model patient in special hospital for many years. However, he had always denied the offence, and the regional secure unit in his home catchment refused to accept him until he admitted his guilt. In the unit's view he would remain unsusceptible to treatment until he developed insight. After several inconclusive hearings over a period of years, the tribunal finally bypassed the usual process of staged release, and discharged him directly into the community. Such assertiveness on the part of a tribunal, however, is rare, and most cases are resolved, if at all, through informal pressure, often after considerable delay.[44]

Similar problems can occur even when the Mental Health Review Tribunal is prepared to direct a conditional discharge. The tribunal may make a deferred direction under section 73(7) to enable the necessary arrangements to be made to meet the conditions it wishes to impose, and those arrangements may never be made. The rmo may strive to set up the required treatment and supervision in the community, but may find that, despite her every effort, no such provision is available. Alternatively, the rmo, if unhappy about the tribunal's decision to discharge, may move reluctantly in search of the necessary arrangements. In either case the patients can face frustrating delays with little obvious means of redress. It is therefore encouraging to note that the court has now recognised that the receiving health authority is under a duty to act 'expeditiously and diligently' in order to make the necessary arrangements.[45]

Thus, while the Mental Health Review Tribunal may be empowered to impose its conclusions in relation to the choice between discharge, whether conditional or absolute, and continued detention in a special hospital, it is not empowered to do so with regard to the choice between special hospital detention and either detention elsewhere or staged release. In practice, these limitations on the adjudicatory powers of tribunals are of considerable significance: they both deprive tribunals of the power to impose their preferred options, and incline them towards a cautious interpretation of the statutory criteria when presented with the stark choice between special hospital detention and discharge.

(3) The Nature of the Evidence and Procedures before Tribunals

A Mental Health Review Tribunal must be satisfied of a negative before it directs the discharge of a restricted patient, but the negative conditions of which it must be satified are rarely susceptible to precise quantification. The notion of psychopathy, for example, is notoriously hard to define, although the 1983 Act does attempt a definition in section 1(2):

44 MHAC, *Fourth Biennial Report 1989–91* (1991, London: HMSO), p. 21.
45 *R* v. *Ealing District Health Authority, ex p. F* [1992] *The Times*, 24 June.

'psychopathic disorder' means a persistent disorder or disability of mind (whether or not including significant impairment of intelligence) which results in abnormally aggressive or seriously irresponsible conduct on the part of the person concerned.[46]

In the case of a patient who has been diagnosed as psychopathic and detained on that basis, a tribunal must satisfy itself, either that the patient is no longer suffering from psychopathy to a nature or degree which makes it appropriate for him to be detained in hospital for medical treatment, or that the patient's detention for treatment is not required for his own safety, or for the protection of others. So the absence of psychopathy or the absence of danger are the keys to discharge. It is hard to imagine the existence of conclusive evidence on either of these issues.

Peay describes the case of a psychopathic patient in a special hospital whose transfer to less secure conditions was recommended by his rmo.[47] At the Mental Health Review Tribunal, the Home Office used the insufficiency of evidence of the absence of disorder to support their opposition to any such change, and expressed particular concern about the 'lack of information on the patient's fantasy life'. According to Peay, the Home Office frequently sought some positive evidence that the patient would not present a danger if released. Positive evidence that something is absent is hard to obtain, particularly when the 'thing' required to be absent is a risk. Nevertheless, from Peay's account it is clear that the lack of such 'positive' evidence can be most influential.

The evidence available to a tribunal on the basis of which it is required to satisfy itself must, according to the relevant regulations, include a statement from the responsible authority, giving the patient's detention details, an up-to-date medical report and, as far as is reasonably practicable, a social circumstances report.[48] In the case of a restricted patient, it should also include a statement from the Secretary of State, the Home Secretary.[49] In practice these reports, in combination with reports from other relevant disciplines, such as psychology, will provide an account of the patient's educational, employment and social background, previous psychiatric history, present mental state, and criminal record, including a full account of his most recent offence.

(a) The Medical Evidence

In many special hospital cases the medical evidence before the Mental Health Review Tribunal will not be restricted to the rmo's written report. The patient's rmo will usually provide oral evidence, and some special hospital doctors will also obtain second opinions. Similarly, most restricted patients will obtain their own independent psychiatric reports.[50] Naturally, in the light

46 See H. Prins, *Dangerous Behaviour, the Law and Mental Disorder* (1986, London: Tavistock), ch. 5, for an account of the evolution of the term, and see chapter 9, *supra*, for a discussion of its use in the 1983 Act.
47 Peay, *supra*, n. 22, p. 113.
48 MHRT Rules, *supra*, n. 24, rule 6 and sch. 1.
49 *Ibid.*, rule 6(2).
50 For patients in receipt of legal aid, independent reports will be covered by the legal aid.

of the discharge criteria, all medical evidence is of considerable significance but, according to Peay, it is the opinion of the rmo that is typically the most influential. Indeed in 85 per cent of cases involving psychopathic disorder, and in 90 per cent of all mental illness cases in Peay's sample, she found that the tribunal endorsed the rmo's recommendations. In the rare cases where the tribunal declined to follow the advice of the rmo it was generally because the tribunal feared that the rmo was being insufficiently cautious. Release decisions taken against the advice of the rmo were rare: in the words of one judicial tribunal member, 'It's a brave tribunal to say that a patient is fit for conditional discharge in the teeth of opposition from the rmo.'[51] This evidence of Mental Health Review Tribunal acquiescence led Peay to conclude that 'rather than making decisions in the sense of exercising choice between real options, the tribunals invariably endorsed the recommendations made to them.'[52] While such a conclusion provides strong evidence of the power of the rmo, it also must cast considerable doubt on the assumption that tribunals fulfil a truly adjudicatory role.

In cases of disagreement between medical experts, Peay's evidence suggests that Mental Health Review Tribunals will accord greater significance to the opinion of the rmo than to that of an independent psychiatrist. Independent psychiatrists are sometimes seen as partial in the sense that they will be selected and, vial legal aid, paid for by the patient, and their contact with the patient will be brief. Further, unless they appear at the hearing, they will not be available to be questioned on their opinions. While this preference on the part of tribunals for the views of the rmo may be understandable, especially if the independent psychiatrist is not present, it would be unfortunate if tribunals were to place automatic trust in the depth of the rmo's knowledge. Many special hospital rmos are undoubtedly conscientious clinicians and possess an intimate knowledge of their patients. However, as the Ashworth Report suggests, this is not always the case; further, recruiting difficulties are such that patients may experience frequent changes in rmo, with the result that tribunal reports may be presented by doctors whose direct knowledge of the patient is limited to one or perhaps two interviews.[53] It is also relevant to note that, despite the recognised significance of the rmo's opinion, patients may be reluctant to challenge it before the Mental Health Review Tribunal, even through their representatives. Any such challenge can lead to the claim that the patient lacks insight, and to the conclusion that no advance can be made in treatment until the patient accepts the diagnosis.

51 Peay, *supra*, n. 22, p. 88. Lawyers now representing special hospital patients suggest that tribunals are becoming more willing to challenge the opinion of the rmo; but recent research data are lacking.

52 *Ibid.*, p. 209.

53 See *Report of the Committee of Inquiry into Complaints about Ashworth Hospital* (The Ashworth Report) (1992, Cm 2028-1, London: HMSO), ch. XVII, for strong criticism of some of the medical care provided at Ashworth. And see MHAC, *supra*, n. 44, p. 21, for comment on the frequent changes of rmo.

(b) The Inquisitorial Model

As was suggested above, Peay's data cast considerable doubt on the practical reality of the tribunal's adjudicatory role. However, before rejecting the adjudicatory classification as inappropriate as well as possibly inaccurate, it is relevant to consider the distinction between the adversarial and the inquisitorial approach.

In chapter 4 it was suggested that the inquisitorial approach might be preferable to the adversarial where facts have to be established, whereas the balance may tip the other way where opinions have to be assessed. On that basis, an adversarial model might be preferred here. However, it was further suggested that, although the parties in dispute might feel greater satisfaction at an adversarial hearing where they maintain more control over the arguments and evidence, a less confrontational approach might be preferred in the event of a need, as here, to maintain a continuing relationship between the parties. Further, the asymmetry between the parties before a Mental Health Review Tribunal in terms of both expertise and information might, as in the case of parole hearings, incline towards the adoption of an inquisitorial model. The evident public interest involved in the decision to discharge might also point to an inquisitorial approach in light of the need to canvass views and opinions beyond those of the parties most directly involved. Certainly, an inquisitorial approach which imposed clear duties on the tribunal to seek expert evidence beyond that provided by the rmo might serve to test the opinion of the rmo more effectively than the present practice of relying primarily on the initiative of the patient. In addition, a more actively inquisitorial approach might encourage tribunals to seek more specific evidence on the public interest from the Home Secretary. Tribunals which adopted such an approach would be providing a more convincingly adjudicatory forum than that apparently provided at present.

At a formal level, the court already regards the tribunal as inquisitorial. In a case involving the disclosure of an independent psychiatric report to the tribunal against the wishes of the patient, the Chancery Division pointed to the Mental Health Review Tribunal Rules, in particular to the duty of the medical member to examine the patient (rule 11), and the tribunal's power to call for further information and reports (rule 15),[54] as evidence of an inquisitorial style. The independent psychiatrist had taken a different and less optimistic view of the patient's disorder and likely dangerousness from that adopted by the rmo, and when the patient's solicitors received his report they withdrew the patient's application to the tribunal. The independent psychiatrist, despite opposition from the patient's solicitors, then revealed the report to the medical director of the special hospital involved, who in turn forwarded it to the Secretary of State, whence it ultimately reached the tribunal. The patient's attempt to prevent further revelation of the report, and to claim damages for the existing revelation on the grounds of breach of confidence, failed. The court took the view that, in the case of a restricted patient applying for

54 *W* v. *Egdell* [1989] 1 All ER 1089.

discharge, the doctor's duty of confidence towards his patient was outweighed by his duty to the public. There was no suggestion that the doctor was under a duty to reveal, merely that his revelation did not in the circumstances amount to a breach of confidence.

On the basis of the approach to process adopted here, this conclusion can be supported in so far as it increases the breadth of evidence before the tribunal, provided patients are not deterred from open disclosures to doctors, and provided they are afforded reasonable access to alternative opinions – both important provisos. The revelation of the independent report to the hospital authorities for the purposes of the patient's future care, on the other hand, raises issues beyond the scope of the present chapter.[55] However, freedom to disclose to the tribunal evidence adverse to the patient must be matched by an equivalent freedom to disclose to the patient evidence in his favour held by the detaining authorities and the Secretary of State. Thus, for example, no duty of confidence should be allowed to prevent the revelation to the patient of a favourable report by the Special Advisory Committee, despite opposition from the Secretary of State.

(c) The Medical Member of the Tribunal

Although no question of breach of confidence arises with regard to the disclosure to the patient of the views of the medical member of the Mental Health Review Tribunal, a reluctance to make such disclosures has been displayed in the past. Evidence would suggest that the medical member of a tribunal, who will have assessed the patient prior to the hearing, can exercise considerable influence over the outcome. Clearly, in cases of disagreement between the rmo and the independent psychiatrist, the medical member might be expected to guide his or her colleagues, but apparently the influence can go further.[56] In the light of the potential significance of the medical member's opinion, the timing and extent of its disclosure becomes a matter of some importance. Peay describes a variety of different practices adopted by tribunals on this point, but concludes that the majority of judicial members did not seek the medical member's assessment until all of the evidence had been heard and the parties had left the room. While such a practice might enable the other tribunal members to hear the earlier evidence ininfluenced by the opinion of their medical colleague, it also prevented the patient from having the opportunity to question the opinion, or to put it to his experts.

In *R* v. *Mental Health Review Tribunal, ex p. Clatworthy*, Mann J suggested that it might be a breach of the principles of natural justice if the tribunal were to proceed 'on some basis unknown to others but known to themselves'.[57] In such circumstances the common law would impose a duty to disclose. Certainly,

---

55 The case is discussed further in H. Lesser and Z. Pickup, 'Law, Ethics and Confidentiality' (1990) 17 Jo. of Law and Soc. 17.
56 Peay, *supra*, n. 22, pp. 113 and 125.
57 [1985] 3 All ER 699, at p. 704.

disclosure to the patient of the medical member's view is essential to the basic common law notion of a fair hearing, but it is also essential to the broader notion of full process since only through disclosure can the view be challenged by other interested parties. Indeed, disclosure can be seen as central to the accountability of an expert decision maker. The medical member is present on the tribunal because of his or her expertise, but in the exercise of that expertise the medical member must be accountable.

(d) Disclosure and the Accuracy of Opinions

Whatever the relative merits of the various medical opinions, however, they *are* only opinions, and their value is highly dependent on the quality of the data on which they are based. In many cases they will be opinions concerning the presence or absence of a specific clinical condition, and will be based on extensive clinical experience, but in others they will effectively be mere predictions as to likely future events, and may be based on records compiled by others. The question of the reliability of records contained in a patient's clinical notes, discussed in chapters 10 and 11, is of obvious relevance here. If a doctor, be she a new rmo, an independent psychiatrist, or the medical member of a tribunal, has to assess a patient, she will have to rely extensively on existing clinical records. It is therefore essential that those records be as accurate as possible, particularly when they relate to the alleged conduct of the patient. The mere mention of a suspected involvement in firesetting or drug abuse, for example, will be of enormous significance. Inaccurate recording of such matters can lead directly to inadequate assessments and erroneous predictions.

An obvious, if not foolproof, means of checking the factual accuracy of reports and records is to disclose them to the patient and others with direct knowledge, and to invite comment. With regard to documents received by it, the tribunal is obliged to send copies to the patient, the responsible authority and, in restricted cases, the Secretary of State, all of whom may submit comments. However, the patient may not see everything. Under rule 6(4) the rmo can request that specific parts of his or her report be not disclosed to the patient; further, under rule 12(2) the tribunal can deny disclosure to the patient of a document before it if it is satisfied that disclosure would 'adversely affect the health or welfare of the patient or others'. In the period immediately following the introduction of the new rules rmos frequently sought to use rule 6, prior to the hearing, to prevent disclosure of their reports. Such requests were not, apparently, treated with much favour by the regional tribunal chairs, who would often receive and decide the requests before the individual tribunals sat, and such requests have as a result become much less frequent. Applications for non-disclosure can, however, still be made to individual tribunals under rule 12.[58]

While the presumption is in favour of disclosure where medical and other

58 Peay, *supra*, n. 22, p. 92.

reports are concerned and specific applications have to be made for non-disclosure, the same was not until recently true in relation to the case notes themselves. Only rarely would they be disclosed to the patient or to his representative, and when they were so disclosed, that disclosure would be partial only, and would relate to specific entries in dispute. There was always a case for arguing that medical records should be regarded as documents before the tribunal, and thus subject to disclosure under rule 12, particularly if they were consulted directly by tribunal members other than the medical member; but in practice this argument was widely ignored. The situation should now be improved by the Access to Health Records Act 1990, which provides patients with a right of access to their medical records. However, as was explained in chapter 10, this Act applies only to records after November 1991, except where access to earlier records is required to make sense of records to which the right applies, and access can be refused under section 5(1) where the records would disclose 'information likely to cause serious harm to the physical or mental health of the patient'.

According to any notion of full process, the non-disclosure of critical data such as medical records is hard to justify. Indeed, although it may lead to some apprehension on the part of patients and their representatives, disclosure of the medical notes should extend not just to the patient but, as would be the case if the notes were regarded as documents received by the tribunal under rule 12, to the Secretary of State as well. It is essential to the notion of full process that the public interest be properly represented and, if under the present structure the Secretary of State is, however inadequately, the vehicle for that representation, he must be fully informed. However if, as would seem to be the case, some notion of selective representation has been applied here, and the public interest is to be represented before the tribunal by the Home Secretary, not by individual members of the public, then no useful purpose can be served by wider dissemination of information regarding the patient.[59]

Whatever the real merits of selective representation, and the issue is discussed further below, its implementation at the application stage does place a considerable responsibility on the Secretary of State. Indeed, under the present system it would not be the fact of disclosure to the Secretary of State itself that would cause concern, but the interpretation of the public interest to which Secretaries of State are prone, and the immunity from challenge of that interpretation.

(e) Non-medical Evidence

In psychiatric hospitals, nursing staff have a far greater opportunity to observe patients than do the medical staff. However, Mental Health Review Tribunals rarely receive evidence from nurses. The rmo's report will, of course, be based on the combined experience of the multi-disciplinary team responsible for the patient's care, but the reality of the hospital hierarchy is such that the views of

59 For discussion of the notion of selective representation see D. Galligan, *Discretionary Powers* (1986, Oxford: Oxford University Press), ch. 7. The issue is also discussed in *supra* chapter 4.

the consultant are bound to prevail. In the context of mental rather than physical disorder, where much expert opinion has to be based on the interpretation of observed behaviour, it is particularly unfortunate that tribunals do not more often demand evidence from those who observe the patients most closely. Similarly, although a psychologist will provide a report if he or she has been specifically required to do so, psychology reports are not automatically obtained. A more actively inquisitorial approach on the part of the tribunal could remedy this particular omission.

(f) Reasons

Finally, Mental Health Review Tribunals are by regulation required to provide written reasons for their decisions (rule 23), and a line of cases has established that this duty is not met by the mere recitation of the tribunals failure to be satisfied as to the necessary conditions for discharge.[60] In cases where discharge is refused and the patient's account of his mental state rejected, the reasons for this rejection must be clearly explained.[61] In the reported cases, the Divisional Court's attitude seems to have been influenced both by the traditional view that reasons must be sufficient to indicate whether or not there has been an error of law, and by the view that reasons must be full enough to indicate what is required to attract a more favourable outcome next time. No express reference is made to the possibility that an obligation to give reasons might improve the quality of the decision making itself. However, the case of *Pickering* is interesting in so far as it provides a clear example of a tribunal's failure adequately to distinguish between the diagnostic issue – was the patient still suffering from a psychopathic disorder? – and what Forbes J described as the 'policy question' – was it safe to release him?[62] The tribunal's failure to make explicit the necessary distinction was reflected in the inadequacy of its reasoning. Arguably, the discipline of providing reasons should deter such muddled thinking in the future.

(4) Preliminary Conclusions: Practice

Mental Health Review Tribunals provide an apparently adjudicatory structure for deciding whether or not to discharge a detained patient. However, the statutory criteria according to which they are required to reach their decisions are worded in such a way as to present the patient with the need to establish his fitness for discharge, and to encourage caution on the part of the tribunals. This tendency towards caution is further encouraged by the paucity of the tribunal's powers, particularly their lack of power to order transfer, and by the nature of the factors they have to assess: psychopathy and risk of dangerousness, for example. The cumulative effect of these influences may well result in

60 *Bone* v. *Mental Health Review Tribunal* [1985] 3 All ER 330.
61 *R* v. *M.H.R.T. ex p. Clatworthy* [1985] 3 All ER 699 and *R* v. *M.H.R.T. ex p. Pickering* [1986] 1 All ER 99.
62 *Ibid.* p. 101.

the production of over-cautious outcomes which do not fully reflect the public interest. Indeed, Peay's data suggest that tribunal's are (or possibly were) not truly adjudicatory in practice: they do not reach an independent assessment of conflicting opinions, but typically serve merely to endorse the views of the rmo. While the need to give reasons for their decisions may deter some loose reasoning on the part of tribunals, it is unlikely on its own to introduce the necessary rigour.[63]

In the face of these reservations, there are strong arguments for revising the statutory criteria in order to make it clear that the case for further detention must be established, rather than the case for discharge: the initial presumption should be in favour of discharge. The powers of the tribunal should also be extended to encompass the intermediate solutions of transfer and leave of absence. Without the possession of these powers the tribunal's effective decision making is severely restricted. Further, if tribunals are to be fully adjudicatory, their inquisitorial characteristics must be emphasised. In order to counteract the possibly disproportionate influence of the rmo, and to ensure the presentation of all relevant views and evidence, the tribunals must become actively investigative. They must, for example, seek out evidence from nurses, psychologists and independent psychiatrists, even if such evidence is not called by the patient. They must also be encouraged to challenge the evidence of the Secretary of State as to the nature of the public interest involved. The quality of such evidence is vital to the decision making process and, if the Secretary of State is to be the primary presenter of the public interest, his role must be examined and the true basis for his assessments sought.

While the Access to Health Records Act 1990 and the decision in *Clatworthy* have improved the openness of proceedings, the assumption must be in favour of the fullest possible disclosure to the patient. The degree of disclosure to parties other than the patient presents greater difficulties. All disclosure must be for the purposes of the tribunal only. The information at issue is of a personal nature, and the only public interest involved in its dissemination relates to the proper functioning of the tribunal. There can be no assumption that the patient has agreed to its disclosure for any other purpose. Thus, disclosure of information to parties other than the patient is justified only in so far as it improves the quality of the evidence before the tribunal. A witness to independent fact, for example, will have no need to see medical reports, since such reports should not affect the quality of the witness's evidence. On the other hand, the Secretary of State, or the clinician offering to provide care after discharge, will require more extensive access to enable them to base their assessments on all relevant information. A test of relevance should therefore be applied, and the extent of disclosure should be dictated by the nature of the evidence sought from the disclosee.

While greater disclosure should improve the quality of the evidence presented to the tribunal, it will not necessarily improve the quality of tribunal

63 Peay, *supra*, n. 22, p. 216.

deliberations. Peay provides disturbing evidence of the influence of the medical member during such deliberations:

more worrying still was the powerful impact remarks could have when made by the medical member during the tribunal's deliberations. Such off the cuff observations made at this stage could be damning, yet they would be considered unchallenged by any other medical view.[64]

There is clearly a dilemma here, created by the need to ensure not only expertise on the part of the decision maker, but accountability and impartiality as well. Peay suggests that some medical members are partial, in the sense of being predisposed towards one interpretation of the facts, predisposed towards treatment and caution. Procedural stringency at the hearing cannot guard against the influence of partiality during private deliberations, and the requirements of *Clatworthy* would not be sufficient to provide the necessary safeguards. A possible solution might lie in the enhancement of the role of the tribunal clerk, but the experience of a comparable experiment in relation to boards of visitors would suggest that little is likely to be achieved through such a ploy alone.[65]

If tribunals are to become effective independent decision makers the structure of their reasoning must be more closely regulated. The statutory criteria must expressly direct them to a sequence of questions, and to the nature of the consequences flowing from the possible conclusions, and must require them to provide full reasons for their sequence of conclusions. In theory, the obligation such an approach would impose on the legislature to provide more specific policy guidance would enhance the process of policy formulation, and reduce the scope for the sort of judicial policy making described earlier.

(d) Alternative Structures?

Although in practice Mental Health Review Tribunals perform valuable functions beyond their direct powers in relation to discharge, they encourage the periodic review of a patient's progress, for example, and oblige those treating the patient to explain their views and intentions; it is their direct role in the discharge process that is of central relevance here. In the previous section certain changes to the present structure were proposed in order to enable tribunals properly to fulfil their discharge role. Tribunals must be given wider powers, must become more actively inquisitorial, and the statutory criteria they are required to apply must be expressed with greater precision. However, the more fundamental question remains whether the tribunal structure, however improved, constitutes the preferred process for application decisions concerning the discharge of individual patients.

64 *Ibid.* p. 217.
65 See chapter 7.

As explained above, under present legislative policy a mentally disordered offender may receive indeterminate detention and treatment in hospital, instead of a prison sentence, if he is suffering from one of the specified mental disorders to

a nature or degree which makes it appropriate for him to be detained in a hospital for medical treatment and, in the case of psychopathic disorder or mental impairment, that such treatment is likely to alleviate or prevent a deterioration of his condition (section 37).

The 1983 Act further provides that restrictions may be placed on the discharge of a mentally disordered offender if 'it is necessary for the protection of the public from serious harm' (section 41). The need for medical treatment in detention is therefore essential to the initial imposition of a hospital order, while the demands of public protection should determine the introduction of additional restrictions.

In the case of a restricted patient, a Mental Health Review Tribunal must direct discharge, and thus end the indeterminate detention, if the patient is not suffering from one of the mental disorders under the 1983 Act, or is not suffering from them to a nature or degree that makes liability to detention in hospital for treatment appropriate, or 'that it is not necessary for the health or safety of the patient or for the protection of other persons that he should receive such treatment', section 72(1)(b)(ii). The first two criteria essentially involve the clinical assessment of an existing condition, but the third involves the assessment of some future state: a prediction.[66] While, according to the statutory wording, prediction or risk assessment should only be relevant if the patient is still mentally disordered to the necessary degree, it is clear from the research that it prevails even in the absence of mental disorder.[67]

Whether the prediction of future harm, that is, dangerousness, should determine the release decision deserves and has received extensive discussion.[68] It raises the whole question of the propriety of preventive detention solely on the grounds of predicted dangerousness. Whatever the eventual outcome of that debate, however, and irrespective of the wording of the existing statute, it is clear that the discharge of a 'mentally disordered' offender from secure provision is, in practice, dependent on the degree of risk perceived, often irrespective of the continuance of disorder, and there are strong arguments for deploring this empirical reality. If preventive detention is to be

66 D. Gottfredson, 'Prediction and Classification in Criminal Justice Decision Making', in D. Gottfredson and M. Tonry (eds), *Prediction and Classification* (1987, Chicago: University of Chicago Press), ch. 1.

67 Peay, *supra*, n. 22, p. 207.

68 See, for example, A. Bottoms, 'Reflections on the Renaissance of Dangerousness' (1977) 16 Howard Jo. of Crim. Jus. 70; J. Floud and W. Young, *Dangerousness and Criminal Justice* (1981, London: Heinemann); A. Bottoms and R. Brownsword, 'The Dangerousness Debate after the Floud Report' (1982) 22 Brit. J of Crimin. 229; L. Wilkins, 'The Politics of Prediction', in D. Farrington and R. Tarling (eds), *Criminological Prediction* (1983, Albany: State University of New York Press) ch. 2; and M. Tonry, 'Prediction and Classification: Legal and Ethical Issues', in Gottfredson and Tonry, *supra*, n. 66 ch. 11.

allowed it should be expressly authorised by legislation evolving through open and informed public debate in the full understanding of its implications; it should not occur through default.

Whatever the nature of the formulation process behind the existing practice, however, Mental Health Review Tribunals are making predictive decisions: they are assessing the risks involved in discharge. The literature suggests that there are two principle models for the assessment of risk in criminal justice in general, and in relation to mental disorder in particular: the clinical and the actuarial. The clinical model relies on the professional judgment of the decision maker in the consideration of all the circumstances of an individual case, while actuarial models produce decisions through the application of statistical tools based on past experience. According to such a classification, Mental Health Review Tribunals adopt a clinical approach. Indeed Peay, who suggests that the relationship between criminal behaviour and mental disorder is very weak, argues that the individual clinical approach is essential:

the attribution of dangerousness in individuals, and the consequent erosion of their rights for the benefit of others, needs to be spelt out and to acquire the status of a justiciable issue; rights apply to individuals, their erosion should be determined on an individual basis and subject to strict procedural safeguards.[69]

Nevertheless, attributions of dangerousness should be as accurate as possible, and it is relevant to note Gottfredson's opinion of clinical predictions: these

are apt to rely on the decision maker's own experience, probably from biased samples and unsystematically observed, using combinations of evidence, conceptualisations, hunches, and untested hypotheses that are difficult to articulate. Viewed in this way it is not surprising that the available evidence strongly suggests that carefully and systematically derived statistical tools are more accurate than are trained decision makers.[70]

In the light of these strongly expressed reservations it is relevant to consider the actuarial alternatives to the present clinical approach.

The assessment of a risk involves the identification of an outcome, and estimation of its likely occurrence. In the case of mentally disordered offenders the predicted outcome is likely to be a crime of violence. Under the present structure the tribunal members will arrive at some estimate of its likely occurrence in the light of their own experience and the expert opinions before them. Research into the histories of 125 men discharged from Broadmoor in the 1960s indicates that subsequent dangerous acts are rare even among a sample who from their past records might be thought dangerous. Nevertheless, the research succeeded in developing a statistical instrument which did, retrospectively, identify half of those who became re-offenders, and led the authors to conclude that 'the development of prediction instruments could

69 Peay, *supra*, n. 22, p. 208. See J. Gunn, 'Criminal Behaviour and Mental Disorder' (1977) Brit. Jo. of Psychiatry 130, and P. Bowden, 'Psychiatry and Dangerousness: a Counter Renaissance', in L. Gostin, *Secure Provision* (1985, London: Tavistock), ch. 9.
70 Gottfredson, *supra*, n. 66, p. 8.

have some utility in at least identifying those patients particularly prone to fail.'[71]

The success of such prediction tools must, of course, depend on the accuracy with which the relevant characteristics of the individual are recorded. In many cases these characteristics, or predictor variables, can be independently verified since they relate to past criminal record, age etc., as is generally the case with the reconviction prediction scales mentioned in chapter 8. Where they relate to clinical diagnoses and judgement, such independent verification is more difficult to achieve. Nevertheless, provided the success rate of the particular statistical technique is disclosed and the patient given the opportunity to challenge the information on which the prediction is being made, the use of these tools might help to extend the information available to the decision maker. Such a technique could not, however, weigh the statistical risk of the feared outcome against the known costs of continued detention. That assessment of the public interest would still have to be made on an individual basis. In theory, a sophisticated decision tree might be constructed which could attach a value to all possible outcomes and assess the statistical likelihood of each,[72] but until such exists, it is hard to envisage a risk assessment process in relation to discharge decisions which does not involve the application of personal judgement to the circumstances of an individual case.

The answer may lie somewhere between Peay and Gottfredson, with the introduction of a more rigorous clinical approach, coupled with a review of the context in which these assessments have to be made. The present tribunal structure tends to encourage a view of risk assessment which sees it as static and final. The tribunal is forced to reach a decision on the information available at a specific point and is given little flexibility. It must choose between taking the risk and ordering discharge, albeit on conditions, or avoiding the risk and refusing discharge. It is given no effective middle path. These unrealistic constraints on a tribunal's choice must be lifted, and the tribunal must be provided with sufficient flexibility to enable it to avoid such all-or-nothing decisions.

Full process, it has been argued, should be designed to encourage the achievement of decisions reflective of the true public interest. The realisation of this objective in the context of Mental Health Review Tribunals poses particular dilemmas. In any individual case there is a tendency to interpret the public interest solely in terms of the protection of the public from further violence: the interests of the individual patient must be balanced against the need to protect the public. It is a stark and over-simplified calculation, the outcome of which is virtually inevitable.

---

71 T. Black and P. Spinks, 'Predicting Outcomes of Mentally Disordered and Dangerous Offenders', in Farrington and Tarling (eds), *supra*, n. 68, ch. 9.

72 Such a decision tree was described in J. Downie, 'Clinical Decision Making: Risk is a Dangerous Concept and Hubris a Sin', paper presented to a conference on Risk-Taking and Mental Disorder, at the University of Southampton, 1990. Similar issues are, of course, raised by parole and life licence decisions.

In order to avoid such crude reasoning in individual cases it is necessary to encourage a wider discussion of the public interest at an earlier stage in the process of policy implementation. At some distance from the emotionally charged atmosphere of individual decisions, a wide and informed debate must be undertaken in order to identify the true nature of the public interest. The questions which must be aired include: the relationship, if any, between mental disorder and violence, the nature of psychopathy, its identification and its susceptibility to treatment, the ability of the relevant professionals to predict future violence in individuals, and the level of resources available for the provision of the necessary facilities. In the light of the information generated by such inquiries the case for prevention detention, even in the absence of treatment, can be assessed, and the alternatives both canvassed and costed. The resulting conclusions should then be refined into legislation, which must be of sufficient specificity to avoid any disproportionate tendency towards caution in individual cases, and which must emphasie the duties imposed on the relevant authorities to provide the necessary facilities. Unless a sufficient breadth of facility is provided, individual cases will continue to pose unrealistic all-or-nothing choices. Against such a legislative background individual application decisions might still appropriately be made by an expert adjudicatory panel, provided that panel was both adequately empowered to impose its conclusions and actively inquisitorial.

While such a tight and structured legislative framework should obviate the need to re-open the fundamental debate at the application stage, some assessment of the public interest might still have to be made in individual cases. A form of selective representation with regard to both the interests represented and the issue discussed is, in effect, required. At the policy formulation stage, wide issues must be aired and the broadest possible participation encouraged. With whatever skill the resulting policy is expressed in statute, however, it is likely to leave some assessment of the public interest to be made at the application stage, in the light of the particular circumstances of the case, including the provision available for the patient. In such cases, where the accurate application of the legislative requirements requires an inquiry stretching beyond the interests of the patient concerned, the articulation of the public interest might appropriately be entrusted to a representative figure. Such a person or body could provide the necessary information and, where relevant, could reflect the views of those members of the public most directly concerned: the family of the original victim for example. Wider participation and publicity at the applicaction stage would not be required.

Part IV

Summary and Conclusions

13
Summary and Conclusions

In chapters 2 and 3 it was argued that the real justification for the law's involvement in the regulation of process lies in the ability of full process to facilitate authoritative or legitimate public decision making. According to the traditions of liberal pluralism, the requirement that all decisions be taken in the full reflection of the public interest is one of the essential characteristics of the legitimate exercise of state authority. For the proponents of strong democracy, on the other hand, the processes of direct participation and self-regulation are sufficient on their own to provide the necessary authority for the decisions they produce.

Although different in emphasis, both these approaches see the requirements of full process, whether they relate to process in the broad and structural sense or to process in the narrow and procedural sense, as designed to facilitate decision making in the full reflection of the public interest. By contrast, it was suggested that the judiciary traditionally regard the imposition of process requirements by the common law as justified, primarily, by reference to the ability of those requirements to protect the substantive interests of individuals from interference through the inaccurate decisions of public officials.

Decisions made regarding the implementation of public policy can be said to fall into three inter-related stages: policy formulation, application and validation, and at any of the three stages the choice of decision making mechanism will involve questions of structure (process broadly defined) and questions of procedure (process narrowly defined). With their emphasis on the protection of an individual's substantive rights, the process requirements of the common law are primarily concerned with the application and validation stages of policy implementation, and the domestic courts are accordingly unwilling to involve themselves in the process of policy formulation. They also limit their intervention to decisions affecting the interests or legitimate expectations of individuals, and tend to model the procedural requirements they impose on their experience of adversarial adjudication. Further, their constitutional position greatly hampers their freedom to consider questions of structure as opposed to procedure. Thus, it was suggested, the ability of the common law to facilitate the pursuit of full process is at present significantly limited. The law in other guises as the creator and empowerer of public decision makers is, however, directly concerned with all matters of process, and in chapter 4 some attempt was made to identify the factors which might properly guide the choice of decision making structure and procedure with a view to the promotion of full process. More specifically, the essential characteristics of the main forms of process relevant to custodial decision making, Parliamentary legislation, administrative decision making, adjudication and commissions of inquiry, were discussed, together with the nature of the procedures required by the demands of full process. The proper role of each decision making structure and their relationships one with another were then considered.

In the remaining chapters an attempt was made to examine the processes of decision making in prisons and special hospitals at all stages of policy implementation, and to consider how far the existing structures and procedures met the demands of full process, and what the implications of those demands in practice might be.

(a) Policy Formulation

(1) Primary Legislation

In order to be authoritative, public policy must reflect the broad public interest, and must thus evolve through a process designed to facilitate the true participation of all relevant interests. Although some reservations were expressed concerning the breadth of discussion preceding certain pieces of legislation and the ability of the House of Commons to challenge the government's identification of the public interest, it was assumed, for the sake of analysis, that the Parliamentary stages through which primary legislation must pass promote the necessary participation. Whatever its real claim to authority, however, Parliamentary legislation alone could never provide a comprehensive statement of public policy and, within the custodial sphere, policies also emerge through administrative decision making, adjudication and public inquiries. The delegation of policy formulation by Parliament in this way is not of itself objectionable, indeed there are strong arguments in terms of expertise and accountability in support of such delegation, but certain conditions of acceptability attach, and in practice it seems these conditions are seldom met.

If Parliament is to delegate large areas of policy formulation to other agencies, that delegation should be express; it should provide the clearest guidance possible as to the principles which should govern the emergent policy, and it should specify the processes to be followed by the agency in reaching its formulation. With regard to prison policy, virtually no attempt is made to meet these conditions. First, the Prison Act 1952 provides neither a definition of imprisonment nor a statement of its purpose, neither does it provide any statement of the purposes of the Prison Service. At a slightly more detailed level, the legislation gives no real guidance as to the conditions within which prisoners are held, nor the regimes to which they are subject: primary legislation, for example, expresses no preference between strict cellular separation and full association. Admittedly, the 1952 Act does specifically delegate to the Secretary of State the power to make rules, but it does so in very general terms, and imposes only the most rudimentary of procedural requirements on the exercise of that power.

The extent of the policy formulation effectively delegated to the Prison Service may be illustrated by the fact that in recent years it has been possible to revise the aims and objectives of the Service, fundamentally to alter the structure of prison discipline, and to introduce both an independent complaints adjudicator and a Code of Standards, without any alteration to the primary legislation. Whatever its shortcomings, Parliament does represent the primary forum for the articulation of the public interest within our constitution, and for it to be bypassed in this way is in direct opposition to the demands of full process.

The 1952 Prison Act is now 40 years old, and it might be hoped that its willingness to delegate the task of policy formulation so generously would never be tolerated in a modern statute. The approach adopted by the Criminal Justice Act 1991, however, must belie any such hope. While the system of discretionary release introduced by the 1991 Act in relation to fixed-term prisoners closely resembles that recommended, after extensive consultation, by the Carlisle Committee, and can thus, to some extent, be said to have evolved through a process designed to reflect the public interest, the 1991 Act still delegates significant areas of policy to the Secretary of State. The Secretary of State is empowered to issue rules governing the procedures to be adopted by the Parole Board and the factors to be taken into account. With regard to the latter, some advance has been made on the previous legislation of 1967, since the 1991 Act does at least contain a brief statutory statement of the factors to which the Secretary of State is to have regard when issuing directions to the Parole Board. However, no guidance is given in the 1991 Act with regard to the procedures to be imposed on the Parole Board. Further, neither the rules nor the directions need be issued by way of a statutory instrument and no duties of consultation are imposed on the Secretary of State. The 1991 Act, like the 1952 Prison Act before it, fails either to provide a comprehensive statement of policy, or to create a structure for the subsequent formulation of policy by specialised agencies which meet the demands of full process.

The legislative structure governing special hospitals is similar to that governing prisons, in that wide areas of policy formulation are left by implication to the Secretary of State or the hospital authorities. This is especially true with regard to the nature of the regime a patient is entitled to expect and the extent of the restrictions which may be imposed. However, unlike the position with regard to imprisonment, there is more statutory guidance as to the purpose of hospital detention and the specific role of special hospitals.

The provisions of the Mental Health Act 1983 indicate that the purpose of a hospital order is to facilitate the medical treatment in hospital of a convicted offender who is suffering from a mental disorder under the 1983 Act. The imposition of additional restrictions is further justified by the need to protect society from serious harm. The National Health Act also makes it clear that special hospitals are required to provide treatment for 'dangerous' patients in conditions of special security. Further, in relation to certain aspects of the hospital regime, the 1983 Act provides considerable detail by comparison to its prison counterpart. The consent to treatment provisions, for example, which emerged from a process of wide participation (albeit chiefly on the part of articulate interest groups) are unusually detailed in their requirements. Finally, the creation of a Code of Practice is specifically, if ambiguously, authorised by the 1983 Act and, in direct contrast to the position under the Criminal Justice Act 1991, the rules relating to the procedures of the Mental Health Review Tribunals are required to be contained in a statutory instrument. To some extent, therefore, patients in special hospitals are better served by Parliament than are their prison counterparts.

(2) Administrative Decision Making

The policy vacuum left by primary legislation is to a large extent filled by policies which have evolved through administrative decision making. In the case of the Prison Rules, for example, and the Mental Health Review Tribunal Rules, the rule making power is specifically delegated by Parliament, and some formal control is retained through the statutory instrument procedures. In other cases, although the delegation may be formal, as in the case of the directions and rules issued to the Parole Board by the Secretary of State under the 1991 Act, Parliament retains no formal control. In the vast majority of cases, however, there is no express delegation, no direct Parliamentary control, save through ministerial responsibility, and no legislative imposition of procedural requirements on the eventual policy formulator.

In terms of full process, as explained above, the delegation of policy formulation to an administrative body might be quite appropriate, provided that body is both expert and accountable. Accountability can be achieved either through the careful stipulation of the criteria to govern the body's policy choices and the rigorous monitoring of its compliance with those criteria by the various mechanisms of validation, or through the direct participation of relevant interests on or before the body during the process of formulation itself. In either event, accountability demands both openness and wide participation and consultation. Whatever the formal status of administrative policy formulators in the field of custodial policy, few if any meet these requirements.

In the past the formulation of prison policy by administrative decision at the national level tended to be internal to the Prison Department, with little outside consultation – the creation of the system for security categorisation by circular instruction, for example, and the criteria to govern release decisions under the 1967 Act. More recently the processes of administrative policy formulation have opened up significantly.

Even before the Woolf Inquiry the practice of wider consultation was developing – the reforms to rule 43, for example; and the introduction of a new application and grievance procedure in 1990. Without doubt, however, the Woolf Inquiry gave these tentative moves towards broader participation a considerable boost. Not only were the procedures before the inquiry itself open and facilitative of wide participation and debate, but, perhaps of even greater significance, the administrative policy formulation which has followed, particularly in relation to the proposed code of standards and the independent complaints adjudicator, has adopted a similar style of open consultation and debate. However, in none of these cases, save those few which have involved amendment to the Prison Rules, has Parliament been involved either in designing the formulation process or in approving the substance of the policy. Indeed, as suggested in chapter 5 in relation to the code of standards, the desire seems to be to achieve feelings of 'ownership' towards the policy by those directly involved, rather than to encourage the broader discussion of the public interest which would in theory be provided by Parliamentary debate.

In relation to special hospitals, the Code of Practice constitutes the major piece of administrative policy making at the national level and there, as described in chapter 9, the ambiguity with which Parliament delegated the task created considerable difficulties and delay in its formulation.

While it can plausibly be assumed that the administration policy makers mentioned in the preceding paragraphs have some claims to expertise, a similar assumption is hard to maintain in relation to the 1983 policy initiative with regard to the release of long-term and life-sentence prisoners announced by Leon Brittan. On the contrary, the more plausible assumption must be that had Brittan consulted the official experts in the field – the Parole Board – such a flawed policy would never have emerged. It is therefore greatly to be regretted that still no statutory duty to consult has been imposed on the Secretary of State by the 1991 Act in relation to his power to issue directions to the Parole Board. That he has so far chosen to consult is no guarantee that he will invariably do so in the future.

In both prisons and special hospitals many policies are formulated at a more local level, and here again the administrative decision makers must be urged to encourage greater participation on the part of prisoners and patients. Such participation would serve both to enhance the true authority of the resulting policy by enabling a more accurate assessment of the public interest to be reached, and to render the policy more acceptable to those subjected to it: the prisoners and patients. On the assumption that the local policy would reflect the requirements of any relevant national guidance, the participation of prisoners and patients would constitute selective representation of the public interest at the local level.

(3) Adjudication

Adjudication, in its classic adversarial form, is seldom regarded as an appropriate mechanism for the formulation of policy. In the first place, the ability of the adversarial adjudicator to assess the broad public interest is severely limited by the nature of the evidence presented. Secondly, where the adjudicator is a judge, he or she is unlikely to be an expert in the relevant policy field, and will not be accountable to the general public in any real sense. However, where legislative policies are stated in ambiguous terms the courts can be asked, in the exercise of their common law review jurisdiction, to state the law, and any such statement will constitute the authoritative definition of the legal position until either overturned by a subsequent court or overruled by specific legislative amendment. In such cases the courts are effectively creating policy and, in the light of the inevitable inadequacies of courts as policy formulators, it was suggested in earlier chapters that they should do so with care. It was accepted that the courts can properly police the legislative boundaries, but in cases of ambiguity it was suggested that they should do so restrictively. They should favour the interpretation that would deny any extension of the power in question. Such an approach requires those seeking the extension to apply to Parliament for its express authorisation, and is particularly important in cases involving the liberty and bodily integrity of prisoners and patients, where infringement should never occur without the express authority of Parliament.

While several of the cases considered did, in fact, adopt such an approach – the Court of Appeal in *Hague* for example, and the courts in *R* v. *Hallstrom, ex p. W* and *R* v. *Mental Health Act Commission, ex p. W* – it was not universal. In *R* v. *Merseyside MHRT, ex p. K*, for example, the court took a generous view of the power to impose a conditional discharge.

Finally, on questions of substantive policy, the courts are placed in a very invidious position if, as in *Bradley*, they are required to state a policy where none is articulated by statute. It is quite inappropriate to leave the articulation of policy in an area as complex and sensitive as the release of life-sentence prisoners to the courts on a case-by-case basis. While the 1991 Act has done something to produce statutory criteria for both fixed-term and discretionary life-sentence prisoners, the courts are still likely to be asked to intervene, since those criteria are woefully inadequate and will require extensive amplification.

With regard to procedural policy, it was suggested that the courts should be encouraged to become active policy formulators. According to the broad approach to process outlined in chapter 3, it was claimed that the pursuit of full process by the courts should be seen as supportive of democracy, not hostile to it. The court's reluctance to intervene and impose additional procedural requirements in *Payne, Gunnell and Hague* was therefore regretted.

However, the possible dangers involved in court intervention were recognised in relation to prison discipline. Court intervention is to be encouraged when it serves to promote full process; but, just as the courts in adjudicating substantive matters possess only limited expertise and receive only limited evidence, so in devising procedural requirements they may have little experience of the context in which the procedure is to apply, and they may receive little objective advice. They are also operating with a narrow view of the purpose of procedural regulation. The procedures which emerge may therefore fall short, as in *Tarrant*, of those required by full process. Similarly, in relation to internal special hospital decisions it was suggested that the procedures which might be required by the common law, being influenced by adversarial adjudication, might not be those most ideally suited to the speical hospital context. Finally, as was arguably the case in relation to prison discipline, the introduction of some common law requirements, however inadequate, might in fact serve to introduce sufficient improvement to the overall decision making process to deflect more radical, but essential, reform.

However, it should be remembered that the courts' impact on procedural policy formulation is not limited to cases in which judges intervene to impose additional requirements: a refusal to intervene by a senior court in one context will, if followed in other contexts, effectively deny procedural improvements in those other areas, as was so clearly illustrated by *Payne*. The dangers of such negative policy formulation may well outweigh the problems attaching to positive but inadequate procedural intervention by the courts. Very strong arguments in terms of both policy and fairness were required before the influence of *Payne* could be successfully challenged. Indeed, counsel for the prisoner in *Wilson* produced far wider and more substantial policy arguments than are generally available in simple adversarial proceedings.

In sum, the difference in attitude towards substantive and procedural policy formulation by the courts advocated initially should be maintained. On the one hand, the courts should be urged to take a restrictive approach to the resolution of ambiguity in substantive policy and to return the decision to Parliament, while on the other, as potential promoters of authoritative decision making through the imposition of procedural requirements, the courts should be encouraged to formulate appropriate procedural policy themselves rather than to return the question to Parliament. Such procedural intervention by the courts can be justified 'constitutionally' since, by promoting full process, the courts would be acting in furtherance of democracy, not in opposition to it. The intervention can also be justified more pragmatically, on the grounds that non-intervention by the courts would leave an inadequate decision making process in place, which the authorities would be unlikely to encourage Parliament to disturb.

In relation to prisons and special hospitals, however, the domestic courts are not the only adjudicators who can influence policy; the decisions of the European Court of Human Rights (ECHR) have had a considerable policy impact on both substance (*Silver* and *Golder*) and process (*X, Weeks* and *Thynne, Wilson and Gunnell*). Indeed, in relation to the last three cases, the decision of the ECHR provided the necessary pressure to force fundamental process reform through Parliament despite lack of enthusiasm from the domestic authorities.

Arguably, the ECHR in such cases is merely policing the boundaries of the European Convention and, when it finds non-compliance, is returning the issue to the domestic legislature for it to decide how best to comply. Like much domestic legislation, however, the European Convention is often ambiguous or unclear, and it might be argued that the ECHR, like the domestic courts, should exercise caution in determining the 'correct' interpretation. Whatever the merits of that argument in the adversarial domestic context, the ECHR does not adopt an adversarial approach, it receives the assistance of the Commission, it takes evidence as to the position in other member states, and it was created specifically by the signatory states as the interpreter of the Convention. As a policy formulator it is not, therefore, vulnerable to the same criticisms as the domestic courts. Further, the 'policy' it is interpreting is simply that contained within the Convention. It is not designing domestic policy, merely announcing certain constraints upon that design, and in that role it has provided the necessary incentive to achieve structural change to the process of release for both discretionary life-sentence prisoners and restriction order patients.

(4) Contract

Until recently, contract has played only a very minor role in the formulation of policy within prisons and special hospitals; with the introduction of the privatisation of prisons that role is likely to grow. Contracts are now being used to set the standards applicable within private establishments. At this early stage it is hard to determine how far this use of contract will meet the requirements of full process, but doubts have already emerged concerning the secrecy surrounding the financial components of the contracts. The standards demanded by these contracts must be those which reflect the interests of the public beyond the contracting parties, thus the greatest openness and participation must be ensured.

(5) Inquiries

In chapter 4 it was suggested that, in certain circumstances, policy formulation might properly be conducted by a commission of inquiry, which would possess the independence absent in the administrative decision maker, and would have greater procedural flexibility than the adjudicator. Such a body might formulate policy for submission to Parliament. As far as independence and procedures are concerned, public inquiries, such as that conducted by Lord Justice Woolf, clearly fulful the requirements of such a commission. However, while the Woolf Inquiry was empowered to make recommendations to the Secretary of State, and those recommendations inspired Parliamentary debate, the Inquiry was not empowered to make specific policy recommendations direct to Parliament. Indeed, under present practice, where inquiries are set up by Secretaries of State, who in turn are responsible to Parliament, any other structure is unlikely to be acceptable. Thus, however participatory and responsive inquiries might be in their investigations, and however authoritative their policy recommendations, under our present constitutional practice they are unlikely to possess the power to make those recommendations direct to the legislature. Their policy making function is thus restricted by their subordination to the Secretary of State, who is, of course, free to dilute their recommendations in any way he or she might regard as politically expedient.

(b) Application Decisions

In prisons and special hospitals the vast majority of application decisions are made by administrative decision, and most of the remainder by adjudication. In chapter 4 it was suggested that administrative decision making might be acceptable for simple allocative decisions and simple disputes, where local knowledge and speed were important, but that the procedures for such decisions should be modelled on adjudication, and should involve disclosure and participation. Reasons should also be given. The structure of routine allocative decision making within prison and special hospitals is thus acceptable in terms of full process, but in practice the procedures often fall far short of the ideal.

Prisoners and patients are not always aware of the basis for decisions, are not always invited to participate, and are not always given reasons. These deficiencies are often exacerbated, in special hospitals particularly, by the scope left to clinical judgement in the relevant policies. Where no specific outcome is ordained by existing policy, even greater care must be taken to explain the relevant criteria, to invite a response, and to explain the ultimate outcome. The demands of security and order require similarly careful handling within prisons. In both prisons and special hospitals, where compliance with the full requirements of openness and participation would be likely to evince some hostility from staff, it is important that the practical benefits flowing from full process be stressed. Openness and participation are not merely reflective of sterile legalism; they are designed to facilitate more authoritative, and thus more acceptable, decision making.

Disputes can arise within prisons and special hospitals in a wide variety of circumstances, and call for a similarly wide variety of processes for their resolution; however, in many cases administrative decision making is still relied upon, either with or without procedural safeguards. Discipline in both prisons and special hospitals provides a good example.

In chapter 7 it was accepted that a code of discipline within prisons was justified, provided its scope and powers of sanction were limited to the minimum necessary to meet the proper demands of security and control. Since April 1992 any charges brought under this code are resolved by administrative decision: they are heard by the governor, who does not possess the independence essential to true adjudication. The procedures are appropriately inquisitorial but, in the light of the retention of loss of liberty as a disciplinary sanction, it was argued that true independent adjudication would have been the preferred structure.

Whatever the shortcomings of the current prison disciplinary system, however, it represents a marked improvement both on what went before and on what applies within special hospitals. Within the latter there is no formal disciplinary system, but patients are 'punished' for certain types of behaviour, and such punishments are imposed informally by way of administrative decision. In chapter 10 it was suggested that, since some system of discipline is both inevitable and justified within the closed community of a special hospital, a disciplinary code should be formally recognised, and infractions formally dealt with. Full independent adjudication was not urged; instead inquisitorial investigation of the charge by someone independent of the clinical team was advocated, and particular emphasis was placed on the need to neutralise any bias against believing the evidence of the patient. The patient should be allowed fully to participate, and should be given reasons for both the finding and any consequent sanction. Again, such requirements should be viewed positively as supportive of the therapeutic endeavour, not negatively as legalistic meddling.

Within special hospitals the question of consent to treatment raises particular difficulties. In the case of the capable but non-consenting patient, a dispute exists which is determined by an independent specialist 'adjudicator', who has the authority to overrule the wishes of the patient. Where the patient is regarded as incapable of consent, no dispute exists, and the independent specialist is required to either endorse or reject the rmo's treatment plan. The real difficulties, however, occur in the identification of both the non-consenting patient and the patient incapable of consent, since there is little effective control on the validity of the rmo's certification of capacity and/or consent. The efficacy of the independent element is therefore much reduced by the powerful gatekeeping role played by the rmo, one of the parties to the 'dispute'.

The decision to release must be the most important decision reached in the entire course of an individual's prison or hospital career. In the case of long-term and life-sentence prisoners and restricted patients it will involve the assessment of risk by an independent body. Where, as in the case of patients and discretionary lifers, that body has the power to order discharge or release, and some form of hearing involving disclosure, participation and reasons is required, the structure is essentially adjudicatory.

In both cases, however, the criteria to be applied are such as to encourage caution, a tendency which is increased in the case of Mental Health Review Tribunals by the inflexibility of their powers. If the decisions reached by these bodies are to be truly reflective of the public interest, therefore, it is particularly important that they be encouraged to be actively inquisitorial and searching of the case against release. Further, every effort must be made to improve the performance of the Secretary of State as the representative of the public interest.

In relation to the Mental Health Review Tribunal, it was suggested that many of the difficulties arising from their 'clinical' assessment of risk on an individual basis could be resolved by clearer legislative guidance, and the granting to them of wider powers. It is particularly unfortunate, therefore, that the discretionary lifer panels have been presented with a statutory structure which is similar to that governing the tribunals and which contains equally little specific guidance. Since it seems likely that the panels will confront the same problems as face the tribunals, the opportunity presented by the recent reforms should have been used to consider the question of risk and preventive detention in depth, and to devise some appropriate and more helpful statutory guidance.

(c) Validation Decisions

Validation provides the formal means of checking that an application or formulation decision is authoritative, in the sense of having been taken in the full reflection of the public interest. Validation can be provided through general monitoring, or through the checking of individual decisions when challenged. In either event, both the essential characteristics and the task required of the validator will be affected by the nature and outcome of the preceding process of formulation and application. In the first place, an application decision which is based on clear, open criteria and for which full reasons are given, is more readily monitored than one based on vague criteria and for which no reasons are recorded. Secondly, where independence is to be desired at the application stage, but is in practice lacking, the obligation to provide independence at the validation stage is particularly strong.

(1) Extra-judicial Monitoring and Complaints Investigation

Processes of validation can take many forms, from internal monitoring to Parliamentary scrutiny, to judicial review. Indeed, as suggested above, there is an important distinction between general monitoring and the investigation of specific complaints. Monitoring can be achieved internally by senior management (as is increasingly the case in prisons), externally by specifically empowered bodies such as boards of visitors and Her Majesty's Chief Inspector of Prisons, and through Parliament. In all cases, the efficacy of the monitoring is likely to depend in part on the specificity with which the policy is enunciated. Thus a decision dependent on the exercise of clinical judgement is much harder to monitor than is the frequency with which a secluded patient is observed. Indeed, it was suggested that, because of the difficulties involved in assessing the validity of any single exercise of clinical judgement, it was an inappropriate basis on which to restrict the freedoms of an individual. The particular need for independent validation of the initial decisions of the rmo under the consent to treatment provisions was also mentioned above, and would suggest that a specialist monitoring mechanism is required.

With regard to Parliamentary scrutiny, the limitations of the notion of ministerial responsibility were considered, and it was suggested that the acquisition of agency status by the Prison Service should be used as an opportunity to evolve alternative mechanisms for Parliamentary oversight. In relation to the new independent adjudicator for prisons, the possibility of employing Parliament as the ultimate monitor of the Prison Service's complicance with his or her recommendations was also considered. However, the continuous marginalisation of Parliament as a formulator of prison policy does not augur well for any proposed increase in its role as monitor. Indeed, the one proposal contained in the Woolf Report that would have given Parliament real influence over the question of prison overcrowding was speedily rejected by the government.

The investigation of individual complaints can also be performed internally or externally, and is again dependent in part for its success on the specificity of the initial policy. Independence is ultimately essential in both prisons and special hospitals, and is now available through the recent introduction of the independent adjudicator and the continued presence of the Mental Health Act Commission. Both bodies are, however, significantly underpowered, and their independence is vulnerable to being undermined by their lack of investigative powers.

In addition to the question of complaints investigation in general, certain decisions present particular problems for validation. The decision to transfer a prisoner under CI 37/1990, for example, has, by necessity, to be taken by an internal decision maker in the first instance. However, the consequences for the individual concerned can be so disruptive that immediate and effective validation is essential, which in this context must mean speedy validation by a body with the power to return the prisoner to his home prison. In practice, only the area manager has this power, and he or she might not always be available at short notice to make the necessary investigations. It is possible, therefore, that in this context as in others – the seclusion of patients, for example – the processes required to facilitate the authoritative exercise of power are so exacting as to make the policy unworkable if they are met, and unacceptable if they are not.

(2) Inquiries

Public inquiries are sometimes used as an additional mechanism for validation in relation to both prisons and special hospitals. In the case of those which are adequately independent, resourced and empowered, such as the Ashworth and the Woolf Inquiries, public inquiries can provide a validation mechanism similar to the board commission advocated in chapter 4. Inquiries on the scale of the two mentioned, however, are expensive and time-consuming, and cannot be used as a matter of routine. Indeed, since they tend to be used when the usual mechanisms have proved to be inadequate, the need to employ them as validators should decrease as the performance of the normal structures improves. Despite their cost, however, inquiries do have a useful role to play in validation. The fresh and rigorous scrutiny employed by the Ashworth Inquiry revealed serious inadequacies in the existing mechanisms which might never otherwise have attracted attention. The occasional resort to such intense investigation is therefore valuable provided it is reserved for exceptional circumstances.

(3) The Courts

In both the exercise of their review jurisdiction and in their enforcement of private law rights, the courts provide an obvious mechanism for the validation of prison and hospital decisions. The *ultra vires* principles of judicial review allow the courts to oversee the substantive legality of application decisions by reference to both the express and the implied boundaries of the statute. The court of Appeal in *Hague* performed such a role when it declared CI 10/1974 to be *ultra vires* the Prison Rules. So, in different contexts, did the courts in *Hallstrom ex p. W* and *R* v. *Mental Health Act Commission*. The ability of the court to intervene in all three cases, however, depended on the existence of a statutory statement of sufficient specificity to enable a finding of *ultra vires* to be made. As has been constantly emphasised throughout, a high proportion of application decisions are reached in the pursuit of policies whose statutory base is far less specific, and the notion of *ultra vires* far more elusive as a result. The *Bradley* court, for example, refused to allow the prisoner's challenge to the Parole Board's application of their release criteria, and the court in *McAvoy* was reluctant to question the Secretary of State's decision to transfer a remand prisoner. In the context of formulation, the House of Lords in *Findlay* was similarly reluctant to question the legality of the substance of the new restrictions on parole.

Further, even if illegality is found, the public law remedies are discretionary as the court in *Hague* was at pains to emphasise, and great care will be exercised in their imposition. The ability of the courts to employ the *ultra vires* principles of public law in the effective validation of the substance of prison and hospital decisions is, therefore, patchy at best. For the policing of legislative boundaries to constitute an effective means of validation, those boundaries must be clearly and specifically defined by Parliament.

With regard to the private law, validation by the courts would appear to be even less effective. As has been explained, the statutory framework within which prisons operate creates few private law rights in prisoners, while the Mental Health Act specifically restricts a patient's access to private legal remedies. The courts thus have little opportunity to intervene. Any residual hope that the Prison Rules might be held to have created private law rights in prisoners was finally dashed in *Hague*, as was any thought that an action in false imprisonment might lie against the prison authorities on the basis of a deterioration of the conditions in which a prisoner was held. Further, in certain cases – *Egerton*, for example, and *Knight* – where the potential for intervention was clearly present, the courts appeared reluctant to challenge the decision of the prison authorities.

It is in relation to the process of prison and hospital decisions that the courts have provided the most effective validation. Where the procedural requirements are stipulated by statute the courts have, in certain circumstances, been assiduous in their pursuit of compliance, as in the case of the Mental Health Review Tribunal's duty to give reasons. It remains to be seen how rigorously the courts will police the procedural requirements imposed by the rules relating to the discretionary lifer panels. Similarly, where courts have been prepared to impose their own common law procedural requirements, their insistence on compliance with those requirements has been quite exacting. Their condemnation of the procedures before boards of visitors and its impact on future disciplinary 'adjudication' is well-known. Finally, the courts are now opening up new areas to their scrutiny by displaying a willingness to question the adequacy of both the structures and the procedures for the release of life-sentence prisoners.

However, there are still significant limitations to the court's intervention, which tend to reflect those limitations arising directly from the judicial attitude to the purpose of common law procedural regulation. In the first place, the courts were quite unwilling to interfere with the process of ministerial policy formulation by imposing a duty to consult the Parole Board in *Findlay*. Judicial intervention, it seems, will not extend to the processes of formulation. Secondly, a reluctance to attribute much importance to the prisoners' substantive interests at stake in cases such as *Payne* and *Hague* enabled the courts to find the case for increased procedural stringency easily outweighed by the arguments of administrative convenience. Where the justification for procedural intervention rests primarily on the need to project the substantive interest of an individual, the weight attaching to that interest will greatly influence any calculation of the benefits to be derived from increased procedural stringency, set against the direct costs of such procedures. A broader approach to process regulation would allow factors unrelated to the direct outcome of the decision to be taken into account. Finally, if the procedural requirements imposed by the courts are themselves either inadequate or inappropriate, the courts' assiduous monitoring of compliance will not necessarily promote full process, and through it the authoritative exercise of power.

In relation to both prisons and special hospitals, the importance of the judicial notion of a legitimate expectation has been frequently emphasised. It is seen as potentially providing the necessary bridge to enable the courts to intervene in the validation of internal application decisions. In particular, the judicial role could be significantly enhanced if the courts were prepared to impose rigorous procedural requirements in the protection of expectations generated by administrative policies within prisons and special hospitals. However, so long as the purpose of the common law intervention is seen primarily in terms of the protection of the interests directly affected by the decision outcome, the court's assessment of the degree of procedural stringency that it is appropriate to ask of the administrator will remain subject to the reservations expressed above in relation to *Payne* and *Hague*.

The review of custodial decision making provided by this book has revealed the presence of both structures and procedures which fall far short of the requirements of full process. Most notably, the poverty of legislative involvement has been condemned as unacceptable. This absence of Parliamentary interest not only reflects poorly on the formal democratic element in policy formulation, but also affects the standard of decision making at subsequent stages in the implementation of policy. In practice, large areas of policy at all three stages are left to be determined by administrative decision. While structurally this might be acceptable, since adjudication is not always to be preferred, the procedures adopted are frequently inadequate. Similarly, where adjudication is, in fact, indicated, due to the presence of a dispute and the particular importance of independence, the actively inquisitorial model that is often required is seldom achieved in practice. While significant reservations were expressed concerning the role of the courts in the formulation of substantive policy, their formulation of procedural policy was encouraged, provided the procedures evolved were such as to further the pursuit of full process. In their role as validators, the courts' potential is seriously restricted, both by the inadequacy of the statutory framework within which prisons and special hospitals operate, and by the judiciary's own prevailing attitude to the purposes of procedural regulation.

Finally, if any general comparisons are to be drawn between prisons and special hospitals, it can only be remarked that, while special hospital patients might have attracted more Parliamentary interest than prisoners, the daily regimes they experience are subject to even more unregulated administrative discretion than are those experienced by prisoners. Further, their ability to obtain effective validation, whether it be judicial or extra-judicial, is significantly more restricted than is that of prisoners. Special hospital patients are regarded as requiring not just segregation from society, but treatment as well, and it is from this additional ingredient that their particular powerlessness appears to spring.

SELECT BIBLIOGRAPHY

Allan, T. R. S., 'Legislative Supremacy and the Rule of Law' (1985) 44 CLJ 111.

Ashworth, A., *Sentencing and Criminal Justice* (1992, London: Weidenfeld and Nicolson).

Baldwin, R. and Houghton, J., 'Circular Arguments: The Status and Legitimacy of Administrative Rules' (1986) *Public Law* 239.

Baldwin, R., '"Next Steps": Ministerial Responsibility and Government by Agency' (1988) 51 Mod. LR 622.

Barber, B., *Strong Democracy: Participatory Politics for a New Age* (1984, Berkeley: University of California Press).

Bayles, M., *Principles of Law: A Normative Analysis* (1987, Dordrecht: Kluwer Academic Publishers).

Bayles, M., *Procedural Justice: Allocating to Individuals* (1990, Dordrecht: Kluwer Academic Publishers).

Bean, P., *Compulsory Admissions to Mental Hospitals* (1980, Chichester: John Wiley).

Bean, P., *Mental Disorder and Legal Control* (1986, Cambridge: Cambridge University Press).

Beardshaw, V., *Conscientious Objectors at Work* (1981, London: Social Audit).

Birkinshaw, P., 'An Ombudsman for Prisoners', in Maguire *et al.* (1985).

Black, T. and Spinks, P., 'Predicting Outcomes of Mentally Disordered and Dangerous Offenders', in Farrington and Tarling (eds.).

Bottomley, K., 'Dilemmas of Parole in a Penal Crisis' (1984) 23 Howard Jo. of Crim. Jus. 24.

Bottoms, A. E., 'Reflections on the Renaissance of Dangerousness' (1977) 16 Howard Jo. of Crim. Jus. 70.

Bottoms, A. E. and Brownsword R., 'The Dangerousness Debate after the Floud Report' (1982) 22 Brit. Jo. of Crimin. 229.

Bottoms, A. E. and Preston, R. H. (eds), *The Coming Penal Crisis* (1980, Edinburgh: Scottish Academic Press).

Bowden, P., 'Psychiatry and Dangerousness: a Counter Renaissance', in Gostin (1985).

Braithwaite, J. and Pettit, P., *Not Just Deserts* (1990, Oxford: Oxford University Press).

Breyer, S. and Stewart, R., *Administrative Law and Regulatory Policy* 2nd edn (1985, Boston: Little Brown).

Butler, Lord, *Report of the Committee on Mentally Abnormal Offenders* (The Butler Report) (1975, London: HMSO).

Carlisle, Lord, *The Parole System in England and Wales* (The Carlisle Report) (1988, Cm 532, London: HMSO).

Casale, R. and Plotnikoff, J., *Minimum Standards in Prison: A Programme for Change* (1989, London: NACRO).

Casale, R. and Plotnikoff, J., *Regimes for Remand Prisoners* (1990, London: Prison Reform Trust).

Cheadle, J. and Ditchfield, J., *Sentenced Mentally Ill Offenders* (1982, London: Home Office Research and Planning Unit).

Cohen, S. and Taylor, L., *Prison Secrets* (1979, London: NCCL).

Comittee for the Prevention of Torture, *The Report to the U.K. Government on the Visit to the U.K. by the European Committee for the Prevention of Torture and Inhuman and Degrading treatment or Punishment* (1991), available from the Home Office, London, together with the *Response of the U.K. Government* (1991).

Cooke, D., 'Violence in Prisons: The Influence of Regime Factors' (1991) 30 Howard Jo. of Crim. Jus. 95.

Craig, P., *Administrative Law* 2nd edn (1989, London: Sweet and Maxwell).

Craig, P., *Public Law and Democracy in the United Kingdom and the United States of America* (1990, Oxford: Oxford University Press).

Davis, K. C., *Discretionary Justice* (1969, Urbana: University of Illinois Press).

Dell, S. and Robertson, G., *Sentenced to Hospital: Offenders in Broadmoor* (1988, Oxford: Oxford University Press).

Dell, S., Grounds, A., James, K. and Robertson, G., *Mentally Disordered Remand Prisoners* (1991, London: Home Office).

Department of Health, *Report of Interdepartmental Working Group of Home Office and D.H.S.S. Officials on Mentally Disturbed Offenders in the Prison System in England and Wales* (1987, London: DoH).

Department of Health, *Code of Practice* (1990, London: HMSO).

Department of Health, *Report of the Committee of Inquiry into Complaints about Ashworth Hospital* (The Ashworth Report) (1992, Cm 2028, London: HMSO).

DHSS, *Report of the Review of Procedures for the Discharge and Supervision of Psychiatric Patients Subject to Special Restrictions* (The Aarvold Report) (1973, London: HMSO).

DHSS, *The Review of the Mental Health Act 1959* (1976, London: DHSS).

DHSS, *The Review of the Mental Health Act 1959* (White Paper, 1978, Cmnd 7320, London: HMSO).

DHSS, *Report of the Review of Rampton Hospital* (1980, Cmnd 8073, London: HMSO).

DHSS, *Reform of Mental Health Legislation* (White Paper, 1981, Cmnd 8405, London: HMSO).

DHSS, *Report to the Secretary of State for Health and Social Services concerning the Death of Michael Dean Martin at Broadmoor Hospital on 6 July 1984* (1985, London: DHSS).

Ditchfield, J. and Austin, C., *Grievance Procedures in Prisons* (1986, HORS 91, London: HMSO).

Ditchfield, J., *Control in Prisons: A Review of the Literature* (1990, HORS 118, London: HMSO).

Dworkin, R., *Taking Rights Seriously* (1977, London: Duckworth).

Dworkin, R., 'The Forum of Principle' (1981) 56 New York Univ. LR 469.

Dworkin, R., *A Matter of Principle* (1986, Oxford: Oxford University Press).

Dworkin, R., *Law's Empire* (1986, London: Fontana Press).

Eisenberg, M., 'Participation, Responsiveness and the Consultative Process' (1978) 92 Harv. LR 410.

Ely, J. H., *Democracy and Distrust: A Theory of Judicial Review* (1980, Cambridge, Mass.: Harvard University Press).

Evans, M. and Morgan, R., 'The European Convention for the Prevention of Torture: Operational Practice' (1992) ICLQ 590.

Faden, R. and Beauchamp, T., *A History and Theory of Informed Consent* (1986, New York: Oxford University Press).

Farrington, D. and Tarling, R. (eds), *Criminological Prediction* (1983, Albany: State University of New York Press).

Fennell, P., 'Mental Health Review Tribunals: A Question of Imbalance' (1977) 2 Brit. Jo. of Law and Soc. 186.

Fennell, P., 'Law and Psychiatry: the Legal Constitution of the Psychiatric System' (1986) 13 Jo. of Law and Soc. 35.

Fennell, P., 'Sexual Suppressants and the Mental Health Act' (1988) Crim. LR 660.

Fennell, P., 'Inscribing Paternalism in the Law: Consent to Treatment and Mental Disorder' (1900) 17 Jo. of Law and Soc. 29.

Fitzgerald, E., 'Prison Discipline and the Courts', in Maguire *et al.* (1985).

Fitzgerald, M. and Sim, J., *British Prisons* 2nd edn (1982, Oxford: Basil Blackwell).

Floud, J. and Young, W., *Dangerousness and Criminal Justice* (1981, London: Heinemann).

Forsyth, C., 'The Provenance and Protection of Legitimate Expectations' (1988) 47 CLJ 238.

Frug, G., 'The Ideology of Bureaucracy in American Law' (1984) 97 Harvard LR 1276.

Fuller, L., 'Adjudication and the Rule of Law' (1960) 54 Proceedings of the Am. Soc. of Internat. L 1.

Fuller, L., *The Morality of Law* (1969, New Haven: Yale University Press).

Fuller, L. 'The Forms and Limits of Adjudication' (1978) 92 Harvard LR 353.

Galligan, D., 'Judicial Review and the Textbook Writers' (1982) 2 Ox. Jo. of Leg. Stud. 257.

Galligan, D., *Discretionary Powers: A Legal Study of Official Discretion* (1986, Oxford: Oxford University Press).

Ganz, G., *Quasi-Legislation: Recent Developments in Secondary Legislation* (1987, London: Sweet and Maxwell).

Garland, D., *Punishment and Modern Society* (1990, Oxford: Oxford University Press).

Genders, E. and Player, E., *Grendon: A Study of a Therapeutic Community Within the Prison System* (1989, Oxford: Oxford University Press).

Genders, E. and Player, E., *Race Relations in Prisons* (1989, Oxford: Oxford University Press).

Gostin, L., *A Human Condition*, vol 1 (1975, London: MIND).

Gostin, L., *A Human Condition*, vol. 2 (1977, London: MIND).

Gostin, L. (ed.), *Secure Provision* (1985, London: Tavistock).

Gostin, L., *Mental Health Services: Law and Practice* (1986, London: Stevens).

Gostin, L. and Staunton, M., 'The Case for Prison Standards', in Maguire *et al.* (1985).

Gottfredson, D. and Tonry, M. (eds), *Prediction and Classification* (1987, Chicago: University of Chicago Press).

Grant, W. *Pressure Groups. Politics and Democracy in Britain* (1989, London: Philip Allan).

Greenland, C., *Mental Illness and Civil Liberty* (1970, Birkenhead: Wilmer Bros).

Grounds A., 'The Transfer of Sentenced Prisoners to Hospital 1960–83: A study in One Special Hospital' (1991) 31 Brit. Jo. of Crimin. 54.

Gunn, J., 'Criminal Behaviour and Mental Disorder' (1977) Brit. Jo. of Psychiatry 130.

Gunn, J., 'The Role of Psychiatry in Prisons and "the Right to Punish"', in Roth, M. and Bluglass, R. (eds), *Psychiatry, Human Rights and the Law* (1985, Cambridge: Cambridge University Press).

Gunn, J., Maden, T. and Swinton, M., *Mentally Disordered Prisoners* (1991, London: Home Office).

Gunn, J., Robertson, G., Dell, S. and Way, C., *Psychiatric Aspects of Imprisonment* (1978, London: Academic Press).

HM Chief Inspector of Prisons, *Annual Reports* (London: HMSO).

HM Chief Inspector of Prisons, *Prison Categorisation Procedures* (1984, London: Home Office).

HM Chief Inspector of Prisons, *A Review of the Segregation of Prisoners under Rule 43* (1986, London: Home Office).

HM Chief Inspector of Prisons, *Feltham Young Offenders Institution* (1988 and 1992, London: Home Office).

HM Chief Inspector of Prisons, *A Review of Prisoners' Complaints* (1987, London: Home Office).

HM Chief Inspector of Prisons, *H.M. Prison Brixton* (1990, London: Home Office).

HM Chief Inspector of Prisons, *Report of a Review of Suicide and Self-harm in Prison Service Establishments in England and Wales* (1990, Cm 1383, London: HMSO).

HM Chief Inspector of Prisons, *H.M. Prison Pentonville* (1991, London: Home Office).

HM Chief Inspector of Prisons, *Inquiry into the Escape of Two Category A Prisoners from H.M. Prison Brixton on 7 July 1991* (1991, London: Home Office).

Harden, I., 'Review Article: The Constitution and its Discontents' (1991) 21 Brit. Jo. of Pol. Sci. 489.

Harlow, C., 'Power from the People? Representation and Constitutional Theory', in McAuslan and McEldowney (1985).

Harlow, C. and Rawlings, R., *Law and Administration* (1984, London: Weidenfeld and Nicolson).

Harlow, C. and Rawlings, R., *Pressure Through Law* (1992, London: Routledge).

Hart, H. L. A., *Concept of Law* (1961, Oxford: Oxford University Press).

Hart, H. L. A., *Punishment and Responsibility* (1968, Oxford: Oxford University Press).

Hawkins, K., 'Parole Procedure: an Alternative Approach' (1973) 13 Brit. Jo. of Crimin. 6.

Hawkins, K., 'Assessing Evil' (1983) 23 Brit. Jo. of Crimin. 101.

Hawkins, K. (ed.), *The Uses of Discretion* (1992, Oxford: Oxford University Press).

Hayhurst, J. and Wallington, P., 'The Parliamentary Scrutiny of Delegated Legislation' (1988) *Public Law* 547.

Health Advisory Service, *Broadmoor Hospital* (1988, London: DoH).

Heap, M., 'Adjudications in Prison Department Establishments Qualified Clerks Pilot Scheme' (1990), evidence to the Woolf Inquiry.

Hirst, P. and Jones, P., 'The Critical Resources of Established Jurisprudence' (1987) 14 Jo. of Law and Soc. 21.

Hoggett, B., *Mental Health Law* 3rd edn (1990, London: Sweet and Maxwell).

Home Affairs Select Committee, *Third Report, Session 1986–7, The State and Use of Prisons* (1987, HC 35–1, London: HMSO).

Home Office, *Annual Reports of the Prison Service* (London: HMSO),

Home Office, *The Adult Offender* (White Paper, 1965, Cmnd 2852, London: HMSO).

Home Office, *Report of the Inquiry into Prison Escapes and Security* (The Mountbatten Report) (1966, Cmnd 3175, London: HMSO).

Home Office, *Committee of Inquiry into U.K. Prison Services* (The May Inquiry) (1979, Cmnd 7673, London: HMSO).

Home Office, *Review of Parole in England and Wales* (1981, London: Home Office).

Home Office, *Managing the Long-Term Prison System: The Report of the Control Review Committee* (1984, London: Home Office).

Home Office, *Report of the Committee on the Prison Disciplinary System* (The Prior Report) (1985, Cmnd 9641, London: HMSO).

Home Office, *The Prison Disciplinary System in England and Wales* (White Paper, 1986, Cmnd 9920, London: HMSO).

Home Office, *Special Units for the Long-Term Prisoner: Regimes, Management and Research* (1987, London: HMSO).

Home Office, *Private Sector Involvement in the Remand System* (1988, London: HMSO).

Home Office, *Manual on the Conduct of Adjudications in Prison Department Establishments* (1989, London: Home Office).

Home Office, *Prisoners' Complaints and Grievances* (1989, London: Home Office).

Home Office, *The Management of Vulnerable Prisoners: Report of a Prison Department Working Group* (1989, London: Home Office).

Home Office, *Crime, Justice and Protecting the Public* (White Paper, 1990, Cm 965, London: HMSO).

Home Office, *Prison Statistics England and Wales 1990* (1990, Cm 1800, London: HMSO).

Home Office, *Report of an Efficiency Scrutiny of the Prison Medical Service* (1990, London: HMSO).

Home Office, *Custody, Care and Justice: The Way Ahead for the Prison Service in England and Wales* (White Paper, 1991, Cm 1647, London: HMSO).

Home Office, *Directions for Release and Recall* (1992, London: Home Office).

Hood, R., *Tolerance and the Tariff* (1974, London: NACRO).

Hood, R., 'The Case Against Executive Control over Time in Custody' (1975) Crim. LR 545.

House of Lords Select Committee, *Report of the Select Committee on Murder and Life Imprisonment* (1989, HL 78-1, London, HMSO).

Howard League, *Remands in Custody* (1992, London: Howard League).

Institute of Race Relations, *Deadly Silence* (1991, London: Institute of Race Relations).

Jenkins, K., Caines, K. and Jackson, A., *Improving Mangement in Government: The Next Steps* (1988, London: HMSO).

Jones, K., *Lunacy, Law and Conscience 1744-1845* (1955, London: Routledge).

Jones, R., *Mental Health Act Manual* 3rd edn (1991, London: Sweet and Maxwell).

Jowell, J., 'The Legal Control of Administrative Discretion' (1973) *Public Law* 178.

Jowell, J., 'The Rule of Law Today', in Jowell and Oliver (1989).

Jowell, J. and Oliver D. (eds), *The Changing Constitution* 2nd edn (1989, Oxford: Oxford University Press).

Justice, *Justice in Prison* (1983, London: Justice).

Kaufman, C., 'Informed Consent and Patient Decision-Making; the Reasoning of Law and Psychiatry' (1981) 4 Int. Jo. of Law and Psychiatry 345.

Lacey, N., Wells, C. and Meure, D., *Reconstructing Criminal Law* (1990, London: Weidenfeld and Nicolson).

Law Commission, *Mentally Incapacitated Adults and Decision-Making: an Overview* (1991, London: HMSO).

Lesser, H. and Pickup, Z., 'Law, Ethics and Confidentiality' (1990) 17 Jo. of Law and Soc. 17.

Lewis, N. and Harden, I., *The Noble Lie* (1986, London: Hutchinson).

Lind, E. A. and Tyler, T. R., *The Social Psychology of Procedural Justice* (1988, New York: Plenum Press).

Loughlin, M., 'Procedural Fairness: A Study of the Crisis in Administrative Law Theory' (1978) 28 Univ. of Toronto LJ 215.

Lygo, R., *Management of the Prison Service* (1991, London: Prison Service).

MacDonald, R., 'Judicial Review and Procedural Fairness in Administrative Law' (1980) 25 McGill LJ 520.

Maguire, M., 'Prisoners' Grievances: The Role of the Boards of Visitors', in Maguire *et al.* (1985).

Maguire, M., Pinter, F. and Collis, C., 'Dangerousness and the Tariff' (1984) Brit. Jo. of Crimin. 250.

Maguire, M. and Vagg, J., 'Who are the Prison watchdogs? The membership and Appointment of Boards of Visitors' (1983) Crim. LR 238.

Maguire, M. and Vagg, J., *The Watchdog Role of Boards of Visitors* (1984, London: Home Office).

Maguire, M., Vagg, J. and Morgan, M. (eds), *Accountability and Prisons: Opening up a Closed World* (1985, London: Tavistock).

Martin, J., *Boards of Visitors of Penal Institutions* (The Jellicoe Report) (1975, London: Barry Rose).

Martin J., *Hospitals in Trouble* (1984, Oxford: Basil Blackwell).

Mashaw, J., 'Administrative Due Process: The Quest for a Dignitary Theory' (1981) 61 Boston Univ. LR 885.

Mashaw, J., *Bureaucrtic Justice: Managing Social Security Disability Claims* (1983, New Haven: Yale University Press).

Mashaw, J., 'Dignitary Process: A Political Psychology of Liberal Democratic Citizenship' (1987) 39 Univ. of Florida LR 433.

Matthews, P. and Foreman, J., *Jervis on the Office and Duties of Coroners* 10th edn (1986, London: Sweet and Maxwell).

McAuslan, P. and McEldowney, J. (eds), *Law, Legitimacy and the Constitution* (1985, London: Sweet and Maxwell).

McCabe, S., 'The Powers and Purposes of the Parole Board' (1985) Crim. LR 489.

McDermott K. and King, R., 'Mind Games: Where the Action is in Prisons' (1988) 28 Brit. Jo. of Crimin. 357.

Mental Health Act Commission, *Biennial Reports* (London: HMSO).

Mental Health Act Commission, *Evidence to the Committee of Inquiry into Complaints about Ashworth Special Hospital* (1992, Nottingham: MHAC).

Michelman, F., 'Forewood: Traces of Self-Government' (1986) 100 Harvard LR 4.

Miers, D. and Page, A., *Legislation* 2nd edn (1990, London: Sweet and Maxwell).

Mill, J. S., *Considerations on Representative Government* (1911, London: Longmans).

Morgan, N., 'The Shaping of Parole in England and Wales' (1983) Crim. LR 137.

Morgan, R., 'Her Majesty's Inspectorate of Prisons', in Maguire *et al.* (1985).

Morgan, R., 'Woolf in Retrospect and Prospect' (1991) 54 Mod. LR 713.

Morgan, R., 'Prison Accountability Revisited,' paper presented at a *Public Law* workshop, London, June 1992.

Morgan, R. and Jones, H., 'Prison Discipline: The Case for Implementing Woolf' (1991) 31 Brit. Jo. of Crimin. 280.

Morris, N., *Madness and the Criminal Law* (1992, Chicago: Chicago University Press).

Murphy, J., 'Therapy and the Problem of Autonomous Consent' (1979) 2 Int. Jo. of Law and Psychiatry 415.

Nelson, W. N., *On Justifying Democracy* (1980, London: Routledge).

Oliver, D., *Government in the United Kingdom: the Search for Accountability, Effectiveness and Citizenship* (1991, Buckingham: Open University Press).

O'Riordan, T., Kemp, R. and Purdue, M., *Sizewell B: An Anatomy of the Inquiry* (1988, London: Macmillan).

Parker, E., 'The Development of Secure Provision', in Gostin (1985).

Parole Board, *Annual Reports* (London: Home Office).

Partington, M., 'The Reform of Public Law in Britain: Theoretical Problems and Practical Considerations', in McAuslan and McEldowney (1985).

Pateman, C., *Participation and Democratic Theory* (1970, London: Cambridge University Press).

Peay, J., 'Offenders Suffering from Psychopathic Disorder: the Rise and Demise of a Consultation Document' (1988) Brit. Jo. of Crimin. 67.

Peay, J., *Tribunals on Trial* (1989, Oxford: Oxford University Press).

Pennock, J. and Chapman, J. (eds), *Participation in Politics: Nomos 16* (1975, New York: Atherton).

Pennock, J. and Chapman, J. (eds), *Due Process: Nomos 18* (1977, New York: New York University Press).

Pennock, J. and Chapman, J. (eds), *Authority Revisited: Nomos 29* (1987, New York: New York University Press).

Pincoffs, E., 'Due Process, Fraternity, and a Kantian Injunction', in Pennock and Chapman (1977).

Polvi, N. and Pease, K., 'Parole and its Problems: a Canadian–English Comparison' (1991) 30 Howard Jo. of Crim. Jus. 218.

Prins, H., *Dangerous Behaviour* (1986, London: Tavistock).

Prison Advisory Group, *Report* (1991, London: DoH/Home Office).

Prison Reform Trust, *Implementing Woolf: The Prison System One Year On* (1992, London: Prison Reform Trust).

Prison Service, *A Code of Standards for the Prison Service: A Discussion Document* (1992, London: Prison Service).

Prison Service, *An Independent Complaints Adjudicator for Prisons: A Consultation Paper* (1992, London: Prison Service).

Prosser, T., 'Towards a Critical Public Law' (1992) 9 Jo. of Law and Soc. 1.

Prosser, T., 'Democratisation, Accountability and Institutional Design', in McAuslan and McEldowney (1985).

Radzinowicz, L. and Hood, R., *The Emergence of Penal Policy* (1990, Oxford: Oxford University Press).

Rassaby, E. and Rogers, A., *Psychiatric Referrals from the Police* (1986, London: MIND).

Raz, J., 'The Rule of Law and its Virtue' (1977) LQR 195.

Redish, M. and Marshall, L., 'Adjudicatory Independence and the Values of

Procedural Due Process' (1986) 95 Yale LJ.

Richardson, G., 'Judicial Intervention in Prison Life', in Maguire *et al.* (1985).

Richardson, G. 'The Case for Prisoners' Rights', in Maguire *et al.* (1985).

Richardson, G., 'The Duty to Give Reasons: Potential and Practice' (1986) *Public Law* 437.

Richardson, G., 'The Select Committee and the Sentencing Structure for Murder' (1990) Howard Jo. of Crim Jus. 300.

Rose, N., 'Unreasonable Rights; Mental Illness and the Limits of the Law' (1985) Jo. of Law and Soc. 199.

Roth, M., 'Modern Neurology and Psychiatry and the Problem of Criminal Responsibility', in Hucker, S., Webster, C. and Ben-aron, M. (eds), *Mental Disorder and Criminal Responsibility* (1981, Toronto: Butterworths).

Saphire, R., 'Specifying Due Process Values' (1978) 127 Univ. of Penn. LR 111.

Special Hospitals Service Authority, *Report of the Inquiry into the Circumstances Leading to the Death in Broadmoor Hospital of Mr Joseph Watts on 23 August 1988* (1989, London: SHSA).

Special Hospitals Service Authority, *S.H.S.A. Review* (1991, London: SHSA).

Stewart, R. B., 'The Reformation of American Administrative Law' (1975) 88 Harvard LR 1667.

Summers, R., *Lon L. Fuller* (1984, London: Edward Arnold).

Sunstein, C., 'Interest Groups in American Public Law' (1985) 38 Stanford LR 29.

Sunstein, C., 'Beyond the Republican Revival' (1988) 97 Yale LR 1539.

Taylor, M. and Pease, K., 'Private Prisons and Penal Purpose', in Matthews, R. (ed.), *Privatising Criminal Justice* (1989, London: Sage).

Thibaut, J. and Walker, L., *Procedural Justice: A Psychological Analysis* (1975, Hillside NJ: Laurence Erlblaum Associates).

Treacy, V., 'Prisoners' Rights Submerged in Semantics' (1989) 28 Howard Jo. of Crim. Jus. 27.

Tribe, L., *Constitutional Choices* (1985, Cambridge Mass.: Harvard University Press).

Unsworth, C., *The Politics of Mental Health Legislation* (1987, Oxford: Oxford University Press).

Van Alstyne, W., 'Cracks in the "New Property": Adjudicative Due Process in the Administrative State' (1977) 62 Cornell LR 445.

Wade, H. W. R., *Administrative Law* 6th edn (1988, Oxford: Oxford University Press).

Walker, N., 'Release by Executive Discretion: A Defence' (1975) Crim LR 540.

Walker, N. and McCabe, S., *Crime and Insanity in England* (1973, Edinburgh: Edinburgh University Press).

Wasik, M. and Pease, K., 'The Role Veto and Party Politics' (1986) Crim. LR 379.

Woolf, Lord Justice, *Prison Disturbances April 1990* (The Woolf Report) (1991, Cm 1456, London: HMSO).

INDEX